PENGUIN CLASSICS

THE QUR'AN

TARIF KHALIDI was born in Jerusalem in 1938. He received degrees from University College, Oxford, and the University of Chicago, before teaching at the American University of Beirut as a professor in the Department of History from 1970 to 1996. In 1996, Tarif Khalidi left Beirut to become the Sir Thomas Adams's Professor of Arabic at Cambridge University, the oldest chair of Arabic in the English-speaking world. He was also Director of the Centre for Middle East and Islamic Studies and a Fellow of King's College, Cambridge. After six years, Professor Khalidi returned to the American University of Beirut, taking on the Sheikh Zayed Chair in Islamic and Arabic Studies. His books include *The Muslim Jesus* (2001), *Arabic Historical Thought in the Classical Period* (1994) and a forthcoming study of the Prophet Muhammad and the evolution of his image across time in the Islamic literary tradition.

The Qur'an

A New Translation by TARIF KHALIDI

PENGUIN BOOKS

PENGUIN CLASSICS

Published by the Penguin Group
Penguin Books Ltd, 80 Strand, London WC2R ORL, England
Penguin Group (USA) Inc., 375 Hudson Street, New York, New York 10014, USA
Penguin Group (Canada), 90 Eglinton Avenue East, Suite 700, Toronto, Ontario, Canada M4P 2Y3
(a division of Pearson Penguin Canada Inc.)
Penguin Ireland, 25 St Stephen's Green, Dublin 2, Ireland (a division of Penguin Books Ltd)
Penguin Group (Australia), 250 Camberwell Road, Camberwell, Victoria 3124, Australia
(a division of Pearson Australia Group Pty Ltd)
Penguin Books India Pvt Ltd, 11 Community Centre, Panchsheel Park, New Delhi – 110 017, India
Penguin Group (NZ), 67 Apollo Drive, Rosedale, North Shore 0632, New Zealand
(a division of Pearson New Zealand Ltd)
Penguin Books (South Africa) (Pty) Ltd, 24 Sturdee Avenue, Rosebank, Johannesburg 2196, South Africa

Penguin Books Ltd, Registered Offices: 80 Strand, London WC2R ORL, England

www.penguin.com

This translation first published in hardback 2008
Published in paperback in Penguin Classics 2009

014

Translation and editorial material copyright © Tarif Khalidi, 2008
All rights reserved

The moral right of the Translator has been asserted

Typeset by Rowland Phototypesetting Ltd, Bury St Edmunds, Suffolk
Printed in England by Clays Ltd, ElcografS.p.A.

978-0-140-45544-1

www.greenpenguin.co.uk

Contents

Introduction

PROBLEMS OF INTERPRETATION

The Qur'an is the axial text of a major religious civilization and of a major world language. For both Islamic civilization and the Arabic language the Qur'an consecrates a finality of authority granted to few texts in history. Muslim piety regards the Qur'an as supremely eloquent, supremely wise, and immune from all error or falsehood. Its immaculate nature extends to its physical copies, which are considered inviolable and untouchable except by one in a state of ritual purity. Good Muslim manners dictate that copies of the Qur'an cannot be bought, only piously bestowed in return for a pious gift from the buyer. Through the centuries, Islamic art and calligraphy have lavished upon it many of their most enduring and magnificent masterpieces. When recited, it flows with a sonority which common Muslim opinion holds to be capable of causing tears of repentance and comfort or else a shiver of fear and trembling.

As the 'Book of God', the divine arbiter of Muslim life and a model of Arabic usage, it sits inside a vast tradition of commentary and scholarship, Islamic and non-Islamic, pre-modern as well as modern. In the pre-modern Islamic tradition, Qur'anic commentary and exegesis (*tafsir*) was widely regarded not only as the most meritorious of the religious sciences but also as the one most fraught with danger, because of the grave consequences of error. This, however, did not prevent Muslim parties and groups from engaging in *tafsir* with the object of fortifying their ideological positions. The resultant corpus of *tafsir* contains a wide spectrum of views on the irreversible justice of God, the freedom of the human will, the divine attributes, the ultimate destiny of sinners and a host of other theological, legal and historical issues embedded in the sacred text. The greatest of these *tafsirs* must rank as among the most subtle and sophisticated commentaries on sacred scriptures in world literature, holding considerable interest for students of comparative religion. Unfortunately their very bulk makes their translation a colossal undertaking, denying them the wider non-Arabic readership they so thoroughly deserve.

The question now arises: can one really understand or appreciate the Qur'an without its tradition of commentary? Can a reader who knows little or nothing of its cultural background make sense of its allusive references or its frequent ad hoc pronouncements? For the scholars of Islam, mastery of the various sub-disciplines of Qur'anic exegesis has always been regarded as an essential prerequisite to authoritative understanding. Among these disciplines are the subsidiary sciences of *tafsir* such as *asbab al-nuzul* (historical context), *al-nasikh wa'l mansukh* (harmony of laws), *gharib al-Qur'an* (linguistic obscurities), *qira'at* (variant readings), *i'rab* (grammar), *isti'arat* (metaphors), *bada'i'* (rhetorical excellences) and *i'jaz* (divinely ordained inimitability). It was upon these sciences that the great exegetes of the Qur'an built their authority. Yet within these fields, controversy was always rife and vivid. No scholar of exegesis would advance an opinion without first engaging with his fellow exegetes, past and contemporaneous. Consensus on a point of interpretation was hard to come by, even on what appear to be simple or straightforward legal or linguistic points. On the larger and more divisive theological issues the debate among exegetes has always contained a wide spectrum of views.

However, despite the claims of the exegetes that full understanding of the Qur'an must pass through their scholarly portals, it was recognized from an early period that the Qur'an was, in a memorable phrase, *hammalu awjuhin* (a bearer of diverse interpretations), somewhat akin to A. N. Whitehead's phrase 'patient of interpretation', cited by Frank Kermode in his definition of a classic.[1] The leeway granted to interpretation issued from the Qur'an's own classification of its verses as *muhkam* or *mutashabih* (Q. 3:7). The word *muhkam* has commonly been understood to mean 'explicit', 'clear-cut', 'fully intelligible', while *mutashabih* has been taken to mean 'indeterminate', 'with multiple meanings' or even 'ambiguous'. Under *muhkam,* the exegetes typically included the body of detailed legislation and moral injunctions in the Qur'an, while *mutashabih* included words and verses which, among other matters, referred to God's attributes and His relationship to the created world. Here, for example, is how the renowned theologian and exegete Fakhr al-Din al-Razi (d. 1209) dealt with the question of certain problematic attributes of God such as His anger, joy, cunning and love. If taken literally, these can bring God dangerously near to human emotions:

> All psychic symptoms, by which I mean such things as mercy, joy, pleasure, anger, shyness, cunning and mockery, have their origins and their ends. Take anger for example. Anger originates with the boiling of the blood of the heart while its end is the desire to inflict harm upon the object of anger. When applied to God, the term 'anger' cannot be taken to refer to its origin, which is the boiling of the heart's blood, but to its end, which is the desire to inflict harm.[2]

This is an example of how certain exegetes, particularly the rationalists among them, have dealt with the problem of God's seemingly human attributes, though other exegetes would argue that such attributes must be accepted on faith and are beyond rational investigation. Regardless of the interpretive strategy adopted, a common view held among exegetes is that the ambiguous or *mutashabih* terms or phrases of the Qur'an were deliberately designed by God to stimulate thinking, and are thus very much in line with the Qur'an's frequent exhortations to mankind to reflect upon the created universe. The exegetes have quite naturally insisted upon mastery of the scholarly curriculum before interpretation can be undertaken, and yet the repeated invitation to mankind to exercise their reason is as timeless, universal and imperative as anything else in the Qur'anic text itself.

If we turn back to the questions posed above, we might argue that a knowledge of, say, conditions in pre-Islamic Arabia would clearly enhance contextual understanding of the Qur'an. But the very allusiveness of the text, its impersonality, its meta-historical tone, seem almost deliberately to de-emphasize context, and to address its audience or readers in a grammatical tense that I have elsewhere called 'the eternal present tense'.[3] Yes, the Qur'an explicitly recognizes the danger of a wilfully perverted reading of the text, but if approached in a pious frame of mind, or what today we might call sympathy, interpretation must in theory be limitless, since God alone is its perfect interpreter (Q. 3:7). Thus, of all sacred texts, the Qur'an is perhaps the one that most self-consciously invites its readers to engage with it exegetically.

A BRIEF HISTORY

So far as one can determine its general contours, early Muslim scholarship on the Qur'an emanated from circles close to the Prophet Muhammad (c. 570–632) and involved, in its beginnings, the collection and preservation of revelation. For the first twenty or so years of its existence, copies of the Qur'an, in whole or in part, were in the possession of venerable collectors dispersed by the Muslim conquests in the diverse regions of the new empire. Because of this dispersal and subsequent political and ideological alignments we possess several contrasting, sometimes conflicting, accounts of the Qur'an's earliest history. Eventually a dominant narrative emerged which held that a committee appointed by the third caliph 'Uthman (r. 644–56) assembled one definitive copy of the text, disseminated it in the major urban centres of the new empire and ordered all other copies destroyed. This master narrative holds that the caliph's edict caused a great deal of distress to possessors of private or family copies of the pre-'Uthmanic text and was indeed one of the causes of the rebellion which ended in the caliph's murder in 656. Nevertheless, Muslim scholarship has preserved examples, in the form of lists, of the variant readings of these early texts. In almost all cases, however, such readings concern very minor variations in grammar or dialect and add nothing of substance to the 'Uthmanic text, the one that is in our hands today. This narrative has not gone unchallenged in both Muslim and non-Muslim circles, but it has withstood the test of time and of recent and dramatic epigraphic and textual discoveries. The result is that Islam has possessed a definitive sacred text from a very early point in its history. There are simply no 'apocrypha' where the Qur'an is concerned. We can therefore be confident that what we possess today is in all essential respects the Qur'an that Muslim narrative tells us was circulated by caliphal fiat somewhere around the year 650. Numerous historical problems remain, but these need not concern a reader who wishes to encounter the text directly, with minimal contextual demands.

Another aspect of the Qur'an's history is the history of its revelation. Here also the immensely rich corpus of Muslim writings, layers of which go back to very early days, preserve a wide and diverse body of narratives and views. The most convenient classical work of reference for these views is *Al-Itqan fi 'Ulum al-Qur'an* (*Exactitude regarding the Sciences of the Qur'an*) by the great Egyptian polymath Jalal al-Din al-Suyuti (d. 1505). In this work Suyuti records the opinions of earlier scholars on numerous aspects of Qur'anic studies and includes a large section on what is called the 'descent' of the Qur'an. What we find in Suyuti is still accepted in essence by Muslim piety as the received wisdom on this topic, even though some modern Muslim scholars question the literal and theological implications of these narratives.[4]

In Suyuti's composite account, the 'descent' of the Qur'an took place in stages. It originated in a heavenly prototype called *al-Lawh al-Mahfuz* ('the well-guarded Tablet'; see Q. 85:22). From this heavenly tablet, the source of all divine revelations, the Qur'an was first made to descend in its entirety to the nether heaven, or sublunary world, in the Night of Power (Q. 97:1) and was then revealed piecemeal over some twenty years to the Prophet Muhammad by the angel Gabriel (Q. 17:106). Suyuti contends that this two-stage descent distinguishes the Qur'an from other revealed scriptures, all of which were imparted in one piece and in one instant of time. The Qur'an was thus both an eternal text and one that addressed specific or ad hoc problems of the Muslim community.[5] The second reason for its piecemeal descent is said to be provided by the Qur'an itself at Q. 25:32–3, namely, to 'confirm your heart with it'. The reference is of course to Muhammad and the manner in which his faith was renewed and reinforced through intermittent revelation.

As a divine revelation carrying the words of God to Muhammad across some twenty years of history, Muslim scholarship was interested first of all in how that revelation descended on the Prophet and, later on, in how his soul was readied for its descent. Three Qur'anic passages were singled out as the very earliest revelations: *Sura* 96 (The Blood Clot), verses 1–5; *Sura* 74 (Enfolded), verses 1–7; and *Sura* 53 (The Star), verses 1–18. In all three passages, there exists an elaborate and vivid narrative entourage. Thus, in *Sura* 96, according to Muslim tradition, Muhammad is choked and stifled three times by the angel who orders him to 'Recite!' before he is finally able to give voice to the verses. This act of stifling is explained by some commentators as a test to make sure he is not reciting anything of his own making. In *Sura* 74, Muhammad, terrified by the encounter with the divine, asks his wife Khadija to wrap him up in his cloak but is then ordered to remove this cloak, cleanse himself, stand up and deliver the message entrusted to him. In *Sura* 53, there is a powerful vision of a divine being who fills the horizon, then continues to approach until he is near enough to deliver the divine words.

All three of these inaugural moments involve visual encounters of some kind. Eventually, the messages descended aurally. When asked directly by a companion how these messages descended upon him, Muhammad compared it to the clanging of a bell, followed by an agonizing ordeal, then by a feeling of great relief when the ordeal was over, leaving him conscious of what he had been taught. The great thinker Ibn Khaldun (d. 1406) was to argue that in time the descent of revelations grew less onerous, to the point where most of *Sura* 9 (Repentance) descended on the Prophet while mounted and during a military expedition.

As regards Muhammad's soul and its readiness to receive revelation, there exist in traditional biographies of Muhammad vivid narratives which show how at various stages of his life divine beings descended and cleansed his heart of its 'black spot'. Later, Muslim theologians and philosophers sought 'natural' explanations for the phenomenon of prophecy and of inspiration (*wahy*), among the more interesting of which is, once more, Ibn Khaldun's. Recalling the great chain of being, Ibn Khaldun asserted that the prophetic soul was the highest on the human ladder, thus overlapping with the angelic realm. God grants prophetic souls the ability to rise to a station where divine revelation, in various forms, can descend upon them. The painful ordeal experienced by Muhammad when revelation came down upon him was simply the soul's agony as it shed its human form and assumed that of the angelic. The Qur'an is thus the product of a revelation descending and of a prophet ascending to receive it.

ISSUES OF CONTENT AND STYLE

Muslim tradition, seeking neatness in chronology, claimed that revelation descended over two periods of Muhammad's life, each lasting ten years, and corresponding to his years in Mecca and Medinah. But the editors of the 'Uthmanic Qur'an did not arrange the text accordingly. Thus Meccan and Medinese revelations are often intermixed, and such intermixture is normally indicated in modern copies of the Qur'an directly under the title of each *sura* or chapter; for example, *Sura* x is Medinese except for verses a, b and c, which are Meccan. A very rough rule of thumb, however, is that if a reader wishes to read the Qur'an in the chronological order of revelation, he or she can start at the end and read back to the beginning. This order of reading might in fact provide a more immediate introduction to the many voices in which the Qur'an speaks to its readers or listeners.

These diverse voices of the Qur'an find their origin in a saying of the Prophet: 'The Qur'an was revealed in seven *ahruf*.' One of the many interpretations of the word *ahruf* is that it refers to the seven registers, or perhaps tropes, of the Qur'an, cited most commonly by the exegetes as follows: command, prohibition, glad tidings, warnings, sermons, parables and narratives. A modern reader is likely to find the narrative mode the most problematic, not only because the dominant grammatical tense of the Qur'an is the 'eternal present tense', but also because the narratives are cast as meta-historical tales and parables of the human spirit and of the perilous journey to faith, rather than as stories. In almost all cases, the Qur'an assumes familiarity with the outlines of the tale in question, and so seeks to remind its audience of the tale's true import and moral. Indeed, the 'Reminder' (*al-Dhikr*) is one of the most frequently occurring epithets for the Qur'an within the text itself. Yet there is much in the Qur'an which concerns itself with, or responds to, the everyday, whether this be a sudden event, a looming crisis or even the mildly irritating conduct of some of the faithful. But even at its most ad hoc or immediate, the Qur'an wraps up these everyday 'asides' with a formula that suggests the aegis of eternity such as 'God is All-Forgiving, All-Wise'. This trans-figuration of narrative, this shift from narrative to mnemonic, may not be easy to appreciate for readers familiar with Bible stories, especially when several of them will be found recast in Qur'anic mode.

Uncommon too in other sacred scriptures is the manner in which the Qur'an registers the voices of those who opposed both the message and the messenger. Accordingly, the central image of faith is that of a process of growth in certainty (*yaqin*), a process that involves polemic and the constant divine invi-tation to ponder and reflect. Humans in the Qur'an are hasty and argumentative, but also stubbornly attached to opinion or creed. For faith to grow, the murmurings of Satan and his followers must be silenced. These murmurings of dissent, these arguments and counter-arguments, are scattered all over the Qur'anic text, to be met in each case by the appropriate response. They range from those who argue for an eternal, fate-dominated universe (*dahr*) (e.g. Q. 45:24) to those who question the resurrection of the body (e.g. Q. 17:49), to those who deny the veracity of the messenger or mock his message (e.g. Q. 3:184). The phrase 'they cry lies' or its equivalent, denoting a highly charged, discordant environment where the message was challenged at every turn, is found frequently. These challenges are met by a divine polemic constantly expanding in scope and rhetoric. In addition to narratives of earlier prophets and nations, nature is brought in to demonstrate God's presence as the rhetoric comes to include an ever-widening circle of invocations: to plants, winds, animals, as well as to ancient peoples, tribes and religious sects. But perhaps the most startling aspect of its rhetoric is the deliberate address to women alongside men, rendering the Qur'an among the most gender-conscious of all sacred texts. It is both men *and* women who are repeatedly addressed in admonition or praise and made to be equally responsible moral agents.

Noteworthy, too, is the gradual transformation of Muhammad himself under the impact of revelation. Classical exegetes had observed how Muhammad evolved from simple warner or bearer of glad tidings to exalted messenger and law-maker, thus running the gamut of prophetic experience. Like any person of faith, he too was on a journey of discovery, reflected in the Qur'an, during which he was often assailed by doubts and temptations and where his sincerity as well as his leadership were constantly challenged. In the Qur'an we find a messenger who, though the deliverer of the message, nevertheless stands and listens to the words of God alongside the rest of his community, who is even scolded by God on occasion for common human failings. Faith is a painful ordeal even for the message-bearer, and much must be endured before final vindication.

Another theme might be the many images of heaven and hell which overhang the Qur'anic text. It has often been noted that these visions of the afterlife involve two contrasting visions of nature, the one perverted, the other perfected. Hell is like a boiling cauldron, whose inmates are neither alive nor dead. They are made to drink fiery or revolting substances and their faces and bodies carry the scars of their torment. Hell is also a place of noisy discord and utter selfishness, where humans are reduced to fending for themselves without regard for family or loved ones. Heaven on the other hand is a garden blessed by shade, soft breezes and running streams, whose fruits are ever ripe and ever at hand. Its inhabitants lie on facing couches, as if at a banquet of friends, and converse quietly and in total harmony of spirit. The maidens and youths of paradise, sometimes a target of ridicule by modern-day sceptics, might be seen as part of the same idyllic scene, since the Qur'an explicitly denies carnal pleasures in paradise (e.g. Q. 52:23). In both places there is a correspondence between the sin itself and its punishment, as well as between a life of virtue and its reward.

In other words the punishment is frequently the sin itself revealed and experienced in its true horror while the reward of virtue is its fruit: amity and peace.

In sum, the Qur'an is both a challenging and a challenged scripture. Read as an invitation to a faith that came into the world when the world was first created, it deliberately provokes a never-ending dialogue between God and his creatures centred principally on their ability to observe, to ponder, to remember, to deduce, to obey. In doing so, the Qur'an also opened itself to challenge. Thus Qur'anic scholarship from its early days preserved a large body of invective (*mata'in*) against the Qur'an, whether genuine or fabricated for polemical purposes. Objections, we are told, were raised against its internal consistency, its repetitiveness, its metaphorical usage and even its grammatical mistakes. Appropriate responses were of course provided to all these objections, but the arena of debate that the Qur'an laid open has remained a central and vivid characteristic of its message: faith as a process of dialectic and discovery.

THIS TRANSLATION

I ought first to express my warm gratitude to three friends at Penguin Books who made this translation possible and took a deep interest in its progress: Adam Freudenheim, Keith Taylor and Caroline Pretty. No translator could hope for more considerate or more astute 'minders'. The first two believed firmly in a new translation of the Qur'an and the third made innumerable suggestions for its improvement. Any new translation must of course be indebted to earlier translations and all three were a constant source of encouragement and wisdom as I laboured to locate my translation within a tradition now both long and distinguished.

In the last two or three decades a large number of new English translations of the Qur'an have appeared, some of which are of considerable accuracy and merit. The translation by George

Sale, first published in 1734, remains to the present day the *fons et origo* of all subsequent scholarly translations, while that of A. J. Arberry in 1954 is the one which has striven most elegantly to capture the resonance of the original Arabic, and to move away from the one-dimensional prose translations hitherto, and thereafter, dominant. Thus the question to be answered by any new translation must be: does a new translation bring new insight?

When I began this translation there were several issues, of varying import, to be considered. To many ancient and modern readers, the Qur'an progresses through what one might call bursts of revelation, and some classical scholars such as Suyuti argued that revelation descended 'according to need, with five or ten verses (*ayat*) at a time, and more and less', while a more ancient authority, 'Ikrima (d. 724), stated that the Qur'an was revealed 'in instalments' (*nujuman*) of three, four or five verses at a time. Any translator of the Qur'an must therefore come to some sort of decision as to where these 'bursts' begin and end, and reflect this in the arrangement of the text. Consequently, it became evident to me that a prose rendering tends not to reflect the Qur'an's structure. By dividing my translation into paragraphs, I hope to highlight the pericopes upon which the text is built, without of course any claim to authority as to the exact boundaries of these divisions. In addition, I have deliberately retained such peculiarities of the original text as the shift in pronouns within a single verse and the occasional incongruity of verb tense, and I have taken a few liberties in translating the same Arabic term in different ways, a matter already discussed by the early exegetes, who held that the same word could mean different things in different contexts.

More substantial is the issue of translating the many voices in which the Qur'an speaks to us. The reader will doubtless notice that the 'register' of the Qur'an constantly shifts, from narrative to exhortation, from homily to hymn of praise, from strict law to tender sermon, from fear and trembling to invitations to reflection. These, I decided, *had* to look different;

hence the horizontal and vertical disposition of the translation.
By and large, where the Qur'an is narrating or legislating, I have
opted for a horizontal prose format. Where it is in any sense
'dramatic', I have arranged the lines in a vertical 'poetic' fashion.
But here too I cannot claim to have done anything other than
to highlight a problem of translation and offer a tentative sol-
ution to it.

Most pressing of all is the issue of the style of language one
chooses. Without wishing to engage with the many and fertile
theories of translation on offer today, or with the fascinating
controversy over the 'familiarity' versus 'alienation' of the
foreign text, I unconsciously slipped into what I like to think of
as measured modern English. Where some verses of the Qur'an
are *mutashabihat* (uncertain in meaning) or abrupt, I have not
tried to force meaning into them, nor have I altered the frequent
mixture of singular and plural verbal forms in the same sentence.
At the same time, it appeared to me to be highly desirable to
preserve the sentence structure and word order of the Arabic,
as well as its idioms, so long as this did not obscure the sense.
In other words, I attempted a balance between the familiarly
modern and the alienating archaic, while preferring at all times
as literal a rendering as possible. In his translation of *Beowulf*,
Seamus Heaney expresses the translator's dilemma as follows:

It is one thing to find lexical meanings for the words and to have
some feel for how the metre might go, but it is quite another
thing to find the tuning fork that will give you the note and pitch
for the overall music of the work.[6]

In my search for that 'tuning fork' I was painfully aware that
the cadence of the Arabic could never be truly reproduced,
but nevertheless strove for what Heaney calls a 'directness of
utterance', in order to convey something of the power of juxta-
positions, rhythmic recurrence, sonority, verbal energy and
rhymed endings of the original.

If all this amounts to some kind of answer to the question

posed above about a new translation bringing new understanding, that in itself would be a worthwhile endeavour. But
since all translation is in essence a Sisyphean activity, inevitably
falling short of perfection, my readers must ultimately judge the
distance remaining to the top.

Wa qul rabbi zidni 'ilman. (Q. 20:114).

Tarif Khalidi
American University of Beirut
8 February 2008

NOTES

1. A. N. Whitehead, cited in Frank Kermode, *The Genesis of Secrecy* (Cambridge, Mass.: Harvard University Press, 1979), p. xi.
2. Jalal al-Din al-Suyuti, *Al-Itqan fi 'Ulum al-Qur'an*, ed. Muhammad Abu'l Fadl Ibrahim (Sidon: al-Maktaba al-'Asriyya, 2006), p. 507.
3. Tarif Khalidi, *The Muslim Jesus* (Cambridge, Mass.: Harvard University Press, 2001), p. 10.
4. See Suha Taji-Farouki (ed.), *Modern Muslim Intellectuals and the Qur'an* (Oxford: Oxford University Press, 2004).
5. This ad hoc character of the revelation is one which many modern Muslim exegetes designate a starting point for reinterpretation.
6. Seamus Heaney, *Beowulf: A Verse Translation* (New York: W. W. Norton, 2002), p. xxxvi.

Further Reading

Readers of the Qur'an today are very well served by a number of reference works which are addressed to the general public, reflect the latest scholarship on various Qur'anic themes and include both Muslim and non-Muslim authors. Two works in particular should first be mentioned, both edited by a distinguished Qur'anic scholar, Jane Dammen McAuliffe. The first is *Encyclopaedia of the Qur'an* (Leiden/Boston/Köln: Brill, 2001–6), with nearly a thousand alphabetically arranged entries in five volumes, and a volume of indices. This contains articles by many hands on Qur'anic terms, names and themes, with useful bibliographies appended to each article. The second is *The Cambridge Companion to the Qur'an* (Cambridge: Cambridge University Press, 2006), which contains articles dealing at greater length with such topics as the formation of the Qur'anic text, its transmission, traditions of interpretation and a few contemporary readings of it. While many contributions are admirably clear, not all of these articles can be recommended to a non-expert reader.

For the reader in a hurry, Michael Cook's *The Koran: A Very Short Introduction* (Oxford: Oxford University Press, 2000) is particularly good on the structure and sound of Qur'anic language but is marred by a supercilious tone. From a Muslim standpoint, Fazlur Rahman's *Major Themes of the Qur'an* (Minneapolis: Bibliotheca Islamica, 1980) remains a lucid, empathic and suggestive treatment. In chapter two of his *Understanding Islam* (London: George Allen and Unwin, 1963),

Frithjof Schuon considers the Qur'an from a Sufi perspective and contrasts it with other sacred scriptures. Though occasionally difficult and essentializing, this essay is full of insights and repays careful reading.

The most famous of the classical commentaries on the Qur'an is that of al-Tabari (d. 923). A projected five-volume abridged translation of al-Tabari's vast commentary was cut short by the untimely and much-lamented death of the translator, the Cambridge scholar John Cooper. Only Volume One has appeared, under the title *The Commentary on the Qur'an by Abu Ja'far Muhammad ibn Jarir al-Tabari* (Oxford: Oxford University Press and Hakim Investment Holdings, 1987). But even from this single volume and Cooper's superb translation, readers will acquire a good notion of how al-Tabari and other like-minded classical commentators deployed their strategy of Qur'anic commentary. From an orientalist viewpoint, the commentary by Richard Bell (d. 1952) edited in two volumes by C. E. Bosworth and M. E. J. Richardson under the title *A Commentary on the Qur'an* (Manchester: University of Manchester, Journal of Semitic Studies Monograph 14, 1991) is perhaps the most impressive but can hardly be recommended to beginners except for sampling.

Two journals contain much material of interest on the Qur'an: the first is the *Journal of Qur'anic Studies*, published by the Centre of Islamic Studies at the School of Oriental and African Studies, University of London; the second is the *Journal of Islamic Studies*, published by the Oxford Centre for Islamic Studies and Oxford University Press.

Among modern Muslim scholars of the Qur'an the following might be singled out: the Pakistani Fazlur Rahman, the Algerian-French scholar Mohammed Arkoun and the Egyptian Nasr Hamid Abu Zayd. In their various ways, all three scholars have moved Muslim Qur'anic scholarship in new directions. A convenient collection of modern Muslim readings of the Qur'an is in Suha Taji-Farouki (ed.), *Modern Muslim Intellectuals and the Qur'an* (Oxford: Oxford University Press, 2004). Of con-

siderable interest is a perceptive review article by a young
Muslim scholar of recent Western works on the Qur'an: Walid
Saleh's 'In Search of a Comprehensible Qur'an: A Survey of
Some Recent Scholarly Works' in *Bulletin of the Royal Institute
of Inter-Faith Studies* (Amman), 5:2 (Autumn/Winter 2003).
The author critically reviews, among others, the works of both
Michael Cook (cited above) and Roberto Tottoli (cited below).
Among non-Muslim scholars, the works of Jane D. McAuliffe,
Stefan Wild, Angelika Neuwirth, Harald Motzki and Toshihiko
Izutsu are of particular interest.

The historical background of Arabia is now clearly and
elegantly summarized in Robert Hoyland's *Arabia and the
Arabs: From the Bronze Age to the Coming of Islam* (London:
Routledge, 2001). For its vast erudition and its majestic sweep
of early Islamic civilization in the context of world civilization,
nothing in any European language so far rivals the first volume
of M. G. S. Hodgson's *The Venture of Islam* (Chicago: The
University of Chicago Press, 1974).

Readers of the Qur'an who come to it with a biblical background might find some interesting parallels in Roberto Tottoli's
Biblical Prophets in the Qur'an and Muslim Literature (Rich-
mond: Curzon, 2001). Those interested in the history of the
Qur'an's reception in the European West might well begin with
R. W. Southern's short classic *Western Views of Islam in the
Middle Ages* (Cambridge, Mass.: Harvard University Press,
1962). Of greater scope and coverage is Norman Daniel's *Islam
and the West: The Making of an Image* (Oxford: Oneworld,
2000). Given the immense influence of Martin Luther on later
Christian theology, the recent study by Adam S. Francisco,
Martin Luther and Islam (Leiden/Boston: Brill (HCMR, Vol. 8),
2007) contains a detailed analysis of Luther's views on the
Qur'an. Elegantly written though somewhat repetitive is John V.
Tolan's *Saracens: Islam in the Medieval European Imagination*
(New York: Columbia University Press, 2002).

Moving to early modern times, George Sale's 1734 translation
of the Qur'an is preceded by a historical introduction, divided

into four 'prefaces', which remains to this day a model of calm and balanced argument, and deserves wider recognition among historians of the European historiography of non-European cultures. Rejecting the Qur'an's divine origin, Sale nevertheless affirms the essential sincerity of Muhammad and presents the ethical teachings of the Qur'an with considerable sympathy. Sale's translation remains central to the history of the Qur'an in English, while his prefaces are a literary monument to the European Enlightenment.

The nineteenth century in Europe witnessed what in many ways was a reversal of medieval attitudes towards the Qur'an, possibly under the impact of renewed missionary zeal combined with European colonization of much of the Muslim world. Typical of nineteenth-century scholarship in English is Sir William Muir's *The Life of Muhammad From Original Sources*, first published in 1861 and frequently reprinted. In his conclusion, Muir includes the devastating statement that 'The sword of Muhammad and the Kor'an are the most stubborn enemies of Civilization, Liberty and Truth which the world has yet known.' This work was by far the best-known among English-speaking Muslims of India and Egypt, and occasioned innumerable rebuttals. Unfortunately, Muirism of one description or another still thrives in certain conservative government circles in the West and among their alleged experts on Islam.

But the world of Western scholarship on the Qur'an in the last half century or so has taken a new turn, pioneered, according to some (for example Walid Saleh, above), by German scholarship. Typical of this is *The Qur'an as Text*, edited by Stefan Wild (Leiden: Brill, 1996), which deliberately abandons the nineteenth-century paradigm of reading the Qur'an as if it were an ignorant paraphrase of the Bible, and instead reads it on its own terms with the aid of modern literary hermeneutics. This is one area where collaboration between Muslim and non-Muslim scholarship holds much promise, in terms of both new knowledge to be gained and a better understanding of the place of the Qur'an and of Islam in the contemporary world.

The Qur'an

The Qur'an

The Opening

In the name of God,
Merciful to all,
Compassionate to each!

Praise be to God, Lord of the Worlds:
Merciful to all,
Compassionate to each!
Lord of the Day of Judgement.
It is You we worship, and upon You we call for help.
Guide us to the straight path,
The path of those upon whom Your grace abounds,
Not those upon whom anger falls,
Nor those who are lost.

The Cow

In the name of God,
Merciful to all,
Compassionate to each!

Alif Lam Mim*

Behold the Book!
No trace of doubt in it.
A guide to the pious,
To those who believe in the Unseen,
Who perform prayer,
And who spend from Our bounty;
Those too who believe in what has been revealed to you,
And what has been revealed before you,

And who know for certain that there is an afterlife.
These are truly guided by their Lord;
2:5   These are truly saved.

As for the unbelievers, it is all the same if you warn or do not warn them: they will not believe. God has sealed up their hearts, their hearing and their vision with a shroud, and terrible punishment awaits them.

Among people, there are those who say: 'We believe in God and in the Last Day.' But they are not true believers. They try to deceive God and the believers but, unknown to them, deceive only themselves. Sickness abides in their hearts and God increases their malady. A painful punishment awaits them for the lies they uttered.

And if someone says to them: 'Do not sow discord in the earth,' they answer: 'We are merely trying to bring people together.' In 2:12   truth, they are sowers of discord, but they know it not.

And if someone says to them: 'Believe as other people have believed,' they answer: 'Should we believe like the weak and ignorant?' In truth, they themselves are weak and ignorant, but they know it not.

And when they meet the believers they tell them: 'We believe'; but when alone with their devilish friends, they tell them: 'We are with you. We were merely jesting.' It is God Who jests with them. He gives them rope to go astray in their excess.

These are people who bartered true guidance for waywardness. Their commerce did not profit them, nor are they rightly guided.

In likeness, they are like one who lit a fire. When the fire illumined his surroundings, God extinguished their light and left them in darkness, unseeing.

Deaf.

Dumb.

Blind.

2:18   They do not repent.

Or else like a torrent from on high, with layers of darkness,
    thunder and lightning.
They press their fingers to their ears from the peal of thunder,
    fearing death.
But God engulfs the unbelievers.
The lightning all but robs them of sight.
Whenever it lights their way, they move forward; but when it
    grows dark they stand still.
Had God willed, He would have taken away their hearing and
    their sight.
God has power over all things.   2:20

O People! Worship your Lord Who created you as well as those
who came before you. Perhaps you will fear Him.

It is He Who made the earth a bed for you, the sky a canopy;
Who causes water to descend from the sky with which He brings
forth fruits as sustenance for you. Do not, therefore, set up any
equals to God when you know better.

If you doubt what We revealed to Our servant, bring forth
one *sura* like it. And summon your witnesses, any other than
God, if you are truthful. But if you do not, and surely you will
not, beware of the Fire whose fuel is mankind and stones, made
ready for the unbelievers.   2:24

Proclaim glad tidings to those who have believed and done good
deeds: for them there are Gardens beneath which rivers flow.
Whenever they are offered its fruits as sustenance, they say: 'This
is what we were provided with before' – all alike in excellence is
their provision.

In these Gardens they have immaculate spouses.

In them they abide eternally.   2:25

God shies not from drawing a parable even from an insect, or
    else anything large or small.
Those who believe know it is the truth from their Lord.
Those who disbelieve say: 'What did God intend by this parable?'

God thereby leads many astray,
And guides many.
But the dissolute alone He leads astray,
They who violate God's covenant after God had established it,
Who sever what God commanded to be joined,
Who sow discord on earth.
2:27   These are the losers.

How can you disbelieve in God when you were once dead,
        and He granted you life?
He shall cause you to die,
Then He shall resurrect you,
Then to Him you shall return.
It is He Who created for you all that is on earth. Then He
        ascended to heaven, and arrayed them in seven heavens.
2:29   All-Knowing is He.

And remember when God said to the angels: 'I shall appoint a
deputy on earth,' and they answered: 'Will you place therein
one who sows discord and sheds blood while we chant Your
praises and proclaim Your holiness?'
2:30   God said: 'I know what you do not.'

He taught Adam the names of all things. Then He displayed
them to the angels and said: 'Tell me the names of these things,
if you are truthful.'
      They said: 'Glory be to You! We have no knowledge except
2:32 what You taught us. You! You are All-Knowing, All-Wise.'
      God said: 'O Adam, reveal to them their names.' When Adam
revealed their names, God said: 'Did I not tell you that I know
the Unseen of the heavens and the earth? That I know what you
2:33 make public and what you hide?'

And remember when God said to the angels: 'Kneel before
Adam'; they knelt, all except Satan, who disdained, grew proud
and became an unbeliever.

We said: 'O Adam, inhabit the Garden, you and your wife. Eat from it in comfort and ease, wherever you wish. But do not come near this tree, or else you will transgress.' Satan seduced them away from it, and caused them to leave their earlier abode.

We said: 'Go down, an enemy each to each! On earth you will find habitation and a certain term of life.'   2:36

And Adam obeyed the words of his Lord, and his Lord pardoned him.

He is Ever-Ready to pardon; He is Compassionate to each.

We said: 'Go down from it, all of you. And when My guidance comes to you, whoever follows My guidance, no fear shall fall upon them, nor shall they grieve. But those who disbelieve and call Our wonders lies, these are the people of the Fire, in which they shall abide for ever.'   2:39

Children of Israel, remember My bounty which I bestowed
    upon you.
Fulfil My covenant and I shall fulfil yours. It is Me you should
    fear!
Believe in that which I have revealed, confirming what you
    possess.
Do not be the first to blaspheme against it.
Do not sell away My revelations for a paltry sum. It is Me you
    should revere!
Do not confound truth with falsehood, and knowingly repress
    the truth.
Offer up prayers; hand out alms; kneel in prayer with those
    who kneel.

How can you command people to do good and forget yourselves, all the while reciting the Book? Do you not understand?

Seek help in patience and prayer, prayer that is indeed burdensome except for the devout, for those who believe they will meet their Lord, and that to Him they shall return.   2:46

Children of Israel, remember My bounty which I bestowed upon you, and that I preferred you above all mankind. Fear a Day when no soul can atone one whit for another, when no intercession is accepted from it, no ransom is admitted, and no helpers are at hand.

Remember when We delivered you from Pharaoh and his people, who practised their evil torments upon you, as they killed your children and debauched your women. Grievous
2:49   indeed was that ordeal from your Lord!

Remember how We sundered the sea with you and saved you,
2:50   and how We drowned the people of Pharaoh as you looked on.

Remember when We appointed for Moses forty nights and how you set up the calf after him. Evil was your deed. Later, We
2:52   pardoned you, so that you might render thanks.

Remember when We gave Moses the Book and the Criterion,
2:53   that you might be guided.

Remember when Moses said to his people: 'My people, you sinned against yourselves when you took the calf as idol. Repent before your Creator and kill each other. This is better for you with your Creator.

'God shall relent towards you: All-Forgiving and Com-
2:54   passionate is He.'

Remember when you said to Moses: 'We shall not trust you unless we see God face to face' and the thunderclap struck you down as you said this. Then We brought you back from the dead, that you might give thanks. And We made the clouds to give you shade and We sent down manna and quail – 'Eat from the delights We provided you.'
2:57   They did Us no wrong; it was themselves they wronged.

Remember when We said: 'Enter this city and eat from it in

comfort and ease, wherever you wish. Enter the gate with heads bowed, and profess repentance, so that We may forgive your sins and increase the reward of the righteous.'

However, the sinners altered the words they were commanded to speak; so We caused a torment to descend from heaven upon the sinners, as punishment for their iniquity. 2:59

Remember when Moses prayed for water for his people and We said: 'Strike the rock with your staff' and twelve springs gushed forth from it. Every group recognized their drinking place – 'Eat and drink from God's bounty and do not corrupt the earth with disobedience.' 2:60

Remember when you said to Moses: 'We can no longer bear to eat one kind of food, so pray to your Lord for us that He may bring out what plants there are on earth: green herbs, cucumbers, corn, lentils and onions.'

He said: 'Do you wish to exchange what is of lesser worth for what is better? Then go and inhabit Egypt and your wish will be granted.'

It was thus that humility and wretchedness were decreed upon them. They departed, hard-pressed by the anger of God, for they had blasphemed against the wonders of God and would kill their prophets unjustly, out of disobedience. They had indeed transgressed. 2:61

As for the believers, for the Jews, the Christians and the Sabeans* who believe in God and the Last Day, and who do righteous deeds – these have their wage with their Lord. No fear shall fall upon them, nor shall they grieve. 2:62

Remember when We made the covenant with you, and raised the Mount above you – 'Hold fast to what We have revealed to you! Remember what it contains; perhaps you will grow pious.' But then you relapsed. Were it not for God's bounty upon you and His mercy, you would have been lost. 2:64

You know full well about those among you who transgressed the Sabbath and how We said to them: 'Turn into apes, most wretched!', thus turning it into a punishment for present and future sin, but a moral lesson for the pious.

2:66

Remember when Moses said to his people: 'God commands you to slaughter a cow.'

They said: 'Are you mocking us?'

He said: 'God be my refuge that I should traduce His message!'

They said: 'Pray to your Lord that He spell out for us what she may be.'

He said: 'God says it is a cow, neither old nor a heifer, but midway between. So perform what you have been commanded.'

They said: 'Pray to your Lord that He spell out her colour for us.'

He said: 'He says it is a yellow cow, very bright in colour, a joy to behold.'

They said: 'Pray to your Lord that He point her out to us, for cows are all alike to us and we, God willing, shall be guided.'

He said: 'He says it is a cow neither yoked to plough the earth nor to water the sown, a cow wholesome and all of one colour.'

They said: 'Now you speak the truth.'

2:71   So they slaughtered it, having come close to not doing so.

Remember when you killed a soul, and how you quarrelled about the matter. But God always reveals what you hide.

So We said: 'Strike the dead man with a piece of the cow.'

This is how God resurrects the dead and reveals His wonders to you; perhaps you will understand.

Then your hearts grew hard,

Becoming like rocks, or even harder;

For among rocks there are some from which streams gush,

And some have cracks from which water flows,

And some which roll down from fear of God.

2:74   But God is not unmindful of what you do.

Do you really expect them to believe in the message sent to you, when a group among them would hear the speech of God and then pervert it, knowingly, after having grasped its meaning?

Thus, when they meet the believers, they tell them: 'We believe.' But when they meet one another in private, they say: 'Do you speak to them of what God has revealed to you so that they dispute with you before your Lord? Have you no understanding?'

Know they not that God knows what they conceal and what they proclaim?   2:77

Among them too are unlettered folk who understand Scripture only as false hopes. But they are living in illusion.

Wretched too are those who write Scripture with their own hands and then claim it to be from God, that they may sell it for a small price!

Woe to them for what their hands have written!

Woe to them for the profit they made!   2:79

They say: 'The Fire shall touch us for a few days only.'

Say to them: 'Have you a compact with God? God does not go back on His pledge. Or do you impute to God that which you know not?'

Rather, he who engenders an evil deed, and his sin engulfs him – these are the inhabitants of the Fire, dwelling therein for ever.

But those who believe and do good works, they are the inhabitants of the Garden, dwelling therein for ever.   2:82

Remember when We made a covenant with the Children of Israel that 'You worship none but God; be kind to parents, kinsmen, orphans and the poor; speak kindly to people; perform the prayer and give alms.' Then you turned away, all but a few among you, recanting.   2:83

Remember when We made a covenant with you that 'You shall not shed one another's blood, nor shall you drive one another out of your homes.' You compacted thus and you yourselves stood witness. But there you are, killing one another and driving one party among you from their homes, joining forces against them in sin and aggression. Yet, if they come to you as captives, you pay their ransom, even though their expulsion was a thing forbidden to you.

Do you then believe in one portion of the Book and disbelieve in another?

What recompense for one who does this but shame in this present life, and on the Day of Resurrection, away to a punishment most dire?

2:85   God is not unmindful of what you do.

Those who have purchased the present life in exchange for the afterlife, for them punishment shall not be lightened, nor shall 2:86 they find any to help them.

We revealed the Book to Moses, and We sent after him messengers in succession; and We granted Jesus son of Mary evident miracles and strengthened him with the Holy Spirit. Whenever a messenger came to you with a message contrary to your whims, did you not grow arrogant, calling some liars and killing others? They said: 'Our hearts are shrouded.' Rather, God 2:88 cursed them for their unbelief. Little is their faith.

When there came to them a Book from God, confirming what they had, and they had previously called for God's help against the unbelievers – when there came to them that which they recognized, they blasphemed against it.
God's curse upon the blasphemers!
Wretched the price they paid for their souls:
That they should blaspheme against what God revealed, in
     envy that God would make His grace descend upon
     whomever He wills of His creatures!

So their lot was anger piled upon anger,
And a humbling punishment awaits the unbelievers.   2:90

And if one says to them: 'Believe in what God has sent down,'
they answer: 'We believe in what was sent down to us.' They
blaspheme against what came after, even though it is the Truth
confirming what they themselves possess.
   Say to them: 'Why then did you kill previous prophets of God
if you are true believers?'   2:91

Moses brought you clear signs. Thereafter you idolized the calf,
acting in wickedness.   2:92

Remember when We covenanted with you and raised above you
the Mount: 'Hold fast to what We have revealed to you, and
listen.'
   They said: 'We hear and disobey.'
   They were made to imbibe love of the calf in their hearts
because of their unbelief.
   Say: 'Wretched is that which your faith commands you, if
you are true believers.'
   Say: 'If the Last Abode with God belongs to you alone from
all mankind, then wish for death if you are sincere.'
But they will never wish for death, because of what they had
      committed before.
And God knows full well who the wicked are.
You will find them, of all mankind, those most attached to life.

Among the polytheists you will find one who longs for a
      lifespan of a thousand years.
Yet even such a lifespan will nudge him not a jot from
      punishment.
And God sees full well what they do.   2:96

Say: 'Whoever is an enemy of Gabriel, let him know that it was
He Who made him descend upon your heart, by God's leave,

confirming His revelation, a guidance and glad tidings to the faithful.

'Whoso is an enemy of God, His angels and messengers, of Gabriel and Michael, know that God is the enemy of unbelievers.'

We brought down upon you signs and wonders most evident; only the dissolute can disbelieve in them. Can it be that every time they make a covenant, a group of them disavows it? In truth, most of them have no faith.

2:100

So, when a messenger from God came to them, confirming what they already possessed, a group among those to whom Scripture had been sent turned their backs upon the Book of God, pretending not to recognize it. Instead, they followed what the devils had narrated during the reign of Solomon. But it was not Solomon who disbelieved; rather, it was the disbelieving devils. It was they who taught mankind sorcery and what was revealed in Babylon to Harut and Marut.* But these two taught no one without first telling them: 'We are a mere temptation, so do not disbelieve.'

Yet they learn from them what enables them to separate a man from his wife.

And they do no harm to anyone with their sorcery, save by God's leave.

They learn what harms them and does them no good.

They know full well that he who deals in sorcery has no share in the afterlife.

Wretched is the price they pay for their souls, if only they knew!

Had they believed and feared God, the reward from God would have been best, if only they knew!

2:103

O believers! Do not say 'Hey, listen!' but rather 'Please regard us' and attend.

For unbelievers there is torment most severe.

Unbelievers among the People of the Book* or among the
  polytheists would much prefer it if no bounty descends
  upon you from your Lord.
But God singles out for His mercy whomsoever He wills.
God's grace is most abundant.   2:105

For every verse We abrogate or cause to be forgotten,
We bring down one better or similar.
Do you not already know that God has power over all
  things?
Do you not already know that to God belongs sovereignty of
  heavens and earth?
That apart from God, you have neither patron nor
  champion?
Or do you wish to interrogate your Messenger, as Moses was
  once interrogated?
He who exchanges faith for unbelief has missed the right
  path.   2:108

Among the People of the Book there are many who wish they
could turn you back to unbelief after you have embraced the
faith. This they do out of the envy of their souls, and once the
truth has become clear to them.
Forgive and pardon – that is, until God reveals His command.
God has power over all things.   2:109

Perform the prayer and hand out alms.
Any good deed you do, laid by for your souls in this life,
You shall surely find with God.
God sees full well what you do.   2:110

They say: 'Only Jews and Christians will enter the Garden.'
Such are their fancies!
    Say to them: 'Show me your proof if you speak the truth.'
    Yes, indeed. He who surrenders his face to God in all piety

shall receive his reward from his Lord. No fear shall fall upon
2:112 them, nor shall they grieve.

The Jews say the Christians count for nothing; the Christians
say the Jews count for nothing; yet both recite the Book. The
ignorant repeat their statements.

   God shall judge between them on the Day of Resurrection
2:113 regarding that upon which they differ.

Who is more impious than he who forbids the houses of God's
worship from mention of His name, and devotes himself to their
destruction? These shall not enter them except in fear. Shame is
2:114 their lot in this world, and terrible punishment in the next.

To God belongs the East and the West.
Wherever you turn, there is the face of God.
God is All-Encompassing, All-Knowing.
They say: 'God has fathered a child.'
Glory be to Him! To Him, rather, belongs all that is in the
      heavens and on earth.
All mankind obeys Him.
Marvellous Creator of the heavens and the earth!
2:117 When He decrees a matter, He merely says to it: 'Be!' and it is.

The ignorant say: 'If only God would speak to us! If only a sign
would descend upon us!'

   This too was said by past generations, word for word. Their
minds are much alike.
2:118 But We have made clear these signs to a people of firm faith.

We have sent you with the Truth,
A herald of good tidings,
A bearer of warning.
2:119 You are not accountable for the denizens of hell.

Jews and Christians will not approve of you unless you follow their religion.

Say: 'God's guidance is true guidance.'

If you follow their whims after the Knowledge which has come to you, you will have in God neither patron nor champion. Those to whom We revealed the Book recite it as it should rightly be recited. They believe in it. But those who repudiate it, they are truly lost.   2:121

Children of Israel, remember My bounty, and that I preferred you above all mankind. Fear a Day when no soul can atone one whit for another; when no ransom is accepted for it, when no intercession can do it any good, and no helpers are at hand.   2:123

Remember when his Lord tested Abraham with certain rulings and how Abraham fulfilled them.

God said: 'I shall appoint you an exemplar to mankind.'

Abraham said: 'And also my descendants.'

God said: 'Evildoers shall not enjoy My covenant.'

Remember when We set up the House as a place frequented by mankind, a sanctuary: 'Take the station of Abraham as a place of worship.' And We thus commanded Abraham and Ishmael: 'To sanctify My House for those who circle around it, those who seclude themselves in it and those who bow and prostrate themselves in prayer.'   2:125

Remember when Abraham said: 'Lord, make this city a sanctuary and bless its people with sustenance, those of them who believe in God and the Last Day.'

God said: 'As for him who disbelieves, I shall grant him brief enjoyment and then shall consign him to the torment of the Fire, a wretched fate indeed.'   2:126

Remember when Abraham and Ishmael were raising up the foundations of the House:
'Our Lord, accept this from us,

You are All-Hearing, All-Knowing.
Our Lord, make us surrender ourselves to You,
And from our descendants a nation which surrenders itself
    to You.
Show us our holy rituals,
And forgive us. You are All-Forgiving, All-Merciful.
Our Lord, send them a messenger, of their number,
Who shall recite to them Your verses,
Teaching them the Book and the Wisdom,
And who shall purify them.
2:129 You are the Almighty, the All-Wise.'

Who can wilfully abandon the religion of Abraham unless it be
one who makes a fool of himself? We chose Abraham in this
2:130 world, and in the hereafter he shall be among the righteous.

Remember when his Lord said to him: 'Surrender!' and he said:
'I surrender to the Lord of the Worlds.' Abraham entrusted his
children with this commandment, as did Jacob: 'My children,
God has chosen the pure religion for you. Depart not from this
life except as those who surrender.'
    Or were you witnesses when death came to Jacob?
    When he said to his sons: 'Whom will you worship when
I am gone?'
    They said: 'We shall worship your Lord, and the Lord of your
fathers Abraham, Ishmael and Isaac: One God. To Him we
2:133 surrender.'

That was a nation which passed away.
They have earned their reward, and you have earned yours.
2:134 You will not be held responsible for what they did.

They say: 'Become Jews or Christians and you will be guided
aright.'
    Say: 'Rather, the religion of Abraham, of pristine faith. Nor
was he a polytheist.'

Say: 'We believe in God, and in what was revealed to us,
In what was revealed to Abraham, to Ishmael, to Isaac and
    Jacob and the Tribes,
In what was revealed to Moses and Jesus,
In what was revealed to prophets by their Lord.
We make no distinction between any of them,
And to Him we surrender.'   2:136

If they then believe in what you believe, they are guided aright.
If they turn away, it is they who are in discord. God will deal
with them on your behalf. He is All-Hearing, All-Knowing.
    The hue of God is upon us! And what better hue than God's?
It is Him we worship.
    Say: 'Do you argue with us concerning God, He being our
Lord and your Lord, and we have our works and you have
yours, while to Him we remain sincere? Or are you saying that
Abraham, Ishmael, Isaac, Jacob and the Tribes were Jews or
Christians?'
    Say: 'Are you more knowledgeable or is God?'
    Who is more unjust than he who keeps hidden a testament
he has from God?
    God is not unaware of what you do.   2:140

That was a nation which passed away.
They have earned their reward, and you have earned yours.
You will not be held responsible for what they did.   2:141

Foolish people shall say: 'What turned them away from the
direction of prayer they once followed?'
    Say: 'To God belongs the East and the West. He guides whom-
soever He wills onto a straight path.'   2:142

Thus, We have appointed you as a median nation,
To be witnesses for mankind,
And the Prophet to be a witness for you.
    And We did not appoint the direction of prayer which you

once followed, except to distinguish him who follows the Prophet from him who turns on his heels. This change of direction was indeed a grave matter, except for those whom God has guided. But God would not allow your earlier faith to have been in vain.

   Towards mankind, God is All-Caring, Compassionate to
2:143 each.

We have seen you turning your face from side to side in the heavens,
So We will now turn you towards a direction that will please you:
Turn your face towards the Sacred Mosque.
Wherever you may be, turn your faces towards it.
Those granted the Book know that this is the truth from their Lord.
2:144 God is not unaware of what they do.

Were you to come to those granted the Book with every kind of manifest proof, they would not follow your direction. Nor will you follow their direction. Nor indeed do some of them follow the direction of others. Were you to follow their whims, after having received Knowledge, you would then be truly unjust.

Those to whom We brought the Book know it as well as they know their own children.
   Some of them suppress the truth knowingly.
   This is the Truth from your Lord: be not among those who
2:147 doubt.

For every community there is a direction towards which it turns;
Therefore, hasten to charitable deeds.
Wherever you may be, God will ultimately gather you in.
God has power over all things.
From any place you leave, turn your face towards the Sacred Mosque.

It is indeed the Truth from your Lord;
God is not unaware of what you do.
From any place you leave, turn your face towards the Sacred
    Mosque.
In any place you may be, turn your faces towards it,
So that people can have no argument against you, except for
    the unfair among them.
These you should not fear.
Rather, fear Me, so that I can complete My bounty upon you,
And that you may be guided aright.   2:150

Likewise, We sent among you a messenger, reciting Our verses
    to you, purifying you,
And teaching you the Book and Wisdom:
Teaching you that which you knew not.
So remember Me and I will remember you.
Give Me thanks, and do not blaspheme.   2:152

O believers, seek help in patience and prayer;
God stands with those who are patient.
Do not say about those who are killed in the cause of God
    that they are dead;
They are indeed alive, but you do not perceive them.   2:154

We shall be testing you with some fear and famine, with loss
    of wealth, lives and crops:
But give glad tidings to the patient,
To those who, when calamity strikes,
Say: 'We belong to God, and to Him we shall return.'
Upon them descend blessings from God and mercy.
They are guided aright.   2:157

Al-Safa and al-Marwa* are among the rites of God. As for him
who performs the Greater Pilgrimage to the Sacred House or
else the Lesser, no blame shall attach to him if he circum-
ambulates them. He who voluntarily does so, in piety, to him

God shall be All-Acknowledging, All-Knowing. Those, however, who suppress what We brought down of evident signs
and Guidance, after We have made it clear to mankind in the
Book, those God shall curse, and all who curse shall curse
them – except for those who repent and reform their conduct
and proclaim their faith. These I shall forgive. And I am All-
2:160   Forgiving, Compassionate to each.

Those who blaspheme and die as unbelievers, upon them shall
descend the curse of God, of the angels and of all mankind, and
under that curse they shall abide eternally. Their torment shall
not be lessened, nor shall any defence be accepted from them.
        Your God is One God. There is no god but He, Merciful to
2:163   all, Compassionate to each.

In the creation of the heavens and the earth,
In the cycle of night and day,
In ships that plough the sea, to mankind's benefit,
In what God causes to descend from the sky of water,
Giving life to the earth, hitherto dead,
And peopling it with all manner of crawling creatures,
In varying the winds and clouds, which run their course
        between sky and earth –
2:164   In these are signs for people who reflect.

Among people there are those who, instead of God, attach
themselves to peers whom they love as much as they love God.
But the faithful love God most. If only the unjust would realize,
when they face torment, that all power belongs to God, that
God is terrible in punishment! Those who were followed would
then disown their followers, they would see the torment, and
the links between them would be severed. The followers will
say: 'If only we could have another chance, we would disown
them as they disowned us.' Thus will God show them their
2:167   deeds as deepest remorse. Nor will they ever leave the Fire.

O mankind, eat what issues from the earth: all is licit and good
for you. Do not follow in the footsteps of Satan. He is indeed
your manifest enemy. He merely commands you to commit evil
and debauchery and to speak about God that which you do
not know.   2:169

And when it is said to them: 'Follow what God has brought
down,' they answer: 'We would rather follow that which we
found our ancestors have practised.' How so, when their ancestors understood nothing, nor were rightly guided? The likeness
of those who disbelieve is like one who bellows to a creature
that cannot give ear to anything save 'Come!' or 'Go!'
   Deaf.
   Dumb.
   Blind.
   They do not understand.   2:171

O believers, eat from the good things We have provided you,
and give thanks to God if it is Him you truly worship. He merely
made illicit for you carrion, blood, flesh of pig and whatever
has been consecrated to other than God. But he who is forced
to do so, not in transgression nor in defiance, no sin shall attach
to him.
   God is All-Forgiving, Compassionate to each.   2:172

Those who suppress what God has revealed of the Book, and
sell it for a paltry profit, those shall eat only fire in their bellies.
God shall not speak to them on the Day of Resurrection, nor
shall He cleanse them. A painful torment awaits them. They are
those who bartered error for right guidance, and torment for
forgiveness. How patiently will they endure the Fire! This is
because God has brought down the Book with the Truth, but
they who differ regarding the Book are sunk deep in discord.   2:176

Virtue does not demand of you to turn your faces eastwards or
westwards. Virtue rather is:

He who believes in God, the Last Day, the angels, the Book and the prophets;

Who dispenses money, though dear, to kinsmen, orphans, the needy, the traveller, beggars and for ransom;

Who performs the prayer and pays the alms;

Who fulfil their contracts when they contract;

Who are steadfast in hardship, calamity and danger;

These are the true believers.

2:177   These are truly pious.

O believers, retaliation for the slain is ordained upon you:

A free man for a free man, a slave for a slave, a female for a female.

But if a brother is forgiven by another regarding what is ordained, then gracious pardon must be offered, and seemly deliverance of payment made. This is an act of leniency from your Lord and a mercy. Whoever commits aggression thereafter, painful torment awaits him.

The prospect of retaliation saves lives, O you who are
2:179   possessed of minds – perhaps you will fear God.

It has been ordained upon you, when death is near to one of you, leaving wealth behind, to make a will in favour of parents and close relatives, impartially. This is incumbent upon the pious. If any person alters it after hearing it, sin will fall upon those who alter it. God is All-Hearing, All-Knowing.

But if a person suspects unfairness or sin from a testator, then brings about harmony among them, no sin shall fall upon him.
2:182   God is All-Forgiving, Compassionate to each.

O believers, the fast is ordained upon you, as it was ordained upon those who came before you – perhaps you will fear God – for a number of days. Whoever is sick among you or on a journey, then a number of other days. Upon those who can bear it, a penance: the feeding of a poor person. He who willingly proffers good, this would be better for him. To fast is better for you, if only you knew. The month of Ramadan is the one in which the Qur'an was sent down – right Guidance to mankind, and clear signs of Guidance and Distinction of truth from false-hood. Those among you who witness it, let him fast therein. Whoever is sick or on a journey, then a number of other days.

God desires ease for you, and desires not hardship.

Thus may you fulfil the number of days assigned, magnify God for having guided you, and perhaps you will be thankful.

If My worshippers ask you about Me, I am near.

I answer the prayer of him who prays when he prays to Me.

So let them obey Me, and believe in Me – perhaps they will be guided aright. 2:186

It is licit for you, on a night of fasting, to lie down with your wives. They are as a garment to you, and you are as a garment to them. God knows you used to cheat, but He has turned His face towards you and forgiven you. But now go in and lie with them, and seek what God has foreordained for you, and eat and drink until the white streak of dawn can be distinguished from the black streak. Then complete your fast until night-time. Do not lie with them in periods when you retire for devotional prayers in mosques.

These are the bounds set by God: do not infringe them. Thus does God make clear His signs to mankind – perhaps they will grow pious. 2:187

Do not consume each other's wealth in falsehood, nor argue the matter with judges in order to consume a portion of people's wealth unjustly, knowing well what you are doing. 2:188

They ask you about the new moons.

Say: 'They are times appointed for mankind, and for the Pilgrimage.' It is not a virtue that you approach houses from their backs. Virtue is to be pious. So approach houses from the front, and fear God – perhaps you will achieve your quest. 2:189

Fight in the cause of God those who fight you, but do not commit aggression: God loves not the aggressors. Slay them wherever you fall upon them, and expel them from where they had expelled you; apostasy by force is indeed more serious than slaying. Do not fight them near the Holy Mosque unless they fight you therein. If they fight you therein, slay them: such is the reward of unbelievers. But if they desist, then God is All-Forgiving, Compassionate to each. Fight them until there is no longer forced apostasy, and the religion is God's. If they desist, no aggression is permitted except against the wicked. A Holy Month will substitute for a Holy Month, and sacrilege calls for retaliation. Whoever commits aggression against you, retaliate against him in the same measure as he committed against you.
2:194   Fear God and know that God stands by the pious.

Spend wealth in the cause of God and do not, with your own hands, hurl yourself into destruction. Be generous, for God loves
2:195   the generous.

Carry out the Greater Pilgrimage and the Lesser, for the sake of God. If fear prevents you, make a sacrificial offering of whatever is ready to hand. Do not shave your heads until your offering reaches its appointed place. For those among you who are ill or are diseased in the head, expiation is set: fasting or else a gift of alms, or sacrifice. When you feel secure, then whoever breaks his state of consecration in the period between the Lesser and the Greater Pilgrimage shall make an offering of whatever is ready to hand. He who has nothing to offer must fast for three days during the Greater Pilgrimage and for seven when you return, making ten full days. This is ordained for one whose family is not present at the Holy Mosque. So fear God and
2:196   know that God is severe in punishment.

The Pilgrimage occurs in familiar months. He who undertakes the Pilgrimage during these months, from him no promiscuity, no vice and no discord is allowed during the Pilgrimage. Whatever good you do is known to God. Lay up stores for yourselves, but the best store is piety. Be pious towards Me, O you who are possessed of minds.   2:197

No blame attaches to you if you seek bounty from your Lord. When you return from 'Arafat,* remember God at the Holy Shrine. Remember how He guided you when before you had been astray. Then return by way of the rest of the people, and seek God's forgiveness. God is All-Forgiving, Compassionate to each.

When you have completed your sacred rites, remember God as you remember your own parents, or even more intensely. For among people is one who says: 'Lord, give us in this world.' But he shall have no share of the life hereafter. Among them are those who say: 'Lord, grant us good in this world and good in the world hereafter, and spare us the torment of the Fire.' To these shall fall a share of what they earned. God is swift in reckoning. Remember God during days appointed. He who leaves in haste after two days commits no sin; he who tarries commits no sin, provided he is God-fearing. Fear God and be assured that to Him you will ultimately be gathered.   2:202

Among people is one who speaks of this present life in a manner that pleases you. He calls upon God to witness what is in his heart, all the while being the staunchest of enemies. But when he departs, he plies the land in order to corrupt it, destroying cultivation and flocks. God loves not corruption. If it is said to him: 'Fear God,' he waxes proud of his crime. Let hell suffice him, an evil cradle indeed!   2:206

Among people is one who sells his soul seeking the pleasure of God. God is Tender towards His worshippers.   2:207

O believers! Enter the fold of peace, all of you. Do not follow in the footsteps of Satan, for he is to you a manifest enemy. If you slip after clear signs have been revealed to you, be assured that God is Almighty, All-Wise. Are they really waiting for God

to come to them in the shadowy folds of clouds, with His angels,
2:210 when judgement is pronounced and all revert to God?

Ask the Children of Israel how many a manifest sign We revealed
to them. Whoever traduces the bounty of God after it has come
2:211 to him – God is severe in punishment.

For those who disbelieve, the present life has been made to
appear attractive. They mock those who believe and those who
fear God. Above them looms the Day of Resurrection. God
2:212 bestows His bounty on whomsoever He wills, uncountable.

Mankind was one community. Then God sent forth prophets
as heralds of glad tidings and as warners, and sent down with
them the Book with the Truth in order to judge among mankind
matters in which they disputed. But there disputed concerning
it only those to whom the Book was revealed and after clear
signs were sent to them. They did so out of covetousness. Then
God guided the believers to the truth regarding which they
differed, by His leave. God guides whomsoever He wills to a
2:213 path that is straight.

Or do you reckon you will enter the Garden without undergoing
that which befell those who came before you? Violence and
injury touched them and they quaked, to the point where the
Messenger and the believers with him said: 'When will God's
2:214 victory come?' Truly, the victory of God is near.

They ask you what they should spend. Say: 'What you spend of
wealth goes to parents, near kin, orphans, the poor and the
needy wayfarer.' God is well aware of any good you do.

Fighting has been prescribed for you, although it is a matter
hateful to you.
    And yet, for all you know, you may hate something – and it
is good for you.

For all you know, you may love something – and it is harmful to you.

God knows, and you do not know.   2:216

They ask you about the Sacred Month: is there fighting in it? Say: 'Fighting in it is a grave sin. But obstructing the path to God and blasphemy against Him and the Sacred Mosque, and the expulsion of its inhabitants from it, is a graver sin with God.

'Forcing people into unbelief is a graver sin than slaughter.'

They will persist in fighting you until they turn you away from your religion, if they can. He among you who retracts his religion and dies an unbeliever, these are people whose works shall come to nothing in this world and the next. These are the people of the Fire, in which they shall abide for ever.   2:217

Those who believed, and those who emigrated and exerted themselves in the path of God – these can indeed expect the mercy of God. God is All-Forgiving, Compassionate to each.   2:218

They ask you about wine and gambling.

Say: 'In them both lies grave sin, though some benefit, to mankind. But their sin is more grave than their benefit.'

They ask you what they shall spend.

Say: 'The surplus of possessions.'

Thus does God make clear His signs to you. Perhaps you will reflect, in this world and the next.

They ask you about orphans.

Say: 'Probity in what concerns them is a virtue.

'Should you associate with them, they are your brothers.

'God knows the dishonest from the honest. Had God willed, He could have caused you hardship.' God is Almighty, All-Wise.   2:220

Do not marry polytheistic women unless they believe. A female slave, who is a believer, is better than a polytheistic woman, even if winning your admiration. Do not give in marriage to polytheists unless they believe. A male slave who is a believer is better than a polytheistic man, even if winning your admiration. These people will lead you to the Fire, but God leads to the Garden and forgiveness, by His leave.

2:221 He makes clear His signs to mankind; perhaps they will remember and reflect.

They ask you about menstruation.

Say: 'It is a sore. So keep away from women in menstruation, and do not come near them until they become clean. When clean, approach them from where God ordered you.'

God loves those who constantly repent, who constantly cleanse themselves.

Your women are your sowing field: approach your field whenever you please. Lay up good works for yourselves and fear God, and know that you shall surely meet Him. Proclaim glad 2:222 tidings to the believers.

Do not make an oath by God an excuse for you not to do good works, to fear God or to act honourably towards people. God is All-Hearing, All-Knowing. God does not hold you to account for carelessness in pronouncing oaths, but He holds you to account for what your hearts have earned. God is All-Forgiving, 2:225 All-Forbearing.

For those who forsake their wives is prescribed a waiting period of four months. If they go back on their oath, God is All-Forgiving, Compassionate to each. If they are determined on divorce, God is All-Hearing, All-Knowing. Divorced women shall refrain from remarriage for three menstrual cycles. Nor is it licit for them to hide what God has created in their wombs, if they truly believe in God and the Last Day. Meanwhile, their husbands have a better right to take them back if they desire

reconciliation. Women have the selfsame rights and obligations
in conformity with fairness, but men are a grade more responsible than them. God is Almighty, All-Wise.   2:228

Divorce can be uttered twice, to be followed either by holding
her back in friendship or letting her go in fairness. It is not licit
for you to take back anything you have given them unless
the two of them fear that they cannot conform to the bounds
of God. If you fear that the two of them will not conform to
the bounds of God, no blame attaches to them both if the
woman gives back that with which she sets herself free. These
are the bounds set by God; do not transgress them. Whoso
transgresses the bounds of God, these are indeed sinners. If he
divorces her, she shall not be licit to him again until she marries
another husband. If the other husband divorces her, no blame
attaches to them if they return to each other, provided they
believe they can conform to the bounds of God.

And these are the bounds of God, which He makes plain to
people who understand.   2:230

If you divorce women, and they reach their appointed term,
hold them back in amity or let them go in amity. Do not hold
them back out of malice, to be vindictive. Whoso does this does
himself an injustice. Do not treat the revelations of God as
matters for jesting. Remember the bounties of God upon you
and what He revealed to you of the Book and Wisdom, wherewith He edifies and instructs you. Fear God and know that God
is Omniscient.   2:231

If you divorce women, and they reach their appointed term, do
not deter them from marrying their former husbands, provided
they both freely agree to do so, and in an affable manner.
Through this commandment are edified and instructed those
among you who believe in God and the Last Day. This would
be better for you and more pure in heart.

God knows and you do not know.   2:232

Mothers nurse their infants two full years for one who desires
to complete the course of nursing. Upon the father rests the duty
of maintenance and clothing, affably granted.

No soul is burdened except with what it can bear.

No mother is to be harmed through her child, nor father
through his.

The same duty rests upon the heir.

If the two of them desire to wean their child through mutual
agreement and consultation, no blame attaches to them. If you
wish to deliver your children to a wet-nurse, no blame attaches
to you provided you pay what you have agreed upon, fairly and
affably.

2:233   Fear God and know that God sees all that you do.

As for those among you who die and leave wives behind, their
widows are to hold themselves apart for a period of four months
and ten nights. When they reach their appointed term, no blame
shall attach to you regarding what they might honourably do
with themselves. God is All-Experienced as to what you do. Nor
shall any blame attach to you if you allude to a marriage pro-
posal with these widows or else keep this to yourselves. God
knows that you shall propose to them. But do not make promises
to them in secret, unless it be in fair and honourable speech. Do
not tie the knot of marriage until the recorded period has
reached its term.

Know that God knows what is in your hearts. So fear Him
2:235   and know that God is All-Forgiving, All-Forbearing.

No blame attaches to you if you divorce women, not having
touched them yet or settled any marriage settlement upon them.
But provide for them – a rich man what he can bear and a poor
man what he can bear. Let this be provided fairly and affably,
and let this be an obligation upon men of good conduct. But if
you divorce them, not having touched them yet though having
settled upon them a marriage settlement, then half of what you

settled, unless they forgo this right or else he who holds the knot of marriage in his hand forgoes it. Yet, if you forgo this right, it would be nearer to piety.

Do not forget to be generous one to another. God sees all that you do.   2:237

Perform your prayers regularly and the afternoon prayer, and stand in God's presence in humility and devotion. But if you are in a state of fear, then pray while walking or mounted. When again you feel secure, remember God and how He taught you that which you knew not.   2:239

Those among you who die leaving wives behind are to leave a bequest to their wives: maintenance for a year and no eviction. If they leave, then no blame attaches to you regarding what they do with themselves, if they do so honourably.

God is Almighty, All-Wise.   2:240

For divorced women, maintenance is decreed, fair and affable. This is an obligation upon the pious. Thus does God make plain His revelations to you; perhaps you will understand.   2:242

Have you not reflected upon those who left their homes, in their thousands, fearing death? And how God said to them: 'Die!' then brought them back to life?
God is bountiful to mankind,
But most mankind will not render thanks.   2:243

Fight in the cause of God and remember that God is All-Hearing, All-Knowing.

Who shall be the one who offers up to God a handsome loan, which God shall multiply for him many times over?

It is God Who holds back or gives in abundance, and to Him you shall return.   2:245

Have you not reflected upon the notables of the Israelites when, after the days of Moses, they said to a prophet of theirs: 'Appoint for us a king so that we may fight in the cause of God'?

He said: 'Do you promise, if fighting is enjoined upon you, that you will fight?'

They said: 'What prevents us from fighting when we have been driven out of our homes, along with our children?' Yet when fighting was enjoined upon them, they turned away, all 2:246 but a few of them. God has full knowledge of evildoers.

Then their prophet said to them: 'God has appointed for you Saul as king.'

They said: 'Why should he reign over us when we have a better claim to kingship than he does, nor has he been granted abundance of wealth?'

He said: 'God has chosen him over you and increased him abundantly in knowledge and bodily stature. God grants rule to whomsoever He wills. God is All-Encompassing, All-Knowing.'

Their prophet said to them: 'The sign of his kingship is that the Ark will come to you in which there is tranquillity from your Lord and a relic from the family of Moses and the family of Aaron, borne by the angels. In this is a sign for you if you 2:248 are true believers.'

When Saul set out with his soldiers, he said: 'God is about to test you at a river. Whoever drinks from it is not my follower; whoever drinks not is my follower, save one who scoops a scoop with his hand.' They drank from it, all but a few of them. When he passed across the river, he and those who believed with him, they said: 'We have no might today against Goliath and his troops.' Those who believed they would meet God said: 'How often a small force has overcome a numerous force, by God's 2:249 leave, and God is with those who stand fast.'

When they came out to do battle against Goliath and his troops, they said: 'Our Lord, pour down steadfastness upon us, make

our feet firm and grant us victory over the host of unbelievers.'
So they defeated them by God's leave, and David killed Goliath,
and God granted him kingship and wisdom, and taught him
what He willed.

Had God not restrained mankind, some by means of others, the
earth would have become chaotic. But God is gracious towards
His creation.   2:251

These are the revelations of God, which We recite to you in
truth. And you are indeed one of the messengers. These messengers, some We have preferred over others. Of their number,
there are some to whom God spoke and He raised some in rank.

And We bestowed clear wonders upon Jesus son of Mary, and
strengthened him with the Holy Spirit. Had God willed, those
who came after them would not have fought each other, once
revelations had come to them. But they fell into dissension and
some of them believed and some disbelieved. Had God willed, they
would not have fought each other, but God does what He wills.   2:253

O believers, spend from that which We provided you before a
Day comes when there is neither commerce nor friendship nor
intercession. The unbelievers are the evildoers indeed.   2:254

God,
There is no god but He,
Living and Everlasting.
Neither slumber overtakes Him nor sleep.
To Him belongs what is in the heavens and what is on earth.
Who shall intercede with Him except by His leave?
He knows their present affairs and their past.
And they do not grasp of His knowledge except what He wills.
His throne encompasses the heavens and the earth;
Preserving them is no burden to Him.
He is the Exalted, the Majestic.   2:255

There is no compulsion in religion.
Right guidance has been distinguished from error.
He who repudiates idols and believes in God
Has grasped a handle most firm, unbreakable.

2:256   God is All-Hearing, All-Knowing.

God is the Patron of the believers:
He leads them from the folds of darkness to the light.
As for the unbelievers, their patrons are the idols:
They lead them from the light to the folds of darkness.

2:257   These are the people of the Fire, in which they abide for ever.

Do you not remember him who disputed with Abraham regarding his lord, since God had granted him kingship?

Remember when Abraham said: 'My Lord is the one Who grants life and deals death'?

He said: 'I grant life and deal death.'

Abraham said: 'God brings the sun up from the east, so bring it up from the west.'

2:258   The blasphemer was struck dumb. God guides not the tyrants.

Or else like the man who passed by a town, its buildings utterly ruined.

He said: 'How will God revive this town after its death?'

God caused him to die for a hundred years and then resurrected him.

God said: 'How long did you remain thus?'

The man replied: 'A day or a part thereof.'

God said: 'No, you remained thus for a hundred years. Look at your food and drink – it has not spoilt. And look at your ass. Thus We shall make you a wonder for mankind. Consider the bones and how We resurrect them and cover them with flesh.'

When the man ascertained all this, he said: 'I witness that
2:259   God is Omnipotent.'

Remember when Abraham said: 'Lord, show me how you revive the dead.'

God said: 'Have you not believed?'

Abraham said: 'Yes, but so that my heart can be at peace.'

God said: 'Take four birds, cut them in pieces and place each piece upon a separate mountain. Then call them and they shall come flying to you. Know that God is Almighty, All-Wise.'   2:260

The likeness of those who spend their wealth in the cause of God is like a grain which brought forth seven ears, in each ear a hundred grains. God multiplies His bounty to whomsoever He pleases. And God is All-Generous, All-Knowing. Those who spend their wealth in the cause of God, and do not follow up what they spent by demanding gratitude or causing offence, shall have their reward with their Lord. No fear shall fall upon them, nor shall they grieve.   2:262

A kind word followed by magnanimity is better than charity followed by rudeness.

God is All-Sufficient, All-Forbearing.   2:263

O believers, nullify not your alms-giving by demanding gratitude or causing offence, like one who spends his wealth in order to flaunt it before people but believes neither in God nor in the Last Day. His likeness is like a boulder upon which is some earth. A downpour strikes it, leaving it hard and smooth. Such people can do nothing with what they have earned. God guides not the impious.

But the likeness of those who spend their wealth, desiring the pleasure of God and to fortify their own faith, is like a garden upon a hill. A downpour strikes it and it produces double its harvest; if not a downpour, then a mere shower. God sees full well all that you do. Would any of you wish to have a garden of palm trees and vines, beneath which rivers flow, and in which he has all kinds of fruit, and then old age overtakes him, and he

has heirs who are minors – now a fiery tempest batters it and it
burns down? Thus does God make clear His signs; perhaps you
2:266 will reflect.

O believers, expend from the good things that you have earned,
and from what We brought forth for your benefit from the
earth. Do not give in alms the inferior portion thereof, since you
yourselves would not accept such unless you turn a blind eye to
it. Know that God is All-Sufficient, All-Praiseworthy. Satan
promises you poverty and commands you to commit sin; God
promises you forgiveness from Him and bounty. God is All-
2:268 Encompassing, Omniscient.

He grants wisdom to whomsoever He wills,
And he to whom wisdom is granted has been granted
     abundant good.
2:269 But none remembers except the prudent.

Whatever sum you spend,
Whatever vow you take,
All is known to God.
2:270 The unjust shall have no champions.

If you make public your gifts, freely given, that would be worthy.
But if you conceal them and donate them to the poor, that
would be even better for you. God will thereby pardon your
2:271 sins. God is All-Experienced with what you do.

It is not up to you to guide them. It is God, rather, Who guides
whomsoever He wills.

Whatever good you expend is for your own souls. Do not
expend anything except to seek the pleasure of God, and whatever good you expend will be paid back to you; you shall not
be wronged. It should go to the poor, those who are constrained
in the cause of God and are unable to journey in the land:

an ignorant person would think them rich because of their self-restraint. You will recognize them by their outward appearance. They do not importune people. Whatever good you expend, God knows it well.   2:273

Those who spend their wealth, night and day, in secret or in public, shall have their reward with their Lord. No fear shall fall upon them, nor shall they grieve.

Those who consume usury shall not rise from the dead except like one whom Satan causes to babble from madness. This is because they allege that commerce is the same as usury. But God has made commerce licit and usury illicit. So he to whom a word of counsel from his Lord has reached, and desists, may keep his previous profit, and his affair is up to God. But he who relapses, these are the inhabitants of the Fire, in which they dwell eternally. God annuls usury and augments free gifts. God loves not every impious lawbreaker.   2:276

Those who believe, do good deeds, perform their prayers and offer alms shall have their reward with their Lord. No fear shall fall upon them, nor shall they grieve.   2:277

O believers, fear God and abandon what remains of usury if you are true believers. If you do not, be forewarned of conflict with God and His Messenger. If you repent, you will keep the capital of your wealth, neither wronging nor wronged. If a person is in difficulties, let there be respite until a time of ease. And if you give freely, it would be better for you, if only you knew. Fear a Day in which you shall return to God, when each soul shall be paid back that which it has earned. And they shall not be wronged.   2:281

O believers, if you contract a debt among yourselves for a set term, write it down. Let a scribe write it down in your presence, in all fairness. Let no scribe refrain from writing as God has taught him. So let him write, and let the debtor dictate. Let him fear God, his Lord, and let him not reduce a jot from it. If the debtor is foolish or feeble or is unable to dictate, let his guardian dictate, in all fairness. Summon two witnesses from among your men. If two men are not at hand, then a man and two women from witnesses of whom you approve. If one woman forgets, the one will remind the other. Nor should witnesses be reluctant if summoned. And do not be reluctant to write it down, whether small or large, up to its set term, for this is fairer in God's eyes, more equitable for testimony, and less cause for you to be distrustful. However, if it concerns an immediate commercial deal that you transact among yourselves, no blame attaches to you if you do not write it down. If you trade with one another, summon witnesses and let no scribe or witness come to any harm. If you do them harm, this would be an offence on your part. Fear God and God will instruct you. And God is Omniscient.

2:282

If you are on a journey and do not find a scribe, let there be a surety handed over. If you trust one another, let the trustee fulfil his trust and let him fear God, his Lord. And do not conceal testimony; whoever conceals it, his heart is sinful and God knows full well what you do.

2:283

To God belongs all that is in the heavens and all that is on earth. Whether you reveal what lies in your souls or whether you conceal it, God will hold you to account, forgiving whomever He wills and punishing whomever He wills. God is Omnipotent.

2:284

The Messenger believes in what was revealed to him from his Lord, as do the believers. All believe in God, His angels, His Books and His messengers. We make no distinction between any of His messengers. They say: 'We hear and obey. We await Your forgiveness, O Lord. To You is the journey's end.'

God charges not any soul except with what it can bear. To its credit belongs what it has earned: upon it falls the burden of what it has deserved.

Our Lord,
Take us not to task if we forget or err.
Our Lord,
Do not lay upon us a heavy burden, as You laid upon those
    who came before us.
Our Lord,
Do not lay upon us what we have no power to bear.
Pardon us, forgive us, be merciful towards us.
You are our Patron, so grant us Your support against the
    impious.   2:286

The House of 'Imran*

In the name of God,
Merciful to all,
Compassionate to each!

Alif Lam Mim

God!
There is no god but He!
Ever-Living, Everlasting.
He sent down to you the Book with the Truth,
Confirming His previous Scriptures.
And He sent down the Torah and the Evangel, beforehand:
A guidance to mankind.
And He sent down the Criterion.

Those who blaspheme against the revelations of God shall meet
with terrible torment. God is Almighty, Vengeful.
    From God nothing is hidden on earth or in heaven. It is He
Who gives you shape in wombs, in any manner He pleases.
    There is no god but He, Almighty, All-Wise.   3:6

It is He Who sent down the Book upon you. In it are verses precise in meaning: these are the very heart of the Book. Others are ambiguous. Those in whose heart is waywardness pursue what is ambiguous therein, seeking discord and seeking to unravel its interpretation. But none knows its interpretation save God, while those deeply rooted in knowledge say: 'We believe in it. All is from our Lord.' Yet none remembers save those possessed of minds.

Our Lord, do not make our hearts swerve now that You have
    guided us;
Grant us mercy from on high.
You – You are the All-Bountiful.
Our Lord, You are the Gatherer of mankind on a Day of
    which there is no doubt.
3:9   God fails not His appointed time.

As for those who blaspheme, neither their wealth nor their progeny shall avail them one jot with God. These shall be fuel for the Fire.

Such was the case with Pharaoh's nation and those who came before them. They called the lie to Our signs and God seized them for their sins. God is terrible in punishment.

Say to those who disbelieve: 'You shall be overcome and
3:12   herded into hell – and what a wretched place of rest!'

A sign was once shown to you, when two troops met in battle, one troop fighting in the cause of God, the other blasphemous, who saw them as twice their number, with their very own eyes. And God supports with His victory whomsoever He pleases. In
3:13   this is a lesson to those possessed of understanding.

Mankind is tempted with love of delights such as women, children, heaps upon heaps of gold and silver, horses finely decked out, cattle and fertile land. All this is the infatuation of this
3:14   present life, but with God is the fairest homecoming.

Say: 'Shall I inform you of what is better than all this? For the pious, there shall be with their Lord Gardens beneath which rivers flow, dwelling in them for ever, and pure spouses and God's good pleasure. And God is Ever-Attentive to His creatures.

It is they who say: 'Our Lord, we have believed. Forgive us our sins and spare us the torment of the Fire.' Steadfast are they and sincere, obedient to God, charitable and imploring God's forgiveness at every break of day. 3:17

God bears witness that there is no god but He,
As do the angels and men of knowledge,
Upholding justice.
There is no god but He, Almighty, All-Wise!
The right religion with God is Islam.

Those to whom the Book had been revealed differed among themselves only after Knowledge had come to them, competing in rivalry with one another. Whoso blasphemes against God's revelations, God is swift in reckoning. If they argue against you, say: 'I have surrendered my face wholly to God, I and those who followed me.' Say to those to whom the Book has been revealed and to those without a Book: 'Have you surrendered?' If they surrender, they are guided aright. If they turn away, your duty is merely to announce the message. And God is Ever-Attentive to His creatures. 3:20

Those who blaspheme against the revelations of God, who kill prophets unjustly, who kill those who bid mankind to fairness – to them announce tidings of an agonizing torment. These are the ones whose deeds have come to nothing in this world and the next; no helpers will they have. 3:22

Have you not considered those who were given a portion of the Book and how, when called to the Book of God to judge between them, a group among them turns away, and repudiates it? This is because they allege that 'the Fire will not touch us except for a limited number of days.' They go astray in their religion

through the falsehoods they devise. How will it be for them
when We gather them upon a Day of which there is no doubt,
when each soul is rewarded for what it has earned, nor will they
3:25 be wronged!

Say: 'O God, Possessor of all power!
You grant power to whomever You wish,
And You wrest power away from whomever You wish.
You exalt whomever You wish,
And You abase whomever You wish.
In Your hand lies all bounty.
You are Omnipotent!
You entwine night with day,
And You entwine day with night.
You cause the living to issue from the dead,
And You cause the dead to issue from the living.
And You bestow Your bounty, without reckoning, upon
3:27   whomever You wish.'

Let not the believers adopt the unbelievers as allies in preference
to believers. Whoso does this counts for nothing with God –
unless you stand in fear of them. And God cautions you regard-
3:28 ing Himself. To God is the journey's end.

Say: 'Whether you conceal what is in your breasts or whether
you reveal it, God knows it. He knows what is in the heavens
and what is on earth. God is Omnipotent.'
     A Day shall come when each soul shall discover what good it
did, all readied before it, and what evil it did: a soul would wish
there was a long interval between itself and that Day! And God
cautions you regarding Himself. And God is gentle with His
3:30 worshippers.

Say: 'If you love God, follow me and God will return your love,
and forgive you your sins. God is All-Forgiving, Compassionate
to each.'

Say: 'Obey God and the Messenger.' If they turn away, God
loves not the unbelievers.   3:32

God chose Adam and Noah, the House of Abraham and the
House of 'Imran above all mankind: a progeny one from
another. God is All-Hearing, All-Knowing.   3:34

Remember when the wife of 'Imran said: 'My Lord, I pledge to
You what is in my womb. It shall be dedicated to Your service.
Accept this from me for it is You – You Who are All-Hearing,
All-Knowing.'

When she gave birth to a female, she said: 'My Lord, I have
given birth and it is a female' – and God knew best what she
had given birth to – 'and a male is not like a female. I have
called her Mary. I seek refuge in You for her and her progeny
from Satan, ever deserving to be stoned.'

God accepted her offering graciously and caused her to grow
up admirably, and entrusted Zachariah with her upbringing.
Whenever Zachariah entered in upon her in the sanctuary, he
found food by her side.

He said: 'Mary, from where do you have this?'

She said: 'It is from God. God provides for whomever He
wills, without reckoning.'

It was then that Zachariah prayed to his Lord, saying: 'My
Lord, grant me from on high a blameless progeny. You always
hear prayers.'

The angels called out to him while he stood in prayer in
the sanctuary: 'God brings you glad tidings of the coming of
John, confirming the truth with a word from God – a lord
among men, chaste, and a prophet from among the righteous.'

He said: 'My Lord, how will I have a son when old age has
come upon me, and my wife is barren?'

He said: 'Thus is God. He does whatever He pleases.'

He said: 'My Lord, grant me a sign.'

He said: 'Your sign is that you shall not speak to people for

three days, except in gestures. Remember your Lord frequently,
3:41 and glorify Him each evening and dawn.'

Remember when the angels said: 'O Mary, God has chosen you,
made you pure and chosen you above all the women of the
world. O Mary, pray constantly to your Lord, and bow down
3:43 in worship, and kneel alongside those who kneel.'

These are reports from the Unseen which We reveal to you. For
you were not with them when they threw down their quills to
determine which of them would care for Mary. Nor were you
3:44 there when they quarrelled among themselves.

Remember when the angels said: 'O Mary, God gives you glad
tidings of a Word from Him. His name is the Christ Jesus son
of Mary, greatly honoured in this world and the next, and
among those drawn nearest to God. He shall speak to mankind
from the cradle, and in maturity, and shall be among the
righteous.'
    She said: 'My Lord, how shall I have a child when no human
has touched me?'
    He said: 'Thus is God. He creates whatever He pleases. When
He decrees a matter, He merely says to it: "Be!" and it is.'
    He shall teach him the Book and the Wisdom, the Torah and
the Evangel. He shall be a messenger to the Children of Israel,
declaring: 'I bring you a sign from your Lord. I will fashion for
you from clay the likeness of a bird, and I shall breathe upon it
and it will become a bird, by God's leave. I shall cure the blind
and the leper and revive the dead by God's leave. I shall reveal
to you what you eat and what you store in your homes. In this
assuredly is a sign for you, if you are true believers. I confirm
what lies before me of the Torah and to make licit for you some
of what had been made illicit. I come to you with a sign from
your Lord. So fear God and obey me. God is my Lord and your
Lord; so worship Him, for here lies a path that is straight.'
    When Jesus detected unbelief from them, he said: 'Who are

my supporters on the path to God?' The Apostles said: 'We are the supporters of God and believe in God. Witness that we are Muslims. Our Lord, we believe in that which You have revealed, and follow the messenger. So inscribe us among those who bear witness.'   3:53

They schemed. But God schemed; and God is the best of schemers.   3:54

Remember when God said: 'O Jesus, I shall cause you to die and make you ascend to Me. I shall purify you from those who blasphemed, and I shall raise those who followed you above those who blasphemed until the Day of Resurrection. Then to Me is your return, and I shall judge between you concerning that in which you disputed. As for those who blasphemed, I shall torment them most severely in this world and the next, and no helpers will they have.' As for those who believed and performed good deeds, He shall pay them their wages in full. God loves not the evildoers.   3:57

These are verses We recite to you, and a Wise Remembrance.   3:58

The likeness of Jesus in God's sight is like Adam. He created him of dust then said to him 'Be!' and he was. This is the truth from your Lord, so be not among those who doubt. Whoso argues with you about him after the Knowledge that has come to you, say: 'Come, let us call together our children and your children, our women and your women, ourselves and your-selves, and let us devoutly pray, and call down God's curse upon those who lie.'

This is the true narrative. There is no god but God. It is God Who is the Almighty, the All-Wise. If they turn away, God knows full well who are the sowers of discord.   3:63

Say: 'People of the Book, let us rally around a discourse common to us and you: that we worship none but God, that we associate nothing with Him, that we do not take each other as lords apart from God.'

3:64   If they turn away, say: 'Bear witness that we are Muslims.'

O People of the Book, why do you dispute concerning Abraham? The Torah and Evangel were revealed only after his time. Will you not be reasonable? Consider. It was you who argued about a matter of which you have knowledge. Why then do you argue about a matter of which you have no knowledge? God knows and you do not know. Abraham was neither a Jew nor a Christian, but a man of pristine faith, a Muslim, nor was he an idolater. Of all mankind, those most deserving of Abraham are his followers, and this prophet standing before you, and those
3:68   who believe. God is the Patron of believers.

A group among the People of the Book longs to lead you astray, but it is only themselves they lead astray, and they know it not.
    O People of the Book, why do you blaspheme against the signs of God, though you witness them?
    O People of the Book, why do you confound truth with
3:71   falsehood, and conceal the truth, even though you know it?

A group among the People of the Book say: 'Believe in what was revealed to the believers at start of day, and repudiate your belief at its end; perhaps the believers will recant. Believe not anyone except him who follows your religion.'
    Say: 'True guidance is God's guidance.'
    They say: 'Believe not that anyone could be given what you have been given, or can argue with you in the presence of your Lord.'
    Say: 'Favour rests in God's hand. He bestows it on whomever He pleases. God is All-Encompassing, Omniscient. He singles out
3:74   for His mercy whomever He wills. God is abounding in favour.'

Among the People of the Book is one who, if you entrust him with a hoard of money, will give it back to you; and among them is one who, if you entrust him with a *dinar*, will give it back to you only if you keep standing over him. This is because they say: 'We have no obligation towards people without Scripture.' They utter falsehood in God's name, and they know it. Not so! He who fulfils his pledge and fears God – God loves the pious. Those who sell the covenant of God and their vows for a paltry sum, no share shall they have in the afterlife. God will not speak to them or regard them on the Day of Resurrection, nor will He purify them. Agonizing punishment awaits them.   3:77

Among them is a group who twist their tongues while reading the Book, so that you might suppose it to be part of the Book, but it is no part of the Book. They claim it is from God, but it is not from God. They utter falsehood in God's name, and they know it. It befits no human being that God should reveal to him the Book, the Wisdom and Prophecy, then says to mankind: 'Be my worshippers apart from God.' Rather should he say: 'Be true guides since you teach the Book and you have studied it.' Such a man would not command you to take angels and prophets as your lords. Would he command you to blaspheme after you have become Muslims?   3:80

Remember when God covenanted with the prophets: 'That I revealed to you some part of the Book and of Wisdom; then there comes to you a prophet, confirming what you already possess so that you are to believe in him and support him.'

God said: 'Do you assent? And do you accept My covenant on these terms?'

They said: 'We assent.'

God said: 'Then bear witness and I too am with you, as a witness.'

Whoever turns away thereafter – these are the deceitful.   3:82

Can they truly desire anything other than the religion of God, when to Him have surrendered all who are in the heavens and

on earth, willingly or compelled, and to Him they shall be
3:83 restored?

Say: 'We believe in God,
And what has been revealed to us,
And what has been revealed to Abraham, Ishmael, Isaac,
    Jacob and the Tribes;
We believe in what was revealed to Moses and Jesus and the
    prophets from God.
We do not distinguish between any of them.
To Him we surrender.'
Whoso desires a religion other than Islam, this shall not be
    accepted from him,
3:85 And in the afterlife he will be among the losers.

How can God guide aright a community who blasphemed after
embracing true belief? Who had once borne witness that the
Prophet is truthful and that clear proofs had come to them?
    God guides not those who are undeserving. These – their
penalty is that upon them shall fall the curse of God, of the
angels and of all mankind. In hell they shall dwell for ever, and
their torment shall not be abated, nor shall they be granted
respite; except for those who repent thereafter and make
3:89 amends. For God is All-Forgiving, Compassionate to each.

Those who blasphemed after their belief and increased further
in blasphemy: their repentance shall not be accepted. These are
the truly wayward.
    Those who blaspheme and die as unbelievers: there shall not
be accepted from any of them even an amount of gold which
fills the earth, were he to ransom himself with such. These shall
meet with agonizing torment, and no helpers shall come to
their aid.

You shall not attain virtue until you spend from what you truly
cherish. And whatever you spend, God knows full well.   3:92

All food was made licit to the Children of Israel, all except what
Israel made illicit for himself before the Torah was revealed.
  Say: 'Bring the Torah and recite it if you are sincere. Whoever
fabricates lies against God thereafter, those are the wrongdoers.'
  Say: 'God has spoken the Truth. So follow the religion of
Abraham, a man of pristine faith, who was not an idolater.'   3:95

The first Sanctuary erected for mankind was the one at Bakka,*
a blessed spot and guidance to mankind. In it are manifest signs:
the station of Abraham. Whoso enters it is safe and secure.
Incumbent upon mankind from God is pilgrimage to the Sanctuary; whoever can make his way to it. As for him who defies this
commandment, God is assuredly Self-Sufficient, needing not
mankind.   3:97

Say: 'O People of the Book, why do you blaspheme against the
signs of God when God is a witness of what you do?'
  Say: 'O People of the Book, why do you obstruct the path of
God before those who believe? Do you wish this path were
crooked while you yourself bear witness to the Truth? God is
not unmindful of what you do.'   3:99

O believers, if you obey a group to whom the Book has been
given, they shall turn you into unbelievers after you have
believed. How can you recant your faith when the signs of God
are being recited to you? And when His Messenger is among
you? Whoever holds fast to God has been guided to a straight
path.   3:101

O believers, fear God as He should truly be feared, and die not
except as Muslims. And hold fast, all of you, to the rope of God
and do not fall into dissension. Remember God's bounties upon

you, when you were enemies to one another, and how He brought harmony to your hearts so that, by His blessing, you became brothers. You had once been on the edge of a precipice of fire, and He saved you from it. Thus does God make plain
3:103 His signs to you; perhaps you will be guided.

Let there be among you a group who call to virtue, who command the good and forbid vice. These shall indeed prosper. Do not be like those who scattered and fell into dissension after manifest signs had come to them. These shall meet with terrible torment, upon a Day when some faces will have turned white, and some faces black. As for those whose faces have turned black, to them will be said: 'Have you indeed blasphemed after belief? Then taste the torment for what you blasphemed.' As for those whose faces have turned white, they shall rest in the
3:107 mercy of God, abiding therein eternally.

These are the revelations of God which We recite to you in truth. Nor does God intend injustice towards mankind. To God belongs all that is in the heavens and on earth. And all matters
3:109 shall revert to God.

You are the best community ever brought forth among mankind, commanding virtue and forbidding vice, and believing in God.

If only the People of the Book come to believe, this would be best for them. Among them are believers – but most are dissolute. They shall not harm you, but are merely a little nuisance. And when they fight you, they turn tail; and then no helpers will come to their aid. Abasement is decreed upon them wherever they may be found, unless they are in covenant with God or in covenant with some people. They shall suffer the anger of God and humiliation is decreed upon them. For they would blaspheme against the revelations of God and kill prophets unjustly. And all this because of their disobedience and their
3:112 aggression.

They are not all alike. Among the People of the Book is a group upstanding. They recite the revelations of God through the hours of the night and prostrate themselves. They believe in God and the Last Day; they command virtue and forbid vice; they hasten to do good deeds. These are among the righteous. What good they do will not be denied them; and God knows full well those who are pious.   3:115

As for those who blaspheme, neither their wealth nor their progeny shall avail them one jot with God. These are the inhabitants of the Fire, abiding therein for ever. The likeness of what they expend in this present life is like an icy gale which batters the tilled land of a people who have done themselves wrong, destroying it utterly. It was not God Who wronged them but themselves it was they wronged.   3:117

O believers, do not adopt as intimate friends those outside your circle. These do all in their power to corrupt you, and long to do you harm. Hatred is obvious from their mouths, and what their breasts conceal is even worse. We have made the revelations clear to you, if only you would reflect.

Here you are: you love them and they do not love you. You believe in the whole Book and when they meet you they say: 'We believe.' When alone with themselves, however, they bite their fingers at you, in angry frustration. Say: 'Die in your frustration!' God knows full well what lies within breasts.

When good fortune touches you, it irritates them; when bad fortune afflicts you, they exult in it. But if you bear with patience and fear God, no harm whatever shall come to you from their slyness. God encompasses all that they do.   3:120

Remember when you left your family one morning to assign battle stations to the believers – and God is All-Hearing, Omniscient. That was when two factions among you were about to falter, though God was their Guardian; so let the believers entrust themselves to God, for God gave you victory at Badr*

when you were weak and small in number. Therefore, fear God
3:123   and perhaps you will give thanks.

Remember when you said to the believers: 'Will it not suffice
you that your Lord will send you as reinforcement three thousand angels, descending?' Yes indeed. If you bear patiently and
fear God, and they advance against you filled with that fury of
theirs, your Lord will send you as reinforcement five thousand
angels, marked for battle. Nor did God intend this act except
as glad tidings to you and so that your hearts may be reassured
by it. Victory comes solely from God, the Almighty, the All-
Wise. And this, in order that He may cut down some blasphemers or repulse them, following which they retreat,
3:127   frustrated.

You have nothing to do with the matter, whether He forgives
or torments them, for they are wicked. To God belongs what is
in the heavens and what is on earth. He forgives whomsoever
He wills and He torments whomsoever He wills. God is All-
3:129   Forgiving, Compassionate to each.

O believers, do not consume usury, multiplied many times over.
Fear God and perhaps you may be saved. And fear the Fire
made ready for the unbelievers. Obey God and the Messenger;
perhaps you will be shown mercy. Hasten to pray for forgiveness
from your Lord, and for a Garden as wide as the heavens and
the earth, made ready for the pious:
For those who expend their wealth in easy times and in
    hardship,
Who restrain their anger,
Who pardon people's offences – God loves those who do
    good –
Who, when they commit a sin or wrong themselves, remember
    God and beg forgiveness for their misdeeds – none forgives
    misdeeds save God –

And who do not stubbornly persist in their actions,
  knowingly.
These – their reward is their Lord's pardon and Gardens
beneath which rivers flow, abiding therein for ever. How
glorious the reward of those who strive!   3:136

Many generations have passed away before your time, so journey in the land and observe to what end the blasphemers have
come!
  This is Speech, manifestly clear, to mankind, a Guidance and
a homily to the pious. Be not faint of heart nor grieve, and you
shall have the upper hand if you truly believe. If a battle wound
touches you, so has a like wound touched the enemy. These are
battle-days We alternate among mankind, that God may know
those who truly believe and may receive some of you as martyrs
– God loves not those who do wrong – and that God may put
the believers to the test, and overwhelm the blasphemers.
  Or did you imagine that you will enter the Garden if God
knows not those among you who exerted themselves or those
who bore with patience? You used to long for death before you
met it, but now you have seen it with your own eyes.   3:143

Muhammad is but a Messenger, and messengers before him
have passed away. If he were to die or be killed, would you
revert to your old ways? Whoso reverts to his old ways shall
harm God not one whit, and God shall reward those who give
thanks.
  A soul cannot die save by God's leave, at a date to be determined. Whoso desires the reward of this world, We shall give
him thereof, and whoso desires the reward of the other world
We shall give him thereof. We shall recompense those who give
thanks.   3:145

How many a prophet there has been, alongside whom numerous
men of virtue and knowledge have fought, but they weakened

not because of what afflicted them in the cause of God, nor became faint-hearted or helpless! God loves those who bear in patience. They spoke not but to say: 'Our Lord, forgive us our sins and our excesses in living. Make firm our feet and grant us victory over the unbelievers.' So God granted them the reward of this world and the glorious reward of the hereafter. God loves

3:148 those who do good.

O believers, if you obey those who disbelieve, they will turn you back to your old ways, and you shall end up lost. It is God, rather, Who is your Patron, and He is the best of Supporters. We shall cast terror in the hearts of those who disbelieve, because they associated with God that regarding which He revealed no sanction. Their shelter will be the Fire – and what

3:151 a wretched resting place for evildoers!

God made good His promise to you as you slew them by His leave, until the moment when you grew weak-hearted and disputed the matter among yourselves, and rebelled, after He had made you see what you longed for. Some of you desired this world and some desired the next. Then He caused you to retreat before them in order to put you to the test. He has now pardoned

3:152 you and God is gracious towards the believers.

Remember when you fled, not caring for anyone, while the Messenger called you from the rear. So He rewarded you with misery piled upon misery, in order that you do not grieve for what you missed or what afflicted you. God knows full well whatever you do. Then, following misery, He sent down upon you a feeling of security, a slumber overcoming a party among you, while another party cared only for themselves, thinking false thoughts about God, thoughts fit for the Age of Idolatry.*
They would say: 'Have we any role in this affair?'
Say: 'Indeed, this affair belongs entirely to God.'
They conceal in their hearts what they do not reveal to you.
They say: 'Had we any role in this affair, we would not have

been killed in this place.' Say: 'Even had you stayed in your homes, those upon whom fighting was decreed would have marched forth to the sites of their death, that God may put to the test what lies in your breasts, and gauge what is in your hearts.' God knows full well what lies within breasts. Those among you who turned tail on the day of battle when two armies met – it was Satan who caused them to slip up for some sin they had earned. But God has pardoned them. God is All-Forgiving, All-Forbearing.

3:155

O believers, do not be like those who blasphemed, and said to their brethren, when others were travelling in the land or on a military expedition: 'Had they remained among us they would not have died, nor been killed.' This is so in order that God may implant grief in their hearts. But it is God Who grants both life and death, and God knows full well what you do. And were you to be killed in the cause of God, or to die, forgiveness from God and mercy is assuredly better than all the wealth they amass. Were you to die or be killed, then assuredly to God you will be gathered.

3:158

It is through God's mercy that you are gentle towards them. Had you been cruel and hard of heart, they would have dispersed from your presence. So forgive them and ask God's pardon for them and seek their counsel in all affairs. When resolved upon a matter, put your trust in God, for God loves those who put their trust in Him. If God supports you, none can defeat you. And if He fails you, who can support you, apart from Him? So let the believers put their trust in God.

3:160

It is not fitting for a prophet to betray his trust. Whoso betrays his trust shall come face to face with what he betrayed on the Day of Resurrection. Thereupon each soul shall be paid in full what it has earned, and they shall not be treated unjustly. Is he who abides by the good pleasure of God like him who turns away, under the censure of God? His refuge shall be hell – and

what a wretched place to end! They are graded in ranks with
3:163 God, and God sees full well what they do.

God did the believers a favour when He sent among them a
Messenger, of their number, reciting to them His verses, puri-
fying them and teaching them the Book and the Wisdom, when
before they had been in manifest error. How is it that when a
calamity befalls you, the like of which you have already suffered,
but twice as grievously, you say: 'Where does this come from?'
3:165 Say: 'It comes from your own selves. God is Omnipotent.'

What befell you when the two armies met was by God's leave
and so that the believers may grow in knowledge; that the
Hypocrites* too may know. For it had been said to them: 'Come
and fight in the cause of God, or else pay.' They had answered:
'Had we known fighting was to occur we would have followed
you.' That day, they were nearer to unbelief than they were to
belief. They would utter with their mouths what was not in their
hearts – and God knows best what they conceal. It was they
who told their brethren, while themselves refraining from the
fight: 'Had they obeyed us, they would not have been killed.'
Say: 'Then ward off death from yourselves if you speak the
3:168 truth.'

Do not imagine those killed in the path of God to be dead.
Rather, they are alive with their Lord,
Enjoying His bounty,
Jubilant at what God has granted them from His grace,
Eagerly expecting those who have not yet followed, to come
    after them.
In truth, no fear shall fall upon them, nor shall they grieve.
They look forward with joy to bliss from God and to His
3:171 bounty. In truth, God does not neglect the reward of believers.

As for those who answered the call of God and the Messenger,
after the wounds that afflicted them, and those among them

who did good and feared God, their reward shall be glorious. These are the men to whom people had said: 'A mighty host has been marshalled against you; so ought you to fear them.' But this only increased them in faith and they replied: 'Sufficient for us is God; and most worthy is He of trust.' So they came back with God's blessing and His bounty, no harm having touched them, and followed the course pleasing to God. In truth, God is All-Bountiful. This had been the work of Satan, who terrifies you with his followers. Fear them not; fear Me, rather, if you are true believers. 3:175

Do not be saddened by those who hasten to blaspheme: they harm God not one whit. God wishes to grant them no portion of the world hereafter, and terrible torment awaits them. Those who exchange blasphemy for faith will not harm God one whit, and agonizing torment awaits them. And let not those who blaspheme imagine that by deferring punishment We are doing them a favour; rather, We so defer them that they may increase in sin. Abasing torment awaits them. Nor would God abandon the believers in your present state until He distinguishes the corrupt from the pure. And nor would He acquaint you with the Unseen, but God elects from among messengers whomsoever He wills. Therefore, believe in God and in His messengers. If you believe and are pious, a glorious reward awaits you. 3:179

Let not those who are miserly with what God has bestowed upon them, from His bounty, imagine that this is for their own good. Rather, it is to their detriment. They shall be shackled with that which they withheld in miserliness on the Day of Resurrection. To God belongs the inheritance of the heavens and the earth, and God is well acquainted with what you do. 3:180

God has heard those who say: 'God is poor but we are rich.' We shall record what they said, as well as their killing of the prophets unjustly, and We say to them: 'Taste the torment of the Flame!' This is because of your past misdeeds; God is not unjust towards His creatures. And to those who say: 'God has charged us not to believe in any messenger unless he brings us an offering consumed by fire,' say: 'Messengers have come to you before me with miracles and with what you mentioned. Why then did you kill them if you are telling the truth?' If they spurn you, other messengers have been spurned before you, though they had come with miracles, revealed Scriptures and a Luminous Book.

3:184

Every soul shall taste death. You shall certainly be paid your wages in full on the Day of Resurrection. Whoever has been dragged away from the Fire and made to enter the Garden has indeed won out. And this present life is but the rapture of delusion.

3:185

You shall be put to a hard test as regards your wealth and your souls, and you shall hear much harm from those who were given the Book before you, and from the idolaters. But if you bear with patience and fear God, this will be a course of action upright and resolute.

3:186

Remember when God covenanted with those formerly entrusted with the Book: 'That you should proclaim your Revelation to mankind and not conceal it.' But they cast it behind their backs and bartered it for a paltry sum – wretched indeed is what they bought! Do not imagine that those who are happy with what they did, and enjoy being praised for that which they did not do – do not imagine that they shall succeed in escaping torment! Painful torment awaits them.

To God belongs sovereignty of the heavens and the earth. God is Omnipotent.

3:189

In the creation of the heavens and the earth,
In the rotation of night and day,
Are sure signs for people possessed of minds;
They who make mention of God, standing, sitting or reclining,

Who reflect upon the creation of the heavens and the earth:
'Our Lord, You did not create all this in vain, glory be to
     You!
Spare us thereby the torment of the Fire.
Our Lord, he whom You admit into the Fire – him You have
     truly abased,
And wrongdoers shall find none to support them.
Our Lord, we heard a caller, calling to faith: "Believe in your
     Lord!"
And we believed.
Our Lord, forgive our sins, and wipe away our misdeeds,
And make us die in the company of the virtuous.
Our Lord, grant us that which you promised Your
     messengers,
And do not abase us on the Day of Resurrection.
You fail not Your appointed time.'   3:194

Their Lord answered their prayer:
'I disregard not the works of any who works among you,
Be they male or female,
The one is like the other.
As for those who emigrated, and were driven away from their
     homelands,
Who suffered harm for My sake,
Who fought or were killed,
I shall wipe away their misdeeds,
And I shall admit them into Gardens beneath which rivers
     flow:
A reward from God.
With God is the best of rewards.'   3:195

Be not impressed by the blasphemers, as they stride back and
forth in the lands:

    A temporary pleasure! Then hell shall be their refuge – and
what a wretched resting place! But those who fear their Lord,
for them are Gardens, beneath which rivers flow, abiding therein

for ever, as honoured guests of God. What is with God is better
3:198 for the virtuous.

Among the People of the Book are some who believe in God,
and in what was revealed to you and what was revealed to them,
bowing in piety before God, and bartering not the signs of God
for a paltry price. These shall have their reward with their Lord,
3:199 and God is swift in reckoning.

O believers, bear in patience, be steadfast in the fight, keep to
3:200 your battle stations and fear God – perhaps you will prevail.

Women

In the name of God,
Merciful to all,
Compassionate to each!

O mankind, fear your Lord Who created you from a single soul,
and created from it its spouse, and propagated from both many
men and women. Fear God in Whose name you make requests
one of another, and sever not the ties of kinship. God watches
4:1 well over you.

Deliver their monies to orphans and do not substitute corrupt
for pure. Do not consume their wealth by adding it to your
own, for this would be an outrage most grievous. If you fear
you will not be fair towards orphans, so too with marriage.
Marry whoever pleases you among women – two, three or four;
but if you fear you will not be fair to them all, then one only,
or else what you own of slaves. This would be closer to imparti-
ality. Give women their dowry, a free offering. And if they
willingly offer you any of it, then consume it in peace of mind
and wholesomeness. Entrust not your wealth to spendthrifts,

wealth that God provided you for maintenance. Provide for them from it, and clothe them and speak kindly to them. Put orphans to the test until they reach the age of marriage. If you observe in them maturity of mind, hand their monies over to them. Do not consume it in dissipation or in haste before they come of age. Whoever is rich should hold back, abstemious; whoever is poor should spend it fairly and honestly. When you deliver their monies to them, bring in witnesses thereof. God suffices as Reckoner. 4:6

To males belongs a share of what was left by parents and closest relatives, and to females belongs a share of what was left by parents and closest relatives, be it little or much – a portion decreed. If the division of inheritance is attended by close of kin, orphans or the needy, give to them from it and speak kindly to them. And let those who leave behind progeny that is weak and for whom they fear – let them beware! Let them fear God and let them speak a fitting word. They who consume the monies of orphans unjustly are in truth consuming fire in their bellies, and shall be scorched by a raging Flame. 4:10

God commands you regarding your children: to the male what equals the share of two females. If they are females, and more than two, they inherit two-thirds of what he leaves. If it be one female, she inherits half. To the two parents of the deceased belongs a sixth each of what he leaves, if he has children. If childless, and his parents inherit, his mother receives one-third of what he leaves. If he has brothers, his mother receives one-sixth, after deducting any bequests you may bequeath, or any debts. Your parents or your children – you know not which of them is nearer to you in benefit. This is an apportionment from God. In truth, God is All-Knowing, All-Wise. 4:11

To you belongs half of what your wives leave, provided they have no children. If they have a child, your portion is a quarter of what they leave, after deducting any bequests they have made, or debts. Your wives' share is a quarter of what you leave, if you have no child. If you have a child, their share is one-eighth, after deducting any bequests you may bequeath, or any debts. If a man or woman dies leaving no heirs, but has a brother or sister, then the share of each is one-sixth. If more, they are partners in one-third, after deducting any bequests or any debts, and provided the bequest is not to their detriment. Such is the decree of God. In truth, God is All-Knowing, All-Forbearing.

4:12

These are the bounds set by God. Whoso obeys God and His Messenger, God shall admit him into Gardens beneath which rivers flow, abiding therein for ever. And this is the greatest of triumphs.

Whoso disobeys God and His Messenger, and transgresses His bounds, God shall admit him into a Fire, abiding therein for ever, and abasing torment awaits him.

4:14

As for your women who commit adultery, call four among you to witness against them. If they so witness, confine them to their homes until death overtakes them or else God provides another way for them. And if two males among you commit indecency, rebuke them harshly. If they repent and make amends, leave them alone. God always accepts repentance, and is Compassionate to each. Repentance, however, rests with God only for those who commit an evil unwittingly and soon repent – God shall accept their repentance, and God is All-Knowing, All-Wise. But repentance is not for them who commit evil deeds until, when death comes to one of them, he says: 'I now repent'; nor for those who die as unbelievers. For these We have readied a painful torment.

4:18

O believers, it is not licit for you to inherit women against their will, nor must you coerce them so as to take possession of part of what you had given them, unless they commit manifest adultery. Live with them in kindness. And if you come to loathe them, perhaps you may loathe something in which God places abundant good.

If you desire to substitute one wife in place of another, and you had given the first a heap of riches, take nothing back from it – would you dare take it back falsely and in manifest sin? And how can you take it back when you have been intimate with each other, and your wives have secured from you a most solemn pledge? Do not marry women that your fathers had married, unless that act belongs to the past, for this would be an indecency, a thing most hateful and evil in its consequences.   4:22

Forbidden to you are your mothers, daughters, sisters, aunts paternal and maternal, nieces on your brothers' or sisters' sides, milk-mothers who suckled you and milk-sisters, mothers of your wives, and step-daughters in your custody from wives with whom you have consummated marriage – unless you have not consummated marriage with them, in which case no blame attaches to you. Forbidden too are legal wives of your own sons, and marriage with two sisters – unless that act belongs to the past. God is All-Forgiving, Compassionate to each. Forbidden too are married women, unless they be your slaves.

The Book of God thus commands you. Licit for you is all that lies outside these limits, provided you use your wealth to contract legal marriage, not fornication. To those women among them whom you take pleasure in marrying, you must render their dowries, as a legal obligation. But no blame attaches to you regarding what you have willingly agreed upon, once the legal obligation is fulfilled. God is All-Knowing, All-Wise.   4:24

If there is one among you who has not the means to marry free, chaste and believing women, let him marry from among your female slaves, believing maidens. God knows best your true faith, one and all alike. So marry them with their owners' consent and render them their dowries in kindness, as legal wives

and not as lovers or as prostitutes. Once in legal wedlock, and
if they commit adultery, upon them falls half the punishment of
free and married women. This is a commandment addressed to
those among you who fear fornication. But if you bear with
patience, this is best for you. God is All-Forgiving, Compassion-
4:25 ate to each.

God wishes to make clear to you and to guide you concerning
the laws of those who came before you, and to pardon you.
God is All-Knowing, All-Wise. So also God wishes to pardon
you, but those who pursue their passions wish you to veer
utterly from your path. Yet God wishes to lighten your burden,
4:28 for humans were created feeble.

O believers, consume not the wealth you trade among yourselves
dishonestly, unless it be a commercial deal resulting from mutual
agreement. Do not kill each other, for God is always Compassionate to every one of you. Whoever does so, aggressively
and unjustly, him We shall scorch at a raging Flame, a thing
easy for God. If you shun the major sins you have been forbidden
to commit, We shall expiate your misdeeds and lead you through
4:31 an honourable portal.

Covet not that by which God preferred some of you over others
in bounty. Men have a share of what they earned and women
have a share of what they earned. Ask God to grant you of His
bounty, for God is Omniscient. Each of you We have appointed
as heirs of what parents and close relatives leave, as also those
with whom you compacted in marriage. So give them their
4:33 proper share, for God witnesses all things.

Men are legally responsible for women, inasmuch as God has
preferred some over others in bounty, and because of what they
spend from their wealth. Thus, virtuous women are obedient,
and preserve their trusts, such as God wishes them to be preserved. And those you fear may rebel, admonish, and abandon

them in their beds, and smack them. If they obey you, seek no
other way against them. God is Highest and Mightiest.   4:34

If you fear dissension between a married couple, send forth an
arbiter from his family and an arbiter from her family. If they
desire reconciliation, God will bring them together. God is All-
Knowing, All-Discerning. And worship God, and associate none
with Him.   4:35

To parents is owed kindness, as also to relatives, to orphans, to
the needy, to a neighbour who is a relative, to a neighbour who
is a stranger, to a companion by your side, to a traveller and to
your slaves. God loves not the swaggering and the conceited;
they who are miserly and urge people to miserliness, who conceal what God bestowed upon them from His bounty – to
unbelievers We have readied an abasing torment. So too for
them who spend their wealth in order to flaunt it before people
but believe neither in God nor in the Last Day. Whoever has
Satan for companion, what a wretched companion has he!   4:38

What harm would come to them if they believe in God and the
Last Day, and spend from the bounty that God bestowed upon
them? God knows them full well.   4:39

God wrongs no one, not even by the weight of an atom. If it be
a good deed, God multiplies it, and from on high shall confer
an immense reward. How then will it be when We summon
from each nation a witness and summon you as witness against
these? On that Day, those who blasphemed and disobeyed the
Messenger will wish the earth were levelled over them, nor can
they keep secret from God anything they ever said.   4:42

O believers, do not come near to prayer when you are drunk,
until you know what you are saying; nor when sexually defiled,
unless passing through, until you perform ablutions. If you are
ill, or on a journey, or one of you comes from the toilet, or you

had intercourse with women, and you do not find water, then use some clean earth and wipe your faces and hands. God is
4:43   All-Pardoning, All-Forgiving.

Do you not observe those who were given a portion of the Book, how they barter error for guidance and wish you would lose your way? God knows best about your enemies; let God suffice as Patron, let God suffice as Champion!

Among Jews are some who distort the words of revelation from their contexts. They say: 'We hear and disobey' and 'Hear, may you not hear!' and 'Hey! Listen!', twisting their tongues and insulting the true religion. If they had said: 'We hear and obey' and 'Hear!' and 'Please regard us!' that would have been better for them and more courteous. But God has cursed them for their blasphemy, and they believe not, except
4:46   for a few.

O People to whom the Book has been revealed, believe in what We have revealed, confirming the truth of that which you already have, before We blot out certain faces and turn them back upon their rear, or else curse them as We cursed possessors of the Sabbath. The edict of God is well and truly carried out. God forgives not that He be the associate of anyone, but forgives what is less than this to whomsoever He pleases. Whoso associates another with God has committed a sin most grievous. Have you not considered those who call themselves pure? It is God, rather, who purifies whomever He pleases, and they shall not be wronged one fleck. See how they fabricate lies about God!
4:50   Let this suffice for a manifest sin.

Have you not considered those to whom a portion of the Book has been revealed, how they believe in idols and demons, and how they tell the blasphemers that they are more rightly guided on the path than those who believe? These are the ones God has cursed, and whomever God has cursed you shall find none to support him.

Or do they have a share in sovereignty? If so, they benefit people not a jot.

Or is it that they envy people for what God has bestowed upon them from His bounty? For We have brought down upon the nation of Abraham the Book and the Wisdom, and brought them too a mighty kingdom. Among them, some believed in him and some turned away from him. Let hell suffice for a raging flame!

Those who blasphemed against Our revelations – We shall scorch at a Fire. Whenever their skins are charred, We replace them with new skins, so that they taste the torment. God is Almighty, All-Wise.   4:56

Those who believe and do good deeds We shall lead into Gardens beneath which rivers flow, abiding therein for ever. In it they shall have pure spouses, and We shall lead them into an overspreading shade.   4:57

God commands you to return trusts to their owners and, when you judge between people, to judge with fairness. Admirable indeed is what God admonishes you to do! God is All-Hearing, All-Seeing.   4:58

O believers, obey God and obey the Prophet and those set in authority over you. If you dispute among yourselves over any matter, refer it to God and the Messenger, if you believe in God and the Last Day. This would be best, and best also in consequence.

Have you considered those who allege that they believe in what was revealed to you and what was revealed before you, and how they desire to seek judgement with the idols, though ordered to abhor them? But Satan desires to lead them far astray.   4:60

And if it is said to them: 'Come to what God has revealed, and to the Messenger,' you would see the Hypocrites turning

resolutely away from you. How will it be then, when a calamity befalls them for their past misdeeds and they come to you, swearing by God and saying: 'We merely intended good-will and reconciliation?' These – God knows what lies in their hearts. Turn your face away from them, admonish them, and speak to
4:63 them words that sink deep into their souls.

We sent no messenger except to be obeyed, by God's leave. If only, when wronging themselves, they had come to you and asked God's forgiveness, and the Messenger had asked forgiveness for them, they would have found God to be All-Pardoning,
4:64 Compassionate to each.

No indeed, and by your Lord! They shall not believe until they take you as judge of what they dispute, then find no resentment in their souls regarding your judgement, and submit completely. Had We commanded them to risk death in fighting or to leave their homes, only a few of them would have done so. If only they had performed what they were admonished with, it would have been better for them, and more sustaining of their faith. In consequence, We would have bestowed upon them from on high a glorious wage, and guided them onto a straight path. Whoso obeys God and the Messenger, they shall be among those upon whom God's grace descends: prophets, men of righteousness, martyrs and the virtuous – and what splendid company they are! This is the bounty of God – and God suffices
4:70 as Knower of all things.

O believers, be on your guard, and sally forth in groups or sally forth all together. Among you is one who lingers behind. If a calamity befalls you, he says: 'God has been gracious to me since I was not with them to witness it.' But if a bounty from God descends upon you he would surely say, as if no affection had existed between you and him: 'Alas, if only I had been with
4:73 them, I would have secured a splendid success.'

Let them fight in the cause of God – they who sell the present life for the next. Whoso fights in the cause of God and is killed, or else is victorious, We shall bestow upon him a magnificent wage. Why is it that you do not fight in the cause of God and of the helpless, men, women and children who cry out: 'Our Lord, bring us forth out of this city of impious inhabitants. Appoint for us from on high a protector. Appoint for us from on high a champion'? Those who believe fight in the cause of God, and those who disbelieve fight in the cause of idolatry. So fight the followers of Satan, for Satan's cunning is feeble indeed.   4:76

Have you not considered those to whom it was said: 'Hold back from the fight, and perform prayer and pay the alms' and how, when fighting was decreed upon them, behold, a group among them were found to fear human beings as they fear God or even more? They say: 'Our Lord, why have You decreed fighting upon us? If only You had deferred us for a short while.' Say to them: 'The delights of this life are brief, but the next life is more excellent for those who are pious. Nor will you be wronged one fleck.'

Wherever you may be, death will overtake you, even if you live in loftiest towers.

When good fortune befalls them they say: 'This comes from God,' but when bad fortune befalls they say: 'This comes from you.'

Say to them: 'All is from God.'

What is it with these people? They can barely understand what is said to them.

Whatever good befalls you comes from God; whatever evil befalls you comes from your own selves.

We have sent you forth to mankind as a messenger – and God suffices as witness. Whoso obeys the Messenger thereby obeys God. Whoso turns away, We did not send you as their overseer.

They say: 'We render obedience,' but when they leave your

presence, a group among them contrives by night something contrary to what you said. But God records what they contrive. So turn your face away from them, and place your trust in God 4:81 – and God suffices as worthy of all trust.

Do they not ponder the Qur'an? Had it been from other than God, they would have found much inconsistency therein. When there comes to them a report, bearing news of security or of foreboding, they spread it wide. Were they to refer it to the Messenger and to those set in authority over them, its true import would be ascertained from them by those best fitted to understand it. Were it not for God's bounty upon you and His 4:83 mercy, you would have followed Satan, all but a few.

So fight in the cause of God; you are answerable only to yourself. And encourage the believers – perhaps God will check the might of the unbelievers. For God is more mighty, and more grievous in torment.

He who intercedes a worthy intercession shall have a share thereof, and he who intercedes an evil intercession shall incur the liability thereof, for God holds power over all things.

If you are greeted with a greeting, return the greeting with one more gracious, or else its like. God holds all things in 4:86 account.

God! There is no god but He! He shall gather you together upon the Day of Resurrection, of which there is no doubt. Who is 4:87 more truthful than God in speech?

Why then are you divided in two factions as regards the Hypocrites, when God has condemned them for the ill they gained? Do you wish to guide one whom God has led astray? Whoso God leads astray, for him you shall find no path. They long for you to blaspheme as they have blasphemed, thus becoming like them. Do not take them for friends until they emigrate in the cause of God. If they refuse, seize them and kill them wherever you find them, and do not take them as friend or ally, except for those who arrive at a clan with whom you have a covenant, or come to you, their hearts too despondent to fight you or fight their own clan. Had God willed, He would have set them against you and they would have fought you. Therefore, if they stand aside and do not fight you, and propose submission to you, God grants you no further sway over them.   4:90

Others you will find who wish to live in security with you and with their own clan, but whenever they are tempted back to civil discord, they are plunged deep therein. If they do not stand aside and propose submission to you, nor hold back their hands, then seize them and kill them wherever you find them. Over these We have granted you explicit sway.   4:91

No believer is to kill another save in error. Whoever kills a believer in error, the freeing of a believing slave is decreed and blood-money handed over to his kin, unless the latter forgo this as an act of charity. If he belongs to a clan which is your enemy while he is a believer, the freeing of a believing slave is decreed. If he belongs to a clan with whom you have a compact, then blood-money is handed over to his kin and the freeing of a believing slave. He who finds not the means, then fasting for two consecutive months is decreed, as penance from God. God is All-Knowing, All-Wise. Whoso kills a believer intentionally, his penalty is hell, abiding therein eternally. God shall be angry with him and curse him, and shall ready for him a grievous torment.   4:93

O believers, when you sally forth in the cause of God, be discerning. Do not say to whoever submits to you in peace: 'You are not a believer,' seeking thereby the spoils of the present life, for God has spoils innumerable. This is how you used to behave in the past, but God has bestowed His favour upon you. So be discerning; God knows full well what you do.

Among the believers, those who stay behind, unless disabled, are not the equal of those who exert themselves in the cause of God, with their wealth and their souls. God has preferred those who exert themselves in the cause of God, with their wealth and their souls, one degree of virtue above those who stay behind. But God has promised both a happy end. And yet God prefers those who exert themselves to those who stay behind by granting them a glorious recompense, closeness in rank to Him, forgiveness and mercy. God is All-Forgiving, Compassionate to each.

4:96

Those whom the angels cause to die while wronging themselves – to them the angels shall say: 'What was your former condition?'

They shall respond: 'We were considered weaklings on earth.'

The angels shall say: 'Was not the land of God wide enough for you to emigrate into?'

These people – their refuge is hell, and what a wretched end it is! All except those weaklings among men, women and children who truly had no means to act, or could not find their way out. These God will perhaps pardon for God is All-Forgiving, All-Pardoning.

4:99

Whoso emigrates in the cause of God shall find on earth many places of emigration and abundance. Whoso leaves his home as an emigrant to God and His Messenger and is overtaken by death, his reward falls upon God, and God is All-Forgiving, Compassionate to each.

4:100

When you set out on an expedition in the land, no blame attaches to you if you curtail your prayer, if you fear the unbelievers will take you by surprise; for the unbelievers are your manifest enemy.

If you happen to be present among them, and stand to lead them in prayer, let a group among them stand with you, and let them take up their arms. When they prostrate themselves in prayer let them be in the rear and let another group who have not yet prayed come forward to pray with you; let them be on their guard and take up their weapons. The unbelievers long for you to be negligent with your weapons and equipment, and thus would attack you in one rush.

If pelted by the rain or else you are sick, no blame attaches to you if you put your weapons aside, but be on your guard. God has readied for the unbelievers an abasing torment.

Once having finished prayer, make mention of God, standing, sitting or reclining. Once you feel secure, perform the prayer, for prayer at a set time is decreed upon the believers. And do not falter in pursuit of the enemy: if you are aching, they too are aching as you ache, but you expect from God what they cannot expect. God is All-Knowing, All-Wise. 4:104

We revealed to you the Book with the Truth in order that you may judge among people as God has shown you. Do not be an advocate for those unworthy of trust. Ask God's forgiveness, for God is All-Forgiving, Compassionate to each.

Do not argue in defence of those who betray their souls; God loves not every deceitful sinner. They seek to hide their iniquity from people but cannot hide it from God, though He is with them at night when they contrive speech that is unacceptable. God encompasses all that they do. Here you are, arguing on their behalf in this present life, but who shall argue with God on their behalf on the Day of Resurrection? Or who shall be their advocate? But whoso commits a sin or wrongs himself, then seeks God's forgiveness, will find that God is All-Forgiving, Compassionate to each. 4:110

Whoso reaps sin, reaps it for his own soul. God is All-Knowing, All-Wise.

Whoso reaps a sin or transgression and attributes it to an innocent person has burdened his soul with fraud and a manifest crime. Were it not for God's grace upon you and His mercy, a group among them had endeavoured to lead you astray – but it is themselves they lead astray. Nor will they harm you in any way, for God has revealed to you the Book and the Wisdom and taught you that which you did not know. The bounty of God upon you has been immeasurable.

4:113

No good comes from most of their secret deliberations unless it be one who commands alms-giving or an act of charity or reconciliation among people. Whoso does this, seeking to please God, We shall bestow upon him a glorious recompense. Whoso defies the Messenger after right guidance has become clear to him, and follows a path other than that of the believers, We assign to him the master he chose to obey, and scorch him in hell – and what a wretched place to end!

4:115

God forgives not that He be the associate of anyone, but forgives what is less than this to whomsoever He pleases. Whoso associates anything with God has indeed strayed far. In truth, they worship nothing but females apart from Him, nothing but a rebel demon, cursed by God.
He said: 'I shall select from among Your worshippers a speci-fied portion;
I shall lead them astray;
I shall give them false hopes;
I shall command them and they shall slit the ears of cattle;
I shall command them and they shall deface God's creation.'
Whoso takes Satan for master, apart from God, has suffered a loss most conspicuous.
He promises them, he gives them false hopes – but what Satan promises is nothing save illusion. These – their refuge is hell, and they shall not find a way to escape it.

4:121

But those who believe and do good deeds We shall lead into Gardens beneath which rivers flow, abiding therein for ever. This is a true promise from God, and who is more truthful than God in speech?
No indeed! It shall not happen through your false hopes, nor the false hopes of the People of the Book! Whoso does evil shall

be recompensed for it; and he will not find, apart from God, any supporter or champion.

Whoso does good deeds, whether male or female, and has faith, shall enter the Garden and will not be wronged one fleck.

4:124

Who is more excellent in religion than he who surrenders his face wholly to God, and acts charitably? Who follows the religion of Abraham, of pristine faith? For God had taken Abraham for an intimate. To God belongs what is in the heavens and what is on earth. God encompasses all things.

4:126

They seek your judgement concerning women.

Say: 'God pronounces judgement concerning them, that is, what is being recited to you in the Book concerning orphaned females. To them you do not deliver their allotted share, yet you desire to marry them. So also concerning defenceless children: that you render justice to orphans.' Whatever good you do God knows full well.

If a wife fears antipathy or aversion from her husband, no blame attaches to them both if they arrive at an amicable settlement between them; such settlement is best.

Souls are bent upon greed. But if you act charitably and in piety God knows full well what you do.

4:128

You will not be able to act equitably with your women, even if you apply yourself to do so. Do not turn wholly away from her, leaving her like one suspended. But if you settle with her amicably and fear God, God is All-Forgiving, Compassionate to each. If a couple separates, God shall suffice each from His bounty. God is All-Encompassing, All-Wise.

4:130

To God belongs what is in the heavens and what is on earth. We charged those who were given the Book before you, and you also, to fear God. If you disbelieve, then to God belongs what is in the heavens and what is on earth. God is All-Sufficient,

All-Praiseworthy. To God belongs what is in the heavens and what is on earth, and God suffices as All-Worthy of trust.

If He wishes, O mankind, He can make you disappear and bring others in your stead. And God is fully capable of this. Whoso desires the reward of this world, with God rests the reward of this world and the next. God is All-Hearing, All-Seeing.

4:134

O believers, conduct yourselves with justice and be witnesses in the cause of God, even if against yourselves, your parents or your close relatives, or whether it be a rich man or a poor man, for God is more caring for both of them. Follow not your whims so as to act unjustly. And if you pervert your witness or refuse to give it, God knows full well what you do.

4:135

O believers, believe in God and in His Messenger, and in the Book He revealed to His Messenger and the Book He revealed before. Whoso disbelieves in God, His angels, His Books, His messengers and in the Last Day has strayed far in error. Those who believed then disbelieved then believed then disbelieved, then increased in disbelief – God shall not forgive them nor guide them upon the way. Give tidings to the Hypocrites that a painful torment awaits them. As for those who adopt the unbelievers as allies apart from the believers – do they truly seek power from them? All power belongs to God.

4:139

God has revealed to you in the Book that if you hear the verses of God blasphemed or mocked, do not sit with them until they broach another subject; otherwise you would be like them. God shall herd all Hypocrites and blasphemers into hell. When victory comes to you from God, those who lie in wait for you say: 'Were we not on your side?' But when the unbelievers gain a measure of success they say: 'Did we not hold sway over you and protect you from the believers?' It is God Who shall judge between you on the Day of Resurrection, and God shall grant the unbelievers no ascendancy over the believers.

4:141

The Hypocrites seek to deceive God but it is He Who deceives them. If they rise to prayer, they rise reluctantly, dissembling before people. They mention God but little. They vacillate, being neither of this party nor of that. Whom God deludes, him you shall find adrift.   4:143

O believers, do not take unbelievers for allies apart from the believers. Do you wish God to exercise His manifest might over you? The Hypocrites are in the lowest reaches of the Fire, and you will not find anyone to assist them – all except those who repent, do good deeds, take refuge in God and have sincere faith in God. These shall be with the believers, and God shall bestow on the believers a glorious recompense. What need does God have to torment you if you give thanks and have faith? God is All-Thankful, All-Knowing.   4:147

God loves not the loud and public expression of ill-natured speech, except from him who has been wronged. God is All-Hearing, All-Knowing.

Whether you make public a good deed or whether you conceal it, or forgive a wrong done to you, remember that God is All-Forgiving, Omnipotent. As for those who disbelieve in God and His messengers, and seek to stir up division between God and His messengers, saying: 'We believe in some and disbelieve in others,' and desire to adopt this as an in-between way – these are truly the unbelievers. For unbelievers We have readied an abasing torment. Those who believe in God and His messengers and do not distinguish between any of them – these He shall pay their wages, and God is All-Forgiving, Compassionate to each.   4:152

The People of the Book ask you to bring down upon them a book from heaven. But surely they asked Moses a thing even more outrageous than this. They said to him: 'Show us God face to face,' and were struck by lightning for their sin. Then they took up the worship of the calf even after clear signs

had come to them. But We forgave that sin and granted Moses
manifest authority. And We raised above them the Mountain in accordance with their covenant and We said to them:
'Enter the gate in prostration,' and We said to them: 'Do not
transgress the Sabbath'; and We took from them a most solemn
4:154 covenant.

Therefore, by renouncing their covenant, by blaspheming
against the revelations of God, by killing prophets unjustly and
claiming: 'Our hearts are sealed' – rather, it is God Who sealed
them with their blasphemy – they believe not, except a few. So
also by their blasphemy and their terrible words of slander
against Mary, and their saying: 'It is we who killed the Christ
Jesus son of Mary, the messenger of God' – they killed him not,
nor did they crucify him, but so it was made to appear to
them. Those who disputed concerning him are in doubt over
the matter; they have no knowledge thereof but only follow
conjecture. Assuredly they killed him not, but God raised him
up to Him, and God is Almighty, All-Wise. Among the People
of the Book none there are but shall believe in him before his
death, and on the Day of Resurrection he shall be a witness
4:159 against them.

Thus, through the wrongdoing of the Jews, We forbade them
certain delectable foods which had been made licit to them; by
reason, too, of their obstructing the path to God, repeatedly;
their taking usury, though forbidden to do so; and their
devouring the wealth of people dishonestly – to the unbelievers
4:161 among them We have readied a painful torment.

But those steeped in knowledge, as also the believers among
them, believe in what has been revealed to you and what was
revealed before you. And those who perform the prayer, who
pay their alms, who believe in God and the Last Day – upon
4:162 these We shall bestow a glorious recompense.

We have revealed to you, as We revealed to Noah and the prophets after him. We revealed to Abraham, Ishmael, Isaac, the Tribes; to Jesus, Job and Jonah, Aaron and Solomon; and We revealed the Psalms to David: prophets whose stories We narrated to you already and prophets whose stories We have not narrated to you – And God spoke to Moses in plain speech – prophets, bringers of glad tidings as well as warners, lest mankind have any argument with God after their coming. God is Almighty, All-Wise.   4:165

But God bears witness to what He revealed to you. He revealed it with His knowledge. And the angels bear witness. And God suffices as witness.   4:166

Those who disbelieved and obstructed the path to God have strayed far in error. Those who disbelieved and committed wrong: God is not about to forgive them, nor guide them to any path save the path of hell, there to dwell eternally. This is a matter easy for God.   4:169

O mankind, the Prophet has come to you with the Truth from your Lord. Believe, and it would be best for you. If you disbelieve, to God belongs what is in the heavens and what is on earth. God is Omniscient, All-Wise.   4:170

O People of the Book, do not be excessive in your religion. Do not say about God anything but the truth. The Christ Jesus son of Mary is indeed the prophet of God and His Word which He cast into Mary, and a spirit from Him. So believe in God and His messengers, and do not say: 'Three!' Desist, for this would be best for you. God in truth is One – glory be to Him, that He should have a child! To Him belongs what is in the heavens and what is on earth. God suffices as All-Worthy of trust.

Christ will not disdain to be a servant of God, nor do the angels closest to God. Whoso disdains to worship Him as servant and waxes proud, He shall herd them all to Him.   4:172

As for those who believe and do good deeds, He shall pay them their wages in full and add to this from His bounty. But those who disdain and wax proud, He shall torment a painful torment, 4:173 and they shall find, apart from God, no friend and no champion.

O mankind, proof has come to you from your Lord, and We have brought down upon you a radiant light. As for those who believe in God and hold fast to Him, He shall make them enter into His mercy and a bounty from Him. He shall guide them to 4:175 Himself: a straight path.

They seek your verdict.

Say: 'God shall pronounce His verdict to you as regards a deceased person without heirs. If a man dies leaving no issue, but has a sister, her share is half of what he leaves, and he inherits her if she has no issue. If it be two sisters, their share is two-thirds of what he leaves. If they are siblings, male and female, the male's share is equal to the share of two females.'

God makes matters plain to you, lest you go astray, and God 4:176 is Omniscient.

The Table

In the name of God,
Merciful to all,
Compassionate to each!

O believers, fulfil your legal obligations.

Licit for you are livestock animals, except such as are recited to you. You are forbidden the hunt while consecrated during 5:1 pilgrimage. God judges what He pleases.

O believers, violate not the sacred rites of God, nor the sacred
month, nor the sacrificial animals, nor those with garlands, nor
those making their way to the Sacred House, seeking favour
with their Lord and grace. When no longer consecrated, you
may hunt. Let not the hatred of some who barred your way to
the Sacred Mosque lead you to aggression. Join hands in virtue
and piety, but join not hands in sin and aggression. Fear God,
for God is severe in punishment.   5:2

Forbidden to you are: carrion, blood, the flesh of swine, and
that which is consecrated to other than God; also the flesh of
animals strangled, killed violently, killed by a fall, gored to
death, mangled by wild beasts – except what you can ritually
sacrifice – or sacrificed to idols. Forbidden to you too is resort
to divination by arrows. This is an iniquity.

Today the unbelievers have despaired from your religion.
Fear them not, but fear Me.
Today I have perfected your religion;
I have completed My bounty upon you;
And I have sanctioned Islam as your religion.

If anyone is forced by famine and is not deliberately sinning,
then God is All-Forgiving, Compassionate to each.   5:3

They ask you what has been made licit to them.
   Say: 'Made licit to you are foods good and wholesome, and
what you trained of hunting animals, birds or dogs, which you
train as God taught you; so eat what they catch for you, and
mention the name of God thereon, and fear God, for God is
swift in account. Today made licit to you are good and wholesome foods. The food of the People of the Book is licit to you
and your food is licit to them.'

Licit too are chaste women from among the believers and chaste
women from among the People given the Book before you,

once you have paid them their dowries in marriage and not in
fornication or in secret dalliance. Whoso reneges his faith, his
good work is annulled and in the afterlife he will be counted
5:5   among the fallen.

O believers, if you rise to prayer, wash your faces and your
hands up to the elbows, and wipe your heads and feet to the
ankles. If you are impure, purify yourselves. If ill or on a journey,
or one of you has come from the toilet, or had intercourse with
women and could not find water, then use some clean earth and
wipe your faces and hands with it. God desires not to impose
any hardship upon you but desires to purify you and perfect
5:6   His grace upon you; perhaps you will render thanks.

Remember God's grace upon you and His covenant which He
covenanted with you, when you said: 'We hear and obey.' And
5:7   fear God, for God knows full well what lies within breasts.

O believers, conduct yourselves virtuously before God, and
be fair witnesses. Let not the hatred of some people lead you
away from practising justice. Be just, for this is closer to
piety, and fear God: God knows full well what you do. God
promises those who believe and do good deeds that they shall
have forgiveness and a glorious recompense. But those who
blaspheme and cry lies to Our revelations, these are the denizens
5:10   of hell.

O believers, remember the blessing of God upon you when a
group of people were intent upon stretching their hands forth
to harm you, and how He held back their hands from you. So
5:11   fear God, and let the believers put their trust in God.

God had taken the covenant of the Children of Israel, and We
selected from their number twelve chieftains. God said: 'I am
with you. If you perform the prayer, and pay the alms, and
believe in My messengers, and honour and support them, and

you offer up to God a handsome loan, I shall absolve you of your misdeeds and lead you into Gardens beneath which rivers flow. Whoso among you blasphemes thereafter, he has surely strayed from the right path.'

For violating their covenant We cursed them, and hardened their hearts. They twist words from their context, and have forgotten a portion of what they were asked to remember. You will still find them to harbour treachery, except for a few of them. But pardon them and forgive, for God loves those who do good.   5:13

And from those who say: 'We are Christians,' We took their covenant. But they have forgotten a portion of what they were asked to remember. So We provoked among them enmity and hatred until the Day of Resurrection, and God shall acquaint them with what they used to do.   5:14

O People of the Book, Our Messenger has come to you, making clear to you much of what you used to conceal from the Book, and forgiving much.
There has come to you from God a Light and a Book most
    lucid;
With it God guides him who conforms to His good pleasure to
    the paths of tranquillity;
He shall lead them from the folds of darkness to the light, by
    His leave;
And He shall guide them to a straight path.   5:16

They have blasphemed – those who say that God is the Christ son of Mary!
Say: 'Who can do anything against God's will should He wish to extirpate the Christ son of Mary and his mother, indeed all that is on earth? To God belongs sovereignty of the heavens and the earth, and what lies between. He creates whatsoever He wishes. And God is Omnipotent.'   5:17

The Jews and Christians say: 'We are the children of God and His beloved.'

Say: 'Why then does He torment you on account of your sins? Rather, you are mere humans from among those He created. He forgives whomsoever He wishes and torments whomsoever He wishes.' To God belongs sovereignty of the heavens and the earth, and what lies between. To Him is the journey's end.

5:18

O People of the Book, there has come to you Our Messenger, following an interval between messengers, to make matters clear to you, lest you should say: 'No herald of good tidings and no warner has come to us.' So now a herald of good tidings and a warner has indeed come to you. And God is Omnipotent.

5:19

Remember when Moses said to his people: 'O people, recall God's bounty upon you when He set up prophets among you, and made you kings, and bestowed upon you what He bestowed upon no other human beings. O people, enter the holy land which God has marked out for you, and do not go back to your old ways, only to end up as losers.'

They said: 'O Moses, in this land there are men of great might. We will not enter it until they leave it. When they leave, we will enter it.'

Then two men who feared God, and upon whom God had bestowed His grace, said: 'Break the gate in upon them. Once you enter, you shall be victorious. Put your trust in God if you are true believers.'

They said: 'O Moses, we shall never enter it so long as they are in it. So depart, you and your Lord, and make war. We shall stay right here.'

He said: 'My Lord, I have no power except over myself and my brother, so judge between us and these sinful people.'

He said: 'Then it shall be forbidden to them for forty years. They shall wander aimlessly in the land. So do not grieve for these sinful people.'

5:26

Recite to them the true story of the two sons of Adam, when they offered a sacrifice and it was accepted from one of them but not from the other.

He said: 'I shall slay you!'

The other replied: 'God only accepts from the devout. Were you to stretch forth your hand to kill me, I shall not stretch forth my hand to kill you, for I fear God, the Lord of the Worlds. I want you to bear my sin and yours, and thus become a denizen of the Fire, for this is the reward of wrongdoers.'   5:29

His soul tempted him to kill his brother, so he killed him and ended up among the lost. But God sent a raven clawing out the earth to show him how he might bury the corpse of his brother. He said: 'What a wretch I am! Am I incapable of being like this raven and so conceal my brother's corpse?' And so he ended up remorseful.   5:31

It is for this reason that We decreed to the Children of Israel that he who kills a soul neither in revenge for another, nor to prevent corruption on earth, it is as if he killed the whole of mankind; whereas he who saves a soul, it is as if he has saved the whole of mankind. Our messengers came to them bearing clear proofs, but many of them thereafter were disobedient on earth.   5:32

In truth, the punishment of those who make war against God and His Messenger, and roam the earth corrupting it, is that they be killed, or crucified, or have their hands and feet amputated, alternately, or be exiled from the land. This would be their shame in the present life, and in the next a terrible torment awaits them – except those who repent before you gain mastery over them. Therefore, you must understand that God is All-Forgiving, Compassionate to each.   5:34

O believers, fear God and seek the right way to draw close to Him, and exert yourselves in His cause; perhaps you will

succeed. As for those who disbelieve, had they possessed all that
is on earth, and the double thereof, to offer as ransom from the
torment of the Day of Resurrection, such will not be accepted
from them, and painful torment awaits them. They will desire
to come out of the Fire, but they shall never leave it! Eternal
5:37   torment awaits them.

The male thief and female thief: cut their hand as a penalty for
what they reaped – a punishment from God. God is Almighty,
All-Wise. But whoso repents after his transgression and does
good deeds, God shall pardon him, for God is All-Forgiving,
Compassionate to each. Have you not yet understood that to
God belongs sovereignty of the heavens and the earth, that
He torments whomever He wishes and pardons whomever He
5:40   wishes? God is Omnipotent.

O Messenger, grieve not for those who are quick to blaspheme,
among those who say 'We believe' with their mouths, but
whose hearts do not believe, nor for the Jews who often lend
their ears to falsehood or to other people who have never
visited you. They distort words from already established contexts and say: 'If you have been given such a ruling, abide by it,
but if you have not, then be on your guard.' If God wishes to
ensnare someone, you shall have no authority with God in his
regard. Those whom God wills not to cleanse their hearts –
shame shall be their lot in this world, and in the next terrible
torment.
    Ever willing to lend their ears to falsehood!
    Ever ready to consume forbidden wealth!
    If they come to you, judge among them or turn away from
them. Should you turn away from them, they will not harm you
one jot. But if you judge, then judge among them with fairness,
5:42   for God loves those who act with fairness.

How is it that they elect you to judge between them when they
already possess the Torah, in which is found the judgement of

God, then turn their backs upon it? These cannot be called believers. 5:43

We have revealed the Torah in which there is guidance and light. Prophets who surrendered to God were to judge in accordance with it for the Jews, as did the rabbis and scholars, those who were made to memorize the Book of God and who were its witnesses. So fear not mankind but fear Me, and do not sell away My verses for a paltry sum. Whoso judges not in accordance with what God revealed, they are the unbelievers. 5:44

In the Torah We decreed upon them a life for a life, an eye for an eye, a nose for a nose, an ear for an ear, a tooth for a tooth, and retaliation for wounds. Whoso freely forgoes this right, it shall be counted as expiation for him. Whoso judges not in accordance with what God revealed, these are the wrongdoers. 5:45

Following upon their tracks We sent Jesus son of Mary, confirming what he already possessed of the Torah. To him We revealed the Evangel in which there is guidance and light, confirming what was in his hands of the Torah, a guidance and homily to the pious. So let those who follow the Evangel judge in accordance with what God revealed in it. Whoso judges not in accordance with what God revealed, these are the dissolute. 5:47

To you We revealed the Book with the Truth, confirming previous Scripture and witnessing to their veracity. So judge between them as God revealed and do not follow their whims, to turn you away from the truth revealed to you.

For every community We decreed a law and a way of life. Had God willed, He could have made you a single community – but in order to test you in what He revealed to you. So vie with one another in virtue. To God is your homecoming, all of you, and He will then acquaint you with that over which you differed. 5:48

So judge between them as God revealed and do not follow their whims, and beware lest they tempt you away from certain things that God revealed to you. If they turn away in denial, know that God wishes to chastise them for some of their sins – many are the sinners among mankind! Do they truly desire the law of paganism? But who is fairer than God in judgement for a people 5:50 firm of faith?

O believers, take not Jews and Christians for allies; they are allies one of another. Whoso among you takes them as allies is counted of their number. God guides not the wrongdoers.

You will see those in whose hearts is sickness rushing to please them and saying: 'We fear lest a calamity overtake us.' Perhaps God will bring victory or decree some matter, and such people will regret what they once concealed in their hearts. And the believers will then say: 'What! Are these the ones who swore to God such mighty oaths that they will stand by you?' Their works shall be in vain, and they shall end among 5:53 the lost.

O believers, whoso among you shall apostatize from his religion, let him know that God will bring forth a people whom He loves and who love Him, humble towards the believers but mighty against the unbelievers, who exert themselves in the cause of God, and fear no blame from any quarter. This is a grace from God which He bestows upon anyone He wills. God is All-Encompassing, Omniscient. Your true ally is God, His Messenger and the believers, those who pray regularly and render alms as they prostrate themselves. Whoso takes God and His Messenger and the believers for allies, the party of God 5:56 shall be victorious.

O believers, do not take for allies those who took your religion as a subject of mockery and entertainment among those granted the Book before you, or among the unbelievers. Fear God if you truly believe. When you call to prayer, they take it as subject for mockery and entertainment, for they are a people of no understanding.

Say: 'O People of the Book, do you begrudge us anything other than that we believe in God and in what has been revealed to us, and what has been revealed before, and that most of you are dissolute?'

Say: 'Shall I tell you of a worse recompense from God than this? It is he whom God has cursed and with whom He is angry, turning them into apes and swine and worshippers of idols. These are worse in station and more straying from the right path.'

When they come to you, they say: 'We believe.' But they enter in blasphemy and they depart in blasphemy. And God knows best what they have concealed. You will see many of them hasten to sin and transgression and to consuming forbidden wealth. Wretched indeed is what they do! Would that the rabbis and scholars dissuade them from uttering blasphemy and consuming forbidden wealth – wretched indeed is what they practise!   5:63

The Jews say: 'The hand of God is shackled!' May their own hands be shackled and may they be cursed for what they say! Rather, His hands are spread forth and He dispenses in any manner He wishes. What has been revealed to you from your Lord will increase many of them in violence and blasphemy. We have sown hostility and hatred among them until the Day of Resurrection; whenever they kindle the flame of war, God shall extinguish it. They roam the earth corrupting it, and God loves not the corrupters.   5:64

If only the People of the Book come to believe and fear God, We would expiate their sins and admit them into Gardens of Bliss. If only they practise the Torah and the Evangel and what has been revealed to them from their Lord, they would thrive, eating what is above them and what lies beneath their feet! Among them is a community sound in belief, but many of them – wretched are their deeds!   5:66

O Messenger, convey what has been revealed to you from your Lord. If you do not, you will not have passed on His message; and God shall protect you from mankind. God guides not the unbelievers.

5:67

Say: 'O People of the Book, you follow no religion unless you practise the Torah and the Evangel and what has been revealed to you from your Lord.'

What has been revealed to you from your Lord will increase many of them in violence and blasphemy. So do not sorrow for the blasphemous. But those who believe, as well as the Jews, Sabeans and Christians who believe in God and the Last Day and do righteous deeds – no fear shall fall upon them, nor shall they grieve.

5:69

We made a covenant with the Children of Israel and sent them messengers. Whenever a messenger came to them with a message their souls coveted not, a group they called liars and another they killed. They imagined there would be no ordeal to follow, and thus grew blind and deaf. Then God pardoned them, but then again they grew blind and deaf – many of them. And God sees full well what they do.

5:71

It is blasphemy they utter, those who say that God is Christ the son of Mary! For Christ had said: 'O Children of Israel, worship God, my Lord and your Lord.' Whoso ascribes partners to God, God proscribes the Garden to him, and his final refuge is the Fire. Wrongdoers shall have no champions.

5:72

It is blasphemy they utter, those who say that God is the third of three! There is no god except the One God. If they do not desist from what they say, there shall touch those among them who blaspheme a painful torment. If only they would repent to God and ask His forgiveness – for God is All-Forgiving, Compassionate to each.

5:74

Christ the son of Mary is only a messenger, and messengers have come and gone before him. His mother was a saintly woman and they both ate food. Consider how We make clear Our revelations to them, and then consider how they pervert the truth!

Say: 'Do you indeed worship, apart from God, that which has no power to harm or benefit you?' God is All-Hearing, Omniscient.   5:76

Say: 'O People of the Book, do not be fanatical in your religion, except in truth. Do not follow the whims of a people who strayed before, and made many stray, and stray once again from the right path.' Those who disbelieved among the Children of Israel were cursed by the tongue of David and of Jesus son of Mary – and this because they rebelled and transgressed. They used not to forbid one another from a sin they committed – wretched was that which they did! You will witness many of them making friends with unbelievers – wretched is what their souls have laid in store for them! God is incensed against them, and in torment they shall remain eternally. And yet, had they believed in God and the Prophet, and in what was revealed to him, they would not have adopted them as friends. But many of them are dissolute.   5:81

You will surely find that the most hostile of men to the believers are the Jews and those who ascribe partners to God. And you will surely find that the nearest in amity towards the believers are those who say: 'We are Christians,' and that is because among them are priests and monks, and they do not grow proud. When they listen to what has been revealed to the Messenger, you will see their eyes overflowing with tears from the truth they recognize. They say: 'Our Lord, we believe, so inscribe us among those who witness. Why should we not believe in God and what has come down to us of the truth? We yearn for our Lord to lead us in among the righteous community.' God shall reward them for their speech – Gardens beneath which rivers flow, abiding therein for ever. This is the reward of the righteous. But those who blaspheme and cry lies 5:86 to Our revelations – those are the denizens of hell.

O believers, do not pronounce illicit the delectable foods that God has made licit to you, but do not transgress – God loves not the transgressors. Eat of what God has provided for you, food licit and delectable, and fear God in whom you believe.

God will not take you to task for a muddle in your oaths, but He will take you to task for an oath firmly undertaken. The expiation thereof is the feeding of ten poor persons such food as you would typically offer your family, or else clothing them, or manumitting a slave. Whoso finds not the means, then a three-day fast, this being expiation for your oath if you swore it. And honour your oaths. Thus does God make clear His 5:89 revelations to you; perhaps you will render thanks.

O believers, wine and gambling, idols and divining arrows are an abhorrence, the work of Satan. So keep away from it, that you may prevail. Satan only desires to arouse discord and hatred among you with wine and gambling, and to deter you from the mention of God and from prayer. Will you desist? Obey God and obey the Messenger and be on your guard. If you turn away, know that Our Messenger is enjoined only to convey the manifest message. Upon those who believe and do good deeds no blame shall attach in what they may taste, so long as they fear God, and believe, and do good deeds; then fear God and believe, then fear God and act charitably, for God loves the 5:93 charitable.

O believers, God will surely put you to the test in some of the game that your hands and lances shall garner, in order that God may know who truly fears Him in the realm of the Unseen. 5:94 Thereafter, whoso transgresses, a painful torment awaits him.

O believers, do not kill game while in a state of sanctity. Whoso among you kills it wilfully, his redress shall be the like of what he killed in cattle, judged by two men of good character among you – an offering which shall reach the Ka'ba. Or else expiation: the feeding of poor persons or the equivalent in fasting, so that he may taste the grave consequences of his act. God forgives past sin but he who returns to the offence, God shall exact revenge upon him, and God is Almighty and Avenging.   5:95

Licit for you is the game of the sea and its foods, as provision for you and for those on a journey. Illicit for you is the game on land as long as you are in a state of sanctity; and fear God, to whom you shall be herded.   5:96

God has appointed the Ka'ba, the Holy House, as a haven for mankind, as also the Holy Month, the animals of sacrifice and their garlands. This is in order that you may know that God knows what is in the heavens and what is on earth, and that God is Omniscient. Know that God is severe in punishment and that God is All-Forgiving, Compassionate to each. The Messenger is enjoined only to convey the message, and God knows what you reveal and what you conceal.

Say: 'The impure is not like the pure, even though you are impressed by the abundant wealth of the impure.' So fear God, you who are possessed of minds; perhaps you will prevail.   5:100

O believers, ask not about matters which, if revealed to you, would displease you. However, if you ask about them when the Qur'an is being sent down, they shall be revealed to you. God has pardoned these acts; and God is All-Forgiving, All-Forbearing. A people who came before you once asked about them, but then repudiated them. God did not designate certain animals in veneration to idols, such as the cleft-eared she-camel, or cattle left to roam, cattle forbidden to be slaughtered, or cattle forbidden to be ridden. It is the unbelievers, rather, who fabricate lies in God's name – and most of them have no understanding. If it is said to them: 'Come to what God has revealed and to the Messenger,' they retort: 'Sufficient for us is what we find our ancestors have followed.' What! Even if their 5:104 ancestors knew nothing, and lived without guidance?

O believers, take good care of your souls. A person who strays cannot harm you if you are guided aright. To God is your ultimate homecoming, all of you; and He shall inform you of 5:105 what you used to do.

O believers, witnessing is required among you, when death draws near one of you and it is time to make a bequest. Let there be two men of just character from among you, or two others not from your number, should you be journeying in the land when death's calamity overtakes you. You are to detain them after prayer and they are to swear by God, if you have doubts, as follows: 'We shall not sell our testimony for a price, even if it concerns a relative, nor conceal the testimony of God, or else we are counted sinners.' If it is found out that these two did something to merit the charge of sinning, let two others take their place, these being the victims of the first two. These latter two must then swear by God as follows: 'Our testimony is more truthful than theirs, and we shall not transgress or else we will be sinners.' In this manner, it would be more likely that they would fulfil their testimony to the letter; otherwise they would be afraid that their oath might be shown to be false once they had sworn it. So fear God and take heed. God guides not the 5:108 miscreants.

Beware a Day when God gathers the messengers together, and He will ask: 'What was the response to you?' They answer: 'We have no knowledge of this, for it is You Who are the All-Knower 5:109 of the Unseen.'

Remember when God said: 'O Jesus son of Mary, remember My blessing upon you and upon your mother, when I strength-

ened you with the Holy Spirit, and how you spoke to people in
the cradle and in your manhood;

When I taught you the Book, the Wisdom, the Torah and the
    Evangel;

When you created from clay the likeness of birds, by My
    leave,

Breathing upon them, and they became birds, by My leave;

When you cured the blind and the leper, by My leave,

And when you raised up the dead, by My leave;

When I held back the Children of Israel from you when you
    came to them with miracles,

And those who disbelieved said: "This is nothing but manifest
    sorcery";

When I inspired the disciples to have faith in Me and in My
    messenger,

And they said: "We believe, so witness that we are Muslims";

When the disciples said: "O Jesus son of Mary, can your God
Send down upon us a table from heaven?"

He said: "Fear God if you are true believers."

'They said: "We wish to eat from it so that our hearts are at
peace, and we know that you have spoken the truth to us, and
we be witnesses thereof"; said Jesus son of Mary: "O God our
Lord, send down upon us a table from heaven, and it shall be a
feast-day for first and last among us, and a miracle from You,
and grant us Your bounty – You are the best of providers."'   5:114

God said: 'I shall send it down upon you. Whoso among you
disbelieves hereafter, I shall torment him with a torment the like
of which I shall torment no other human being.'   5:115

Remember when God said to Jesus son of Mary: 'Did you
    really say to people: "Take me and my mother as two
    gods, instead of God"?'

He said: 'Glory be to You! What right have I to assert what
    does not in truth belong to me?

If I had said it, You would have known it;

You know what is in my soul and I know not what is in Your
      soul,
For it is You Who are the All-Knower of the Unseen.
I said nothing to them except what You commanded me:
"Worship God, my Lord and your Lord."
I was a witness to them while I lived among them,
But when You caused me to die, it was You Who kept watch
      over them.
You are a witness over all things.
If you torment them, they are Your servants,
And if You forgive them, it is You Who are Almighty,

5:118   All-Wise.'

God said: 'This is a day when the truthful profit from their
truthfulness. For them shall be Gardens beneath which rivers
flow, dwelling therein for ever. God is well-pleased with them
and they are well-pleased with Him.
      'This is the greatest of triumphs.'
      To God belongs sovereignty of the heavens and the earth and
5:120 what lies therein. God is Omnipotent.

Cattle

In the name of God,
Merciful to all,
Compassionate to each!

Praise be to God Who created the heavens and the earth,
And fixed the folds of darkness and light;
And yet those who blaspheme set up equals to their Lord!
It is He Who created you from clay, then decreed a span of
      time, while another span is named by Him,
And yet you continue to doubt!
He is God, in the heavens and on earth.

He knows what you hide and what you reveal,
And knows also what you deserve.   6:3

There comes to them no miracle from their Lord's miracles
except they turn away from it in denial. They called the lie to
the Truth when it came to them; but there shall come to them
a true account of that which they used to mock. Have they not
seen how many a generation We wiped out before them? We
granted them power on earth, such as We did not grant you.
We poured down the heavens upon them, with plentiful rain,
and caused rivers to flow beneath them. Then We wiped them
out because of their sins. After them, We created other generations.   6:6

Had We sent down upon you a book, inscribed on parchment,
which they touched with their very hands, those who blaspheme
would say: 'This is nothing but manifest sorcery.' They say: 'If
only an angel was sent down upon him!' Had We sent down an
angel, the matter would be judged, and they would receive no
respite; had We made him an angel, We would have given him
a man's form, and confused them even more than they are
already confused.   6:9

Messengers before you were mocked. But those who mocked
them were engulfed by that which they used to mock.
    Say: 'Travel the earth and see what was the destiny of liars.'
    Say: 'To whom belongs what is in the heavens and on
earth?'
    Say: 'To God. He has pledged upon Himself mercy in order
that He may gather you together on the Day of Resurrection,
of which there is no doubt.'
    But those who lost their souls – these do not believe.   6:12

To Him belongs all that find rest by day or night. He is All-
Hearing, Omniscient.   6:13

Say: 'Am I to take other than God as Master,

He Who created the heavens and the earth,

He Who feeds but is not fed?'

Say: 'I have been commanded to be the first to submit' – so do
not ascribe partners to God.

Say: 'If I disobey my Lord, I fear the torment of a terrible
Day;

Whoso is spared that Day, God has shown him mercy. This is
the greatest of triumphs.

If God touches you with harm, none but He can remove it,

And if He touches you with good, He is Omnipotent.

He is All-Powerful over His worshippers,

6:18   All-Wise, All-Experienced.'

Say: 'What is the most solemn witness?'

Say: 'God. He is witness between me and you.

This Qur'an has been revealed to me, to warn you therewith
and whomsoever it shall reach.

Do you indeed testify that there are other gods with God?'

Say: 'I do not testify.'

Say: 'It is but One God, and I am blameless of what you

6:19   associate with Him.'

Those to whom We gave the Book know it as they know their
own children. But those who lost their souls – these do not
believe. Who is more sinning than he who fabricates lies from
God or denies His revelations? The wrongdoers shall not
prevail.

A Day shall come when We shall herd them all, and We shall
then say to those who ascribed partners to God: 'Where are
your partners, those that you alleged?'

Having been tested, their only excuse will be: 'By God, our
Lord, we did not ascribe partners to You.'

See how they lie to themselves! How their fabrication aban-

6:24   doned them!

Some of them that listen to you – upon their hearts We draped veils lest they understand it, and in their ears heaviness. And whatever miracle they see they do not believe, so that when they come to you, they argue with you.

Those who disbelieve say: 'This is nothing but fables of the ancients.' They forbid others to listen to it, and themselves stay far away. But it is their souls that they destroy, and they know it not!

If only you could see them when they are made to stand above the Fire, crying out: 'Would that we could be returned to life and not call the lie to the revelations of our Lord, and be among the faithful!' But now there stands revealed to them what before they used to hide. And were they to be returned to life, they would revert to what was forbidden them. Liars they are!   6:28

They say: 'There is nothing but this our present life, and we shall not be resurrected.'

If only you could see them when they are made to stand before their Lord!

He shall say: 'Is this not the very truth?'

And they shall reply: 'Yes, by our Lord.'

He will then say: 'So taste the torment for the blasphemy you uttered.'   6:30

Lost indeed are those who deny the encounter with God. Thus, when the Hour comes to them unexpectedly, they will say: 'Wretched are we for having wasted our lives!' They shall carry their burden of sins upon their backs – evil is the burden they carry!

The present life is nothing but show and frivolity, but the Final Abode is surely better for the pious. Will you not understand?   6:32

We know you are grieved by what they say. It is not you they call the lie to, but the signs of God that the wrongdoers abjure. Messengers before you were called liars, but they patiently endured the charge of falsehood and the injuries they suffered until Our victory came to them.

There can be no alteration to the words of God.

There have already reached you reports of other messengers. If you find it hard that they turn away from you, then seek, if you can, a tunnel beneath the earth or a ladder in the sky whence you can bring them a miracle! Had God willed, He could have united them in right guidance. So do not be impetuous.

6:36   Only those who listen shall respond. As for the dead, God shall resurrect them, and to Him they shall return.

They say: 'If only a miracle were sent down upon him from his Lord!'

Say: 'God is able to send down a miracle but most of them
6:37   have no understanding.'

There is no creature that crawls on the face of the earth, no bird on the wing, but they are nations like you. We have not neglected any matter in this Book, and then to God they shall be mustered. As for those who cry the lie to Our revelations – deaf and dumb they are, and enveloped in darkness.

Whomever God wishes, He leads astray; whomever He
6:39   wishes, He sets upon a straight path.

Say: 'Consider this: if God's torment overtakes you or else the Last Hour, would you call upon any but God if you are sincere? Rather, it is Him you will call upon; and if He wills, He will relieve your distress as you call upon Him, and you will forget
6:41   your idolatry.'

We sent messages to nations before you, and We inflicted upon them famine and hardship that they might abase themselves. If only they had abased themselves when Our calamity struck! But their hearts had grown hard, and Satan made their deeds appear attractive to them. When they forgot what they had been asked to remember, We opened wide to them the gates of all good things; until, delighted with what they were given, We seized them suddenly, and behold, they were in utter despair. The last remnant of these wrongdoers was brought to an end. Praise be to God, Lord of the Worlds! 6:45

Say: 'Consider this: if God takes away your hearing and your sight, and seals your hearts, what god other than God can restore it to you?' Behold how We multiply Our signs, and yet they continue to avert their gaze! 6:46

Say: 'Consider this: if the torment of God descends upon you suddenly or openly, will any but the wicked be done away with?' We send messengers only as heralds of glad tidings and warners. Whoso believes and does good deeds, no fear shall fall upon them, nor shall they grieve. But those who cry lies to Our revelations, torment shall touch them by reason of their iniquity. 6:49

Say: 'I do not tell you that I possess the treasures of God, nor do I know the Unseen. Nor do I tell you I am an angel. I merely follow what is revealed to me.'

Say: 'Is the blind man the equal of one who sees? Will you not reflect?' 6:50

Warn in your message those who fear to be mustered to their Lord and have, apart from Him, neither master nor intercessor; perhaps they will grow in piety. And do not drive away those who call upon their Lord morning and evening, seeking His face. Upon you falls no part of their accounting, and upon them falls no part of yours. If you drive them away you would be unjust. In this manner We put them to the test, one against another, so that they would say: 'Are these the ones whom God has preferred from among our number?' Does not God know best those who are truly thankful? 6:53

When there comes to you those who believe in Our revelations, say: 'Peace be upon you. Your Lord has pledged upon Himself mercy so that whoso among you commits evil unknowingly and thereafter repents and does good, God is All-Forgiving, Compassionate to each.' This is how We render Our revelations distinct, and in order that the path of sinners be clearly 6:55 marked.

Say: 'I am forbidden to worship those whom you call upon other than God.'

Say: 'I shall not follow your caprice, else I would be lost and not be among those guided aright.'

Say: 'I stand upon a manifest proof from my Lord, and you have pronounced it false. I have no authority over what you seek to quicken. Judgement belongs solely to God. He follows the truth; He is the most decisive of arbiters.'

Say: 'If I had authority over what you seek to quicken, the matter between you and me would receive ultimate judgement. 6:58 God knows best who are the wrongdoers.'

With Him are the keys of the Unseen; none but He has
    knowledge thereof.
He knows all that is on land and in the sea;
Not a leaf falls but He knows it.
Not a seed in the darkness of earth,
Not anything, fresh or dried,
But is inscribed in a Manifest Book.
It is He Who causes you to die by night,
And knows what you earn by day.
Then He sends you forth therein, until a stated term is
    fulfilled.
Then to Him is your return.
Then He shall inform you of your deeds.
He towers in might above those who worship Him,
And sends you guardians,
Until, when death comes to one of you,
Our envoys receive his soul – and they fail not in their task.
Then they are returned to God, their true Master,

For His is the verdict – and quickest of all is He to settle
accounts.   6:62

Say: 'Who delivers you from the darknesses of land or sea? You
call upon him, humbly and in secret: "If You deliver us from
this agony, we shall surely be thankful."'
Say: 'It is God Who delivers you from this, and from every
agony,
But still you associate others with Him!'   6:64

Say: 'He is able to let loose upon you torment from above you
or from below your feet, or confound you in diverse sects, and
let some of you taste the violence of others.'
    Behold how We multiply Our signs; perhaps they will under-
stand.   6:65

Your people called it a lie, though it is the Truth.
Say: 'I am not your keeper;
Every account has its closure.
And you shall surely know.'   6:67

When you see those who wade in and argue about Our revelations, turn away from them until they wade into some other
topic. And should Satan cause you to forget this commandment,
do not, having remembered it, keep the company of evildoers.
In no way will the pious be held to account because of them,
but theirs is only to remind; perhaps they will grow pious.   6:69

And forsake those who take their religion for amusement and
frivolity, those whom the present life has beguiled. Remind them
with it, lest a soul be disgraced by what it has earned, having
no keeper or intercessor apart from God. And were it to offer
every penance, it shall not be accepted from it. Those souls
disgraced by what they earned shall have boiling water to drink,
and painful torment, because of their blasphemy.   6:70

Say: 'Are we to call upon any other than God – that which neither profits nor harms us? Are we to turn back upon our heels now that God has guided us? We would then be like one deluded by the devils on earth, and baffled. Meanwhile his friends are calling him to guidance: "Come to us!"'

Say: 'The guidance of God is true guidance, and we have been commanded to submit to the Lord of the Worlds: "Observe the prayer and fear God." It is to Him you will be mustered.'
It is He Who created the heavens and earth in truth;
Upon a Day when He says 'Be!' and His speech is the Truth;
To Him belongs sovereignty, upon a Day when the trumpet
    shall be blown.
Knower of the Invisible and the Visible,
6:73 All-Wise is He, All-Experienced.

Remember when Abraham said to his father Azar: 'Do you take idols as gods? I find you and your people manifestly astray.' This is how We made Abraham see the kingdom of the heavens and the earth, so that he would have certain faith.
When night enveloped him he saw a star;
He said: 'This is my Lord.'
When the star set, he said: 'I love not things that set.'
When he saw the rising moon, he said:
'This is my Lord,' but when it set, he said:
'If my Lord does not guide me, I shall be among those who go
    astray.'
When he saw the rising sun he said:
'This is my Lord, for it is larger,' but when it set he said:
  'O people, I am quit of your idolatry. I have set my face towards Him Who created the heavens and the earth, pure in my worship, nor am I one who associates anything with
6:79 God.'

His people disputed with him. He said:
  'Do you dispute with me about God now that He has guided me?

'I have no fear of your idol worship, unless my Lord intends some matter.

'My Lord encompasses all in His knowledge. Will you not reconsider?

'How can I fear the idols you worship while you do not fear associating with God that for which no sanction has been revealed to you?'

Which of these two groups has the better right to feel secure, if only you knew?

Those who believe and mix not their faith with evil – these shall feel secure and these are rightly guided.   6:82

This was Our argument which We conveyed to Abraham against his people. We elevate in degrees whomsoever We wish. Your Lord is All-Wise, Omniscient.   6:83

We bestowed upon him Isaac and Jacob, and both We guided – and Noah We had guided beforehand. From his progeny were David and Solomon, Job and Joseph, Moses and Aaron – this is how We reward those who do good – as also Zachariah, and John, Jesus and Elijah, all virtuous; as also Ishmael, Elisha,* Jonah and Lot, all of whom We preferred above mankind. So too their fathers, their progeny and their brothers: We chose them and guided them to a straight path. Such is God's guidance; with it He guides whomever He wishes among His worshippers. Had they worshipped idols, vain would have been their works.   6:88

They are the ones to whom We granted the Book, the law and prophecy. If these people here present disbelieve in it, We have charged with it another people who shall not disbelieve. They are the ones whom God has guided, so emulate their guidance.

Say: 'I ask you no wage for it; it is but a Remembrance to mankind.'   6:90

Nor have they honoured God as He ought to be honoured when they say that God did not reveal anything to a human being.

Say: 'Who was it who revealed the Book that Moses brought, a light and guidance to mankind – the revelation you have committed to scrolls, some of which you show and much of which you hide? And then you were taught what you did not know, neither you nor your fathers?'

6:91   Say: 'It is God,' then leave them to indulge in their frivolity.

This is a Book We have sent down, blessed, and confirming previous revelations, in order that you may warn Mecca, mother of cities, and its surroundings. Those who believe in the here-after shall believe in it, and they shall remain steadfast in their prayers.

Who is more sinful than he who fabricates lies in God's name?

Or he who says: 'It was revealed to me,' and nothing was revealed to him?

Or he who says: 'I shall reveal the like of what God revealed'?

If only you could see the sinners then, sunk deep in the throes of death, as the angels with flailing hands address them:

'Deliver up your souls!

'Today you shall be requited with an abasing torment in return for the untruths you spoke in God's name, when you
6:93   were too proud to accept His revelations.'

You have come to Us singly, just as you were when We first
    created you;

You have abandoned what We charged you with, tossing it
    behind your backs.

We do not see your advocates standing with you,

Those you alleged were your partners.

The ties between you are severed,

6:94   And lost to you is what you used to claim.

It is God Who splits open the seed and the pits.

He causes the living to issue from the dead, and the dead to
    issue from the living.

Behold the works of God! How can you deny?

He is the breaker of dawns,

He made the night for resting,

And the sun and moon as measures of time.

Such is the disposition of the Almighty, the Omniscient!   6:96

It is He Who fixed for you the stars whereby you may be
    guided,

In the darkness of land and sea.

We have made distinct Our revelations to a people who
    understand.   6:97

It is He Who brought you forth from one soul,

Lodged in the womb, or laid to rest in the tomb.

We have made distinct Our revelations to a people who reflect.   6:98

It is He Who brought down from the heaven water,

With which We bring forth vegetation of all kinds,

From which We bring forth greenery,

From which We bring forth close-packed grain,

And from the palm tree, from its wreaths, clusters of dates,
    near to hand,

And gardens of vine, olive and pomegranate,

Resembling and not resembling one another.

Behold their fruits when ripe and ready to pluck!

In these are signs for a people who believe.   6:99

To God they assigned the *Jinn* * as partners, though He created
them, and fabricated for Him sons and daughters, mindlessly.

    Glory to Him! May He be far above what they recount!

    Marvellous Creator of the heavens and the earth!

    How can He have a son when He has no spouse and created
all things? He is Omniscient.   6:101

Behold God your Lord!
There is no god but He, Creator of all things, so worship Him.
He is Guardian over all things.
Eyes reach Him not, but He reaches the eyes,
6:103 All-Refined, All-Experienced is He!

Proofs conspicuous have come to you from your Lord; whoso discerns them, this will be to his soul's credit, but whoso is blind, that will be to his soul's loss. I am not your keeper. Thus do We make explicit Our revelations – lest they say: 'You have been tutored' – and to clarify the message to a people who understand.

Follow what has been revealed to you from your Lord – there is no god but He – and turn away from the idolaters. Had God willed, they would not have worshipped idols. But We did not 6:107 appoint you their keeper, nor are you their guardian.

Do not curse those who call upon what is other than God, for they might curse God back in their mindless violence. This is why We made attractive to each nation their own works; then to their Lord is their return, and He shall inform them of what they used to do. They swear by God the mightiest oath that if a miracle is performed before them they would believe in it.

Say: 'Miracles can only come from God.' But how do you know? It may be that even if a miracle is performed before them they would still not believe. For We would confound their hearts and eyes just as they did not believe in it the first time, and abandon them to stray, aimless in their rebelliousness. Had We brought the angels down upon them, or had the dead spoken to them, or had We mustered all things before their very eyes, they would still not believe unless God wills. But most of them 6:111 are ignorant.

In like manner, and for every prophet, We assigned an enemy, demons of humans and *Jinn*. Each inspires to each vanities of speech, all of it delusion. Had your Lord willed, they would not have done it. So leave them to their deceit. And let the hearts of those who do not believe in the afterlife give heed to it! Let them find it pleasing! Let them reap what they reap!   6:113

Am I to seek anything other than God as judge when it was He Who sent down the Book upon you, lucid and specific? As for those to whom We brought the Book, they recognize that it is revealed from your Lord in truth; so be not among those who doubt.   6:114

Consummate is the Word of your Lord in truth and justice. Nothing can alter His words. He is All-Hearing, Omniscient.   6:115

And were you to give heed to most people on earth, they would lead you astray from the path of God. They follow nothing but conjecture; they merely fantasize. Your Lord knows best who is straying from His path; He knows best who are truly guided.   6:117

Eat of food which God's name has been mentioned upon, if you believe in His revelations. There is no reason for you not to eat food upon which God's name has been mentioned, when God has made plain to you what He forbade you, except such as you are forced to eat through necessity.

Many go astray while following their whims, and with-out knowledge, but your Lord knows best who the deliberate sinners are.   6:119

So avoid sin, manifest or concealed, for those who garner sin will be requited for what they commit. Therefore, do not eat food upon which God's name has not been mentioned, for this is an offence. It is the devils who inspire their friends to argue against you, and if you obey them you would be idol worshippers.   6:121

Consider. Is he who was as if dead and whom We then
    restored to life,

Granting him a light with which he walks among men,
Like one who walks in darkness, from which he cannot
    escape?
Thus has it been made attractive to blasphemers that which
6:122   they do.

Likewise in every city We appointed its most infamous sinners
to plot and scheme therein, but they scheme only against themselves, and they know it not.

Whenever a verse is revealed to them they say: 'We will not
believe unless we are given what other messengers of God were
given.'

God knows best where He places His message. Those who
sinned shall be punished with abasement from God, and with
6:124   terrible torment because of what they schemed.

He whom God wishes to guide, He spreads open his breast to
    Islam;
And he whom God wishes to lead astray, He turns his heart
    narrow and constricted,
Like one clambering up to the sky.
Thus does God inflict His anger upon the unbelievers.
Behold the path of your Lord, made straight!
We have made plain Our verses to a people who recollect.
They shall dwell in the House of Peace with their Lord,
6:127   And He shall be their Protector in return for what they did.

On that Day when He shall muster them all:
'O tribes of *Jinn*, you have indeed seduced many humans.'
Their friends among mankind will say:
'Our Lord, we have done favours to one another,
But now we have reached the term You appointed for us.'
He shall say: 'The Fire shall be your refuge, therein to dwell
    for ever,
Unless God wills otherwise. Your Lord is All-Wise,
    Omniscient.'

Thus do We cause sinners to befriend one another, to requite them for what they earned.   6:129

O tribes of *Jinn* and men, were you not visited by messengers from among you, narrating to you My revelations and warning you of arriving at a Day like this?

They shall say: 'We so witness, against ourselves.'

This present life seduced them, and they testified against themselves that they had blasphemed.

This is because your Lord would not destroy cities unjustly, while its inhabitants were sunk in ignorance.   6:131

For all creatures there are ranks, depending on what they did, and your Lord is not unaware of what they do. Your Lord is All-Sufficient, Possessor of Mercy. If He wishes, He can make you disappear and appoint whomever He wishes as successors after you, just as He created you from the progeny of other nations. That which you have been promised will surely come to pass; nor can you prevent it.   6:134

Say: 'O people, do the best you can, and I too shall do my best. You will surely know to whom belongs the reward of the House. Wrongdoers shall not prevail.'   6:135

To God they assign a portion from what He created of harvest and cattle. They say: 'This portion belongs to God – or so they allege – while that goes to our partners.' Their partners' share does not reach God, while God's share does reach their partners. What a wretched ruling!

Then again, their partners have enticed many idolaters to kill their infants, in order to lead them to their destruction and confuse them in their religion. Had God willed, they would not have done so. So leave them to their fraud!   6:137

They say: 'These cattle and harvest are taboo, not to be eaten except by whomever we wish' – or so they allege. Here too are

cattle whose backs are forbidden and cattle upon which they do not mention the name of God – fabricating falsehood against
6:138   God. He shall requite them for their fraud.

They say: 'That which lies in the wombs of these cattle is dedicated solely to our males but forbidden to our wives. If stillborn they are partners in it.' He will requite them for such false
6:139   commandments. He is All-Wise, Omniscient.

Wretched are they who kill their infants, witless and dumb. They have forbidden what God bestowed upon them, fabricating falsehood against God. They have strayed far, and have not
6:140   been guided aright.

He it is Who created gardens, trellised and untrellised, and palms and plants of diverse fruits, and olives and pomegranates, like and unlike. Eat of its fruit when ripe, and deliver up its due the day it is harvested. Do not be immoderate; He loves not the
6:141   immoderate.

Of cattle He created some for burden, others for slaughter. Eat from what God bestowed upon you and do not follow in the
6:142   footsteps of Satan, for he to you is a manifest enemy.

Consider eight pairs, two pairs of sheep and two pairs of goats. Then say to them: 'Did He forbid the two males or the two females? Or only what is enfolded in the wombs of the female pairs? Let me have the benefit of your knowledge if you speak the truth!'
    Or consider two pairs of camels and two of cattle. Then say to them: 'Did He forbid the two males or the two females? Or only what is enfolded in the wombs of the female pairs? Or were you present as witnesses when God charged you with this commandment?'
    What greater sinner than he who, without true knowledge,

fabricates lies from God in order to mislead people? God guides
not those who are dishonest.   6:144

Say: 'I do not find in what was revealed to me anything illicit
for one who consumes food except it be carrion or blood that
is shed, or flesh of swine. Such food is an abomination or else
an iniquity, dedicated to other than God. However, if one is
forced by necessity, and does so neither deliberately infringing
nor violating this commandment, your Lord is All-Forgiving,
Compassionate to each.'   6:145

Upon Jews We forbade all animals with claws. As for cattle and
sheep, We forbade them their fats except for the fat on their
backs or entrails or what is mixed with bone. This is how We
requited them for their sins – and We are truthful. If they
contradict you, say: 'Your Lord's mercy is wide, but His wrath
against lawbreakers cannot be restrained.'   6:147

Those who ascribe partners to God will say: 'Had God willed,
we would not have ascribed partners to God, nor would our
ancestors; nor would we have declared anything illicit.' In like
manner did those who came before them utter falsehoods, until
they tasted Our wrath!
   Say: 'Have you any knowledge which you can bring forth to
us? You follow nothing but conjecture; you merely fantasize.'
   Say: 'To God belongs the crowning argument. Had He willed,
He would have guided you all.'
   Say: 'Bring me your witnesses who attest that God declared
this illicit.' If they testify, do not join them in their testimony.
Nor must you follow the whims of those who called the lie to
Our revelations, who do not believe in the hereafter, who hold
God to have equals.   6:150

Say: 'Come, let me recite to you what your Lord forbids you:
that you associate nothing with Him; that you show loving

kindness towards parents; that you do not kill your infants for fear of poverty – We shall provide for you and them; that you do not come near indecencies, whether out in the open or else concealed; that you do not kill the soul which God has sanctified except in justice.

'This is what He has charged you with; perhaps you will come to your senses.

'And do not come near the property of the orphan, except with the best intentions, until the orphan has attained the age of full maturity. Be fair in weights and measures, and act equitably. We charge no soul except what it can bear. If you pass judgement, be just even if a kinsman is involved, and fulfil the covenant of God.

6:152 'This is what He has charged you with; perhaps you will remember.'

6:153 Here then is My path, made straight, so follow it and do not follow other paths which will divert you from His path. This is what He has charged you with; perhaps you will grow in piety.

Then We revealed the Book to Moses, to complete Our blessings on one who was righteous, to make clear all things, and as a guidance and a mercy; perhaps they would believe in the encounter with their Lord.

6:155 And this too is a Book We have sent down, blessed; so follow it and be pious; perhaps you will be shown mercy.

Lest you should say: 'The Book was only revealed to two communities before us, and we were unschooled in their religious learning'; or lest you should say: 'If only the Book had been sent down upon us, we would have been more rightly guided than they are,' manifest proof has now come to you from your Lord, a guidance and a mercy. What greater sinner than he who calls the lie to God's revelations and turns away from them? We shall recompense those who disdained Our revelations with a wretched torment in return for their disdain. Are they merely

waiting for the angels to come down upon them, or for your
Lord to come, or else some miracle of your Lord? The Day
when some miracle of your Lord is revealed is a Day when faith
is of no profit to a soul unless that soul had believed beforehand,
or laid a good stock of work through its faith.

Say: 'Wait, and We too are waiting!'   6:158

As for those who divide their religion and turn themselves into
sects, you have nothing to do with them. Their judgement is left
to God, and it is He Who will inform them of what they used
to do. Whoso begets a good deed shall be rewarded tenfold;
whoso begets an evil deed shall only be punished once. And
they shall not be wronged.   6:160

Say: 'My Lord has guided me to a straight path,
A religion upright, the religion of Abraham, of pristine faith,
Nor did he associate anything with God.'   6:161

Say: 'My prayers, my devotions, my very being, my death,
Are in the hands of God, Lord of the Worlds –
No partner has He! Thus was I commanded,
And I am the first of Muslims.'   6:163

Say: 'Am I to seek a Lord other than God,
When He is Lord of all things?
No soul earns except what is charged to its account,
And no soul burdened shall bear the burden of another.
Thereafter to God is your homecoming,
And He will then acquaint you with that over which you
    differed.'   6:164

It is He Who made you inheritors of the earth, and elevated
some of you above others in degree in order to test you in what
He bestowed upon you. Your Lord is swift in punishment; your
Lord is All-Forgiving, Compassionate to each.   6:165

The Battlements

In the name of God,
Merciful to all,
Compassionate to each!

Alif Lam Mim Sad

This is a Book, sent down upon you, so let there be no distress in your breast because of it. You are to warn with it, and it is a Remembrance to the faithful.

Follow what has been sent down to you from your Lord and follow not, apart from Him, any other guardians. Little do you reflect!

How many a town We destroyed! Our wrath came upon it as they slumbered at night or reposed by day.

Their only plea, as Our wrath fell upon them, was to say: 'We were indeed wicked.' Let Us ask those to whom messengers were sent, and let Us ask the messengers! And let Us then give them a true account – for We were never absent! On that Day, the scales will be just. Those whose scales are heavy, they are the winners; but those whose scales are light, they are the ones who shall lose their souls for repudiating Our
7:9 revelations.

We established you firmly upon the earth. We provided you with livelihoods therein – little thanks did you render. We created you, We gave you form, and then We told the angels: 'Bow down before Adam.' They bowed, all except Satan, who was not among those who bowed.

He said: 'What prevented you from bowing down when I commanded you?'

He said: 'I am better than he. You created me of fire but him You created of clay.'

He said: 'Descend from it. It is not fit for you to wax proud in it. Depart! You have been disgraced.'

He said: 'Defer my judgement until the Day when they are resurrected.'

He said: 'You shall be so deferred.'

He said: 'Inasmuch as You have led me astray, I shall lie in wait for them along Your straight path. Then I shall assail them from their front and from their backs, from their right and from their left. Nor will You find most of them to be thankful.'

He said: 'Be gone, accursed and outcast! As for those among them who follow you, I shall fill hell with you all! And you, Adam, dwell with your wife in the Garden, and eat wherever you wish, but do not come near that tree or else you will be sinners.'   7:19

And Satan whispered to them to open their eyes to what had been concealed from them of their shame.

He said: 'Your Lord forbade you to approach this tree only because you would become angels or turn immortal.'

And he swore to them: 'I offer you good advice.' Thus did he deceive them with florid speech. When they tasted the tree, their shame was visible to them, and they went about sewing leaves of the Garden upon themselves.

Their Lord called out to them: 'Did I not forbid you that tree? Did I not tell you that Satan was your undisguised enemy?'

They said: 'Our Lord, we wronged ourselves. If You do not forgive us and be merciful towards us, we shall surely be lost.'

He said: 'Descend, enemies one to another! On earth you shall have a dwelling place and livelihood for a while.'

He said: 'In it you shall live; in it you shall die; from it you shall be brought forth.'   7:25

O Children of Adam, We have sent down upon you a garment to hide your shame, and as adornment. But the garment of piety – that is best. These are some of God's revelations; perhaps they will remember.

O Children of Adam, let not Satan seduce you as he drove out your two parents from the Garden. He stripped them of their garments to show them their shame. He and his clan can see you from where you cannot see them.

We have assigned the devils as masters of those who do not believe. When they commit an indecency, they say: 'We found our ancestors had done likewise, and God commanded us to do so.'

Say: 'God does not command indecency. Do you attribute to God what you do not know?'

Say: 'My Lord commands justice. Turn your faces towards Him at every site of prayer, and call upon Him, sincere in your faith. As He created you so also shall you return to Him. A group He has guided and a group has justly gone astray, for they have taken the devils as masters instead of God, and 7:30 imagine they are rightly guided.'

O Children of Adam, dress properly at every site of prayer; eat and drink, but do not be excessive – God loves not the excessive.

Say: 'Who was it who forbade the fine apparel which God created for the benefit of His worshippers? Who forbade the delights of livelihood?'

Say: 'Such things shall belong to the faithful in this present life, and to them alone of all mankind on the Day of Resurrection.' Thus do We elucidate Our revelations to a people with 7:32 understanding.

Say: 'My Lord did indeed forbid all indecencies, apparent or concealed, as also sin and aggression without due cause; and that you associate with God anything for which no sanction has been revealed from on high, or else impute to God what you do 7:33 not know.'

For every nation there is an appointed span of time; when their time arrives, they can neither delay it nor bring it forward, even 7:34 by an instant.

O Children of Adam, when messengers from among you come to you and narrate to you My revelations, whoso is pious and does good deeds – no fear shall fall upon them, nor shall they grieve. But they who call the lie to Our revelations and are too proud to accept them – these are the inhabitants of the Fire, dwelling therein for ever. What greater sinner than he who fabricates lies from God or calls the lie to His revelations? These shall have their share of what is divinely inscribed as their lot, until, when Our angelic messengers come to carry away their souls, they shall ask them: 'Where are they whom you used to worship instead of God?' and they shall reply: 'They have forsaken us.' Thus will they testify against themselves that they were unbelievers.   7:37

To them God will say: 'Join the company of nations that passed before you, of *Jinn* and humans, heading for the Fire. As each nation enters, it curses its sister nation until, when all are plunged therein, the last shall tell the first: "Our Lord, these people have led us astray, so double their torment in the Fire," and He shall respond: "For each of you torment is doubled, but you know it not." And the first shall say to the last: "You have no advantage over us, so taste the torment for what you have earned."'   7:39

Those who call the lie to Our revelations or are too proud to accept them – the gates of heaven shall not open before them, nor shall they enter the Garden, until the camel enters the eye of the needle. Thus do We requite evildoers. In hell they shall make their beds, and above them its sheets of fire. Thus do We requite wrongdoers.   7:41

But those who believe and perform good deeds – We do not charge a soul except what it can bear – these are the people of the Garden, therein dwelling for ever. We shall remove all malice from their hearts, and rivers shall flow beneath them. They shall say: 'Praise be to God Who guided us to this place. We would not have been guided had it not been for God Who guided us. The messengers of Our Lord came with the Truth.' And they shall be addressed as follows: 'This Garden you have been made 7:43 to inherit in return for your deeds.'

The people of the Garden shall call out to the people of the Fire: 'We have found our Lord's promise to be true. Have you found His promise to be true?'

And these shall answer: 'Yes.'

A clarion voice shall be heard between them, calling out: 'God's curse upon wrongdoers! Those who obstruct the path of God, who seek to deflect it, who blaspheme the hereafter!'

Between them is a wall, and upon its battlements are men who know each group by their outward visage. These call out to the people of the Garden: 'Peace be upon you!' They have not entered it, though eager to do so. And when their eyes are directed towards the people of the Fire, they say: 'Our Lord, do 7:47 not include us among the wrongdoers.'

The people on the battlements call out to men they know by their outward visage, saying: 'What did you gain from all your money making? What did you gain from all your pride? Are these the men you swore would not be touched by God's mercy?'

Enter the Garden. No fear shall fall upon you, nor shall you 7:49 grieve.

The people of the Fire call out to the people of the Garden: 'Pour down upon us water or else some of what God bestowed upon you.' And these shall answer: 'God forbade them to the unbelievers. They are those who took their religion lightly and in jest, and whom this present life seduced.'

Today We shall forget them as they forgot they would encounter this very Day, for they used to blaspheme against Our revelations. We brought them a Book, one which We elucidated with

Our knowledge, a guidance and a mercy to a people who believe. Are they merely awaiting its fulfilment? But on the Day when it shall be fulfilled, those who had previously forgotten it shall say: 'The messengers of Our Lord have come with the Truth. Have we any advocates who can plead for us? Or can we be restored to life and do other than what we did?' They have lost their souls, and that which they fabricated has deserted them.   7:53

Your Lord God is He Who created the heavens and the earth in six days. Then He settled firmly on the throne.
It is He Who veils the day with night – swiftly following.
The sun, the moon and the stars are subject to His command.
His the creation, His the command:
Blessed be God, Lord of the Worlds!   7:54

Call upon your Lord, in humble supplication and in private. He loves not those who transgress. Do not corrupt the land once it has been set right. Call upon Him in piety and in hope, for the mercy of God is within reach of the righteous.

It is He Who sends the winds softly blowing, ahead of His mercy, until, when laden with heavy clouds, We drive them forth to a parched land, and cause water to come down, with which We bring forth all manner of fruit.
    Thus will We revive the dead; perhaps you will reflect.   7:57

A good land yields its produce by leave of its Lord; an evil land brings forth nothing save in hardship and misery. Thus do We expound Our revelations to a people who render thanks.   7:58

We had sent Noah to his people and he said to them: 'My people, worship God. You have no other god besides Him, and I fear for you the torment of a mighty Day.'
    The chieftains of his people said: 'We see you are in manifest error.'
    He said: 'My people, there is no error in me, but I am a

messenger from the Lord of the Worlds. I am here to deliver to you the messages of my Lord and offer you counsel. For I know from God what you do not. Are you surprised that a message from your Lord has come to you by means of a man from among you, here to warn you and call you to piety, so that you might obtain mercy?'

But they called him a liar, so We saved him and his companions in the Ark and We drowned those who called the lie to 7:64 Our revelations. They were indeed a people blind to truth.

To 'Ad* We sent their fellow tribesman Hud.* He said: 'My people, worship God. You have no other god besides Him. Will you not be pious?'

The disbelieving chieftains of his people said: 'We see you are being foolish, and we think you are a liar.'

He said: 'My people, I am not being foolish, but I am a messenger from the Lord of the Worlds. I am here to deliver to you the messages of my Lord and I am a counsellor to you, worthy of trust. Are you surprised that a message from your Lord has come to you by means of a man from among you, here to warn you? Remember how He made you His deputies, following the people of Noah? How He increased you in physical strength? So remember the bounties of God; perhaps you 7:69 will be saved.'

They replied: 'Have you come to ask us to worship God alone, and to forsake what our forefathers worshipped? Bring to pass, then, what you promised us, if you speak the truth.'

He said: 'Decreed upon you is the torment and wrath of God. Do you dispute with me over names that you and your forefathers coined, and for which no sanction has come from God? So wait, and I shall wait with you.'

So We saved him and his companions through Our mercy, and We extirpated all traces of those who cried lies to Our 7:72 revelations. They were assuredly a faithless people.

To Thamud* We sent their fellow tribesman Salih.* He said: 'My people, worship God. You have no other god but He. A sign has come to you from your Lord: here is the she-camel of God, a sign to you. Leave it to graze in the land of God and do it no harm, or else painful torment will befall you. Remember when He made you His deputies following the people of 'Ad, and granted you mastery over the earth, when you seized its plains to build your mansions, and carved houses from the mountains. Remember the bounties of God and do not make mischief in the land, to corrupt it.'

The chieftains of his people, waxing proud towards those deemed weak among the believers, said: 'Do you know for sure that Salih is a messenger from God?' They answered: 'We believe in the message he was sent with.' The proud ones said: 'We, however, disbelieve in what you believe.'

So they hamstrung the she-camel and defied the command of their Lord. They said: 'O Salih, bring to pass what you threatened us with if you are truly a messenger.'

Whereupon a mighty trembling swept down upon them, and they lay dead in their houses. So he withdrew from them and said: 'My people, I delivered to you the message of my Lord. I offered you counsel but you do not like counsellors.'   7:79

Then again, remember Lot, when he said to his people: 'Do you commit an indecency that no people anywhere have ever committed before you? You go lusting after men rather than women. You are indeed a people depraved.'

No answer did his people give but to say: 'Banish them from your town. They are a group who wish to remain chaste.'

So We saved him and his family, except for his wife, who was among those remaining behind. And We rained down upon them a rainstorm: behold what end these sinners met!   7:84

To Midian* We sent their fellow tribesman Shu'ayb,* who said: 'My people, worship God; you have no other god but He. A clear sign has come to you from your Lord, so be fair in weights and measures, and do not cheat people of their rights. Do not corrupt the land once it has been set right. This is better for you if you are true believers. Do not sit by every roadside to make threats and obstruct the way to God for those who believe in Him, seeking to turn that way crooked. Remember when you were few and God increased you in number.

'Consider the fate of the dissolute. If a group among you believe in the mission with which I was sent while another believes not, be patient until God judges between us, for He is 7:87 the best of judges.'

The chieftains of his people, waxing proud, said: 'We shall drive you out of our town, O Shu'ayb, you and those who believe with you, unless you return to our religion.'

He said: 'Even though we detest it? We would be dishonest to God were we to return to your religion, now that God has saved us from it. We cannot return to it unless God our Lord wishes it. Our Lord encompasses all things in His knowledge. In Him we place our trust. Our Lord, judge in righteousness between us and our people for You are the best of arbiters.'

The blasphemous chieftains of his people said: 'If you follow Shu'ayb, you will surely fail.'

Whereupon a mighty trembling swept down upon them, and they lay dead in their homes. It was as if those who called Shu'ayb a liar had never enjoyed these homes. And those who called Shu'ayb a liar were themselves the losers.

So he withdrew from them and said: 'My people, I delivered to you the messages of my Lord and I offered you counsel. How 7:93 can I feel sorry for a blasphemous people?'

Never did We send a prophet to a city but We seized its inhabitants with hardship and injury; perhaps they might repent in humility. Then We substituted good for evil until they grew prosperous and said: 'Our ancestors too were touched by both hardship and ease.' But suddenly We seize them, unawares!

Had the people of the cities believed and grown pious, We

would have opened to them the blessings of heaven and earth. But they lied, so We seized them in recompense for what they earned.

Are the people of the cities confident that Our wrath will not strike them at night, while they sleep?

Or are the people of the cities confident that Our wrath will not strike them in the morning while they amuse themselves?

Do they really feel secure from the cunning of God? None can feel secure from the cunning of God save those who are lost.

Was it not made clear to those who inherit the earth from its former inhabitants that, had We wished, We could strike them down for their misdeeds? Or seal their hearts and turn them deaf?

These cities, We narrate to you some of their tales. Their messengers came to them with manifest signs, but they were not ready to believe in what they had previously called false. Thus does God seal the hearts of blasphemers. We found most of them bound by no covenant. We found most of them to be dissolute.

Following them, We sent Moses with Our wonders to Pharaoh and his court, but they denounced them. Consider what an end these perverts met!

Moses said: 'O Pharaoh, I am a messenger from the Lord of the Worlds. I am bound to report from God only what is true. I come to you with a miracle from your Lord, so send forth with me the Children of Israel.'

He said: 'If you come with a miracle, bring it forth if what you say is true.'

So Moses threw his staff on the ground and it turned into a serpent, undisguised. He drew his hand out and it was white for all to see.

The courtiers of Pharaoh's people said: 'This man is an expert sorcerer.'

Pharaoh said: 'He wishes to expel you from your land, so what is your advice?'

They said: 'Put him off, him and his brother, and send out to all cities to gather for you every expert sorcerer.'

The sorcerers came to Pharaoh and said: 'We must have our wage if we are the victors.'

7:114   He said: 'Yes. Indeed, you will be among my intimates.'

The sorcerers said: 'O Moses, either you throw down first or we throw down.'

He said: 'You throw first.'

When they threw down, they bewitched the eyes of the people and struck fear into their hearts, producing prodigies of sorcery.

Then We revealed to Moses: 'Throw down your staff,' whereupon it swallowed their deceits. The truth burst into view, and their works were proven fraudulent. They were defeated and slunk back in shame. The sorcerers were thrown to the ground,

7:120   prostrate.

They said: 'We believe in the Lord of the Worlds, the Lord of Moses and Aaron.'

Pharaoh said: 'You believe in Him before I grant you leave? This is but a scheme you schemed in the kingdom to drive out its people. You will surely know! I shall cut off your hands and legs, on opposite sides, and then crucify you all.'

They said: 'It is to our Lord that we shall return. You bear us a grudge only because we believed in the wonders of our Lord when they were shown to us. Our Lord, fill us with patience

7:126   and make us die as Muslims.'

The courtiers of Pharaoh's people said: 'Will you allow Moses and his people to corrupt the earth and to abandon you and your gods?'

He said: 'We shall slaughter their sons and debauch their females, and we shall assert our mastery over them.'

Moses said to his people: 'Call upon God for help, and be

patient. The earth belongs to God and He gives it in inheritance to whomever He pleases among His servants. The pious shall prevail in the end.'

They said: 'We were oppressed before you came to us, and we remain oppressed after you have come to us.'

He said: 'Perhaps your Lord will destroy your enemy and make you His deputies on earth. Then He will observe how you shall act.'

7:129

We tested Pharaoh's people by afflicting them with years of drought and failure of crops, in order that they might reflect. So, when the times were good to them they said: 'We deserve this,' but when afflicted they would accuse Moses and his companions of evil omen. Rather, their omen came from God, but most of them knew it not.

7:131

They said: 'Whatever wonder you work to bewitch us, we will not believe in you.' So We brought down upon them the flood, locusts, lice, frogs and blood – wonders most evident. But they grew conceited and were a people reprobate.

7:132

When God's torment fell upon them they said: 'O Moses, call upon your Lord according to the covenant you have with Him – if you take away this torment from us, we shall have faith in you and send out the Children of Israel with you.' But when We relieved them of the torment for a period of time set for them to reach, there they were, breaking their promise. So We took revenge upon them and drowned them in the sea because they called the lie to Our signs and paid them no heed. And to the nation considered weak We gave in inheritance the eastern and western parts of the land which We had blessed. Thus was the good Word of your Lord fulfilled upon the Children of Israel, for they had endured with patience; and We utterly destroyed the works of Pharaoh and his people, together with all the monuments that they had built.

7:137

Then We led the Children of Israel across the sea, where they
came upon a people devoted to the worship of their idols. They
said: 'O Moses, fashion for us a god similar to their gods.' He
answered: 'You are an ignorant lot. What these people follow
is nothing but perdition and their works are all in vain.' He
said: 'Can I possibly seek for you a god other than God, Who
preferred you above mankind?'

Remember when We saved you from Pharaoh's people who
tormented you most cruelly, who killed your sons and
debauched your womenfolk – all of which was a great calamity
7:141 from your Lord.

Thirty nights did We appoint for Moses, and thereto added ten,
so the period with his Lord was complete in forty nights. Moses
said to his brother Aaron: 'Be my deputy among my people; act
with righteousness and do not follow the path of the corrupt.'
When Moses came to Our appointment and his Lord spoke to
him, he said: 'My Lord, show me Yourself that I may look upon
You.' He said: 'You shall not see Me, but look instead upon
that mountain. If it remains firmly in place you shall see Me.'
When the glory of his Lord appeared upon the mountain, it
levelled it to the ground. Moses fell down, unconscious. When
he came to, he said: 'Glory be to You! I have repented before
7:143 You and I am the first among believers.'

He said: 'O Moses, I have preferred you above mankind with
My mission and My speech. So receive what I bring you and be
thankful.' And We inscribed for him on tablets moral precepts
regarding all matters, specific in all their details. 'So grasp them
firmly and command your people to adopt what is best in them.
I shall show you the abode of wrongdoers. I shall turn away
from My wonders those who wax proud on earth, defying
truth.

'If they behold every wonder, they shall not believe in it.

'If they behold the path of right guidance, they shall not
follow it.

'If they behold the path of temptation, they follow it as their own.

'This is because they called the lie to Our wonders and paid them no heed. As for those who called the lie to Our wonders, and to the encounter of the hereafter, their works shall be in vain. Will they be requited save in accordance with their deeds?'   7:147

After Moses had departed, his people fashioned from their jewellery a calf, an effigy that lowed. Did they not see that it neither spoke to them nor guided them to any path? Yet they worshipped it and were truly sinful. But when they rued their handiwork and saw that they had strayed in error, they said: 'If God does not show us mercy and forgive us we shall surely be lost.'

7:149

When Moses returned to his people, furious and grieving, he said: 'Wretched is the way you acted on my behalf while I was away! Do you wish to hasten the decree of your Lord?' He threw down the tablets and grasped his brother's head, dragging it towards him.

He said: 'Son of my mother, the people took me for a weakling and were about to kill me. Do not let my enemies rejoice at my misfortune, and do not count me among those who do wrong.'

He said: 'O Lord, forgive me and my brother, and admit us into Your mercy, for You are the most merciful of those who show mercy. As for those who worshipped the calf, the anger of their Lord shall blaze forth upon them and disgrace will be their lot in this present life.'

This is how We requite those who utter falsehood.

As for those who commit evil deeds and then repent and believe, your Lord thereafter is All-Forgiving, Compassionate to each.

7:153

When the anger of Moses was stilled, he took up the tablets, inscribed with guidance and mercy towards those who piously fear their Lord. Moses then selected seventy men from his people for the time appointed by Us to meet them. When a quake struck them down, he said:

'My Lord, had You wished, You could have destroyed them before, and me with them. Will You destroy us now for what the reprobates among us have done?

'This is nothing but a trial from You; through it You lead astray whomsoever You will, and guide aright whomsoever You will.

'You are our Protector. Forgive us, and be merciful towards us, for You are the Most-Forgiving.

'Inscribe for us a good deed in this present world, and in the hereafter. We have repented to You.'

He said: 'My torment I inflict upon whomsoever I wish;
And My mercy encompasses all things.
I shall inscribe My mercy for those who are pious, those who
  pay the alms, and those who believe in Our revelations;
For those too who follow the Messenger, the Unlettered
  Prophet, he whom they find written down among them, in
  Torah and Evangel;
Who commands them to the good, and forbids them from evil;
Who makes licit to them things that are pure, and illicit things
  that are impure;
Who relieves them from their burdens, and from the chains
  that were upon them.
Those who believed in him, who reverenced and supported
  him,
Who followed the light that was made to descend with him –
  these shall win through.'

7:157

Say: 'O mankind, I am the Messenger of God to you all – He to whom belongs sovereignty over the heavens and the earth. There is no god but He. It is He Who grants life and deals death. So believe in God and in His Messenger, the Unlettered Prophet, who believes in God and His words, and follow him; perhaps you will be guided aright.'

7:158

Among the people of Moses is a community that guides to truth, and thereby acts with justice.   7:159

We divided them into twelve tribes, separate communities. We inspired Moses when his people asked him to pray for water: 'Strike the rock with your staff.' From it gushed forth twelve springs, and every group knew their drinking place. We caused the clouds to give them shade and brought down upon them manna and quail: 'Eat from the good things We have provided you.'

They did not wrong Us; it was their own selves they wronged.   7:160

Remember when it was said to them: 'Inhabit this town and eat therein wherever you wish. Say: "Lighten our burden" and enter the gate, prostrate yourselves, and We shall pardon your sins and multiply the recompense of the virtuous.' But the wicked among them replaced the word given to them with another which had not been given them. So We sent down upon them a wrath from heaven for the evil they did.   7:162

Ask them about a town by the sea, when they broke the Sabbath. Their fish would swim to them from every side on the day of the Sabbath. When they did not keep the Sabbath, the fish would not come to them. This is how We put them to the test because of their iniquity.   7:163

Remember when a group among them said: 'Why preach to a people whom God shall destroy or else torment most severely?' They said: 'To fulfil your Lord's command; perhaps they will revert to piety.' When they forgot what they had been reminded of, We saved those who forbade evil but exacted punishment most harsh from the wrongdoers because of their transgression. When they grew headstrong regarding what they had been forbidden, We said to them: 'Be turned into apes, contemptible!'   7:166

Remember when your Lord announced that He would send against them, until the Day of Resurrection, those who would impose terrible torment upon them. Your Lord is quick in punishment, and yet He is All-Forgiving, Compassionate to each.

7:167

So We scattered them into communities on earth; some virtuous, some less so. And We put them to the test, sending them both prosperity and hardship; perhaps they might come back. And there came after them a progeny who inherited the Book but were engrossed in the goods of this nether world, saying: 'He shall pardon us.' And if similar goods came their way they would still be engrossed in them. Was not the covenant of the Book contracted with them, that they would proclaim nothing but the truth from God? They have surely studied what it contains. The Last Abode is better for the pious: will you not reflect? As for those who hold fast to the Book and perform the prayer, We do not neglect the reward of the upright.

7:170

Remember when We raised up the mountain above them like a canopy of shade, and they thought it was about to fall upon them: 'Hold fast to what We have brought to you, and remember what it contains; perhaps you will be pious.'

7:171

Remember when your Lord took away from Adam's children the seeds from their loins, and made them witness upon themselves: 'Am I not your Lord?' They answered: 'Yes, we witness' – lest you should claim on the Day of Resurrection: 'We were unaware of this.' Or else you might claim: 'But our ancestors too were once guilty of polytheism, and we are merely their later seed. Will You therefore destroy us because of the works of falsifiers?' Thus do We clarify Our revelations; perhaps they will turn back.

7:174

Recite to them the tale of one to whom We brought Our revelations, but who cast them off. Satan took him in hand and he was utterly lost. Had We wished, We could have elevated him through Our revelations, but he inclined to the things of this world and followed his caprice. In likeness, he was like a dog: if you drive it off, it pants, and if you leave it alone, it pants. Such is the likeness of the people who cried lies to Our revelations. So tell them the tale; perhaps they will ponder.   7:176

What a wretched likeness for those who cry lies to Our revelations! It is themselves they wronged. He whom God guides is truly guided; whom He leads astray, these are truly the losers.   7:178

We have consigned to hell many *Jinn* and humans.
They have hearts but do not understand therewith,
Eyes but do not see therewith,
Ears but do not hear therewith.
They are like cattle – indeed more astray!
Those – they are the mindless.   7:179

To God belong the names most exalted. Worship Him through them and forsake those who blaspheme His names. They shall be requited for what they committed.   7:180

Among those We created is a community who guide to the truth and judge accordingly. As for those who cried lies to Our revelations, We shall gradually lure them to their destruction, unawares. I shall lull them for a while, but My plot is tightly woven.

Have they not reflected? There is no madness in their companion. He is merely one who delivers a distinct warning.   7:184

Or have they not contemplated the kingdom of the heavens and the earth and all the things God has created? Do they not see that their destiny has perhaps drawn near? So what other message can they possibly believe in? Whomsoever God leads astray, no guide has he; He abandons them to stumble aimlessly in their impudence.   7:186

They ask you about the Hour and when it will alight.

Say: 'Knowledge of it is with my Lord alone, and none will reveal it when its time arrives but He. This is a weighty matter in the heavens and earth. It shall only come upon you suddenly.'

They ask you as though you had knowledge of it.

Say: 'Knowledge of it rests only with God, but most people
7:187 are ignorant.'

Say: 'I have no power to do myself good or harm save as God wills. Had I known the Unseen I would have done myself much good, and no harm would have touched me. I am merely a
7:188 warner, and a herald of good tidings to a people who believe.'

He it is Who created you from one soul, and from it made a spouse with whom he might find solace. When he embraced her, she became with child, whom she carried lightly. When she grew heavy, the two of them called upon their Lord: 'If you grant us a righteous child we shall give thanks.' But when He granted them a righteous child, they ascribed partners to Him for that bounty which He brought them – may God be far above their ascription! Do they truly associate with Him that which creates nothing while they themselves are created? That which
7:192 has no power to aid them, nor even aid themselves?

When you call them to right guidance, they do not follow you. It is all the same whether you call them or remain silent. Those whom you worship other than God are creatures like yourselves.

So call upon them!

And let them answer your call if you speak the truth!

Do they have feet they walk upon?

Or hands they use to strike?

Or eyes with which to see?

Or ears with which to hear?

Say: 'Call upon your associates, do your worst and give me no respite! My protector is God Who sent down the Book, and

He shall protect the upright. And those you call upon, other than Him, they have no power to aid you nor even aid themselves. If you call them to right guidance they do not hear. You see them looking at you but they do not see.'   7:198

Conduct yourself with forbearance, command to virtue and forsake the ignorant.   7:199

If a surge of anger that issues from Satan sweeps over you, seek refuge with God; He is All-Hearing, Omniscient. When the pious are touched by a passing fancy from Satan, they remember, and at once their eyes are opened. Meanwhile, the devils lead their companions further into confusion, and stop at nothing.   7:202

When you do not bring them a verse of revelation, they say: 'Would that you could make it up!' Say: 'I only follow what is revealed to me from my Lord. Here are visible proofs from your Lord, a Guidance and a mercy to a people of faith.'   7:203

When the Qur'an is recited, listen to it and remain silent; perhaps you will be shown mercy.

Remember your Lord in private, humbly and in awe, and be not loud in your speech, morning and evening. And be not among the negligent.

Those who are in your Lord's company are not too proud to worship Him. They glorify Him, and to Him they kneel in prostration.   7:206

Booty

In the name of God,
Merciful to all,
Compassionate to each!

They ask you about booty.

Say: 'Booty belongs to God and His Messenger. So fear God, settle your disputes, and obey God and His Messenger if you are true believers.'

The true believers are those who, when God is mentioned, their hearts grow fearful; and if you recite to them His revelations, they increase them in faith; they are those who place their trust in their Lord; who perform the prayer and spend from Our bounty. They are the true believers. High in rank they stand with their Lord, and they shall enjoy His forgiveness and glorious
8:4   provisions.

Just as it was in truth your Lord Who drove you out of your home, though a group of believers were most reluctant, so also they dispute with you regarding the Truth after it has become evident, as if they are being led to death with their eyes open.

Remember when God promised that one of the two caravans shall be yours whereas you had wanted the unarmed one to be yours. But God wishes to vindicate the truth with His words, and utterly to uproot the unbelievers, in order to vindicate the
8:8   truth and nullify falsehood, even if the wicked should hate it.

Remember when you prayed fervently to your Lord and He answered you: 'I shall reinforce you with a thousand angels, coming in waves.' God did not bring this about except as glad tidings, and so that your hearts might be calmed thereby. Victory
8:10   comes only from God; God is Almighty, All-Wise.

Remember when He brought drowsiness upon you in order to reassure you, and made water descend upon you from the sky in order to purify you, to rid you of Satan's enticement, to brace your hearts and make firm your feet.   8:11

Remember when God revealed to the angels: 'I am with you, so grant the believers resolve. I shall cast terror into the hearts of the unbelievers. So strike above the necks, and strike their every finger!' For they defied God and His Messenger, and whoso defies God and His Messenger, God is severe in retribution. Here it is: so taste it! For the unbelievers the torment of the Fire!   8:14

O believers, when you meet the unbelievers in combat, turn not your backs to them. Whoso turns his back upon them that day, except to retreat and re-attack, or to join another troop, suffers the burden of God's anger and his refuge is hell – a wretched fate indeed.   8:16

You did not slay them; it was God who slew them. It was not you who threw when you threw, but God it was Who threw, in order to bestow upon the believers, from His grace, a fine achievement. God is All-Hearing, Omniscient. That is so, and God shall subvert the cunning of the unbelievers.   8:18

If you desire a verdict, the verdict has already come to you; and if you desist, it would be best for you. But if you resume your enmity, We too shall resume it, and your army, though numerous, will be of no avail. God stands with the believers.   8:19

O believers, obey God and His Messenger, and do not turn away from him even while listening. Be not like those who say 'We hear' but do not hear. The worst of beasts in God's sight are surely the deaf and dumb, those that do not understand. Had God known of any good in them, He would have made them hear; and had He made them hear, they would still turn away, heedless.   8:23

O believers, respond to God and His Messenger when he calls you to that which grants you life, and know that God comes between a man and his heart, and that to Him you shall be mustered. And beware an ordeal which will afflict not merely the wrongdoers among you, and know that God is grievous in torment. Remember a time when you were few in number and held to be weak on earth, when you feared men would tear you to pieces. He gave you refuge and aided you with His victory; and He bestowed His bounties upon you – perhaps you will
8:26   render thanks.

O believers, do not betray God and His Messenger, nor betray your undertakings knowingly. Know that your property and your children are merely a trial, and that with God is the greatest
8:28   reward.

O believers, if you fear God, He will grant you a decisive victory and will absolve you of your sins, and forgive you. God's grace
8:29   is most abundant.

Remember when the unbelievers plotted to imprison or kill or expel you. Yes, they plotted but God also plotted – and God is the best of plotters!
    Remember, when Our verses were being recited to them, how they said: 'We have heard. Had we wished we could recite their like. This is nothing but fables of the ancients.'
    Remember when they said: 'O God, if this be the truth from You, shower upon us rocks from the sky or bring down upon us a painful chastisement.'
    But God would not have punished them while you remained among them; nor would God punish them while they called for
8:33   forgiveness.

And yet, why should God not punish them when they bar the way to the Sacred Mosque? They can never be His friends, for only the pious can be His friends. But most of them are ignorant.

Their prayer near the House is nothing but whistling and clap-
ping – so taste the punishment for your blasphemy!   8:35

The unbelievers spend their wealth to bar God's way. They
will spend it indeed – and reap regret! And then they shall be
overcome. And the unbelievers shall be herded into hell, in order
that God may distinguish the depraved from the pure. He shall
heap the depraved one upon the other, piling them all up, and
deliver that pile to hell. These are truly the losers.   8:37

Tell the unbelievers: if they desist, past sins will be forgiven
them, but if they persist, the lesson of ancient nations shall
come to pass. Therefore, fight them so that there will be no
discord and the whole of religion belongs to God. If they desist,
God sees best what they do. If they turn away, know that
God is your patron: how excellent a Patron, how excellent a
Champion!   8:40

Know that whatever booty you gain, to God belongs its fifth,
and to the Messenger, to relatives, orphans, the poor and the
needy wayfarer, provided you believe in God and in what We
revealed to Our servant on the Day of Separation, the day the
two armies clashed. God is Omnipotent.   8:41

Remember when you lined up on the nearer rim of the valley,
they on the farther, while the caravan was below you. Had you
promised to keep an appointed time with them, you would
surely have failed your appointment! But it was so that God
might bring to pass a matter already ordained: that whoso
perishes would perish attesting to God's manifest portent, and
whoso lives shall live attesting to God's manifest portent. God
is All-Hearing, Omniscient.   8:42

Remember when God revealed them to you in a dream as few
in number. Had He shown them as many, you would have
hesitated and quarrelled regarding that matter. But God

delivered you safely – He knows full well what lies within
8:43 breasts.

Remember when He showed them to you as few in your eyes,
when you met in battle, and showed you as few in theirs, so
that God might bring to pass a matter already ordained. To
8:44 God all matters revert.

O believers, when you meet a fighting party, stand firm and
mention God often – perhaps you will prevail. Obey God and
His Messenger, and do not quarrel, or else you will falter and
your spirit will flag. Remain steadfast: God stands with the
steadfast. Do not be like those who marched forth from their
homes in arrogance, showing off before people, while barring
8:47 the path to God. God encompasses all that they do.

Remember when Satan made their deeds appear attractive to
them, saying: 'Today, none shall overcome you, for I shall be
by your side.' But when the two armies came in sight of one
another, he turned upon his heels and said: 'I have nothing to
do with you! I see what you do not see. I fear God, and God is
8:48 grievous in punishment.'

Remember when the Hypocrites and those whose hearts are
diseased said: 'Their religion has deceived these people.' But
8:49 whoso puts his trust in God, God is Almighty, All-Wise.

If only you could witness the moment when angels seize the
unbelievers' souls! They strike their faces and backs – 'Taste the
torment of the Fire because of your past misdeeds! And yet God
8:51 is never unjust to His servants.'

So too was it with Pharaoh's people and those gone before.
They denied God's signs and God seized them for their sins –
God is powerful, severe in punishment. That is because God
would never change a favour He bestowed upon a people unless

they themselves had changed their inner selves. God is All-Hearing, Omniscient. 8:53

So too was it with Pharaoh's people and those gone before. They cried lies to their Lord's revelations and We destroyed them for their sins and drowned Pharaoh's people. All were wrongdoers. 8:54

The worst of creatures in God's sight are the unbelievers for they have no faith – those with whom you contract an obligation and they break their word, every time, without fear of God. When you meet them in battle, scatter them utterly as a lesson to those coming after them – perhaps they will reflect. If you fear treachery from a group, renounce your compact with them on equal terms for all, for God loves not the treacherous. Let it not be thought that the unbelievers have the upper hand, for they shall not escape. Prepare against them whatever force and war cavalry you can gather to frighten therewith the enemy of God and your enemy, and others besides them whom you do not know but God does. Whatever you expend in the cause of God will be returned in full to you, and you shall not be wronged. 8:60

Should they incline to peace, incline to it also, and put your trust in God. He is indeed All-Hearing, Omniscient. But if they intend to deceive you, God is sufficient for you. He it was Who vindicated you with His support, and with the believers; and He it was Who brought their hearts together. Had you spent all that is on earth you could not have brought their hearts together, but it was God Who reconciled them to one another. He is Almighty, All-Wise. 8:63

O Prophet, God is sufficient for you and the believers who have followed you.
    O Prophet, urge the believers on to the fight. If there are twenty steadfast among you they will overcome two hundred;

8:65 if there are a hundred of you they will overcome a thousand unbelievers, for they are a people of no understanding.

8:66 God has now lightened your burden, knowing that there is weakness in you. If there are a hundred of you, steadfast men, they will overcome two hundred, and if there are a thousand of you, they will overcome two thousand, by God's leave. God stands with the steadfast.

8:69 It is not fitting for a prophet to hold prisoners until he has achieved supremacy in the land. You desire the glory of this world but God desires the afterlife. God is Almighty, All-Wise. Had it not been for a prior decree from God, there would have touched you a great torment for the ransom you took. So consume what booty you gained, lawfully and well, and fear God – He is All-Forgiving, Compassionate to each.

8:71 O Prophet, say to the prisoners in your hands: 'If God knows of any good in your hearts, He will give you more than what was captured from you, and will forgive you – He is All-Forgiving, Compassionate to each.' If they seek to betray you, they have already betrayed God, but He delivered them into your hands. God is Omniscient, All-Wise.

8:73 Those who believed, who emigrated, and who laboured in the cause of God with their property and their own selves, together with those who gave them shelter and support – these are comrades one of another. Those who believe but have not emigrated – you are not obliged to act as their comrades until they emigrate. If they call upon you for succour in the name of religion, you are obliged to give succour, unless it be against another people with whom you have a treaty. And God knows full well what you do. But those who disbelieve, they are comrades one of another. Unless you act thus, there will be discord on earth and great defilement.

But those who believed, who emigrated, and who laboured in the cause of God, together with those who gave them shelter and support – these truly are the believers. For them there is forgiveness and magnificent provisions. As for those who believed thereafter, who emigrated and laboured alongside you, these are of your number. But blood relatives are more closely obligated one to another in the Book of God. God is Omniscient.

8:75

Repentance

A decree of repudiation, from God and His Messenger, as regards your compact with the polytheists:

Wander the earth for four months and know that you cannot escape the power of God; that God will humble the unbelievers.

A proclamation from God and His Messenger to all mankind on the day of the Greater Pilgrimage:

God is quit of the polytheists, as is His Messenger. If you repent, this shall be better for you. If you turn away, know that you cannot evade the power of God. And announce to the unbelievers a torment most painful. Except for those among the polytheists with whom you had a compact, and who never let you down, nor ever aided anyone against you – with them you are to fulfil their compact until their appointed term. God loves the pious.

9:4

Once the sacred months are shorn, kill the polytheists wherever you find them, arrest them, imprison them, besiege them, and lie in wait for them at every site of ambush. If they repent, perform the prayer and pay the alms, let them go on their way: God is All-Forgiving, Compassionate to each. If a polytheist seeks your protection, grant him protection until he hears the speech of God, then escort him to where he feels safe. For they are a people of no understanding.

9:6

How indeed can polytheists have a compact with God or His Messenger? Except for those with whom you compacted at the Sacred Mosque – so long as they deal fairly with you, you too are to deal fairly with them. God loves the pious. How can it be otherwise since, whenever they gain the upper hand over you, they respect neither kinship nor covenant with you! They give you pleasure with their mouths, but their hearts disdain, and most are sinful. They sold the revelations of God for a paltry sum and barred the way to Him. They – evil indeed is what they have done! Towards a believer, they respect neither 9:10 kinship nor covenant. They are truly the aggressors.

But if they repent, perform the prayer and pay the alms, they are to be your brothers in religion. We make intelligible Our revelations for a people who understand. If they break their oath after their covenant, and insult your religion, fight the ringleaders of blasphemy, for they have no faith, and perhaps 9:12 they may desist.

Will you not fight a people who broke their oath, who undertook to drive out the Messenger, who commenced hostilities against you?
Do you fear them? God is more worthy of your fear, if you truly believe.
Fight them and God will punish them at your hands.
He will humble them and grant you victory over them.
He will appease the hearts of a people who believe.
He will remove the anger from their breasts.
And God shall restore to His grace whomsoever He wills.
9:15   And God is Omniscient, All-Wise.

Did you imagine you would be abandoned, and that God would not know those among you who laboured, and took no intimate to themselves other than God, His Messenger and the believers? 9:16 God knows full well what you do.

It is not fit that polytheists should frequent the mosques of God while professing unbelief. These – their labour shall be in vain, and in hell they shall abide for ever. There shall frequent the mosques of God only he who believes in God and the Last Day, who performs the prayer and dispenses alms, fearing God alone. Perhaps such men shall be guided aright.   9:18

Are you indeed equating provision of water to pilgrims and caring for the Sacred Mosque with one who believes in God and the Last Day, and labours hard in the cause of God? They are not equal in the sight of God, and God guides not the evildoers. For those who believed and emigrated and laboured hard in the cause of God, with their property and persons, are of a higher rank with God. They are the true victors. Their Lord gives them glad tidings of a mercy from Him and His good pleasure, of Gardens in which they abide in constant bliss, therein eternally and evermore. With God lies the greatest reward.   9:22

O believers, take not your fathers and brothers as allies, so long as they prefer blasphemy to faith. Whoso among you does so, these are the wrongdoers.
     Say: 'If your fathers and your sons, your brothers and your spouses and your clans, together with the wealth you acquired and a commerce you fear will find no market, and homes you find pleasing – if all these are more dear to you than God, His Messenger and the struggle in His cause, then wait and attend until God fulfils His decree.' God guides not the dissolute.   9:24

God gave you victory on many a battlefield. Recall the Day of Hunayn,* when you fancied your great number but it did not help you one whit. So the earth, for all its wide expanse, narrowed before you, and you turned tail and fled. Then God made His serenity descend upon His Messenger and the believers, and sent down troops you did not see, and punished the unbelievers. Such is the reward of unbelievers. Thereafter God will restore

to His grace whomsoever He wills – God is All-Forgiving, Com-
9:27 passionate to each.

O believers, the polytheists are indeed a pollution, so let them
not approach the Sacred Mosque beyond this year of theirs. If
you fear poverty, God will supply your needs from His bounty,
9:28 if He wills. God is Omniscient, All-Wise.

Fight those who do not believe in God or the Last Day, who do
not hold illicit what God and His Messenger hold illicit, and
who do not follow the religion of truth from among those given
the Book, until they offer up the tribute, by hand, in humble
mien.
     The Jews say Ezra is the son of God while the Christians say
Christ is the son of God. This is what they say, from their very
mouths, thereby agreeing with the speech of the unbelievers who
came before. May God strike them down! How they pervert
9:30 the truth!

They have taken their rabbis and monks as lords instead of God
– as also the Christ son of Mary. They were commanded to
worship but one God – there is no God but He, glory to Him,
far above their polytheism! They seek to quench the light of
God with their mouths, but God insists on blazoning forth His
light, even if the unbelievers find it abhorrent. It is He Who sent
His Messenger with Guidance and the religion of truth, that He
may exalt it above all religions, even if the idolaters find it
9:33 abhorrent.

O believers, many rabbis and monks consume the wealth of
people unjustly and bar the way to the path of God. And those
who hoard gold and silver, and do not spend them in the cause
of God – warn them of a most painful punishment, upon a Day
when the fire of hell shall be stoked, and with it shall be scorched
their foreheads, sides and backs. 'This is what you hoarded for
9:35 yourselves, so taste what you used to hoard!'

The total number of months with God is twelve months in the Book of God, from the day that God created the heavens and the earth. Of these, four are sacred. This is the correct religious practice. So do yourselves no wrong therein. And fight the polytheists, all of them, as they fight you all. And know that God stands with the pious. 9:36

To postpone the sacred month is to increase in blasphemy. The unbelievers lead others astray with this, for they declare it licit one year and illicit the next, in order to conform to the total number decreed illicit by God, so making licit what God has decreed illicit. Their misdeeds have been made to appear attractive in their eyes. God guides not the unbelievers. 9:37

O believers, what is it with you? When it is said to you: 'March forth in the cause of God,' you pretend you cannot heave yourself off the ground. Do you prefer this present life to the afterlife? The luxuries of this life are but a trifle compared to the life hereafter. If you do not march forth, He will punish you most painfully and will substitute another community in your stead, nor will you harm Him one whit, for God is Omnipotent. 9:39

If you do not rally to his support, God has already supported him when the unbelievers drove him out, one of two men in a cave. It was then that he said to his companion: 'Do not grieve, for God is with us.' Then God made His serenity descend upon him and backed him with troops you did not see. Thus He abased the word of the unbelievers, and the Word of God was supreme. God is Almighty, All-Wise. 9:40

March forth, then, whether light or heavy in armour. Labour hard in the cause of God, with your property and persons; this is best for you, if only you knew. Had it been a source of booty near at hand or a journey easy of access, they would have followed you. But the journey was long and arduous. They will no doubt swear by God: 'Had we been able, we would have marched forth with you.' They merely damn their souls. And God knows that they are lying.

9:42

God forgive you! Why did you give them leave before you found out those who spoke the truth, and you came to know those who lied? Those who believe in God and the Last Day do not ask your permission to labour with their property and persons. God knows full well who the pious are. It is only they who do not believe in God and the Last Day who ask your permission: their hearts are ill at ease and they flounder in their uncertainty.

9:45

Had they wanted to march out, they would have made preparations for it, but God was averse to their joining the expedition, so He slackened them, and it was said to them: 'Stay behind with those who stay behind.' Had they gone out with you, they would only have added to your difficulties, hastening between your ranks and intending to spread discord among you, while some of you would have lent them an ear. But God knows full well who the wrongdoers are. They had once intended to sow discord, and had turned matters topsy-turvy for you, until the truth was at hand and the command of God won the day, even though they detested it.

9:48

Among them are some who say: 'Grant me leave, and do not tempt me.' But it is precisely in temptation that they have fallen, and hell shall engulf the unbelievers!

If any good touches you, it displeases them, and if a calamity strikes you they say: 'We have already taken our precautions,' and they depart, rejoicing.

Say: 'There shall not touch us except what God has decreed for us; He is our Protector; in God let the believers trust.'

Say: 'Are you waiting to see if either of the two most glorious rewards shall be ours? We too are waiting to see whether God will inflict His punishment upon you, or else at our hands. So wait and see, and we are waiting with you!'

Say: 'Whether you spend willingly or unwillingly, it shall not be accepted from you. You have always been a sinful lot.' 9:53

What prevents the acceptance of their offerings is nothing but the fact that they disbelieve in God and His Messenger. They come to prayer but lazily and only spend reluctantly. So do not be impressed by their wealth or their progeny; God only desires to torment them therewith in this present life, and their souls shall expire while still unbelievers. They swear to God they are of your number but they are not, for they are a people that lose heart. If they find any refuge or cave or tunnel, they would flee to it in swarms. 9:57

Among them are some who reproach you regarding voluntary alms: if given a portion thereof, they are content, but if they are not given anything they grow discontented. If only they were content with what God and His Messenger bring them! If only they would say: 'God suffices for us, and God will grant us from His bounty, as too His Messenger; to God we turn for succour.' 9:59

Voluntary alms are for the poor and wretched, for those who collect them, for those whose hearts have been won over, for slaves to buy their freedom, for those in debt, for the cause of God and for the needy wayfarer. This is an ordinance of God – God is Omniscient, All-Wise. 9:60

Among them are some who offend the Prophet, saying: 'He gives ear to all.' Say: 'And a good ear it is for you! He believes in God and trusts the believers, and is a mercy to those of you who believe.' For those who offend the Messenger of God painful punishment is in store. They swear by God in order to satisfy you, but God and His Messenger are more worthy to be satisfied, if they are true believers. Do they not know that he who oversteps the limit with God and His Messenger – for him awaits the fire of hell, abiding therein for ever? That is the greatest disgrace. 9:63

The Hypocrites are anxious that a *sura* might be sent down regarding them, which would reveal to them what lies in their hearts.

Say: 'Go ahead and mock! God shall reveal what you are anxious about.'

If you ask them, they say: 'We were merely gossiping and jesting.'

Say: 'Was it God, His revelations and His Messenger you were mocking? Do not offer any excuse, for you have blasphemed after having believed. If We forgive a group among you, We shall torment another group, for they have been impious.'

9:66

Hypocrites, male and female, are all alike; they command what is forbidden and forbid what is virtuous, and clench tight their hands. They have forgotten God and so He has forgotten them. The Hypocrites are the dissolute. God promises the Hypocrites, male and female, as also the unbelievers, the fire of hell, therein abiding for ever. It is their due. God has cursed them and their punishment is unchanging.

9:68

So too the nations before you: they were greater than you in might, and possessed more wealth and progeny. They enjoyed their lot in life as you enjoy yours, just as those before you had enjoyed their lot. And you too indulge in gossip just as they indulged. These – their deeds have come to nothing in this life and in the hereafter. These are the losers. Have they not heard the history of those who came before them? The people of Noah, of 'Ad and Thamud, the people of Abraham, the inhabitants of Midian and the Towns in ruin? Their messengers came to them with manifest signs. God would not have wronged them; rather, it was themselves they wronged.

9:70

The believers, male and female, are friends of one another. They command to virtue and forbid vice. They perform the prayers and pay the alms, and they obey God and His Messenger. These – God shall show them mercy. God is Almighty, All-Wise.

God promises the believers, male and female, Gardens beneath which rivers flow, therein abiding for ever, and mansions glorious in the Gardens of Eden and, greater than all this, the good pleasure of God. This is the greatest of triumphs.   9:72

O Prophet, exert yourself against the unbelievers and Hypocrites, and deal harshly with them. Their refuge is hell – a wretched destiny. They swear by God they did not utter it, but they did utter the word of blasphemy, and reverted to unbelief after having embraced Islam. They were about to commit what in the final resort they could not. They were resentful just because God and His Messenger granted them sufficiency from His bounty. If they repent, that would be better for them, and if they turn away, God will torment them with a torment most painful in this life and in the hereafter. On earth they shall have neither friend nor champion.   9:74

Among them are some who covenanted thus with God: 'If He brings us some of His bounty we shall surely give alms, and be among the virtuous.' When He brought them some of His bounty, they were miserly with it, and turned away in refusal. So He fomented hypocrisy in their hearts until the Day they face Him, because they reneged on what they had promised God, and because they were liars. Do they not know that God knows their secrets and their most intimate talk? That God is Knower of the Unseen?   9:78

They who reproach believers who volunteer their alms-giving, or who have nothing to offer except their hard labour – these they mock! May God mock them! A painful punishment awaits them. Whether you ask forgiveness for them or whether you do not, were you to ask forgiveness for them seventy times, God would not forgive them. This is because they blasphemed against God and His Messenger, and God guides not those who are perverse.   9:80

Those left behind were pleased with where they squatted, contrary to the wish of the Messenger of God. They hated to labour hard with their property and persons in the cause of God and said: 'Do not march out in the heat.' Say: 'The fire of hell is far hotter, if only they had understanding.' They shall laugh a little and weep a lot, in recompense for what they have earned. Should God bring you back, and you meet a group of them who ask your permission to set out, say: 'You shall never set out with me nor fight an enemy with me. You were content to squat behind the first time, so squat with those who are left behind.'

9:83

You are never to pray over any of them who dies, nor stand over his grave, for they disbelieved in God and His Messenger, and died as sinners. Do not be impressed by their wealth or their progeny; God only desires to torment them therewith in this present life, and their souls shall expire while still unbelievers. When a *sura* is revealed: 'Believe in God and strive with His Messenger,' the men of wealth among them seek your leave and say: 'Let us be with those who squat behind.' They are content to be among those left behind. A seal has been set upon their hearts, so they do not comprehend.

9:87

But the Messenger and the believers with him have laboured hard with their properties and persons. These – to them belong the finest rewards. These shall truly gain success. God has readied for them Gardens beneath which rivers flow, abiding therein for ever. This is the greatest of triumphs.

9:89

The Bedouins come forward, proffering excuses to be allowed to remain behind, while those who disbelieved in God and His Messenger sit tight. Those among them who blasphemed shall be afflicted by a most painful torment.

No blame attaches to the infirm, nor to the sick, nor to those who find nothing to spend, provided they keep faith with God and His Messenger; in no way can the virtuous be faulted. God is All-Forgiving, Compassionate to each.

9:91

Nor are they to be faulted who came to you asking to be mounted for war and to whom you said: 'I find nothing I can mount you upon.' Whereupon they left, their eyes overflowing with tears, in sorrow that they possessed nothing to spend.   9:92

But fault is found with those who ask your leave to stay behind, and are wealthy. They are content to remain among those left behind. God has set a seal upon their hearts so they do not understand. They offer excuses to you when you return to them.
Say: 'Do not make excuses. We do not trust you.
God has apprised us of your news.
God shall see your deeds, as shall His Messenger.
You shall then be returned to the Knower of the Invisible and
   the Visible,
And He will inform you of what you used to do.'   9:94

They will swear by God to you when you turn back to them, to leave off their reproach. So leave them alone. They are indeed a pollution; their final place of rest is hell, in recompense for what they earned. They swear to you to forgive them but even if you do, God will not forgive the corrupt.   9:96

The Bedouins are the most blasphemous and hypocritical, the least worthy to learn the sacred bounds that God revealed to His Messenger. God is Omniscient, All-Wise. Some Bedouins consider what they expend as loss, and lie in wait for you, hoping for a reversal of fortune. Upon them let the cycle of misfortune fall! God is All-Hearing, Omniscient.

Some Bedouins believe in God and the Last Day, and consider what they expend as offerings to draw them closer to God and the prayers of the Messenger. These shall indeed draw them closer, and God shall admit them into His mercy – God is All-Forgiving, Compassionate to each.   9:99

As for the precursors, the first to believe among the Emigrants*
and the Helpers,* and those who followed after them and were
virtuous, God is well pleased with them and they with Him.
He has prepared for them Gardens beneath which rivers flow,
9:100   abiding therein for ever. This is the greatest of triumphs.

Some of the Bedouins who dwell in your vicinity are hypocrites,
as are some of the inhabitants of Medinah. They have become
adamant in their hypocrisy. You know them not, but We do.
We shall torment them twice, and then they shall be conveyed
to a torment most painful. Others have admitted their sins: they
mixed a good deed with another that is evil. Perhaps God will
pardon them – God is All-Forgiving, Compassionate to each.
Take from their wealth freely given alms, to cleanse them therewith and purify their acts. And pray for them, for your prayers
will give them peace of mind – and God is All-Hearing,
9:103   Omniscient.

Do they not know that God accepts repentance from His worshippers, that He accepts freely given alms, that it is God Who
is All-Pardoning, Compassionate to each?
      Say: 'Strive, and God shall see your striving, as also His
Messenger and the believers. You shall be returned to the
Knower of the Invisible and the Visible, and He will inform you
9:105   of what you used to do.'

Others are deferred to the decree of God: He will either torment
9:106   or pardon them. God is Omniscient, All-Wise.

As for those who built a mosque, out of malice and blasphemy
and to sow discord among the believers, and as a spying post
for one who had previously fought against God and His Messenger – they will no doubt swear: 'We only intended a good deed.'
Yet God testifies that they are liars. You are never to pray in it.
A mosque founded on piety from the very first day is more
worthy for you to pray therein. In it are men who desire to be

cleansed – and God loves those who cleanse themselves. Is he who builds its foundations upon piety towards God and His good pleasure better, or one who builds them upon the edge of a tottering precipice which then collapses with him into the fire of hell? God guides not the wrongdoers. The structure they built shall remain questionable in their hearts until their very hearts are torn asunder. God is Omniscient, All-Wise. 9:110

God has purchased from the believers their souls and their wealth and, in exchange, the Garden shall be theirs. They fight in the cause of God, they kill and are killed – a true promise from Him in the Torah, the Evangel and the Qur'an. Who is more truthful to his promise than God? So be of good cheer regarding that business deal you transact. That is the greatest of triumphs.

The repentant,
The worshippers,
The thankful,
The fasting,
They who kneel and prostrate themselves,
The bidders to good and forbidders of evil,
The respecters of the bounds of God – give glad tidings to the believers! 9:112

It is not right for the Prophet and the believers to ask forgiveness for polytheists, even if they are relatives, once it has become clear to them that they are denizens of hell. When Abraham asked forgiveness for his father, this was only to fulfil a promise he had promised him. But once it became clear to him that he was an enemy of God, he washed his hands of him – Abraham was one who sighed much, and was self-restrained. 9:114

God would never lead astray a people once He had guided them until He has made clear to them what they are to fear in piety. God is Omniscient.
To God belongs the kingdom of the heavens and the earth;

He gives life and He deals death;

9:116 Apart from God, you have neither friend nor champion.

God has pardoned the Prophet, the Emigrants and the Helpers, those who followed him in the hour of hardship, after the hearts of a group of them were about to fall into temptation. Then He pardoned them, for to them He is All-Tender, Compassionate to each.

Likewise He pardoned the three who were left behind. Once the earth, so wide in expanse, had become constricted for them, and their very souls were constricted, and they came to believe that there can be no refuge from God except with Him, it was then that God turned towards them in pardon that they might turn to Him. It is God Who is All-Pardoning, Compassionate

9:118 to each.

O believers, fear God and keep the company of those who are

9:119 sincere.

It is not fitting for the people of Medinah and the Bedouins in their vicinity to fail to aid the Messenger of God, nor to prefer their own selves to his. For there shall touch them no thirst, hardship or hunger in the cause of God. Nor will they tread any territory that vexes the unbelievers, nor score any success over an enemy, but a good deed shall be inscribed for them. God neglects not the wages of those who do good. They shall expend no sum, small or great, nor ever cross a valley but it shall be inscribed for

9:121 them. And God will then reward them for the best of their deeds.

It is not fitting for the believers to sally forth, one and all. Therefore, let one group from each contingent embark on the study of religion, so as to warn their people when they return

9:122 to them – perhaps they will learn from experience.

O believers, fight the unbelievers near you, and let them find you harsh, and know that God stands with the pious. When a *sura* is sent down, some of them say: 'Which of you has this increased in faith?' Those who believe – it shall increase them in faith, and they shall regard it as auspicious. As for those with sickness in their hearts, it shall increase them in pollution, adding to their pollution, and they shall die as unbelievers. Do they not see how they succumb to temptation, once or twice a year, and then repent not, nor do they reflect? When a *sura* is sent down, they exchange glances: 'Has anyone seen you?' And they turn away.

May God turn away their hearts! For they are a people who do not understand.   9:127

To you has come a messenger, from among your number,
Aggrieved by the hardship you suffer,
Concerned for you,
Tender and compassionate towards the believers.

If they turn away, say: 'God suffices me. There is no god but He. In Him I trust. Lord of the great throne is He.'   9:129

Jonah

In the name of God,
Merciful to all,
Compassionate to each!

Alif Lam Ra'

Behold the revelations of the Wise Book!   10:1

Was it so strange to people that We revealed to a man among them: 'Warn mankind, but give glad tidings to those who believe that they have precedence in virtue with their Lord?'

The unbelievers say: 'This man is a manifest sorcerer!'   10:2

Your Lord is God Who created the heavens and the earth in six days, then settled firmly on the throne, to order the world's affairs. There is no intercessor except by His leave. This is God, your Lord. So worship Him! Will you not reflect?

10:3

To Him you shall all return: a true promise that He began creation and will then restore it, to reward those who believed and performed good deeds in fairness. For those who disbelieved, there awaits a drink of boiling water and painful torment because of their blasphemy.

10:4

He it is Who made the sun a shining splendour and the moon a radiance, reckoning its phases so that you may know the number of years, and how to calculate. God created this not except in truth, and He makes clear His revelations to a people who understand.

10:5

In the alternation of night and day and what God created in the heavens and the earth – in these are signs for a people who are pious.

10:6

As for those who do not look forward to Our encounter, and are content with life in this nether world, and feel at ease therein, and who ignore Our signs – these shall have hell for refuge, because of what they earned.

But those who believed and performed good deeds – these are guided by their Lord because of their faith. Beneath them shall flow rivers in the Gardens of Bliss.

In them their prayer shall be: 'Glory to You, O God!'

In them their greeting shall be: 'Peace!'

The end of their prayer shall be: 'Thanks be to God, Lord of the Worlds!'

10:10

If God were to hasten evil to mankind, just as they pray for good to be hastened to them, their destined term would already have been fulfilled. But We abandon those who do not seek Our encounter to stumble aimlessly in their impudence.

When harm touches a man, he calls upon Us – lying on his side, sitting or standing. When We draw away his distress, he passes on, as though he had never called upon Us that harm had touched him.

Thus are their works made to appear attractive to the profligate.   10:12

We have destroyed many generations before your time when they transgressed, and their messengers came to them with manifest signs, but they would not believe. Thus do We recompense sinners. Whereupon We made you their successors on earth, after them, so We might see how you would act.   10:14

When Our clear revelations are recited to them, those who do not look forward to Our encounter say: 'Bring us a Qur'an other than this, or else change it.'

Say: 'It is not in my power to change it of my own accord. I merely follow what is revealed to me. If I disobey my Lord, I fear the torment of a terrible Day.'

Say: 'Had God willed, I would not have recited it to you, nor would He have apprised you of it, for I remained a lifetime among you before it. Will you not come to your senses?'

Who, then, is more evil than he who ascribes lies to God or cries lies to His revelations? In truth, the wicked shall not prevail.   10:17

They worship, instead of God, that which neither harms nor benefits them, and they say: 'These are our intercessors with God.'

Say: 'Are you informing God of what He knows nothing about, in the heavens or on earth?' Glory be to God! May He be far above what they associate with Him!   10:18

Mankind was but a single nation but then they fell into discord. Were it not that a prior decree had come from your Lord, a judgement would have been pronounced regarding that over 10:19 which they dispute.

They say: 'If only a miracle were sent down upon him from His Lord!'

Say: 'The realm of the Unseen belongs to God. So wait, and I shall wait by your side.' When We make people taste Our mercy, following a calamity that has touched them, behold how they scheme against Our signs!

Say: 'God is faster at scheming: Our heavenly envoys write 10:21 down what they scheme.'

It is He Who causes you to journey on land and sea. When you are aboard ship and the ships sail along with them before a good breeze, and they are happy therewith, a raging storm arrives, and the waves surround them on all sides, and they think their end is near – it is then that they call upon God, in all sincerity of faith: 'If You deliver us from this ordeal, we shall truly be thankful.' When He saves them, there they are, corrupting the earth in wickedness.

O mankind, you engender corruption only upon yourselves.

It is but the fleeting pleasures of this present life and then to Us is your homecoming, when We shall inform you of what you 10:23 used to do.

The likeness of this present life is like water We made descend from the sky. The plants of the earth, such as men and beasts are wont to eat, grow diverse because of it – until, when earth has assumed its ornament and is decked out in all its finery, and its people think they hold it in their power, Our command descends upon it by night or day, and We turn it into stubble, as though yesterday it had never bloomed. Even so do We make 10:24 clear the signs for a people who reflect.

God calls to the Abode of Peace and guides whomsoever He
wills to a path that is straight.   10:25

To those who do good belongs the fairest reward – and then
  some more.
Neither dust nor humiliation shall cloud their faces.
These are the denizens of the Garden, dwelling therein
  eternally.
But to those who garner evil deeds – a reward of similar evil.
Humiliation shall envelop them,
And from God they shall have no protector.
It is as if their faces have been daubed with streaks of darkest
  night.
These are the denizens of the Fire, dwelling therein eternally.   10:27

There shall come a Day when We shall herd them all, and
then say to the polytheists: 'Keep to your place, you and your
associates!' We will then distinguish between them. Their associates will say: 'It was not us you used to worship. Let God suffice
for witness between us and you that we were not aware of your
worship.'
    It is then that each soul shall experience what it did before-
hand, and they shall be returned to their Lord, their True Protector. And all their fabrications will vanish.   10:30

Say: 'Who provides for you from heaven or earth? Or who possesses hearing and sight? Who brings out the living from the dead,
the dead from the living? Who governs the world's affairs?'
    They shall say: 'God.'
    Say: 'Will you not then be pious?'   10:31

This then is God, your True Lord. What is there, beyond truth,
save error? Where will your faces be turned? This is how the
Word of your Lord shall be fulfilled against the dissolute, for
they have no faith.   10:33

Say: 'Are there among your associates any who can begin creation and then restore it again?'

Say: 'It is God Who begins creation and then restores it. How can you gainsay it?'

Say: 'Are there among your associates any who guide to the truth?'

Say: 'God guides to the truth. Is He Who guides to the truth more worthy to be followed or he who guides not, unless he be guided? What is the matter with you? How do you judge?'

Most of them merely follow conjecture, but conjecture can never substitute for the truth, not one whit. God is All-Knowing as to what they do.

10:36

It is not possible that this Qur'an is forged by other than God. Rather, it is a confirmation of that which preceded it, and the Book made manifestly clear, wherein is no doubt, from the Lord of the Worlds.

Or do they say: 'He forged it'?

Say: 'Bring forth one *sura* like it, and call upon whomever you can, apart from God, if you speak the truth.' But, no! They lie regarding what they do not comprehend, and its interpretation escapes them. Likewise did lie those who came before them. Consider, therefore, how the wicked met their fate!

10:39

Some of them believe in it, some believe not. Your Lord knows best those who are corrupt. If they call you a liar, say: 'I have my works and you have yours. You are quit of what I do, and I am quit of what you do.'

Some of them listen to you. But do you think you can make the deaf hear, even though they do not reflect?

And some of them look at you. But do you think you can guide the blind even though they do not see?

God wrongs not mankind, not one whit. Rather, it is themselves that mankind wrong.

10:44

The Day He herds them – it is as if they had tarried on earth merely an hour of a day. They shall recognize each other. Lost will be those who denied the encounter with God, nor were they guided aright. Whether We show you part of what We promised them or whether We cause you to die, to Us is their homecoming, where God shall be a witness to what they do.

For every nation there is a messenger: when their messenger comes to them, judgement is passed among them with fairness, and they are not wronged.   10:47

They say: 'When will this promise be fulfilled if you speak the truth?'

Say: 'I have no power to do myself good or harm except as God wills. For every nation there is an appointed span of time; when their time arrives, they can neither delay it nor bring it forward, even by an instant.'

Say: 'Consider this. If His torment falls upon you at night or by day, what portion of it will sinners desire to hasten? And then, when torment falls, you believe in it? What! Now? When before you sought to hasten it?' Then it shall be said to those who sinned: 'Taste the torment of eternity! Will you be recompensed for other than what you earned?'   10:52

They inquire of you: 'Is it the truth?'

Say: 'Yes, by my Lord, it is the truth, nor can you invalidate it. If to every soul that sinned belonged all earthly possessions, it would offer them as ransom.'

They shall hide their remorse when they witness the torment. And judgement shall be passed among them with fairness, and they shall not be wronged.   10:54

Assuredly, to God belongs all that is in the heavens and on earth; assuredly, the promise of God is true, but most of them have no understanding. It is He Who grants life and deals death. To Him you shall return.   10:56

O mankind, there has come to you a homily from your Lord, a remedy for what lies within breasts, a Guidance and a mercy to the believers.

Say: 'This is through God's bounty and mercy.' At this let them rejoice, for it is better than all the treasure they amass.

Say: 'Have you considered what bounty God has caused to descend upon you, which you then divided into illicit and licit?'

Say: 'Did God give you leave, or did you fabricate lies upon God?'

What will they think, those who fabricate lies upon God, on the Day of Resurrection?

God is bountiful to mankind,

10:60 But most mankind will not render thanks.

Whatsoever you are engaged in,

Whatever portion of the Qur'an you recite,

Whatever work you do,

Yet still We are witnesses over you the instant you embark upon it.

There does not escape your Lord an atom's weight on earth or in heaven,

Nor smaller than this, nor bigger,

10:61 Except it be in a Manifest Book.

Surely the friends of God – no fear shall fall upon them, nor shall they grieve.

They who believed and were pious – to them glad tidings in this present world,

And in the hereafter.

There can be no change in the words of God.

10:64 This indeed is the greatest of triumphs.

Let not their discourse sadden you: all might belongs to God.

He is All-Hearing, Omniscient.

Surely to God belongs whoever is in the heavens and whoever is on earth.

They follow nothing, those who worship partners apart from
    God – they follow nothing but conjecture; they utter
    nothing but lies.
He it is Who created the night for you to rest therein,
And created the luminous day.
Assuredly in this are signs for a people who hear.   10:67

They say: 'God has taken for Himself a child!' Glory be to Him!
He is All-Sufficient.

    To Him belongs whatever is in the heavens and whatever is
on earth.

    Have you any authority for this utterance? Or are you ascrib-
ing to God what you do not know?

    Say: 'Those who fabricate lies against God shall not prevail.'

    A short span of enjoyment in this life, and then to Us is their
homecoming.

    Then will We make them taste terrible torment for their
blaspheming.   10:70

Recite to them the story of Noah when he said to his people: 'O
people, if it has grown burdensome to you my sojourn among
you and my reminding you of the signs of God, I shall put my
trust in God. So come to a decision, you and your associates,
and let not the matter perplex you. Then pass your judgement
upon me, and do not delay. If you reject my call, I asked you
no wage for it: my wage falls only on God. I was commanded
to be a Muslim.'

    But they called him a liar. So We delivered him with his
companions in the Ark, and made them survive, but drowned
those who cried lies to Our signs. Consider, therefore, the fate
of those who had been warned.   10:73

Then after him We sent messengers to their peoples. They
brought them signs but they were not about to believe in what
beforehand they had cried lies to. This is how We seal the hearts
of transgressors.   10:74

Then We sent after them Moses and Aaron to Pharaoh and his court, with Our signs. But they grew proud and were a sinful people. When there came to them the Truth from Us, they said: 'This is nothing but manifest sorcery.'

Moses said: 'Is this what you call the Truth when it comes to you? Is this sorcery? But sorcerers do not prevail.'

They said: 'Have you come to lead us away from what we found our fathers to have followed, in order that you two should have eminence on earth? Assuredly we shall not believe you.'

Pharaoh said: 'Bring me every expert sorcerer.' When the sorcerers came, Moses said to them: 'Throw down whatever you wish to throw.' When they threw it down, Moses said: 'What you brought forth is sorcery, and God shall nullify it. God does not set straight the actions of the corrupt. And God shall vindicate the truth with His words, even if the wicked should hate it.' But there believed in Moses only a few of his people, fearing that Pharaoh and their own leaders would persecute them.

Yes, indeed; Pharaoh grew high and mighty on earth, one 10:83 who exceeded all bounds.

Moses said: 'My people, if you have faith in God, then put your trust in Him if you are truly Muslims.'

They said: 'In God we trust. O Lord, turn us not into an ordeal for an unjust people. Deliver us, in Your mercy, from a 10:86 blasphemous people.'

We revealed to Moses and his brother: 'Take homes for your people in Egypt, and turn your homes into places of worship. Perform the prayer and give glad tidings to the believers.'

Moses said: 'Our Lord, You have bestowed upon Pharaoh and his court luxuries and wealth in this present life but, Lord, only for them to lead men astray from Your path. Our Lord, blot out their wealth! Harden their hearts so that they will not come to believe until they see the grievous torment.'

He said: 'The prayer of you both has been answered. So remain upright, and follow not the path of the ignorant.' 10:89

Then We led the Children of Israel across the sea, and Pharaoh and his troops pursued them, in their insolence and aggression. When drowning was near, he said: 'I believe that there is no god except Him in Whom the children of Israel believe, and I am a Muslim.'

Now? When before you had disobeyed, and were counted among the corrupt?

Today We shall save you in body, that you might become a wonder to those who come after you; many indeed are heedless of Our wonders. 10:93

We placed the Children of Israel in an abode of truth, and We provisioned them with delicacies. They quarrelled not, until knowledge came to them that your Lord shall judge between them on the Day of Resurrection concerning that over which they quarrelled. If you are in doubt concerning what We revealed to you, ask those who have read the Book before you.

Truth has come to you from your Lord so do not be among those who doubt. And do not be among those who cry lies to God's revelations, for you will surely be among the losers. Those against whom the decree of your Lord has been pronounced will not believe, even if every sign were to come to them – not until they witness the painful torment. 10:97

If only there was one city which believed and whose faith benefited it! Except for the people of Jonah who, when they believed, We relieved from the torment of humiliation in this present life, and gratified their desires for a while. Had your Lord willed it, all on earth, every single one, would have believed. Will you then compel people to become believers? No soul can believe except by God's leave. He shall inflict His wrath upon those who refuse to understand. 10:100

Say: 'Behold what is in the heavens and on earth!' What use are
revelations and threats to a people who do not believe? Can
they expect anything other than days similar to those that men
before them passed? Say: 'Wait, then, and I shall wait with you.'
Then We save Our messengers and those who believe, for it is
10:103   only right that We should save the believers.

Say: 'O mankind, if you are in doubt regarding my religion,
know that I worship not what you worship instead of God;
rather, I worship God, Who causes you to die. I have been
commanded to be among the believers.'

   Then again: 'Set your face towards the true religion, a man
of pristine faith, and be not a polytheist. Do not worship, apart
from God, what neither benefits nor harms you. If you do, you
would truly be a transgressor.' If God should touch you with
some harm, none can relieve it save Him. If He brings you some
good, none can turn back His bounty, which He brings down
upon whomsoever He pleases of His worshippers.
10:107   He is All-Forgiving, Compassionate to each.

Say: 'O mankind, the Truth has come to you from your Lord.
Whoso embraces guidance, embraces guidance for his own
     soul's good;
Whoso goes astray, leads his own soul astray.
10:108   Nor am I your guardian.'

Follow what is being revealed to you.
And bear with patience until God passes judgement – He is the
10:109   best of judges.

Hud

In the name of God,
Merciful to all,
Compassionate to each!

Alif Lam Ra'

Here is a Book,
Its verses made free of error, and then distinct,
From on high, by One
All-Wise, All-Experienced.   11:1

That you worship none but God:
I am to you from Him a herald of glad tidings, and a warner;
That you call upon your Lord to forgive you, and repent to
    Him.
He will then make you enjoy His good pleasure for a
    determined period.
Upon every doer of good He will bestow good.
Should you turn away, I fear for you the torment of a mighty
    Day.
To God is your return – and He holds power over all things.   11:4

And still they slouch, chests bent, meaning to hide from Him!
But even as they don their garments, He knows what they
    conceal, and what they proclaim!
He knows full well what lies within breasts.   11:5

No beast there is on earth but its livelihood rests with God.
He knows its berth and its final resting place.
All is in a manifest Book.   11:6

He it is Who created the heavens and the earth in six days, and

His throne was upon the waters, so as to test you: who among you is the best in works.

When you say: 'You shall surely be resurrected after death,' those who blaspheme respond: 'This is nothing but manifest sorcery.'

And if We postpone their punishment for a set period of time, they will say: 'What is holding it back?'

Indeed that Day shall come upon them, nor shall it be held back from them!

Engulfing them shall be that which before they would mock!

And if We make man taste Our mercy, then wrench it away from him, he grows exceedingly despondent, exceedingly blasphemous.

And if We make him taste prosperity after harm has touched him, he says: 'Adversity has passed me by,' then grows exultant, exceedingly proud – all except those who bear with patience and perform good deeds.

11:11   These – to them belongs forgiveness and a great reward.

Are you perhaps about to set aside some of what is being revealed to you, and with which your heart feels constricted, because they say: 'If only a treasure were sent down upon him or an angel would accompany him'?

You are but a warner – and God it is Who is Guardian over all things.

Or because they say: 'He fabricated it?'

Say: 'Bring forth ten *suras* like it, fabricated, and call upon whomever you can, apart from God, if you speak the truth.'

If they do not respond to you, know that it was only sent down with the knowledge of God, and that there is no god but

11:14   He. Will you become Muslims?

Whoso desires this nether world and its luxuries, to them We pay in full their works therein, and in it they shall not be shortchanged. These – they shall have nothing in the hereafter but the Fire. Failed are their deeds therein! Illusion are all their works!

Can such be compared to one possessed of certainty from his Lord, recited by a witness from Him and, before that, the Book of Moses, a model and a mercy? These believe in it. Whoso disbelieves in it from among various groups, his appointment is with the Fire.

Do not be in any doubt about this, for it is the Truth from your Lord. But most people do not believe.   11:17

Who is more wicked than he who fabricates a lie from God? These shall be passed in review before their Lord, and the witnesses shall say: 'These are the ones who lied about their Lord – God's curse upon the wicked!' They are those who dissuade from the path of God, seeking to make it crooked, and as for the hereafter, they blaspheme it. These will not escape on earth, and apart from God, shall have no protectors. He shall multiply their torment. They were incapable of hearing and could not see. They are those who lost their souls, and that which they fabricated has deserted them.

No indeed! It is only right that in the hereafter they shall lose the most.   11:22

Those who believed and performed good deeds and placed their trust in their Lord – these are the denizens of the Garden, therein remaining eternally.   11:23

The likeness of the two groups is like the blind and deaf, and the one who sees and hears: are they equal in likeness? Will you not reflect?   11:24

We sent Noah to his people, saying: 'I am come to you as a clear warner. You are not to worship anything but God. I fear for you the torment of a grievous Day.'

The chieftains of those who disbelieved among his people said: 'We do not see you as anything but a human being like us.

We do not see that any have followed you except our riff-raff, as it seems. We do not see that you have any advantage over us. Rather, we think you are liars.'

He said: 'My people, tell me this. If I am certain of my Lord, and He has brought me a mercy from Him which was hidden from you, are we to force you to accept it when you are averse to it?

'My people, I ask you no money for it: my wage falls only on God. I am not about to drive away those who believed: they shall encounter their Lord. But I see you are a people that do not understand.

'My people, who will take my side against God if I drive them away? Will you not recollect? I do not say to you that I possess the treasures of God. I do not know the Unseen, nor do I say I am an angel, nor do I tell those whom your eyes despise that God will not bring them good, for God knows best what is in
11:31   their hearts. If I did so I would indeed be wicked.'

They said: 'O Noah, you have argued with us; indeed, you have exceeded the limit in argument. So now bring upon us what you threaten us with, if you are truthful.'

He said: 'It is God Who will bring it upon you, if He wills. Nor can you escape it. My counsel, should I wish to counsel you, will be of no benefit to you if God desires to confound you.
11:34   He is your Lord, and to Him you shall return.'

Or do they say: 'He fabricated it'? Say: 'If I fabricated it, upon
11:35   me falls my sinful act, and I am quit of your sinning.'

It was revealed to Noah: 'None shall believe from your people except those who have already believed, so do not feel sad because of what they do. Build the Ark where We can see you and with Our inspiration, and do not plead with Me regarding those who are wicked. They shall be drowned.'

Noah then builds the Ark. Whenever a group of notables of his people passed by, they would mock him.

He said: 'If you mock us, we mock you as you mock. You will surely know upon whom shall fall a torment that will abase him, upon whom shall fall an everlasting torment.' 11:39

And so it came to pass that when Our command went out, and water gushed forth to the surface, We said: 'Load up on board two of every kind, and your family – except for those foretold – and those who believed.' But the believers with him were few. 11:40

He said: 'Go on board. In the name of God may it sail and anchor! My Lord is All-Forgiving, Compassionate to each.' 11:41

And so it sailed with them amidst waves like mountains. Noah called out to his son, who had kept away: 'My son, embark with us and do not remain among the unbelievers.'
He said: 'I shall find refuge on a mountain which shall protect me from the waters.'
He said: 'Today there is no protector from the command of God, except him to whom God shows mercy.'
Then the waves came between them and he was among those who were drowned. 11:43

It was said: 'O earth, swallow your waters! O sky, desist!' The waters subsided, the judgement was passed. The Ark settled upon Mount Judi and it was proclaimed: 'Away with the wicked!'
Noah then called out to his Lord, saying: 'Lord, my son is of my family. Your promise is the truth, and you are the fairest of judges.'
He said: 'O Noah, he is not of your family. It is an act unrighteous. So ask Me not for that of which you have no knowledge. I counsel you not to be foolish.'
He said: 'My Lord, I seek refuge in You lest I be one who asks You for what I have no knowledge of! If You do not forgive me and show me mercy, I shall surely be lost.'

It was said: 'O Noah, disembark in Our peace, and with Our blessings upon you and upon the nations with you. Other nations We shall grant prosperity, and then there shall touch 11:48 them from Us a torment most painful.'

These are reports of the Unseen which We reveal to you. You knew them not, neither you nor your people, beforehand. So be 11:49 patient: the final outcome will vindicate the pious.

To 'Ad We sent their fellow tribesman Hud.

He said: 'My people, worship God; you have no other god but He. You do nothing but spin lies.

'My people, I ask you no wage for it: my wage falls only on Him Who created me. Will you not be reasonable?

'My people, ask your Lord's forgiveness and repent to Him and He will pour down the heavens in torrents upon you, and increase you in strength above your strength. Do not turn away and be wicked.'

They said: 'O Hud, you bring us no certain sign. We shall not forsake our gods just because of your word, nor will we believe in you. We say only that one of our gods must have afflicted you with harm.'

He said: 'I call God to witness, and you too are to witness, that I am innocent of your associating other gods with Him. So practise your cunning against me, all of you, and do not hesitate. I have put my trust in God, my Lord and yours. There is no beast but that He holds tight by its forelock. My Lord is upon a straight path. If they turn away, I have delivered to you what I was sent to you with. My Lord shall choose a people other than you to be your successors. You cannot harm Him one whit. 11:57 My Lord is Guardian over all things.'

When Our judgement was passed, We saved Hud and those who believed with him, through a mercy from Us. We saved 11:58 them from a torment most onerous.

Such was 'Ad! They repudiated the signs of their Lord and disobeyed His messengers, and followed the lead of every obdurate tyrant. They were pursued by a curse in this world and on the Day of Resurrection.

Yes, indeed! 'Ad blasphemed against their Lord! Away with 'Ad, the people of Hud!   11:60

To Thamud We sent their fellow tribesman Salih.

He said: 'My people, worship God; you have no other god but He. He it was Who raised you up from the earth and made you build upon it. So ask your Lord's forgiveness and repent to Him – my Lord is ever at hand, ever ready to respond.'

They said: 'O Salih, among us you were one from whom much was expected before this matter. Are you forbidding us to worship what our ancestors worshipped when we are in perplexing doubt about what you call us to?'

He said: 'My people, tell me this. If I am certain of my Lord, and He has brought me a mercy from Him, who shall protect me from God if I disobey Him? For then you would merely increase me in loss.

'My people, here is the she-camel of God, a sign for you. Set it free to graze in God's earth, and touch it not with harm lest an imminent punishment should overtake you.'   11:64

But they hamstrung the she-camel.

He said: 'Enjoy your homes for three days – that is a promise not to be denied.'

When Our command came to pass, We saved Salih and those who believed with him, through a mercy from Us, and from the humiliation of that day. Your Lord is All-Powerful, Almighty.

The Scream overtook those who were wicked and, on the morrow, they were found prostrate in their homes, as if they had never prospered therein.

Yes, indeed! Thamud blasphemed against their Lord! Away with Thamud!   11:68

Our envoys came to Abraham, bearing glad tidings.

They said: 'Peace!'

He said: 'Peace!'

At once he brought forth a roasted calf. When he saw that their hands did not stretch forth to it, he was in doubt about them and harboured some fear of them.

They said: 'Fear not. We were sent to the people of Lot.'

His wife, standing by, laughed, so We brought her glad tidings of Isaac, and after Isaac, of Jacob.

She said: 'Alas for me! Am I to give birth, me an old woman, and here is my husband, an old man? That would indeed be a marvel!'

They said: 'Do you marvel at the command of God? May the mercy of God and His blessings descend upon you, O members of the house! He is All-Praiseworthy, All-Glorious.'

11:73

When fear left Abraham, and glad tidings came to him, he began to argue with Us regarding the people of Lot. Abraham was gentle, sighing much, penitent.

'O Abraham, make no mention of this matter. The command of your Lord is come and they – there shall come to them a torment irreversible.'

11:76

When Our envoys came to Lot, he was annoyed and grew impatient with them, saying: 'This indeed is an arduous day.' His people came to him, hurrying in haste – beforehand, they had committed misdeeds.

He said: 'My people, here are my daughters; they are more pure for you. So fear God and do not shame me with my guests. Is there not among you a man of discernment?'

They said: 'You know we have no right to your daughters, and you know well what we want.'

He said: 'If only I had some power against you, or else I could take refuge in a pillar of great strength!'

They said: 'O Lot, we are the envoys of your Lord. They shall not reach out to harm you. So set out with your family in the course of the night, and let none of you turn their heads back except your wife. She will be smitten with that which will smite them. Their appointed time shall be the morning: is not the morning close at hand?'   11:81

When Our command came to pass, We turned it upside down and rained down upon it stones of baked clay, all piled up and marked by your Lord. Nor are these stones remote from the wicked!   11:83

To Midian We sent their fellow tribesman Shu'ayb.

He said: 'My people, worship God; you have no other god but He. Do not shortchange the measure and the balance. I see you are prosperous, and I fear for you the torment of a Day, all-encompassing.

'My people, give full share in the measure and balance, acting justly. Do not cheat people of their goods and do not act wickedly on earth, corrupting it. What remains from God is better for you if you are true believers. But I am not a guardian over you.'

They said: 'O Shu'ayb, is it your mode of worship that commands you that we abandon what our ancestors worshipped? Or are we to do with our wealth what we please? For you are gentle and discerning.'

He said: 'My people, tell me this. Though I am certain of my Lord, and He has granted me a fair livelihood from Him, I desire not to do the opposite of what I forbid you to do. I merely wish to reform you, as much as I can. My good fortune comes solely from God: in Him I trust, to Him I repent.

'My people, let not your enmity towards me bring upon you a calamity such as befell the people of Noah, or of Hud, or of Salih; nor is the example of Lot's people remote from you. Ask your Lord's forgiveness and repent to Him: my Lord is Compassionate to each, All-Tender.'   11:90

They said: 'O Shuʻayb, we do not understand most of what you say. We hold you to be a weak man among us. Were it not for your clan, we would have stoned you; nor are you too powerful for us.'

He said: 'My people, is my clan more powerful against you than God, Whom you have cast behind your backs? My Lord encompasses all that you do.

'My people, do your best, and I shall do likewise. You shall learn to whom shall come a torment that abases him, and who is the liar. So wait and watch, and I shall wait and watch with 11:93   you.'

When Our command came to pass, We saved Shuʻayb and those who believed with him through a mercy from Us, and the Scream overtook those who were wicked. On the morrow they were found prostrate in their homes, as though they had never prospered therein. Away with Midian, as was done away with 11:95   Thamud!

We sent Moses, with Our revelations and with manifest proof, to Pharaoh and his grandees, but they followed the command of Pharaoh, and Pharaoh's command was not guided aright. He shall be at the head of his people on the Day of Resurrection, for he has led them into the Fire – wretched the place he placed them in! They were pursued by a curse in this world and on the 11:99   Day of Resurrection – wretched the lot allotted to them!

These are reports of cities which We narrate to you: some are left standing, some have withered away. We wronged them not, but it was themselves they wronged. Their gods, whom they used to worship instead of God, were of no use to them in any wise when the command of God had come to pass – they merely increased them in loss and destruction. Thus does your Lord seize when He seizes cities that are sinful! His seizure is most 11:102   painful, most grievous.

In this is a sign for him who fears the torment of the hereafter.

That will be a Day at which mankind shall be gathered; that will be a Day witnessed by all. We shall defer it only for a set term – upon a Day when no soul shall speak except by His leave; and some will be wretched and some will be happy. As for those who sinned, they are in the Fire. For them there is groaning and lamentation, abiding therein for ever, as long as the heavens and the earth shall last, save as your Lord desires. Your Lord is ever the disposer of all that He desires. As for those blessed with happiness, they are in the Garden, abiding therein for ever, as long as the heavens and the earth shall last, save as your Lord desires: a wage uninterrupted. 11:108

Therefore, be not in any doubt as to what these people worship. They merely worship as their forefathers had worshipped before. We shall pay them their share in full, undiminished. 11:109

We had brought Moses the Book, and disputes arose concerning it. Were it not for a prior Word from your Lord, judgement would have been passed upon them. They are in perplexing doubt concerning it. To each and every one of them your Lord will pay in full the wages of their deeds – He knows full well what they do. 11:111

So stand straight, as you were commanded, and those who repented with you.

Be not overbearing – He sees full well what you do.

Do not incline to those who did wrong, or else the Fire will touch you. You have, apart from God, no protectors, nor will you be aided.

Perform the prayer at the two ends of the day and for some hours of the night.

Good deeds efface bad deeds.

This is a Remembrance to those who remember.

Bear with patience; God neglects not the reward of those who do good. 11:115

Would that, in ages past before you, there had been a group, a remnant, who forbade corruption on earth! Except for a few, and these We saved. But wrongdoers pursued the luxuries they were plunged in, and grew sinful. And yet your Lord would not have destroyed cities unjustly if their inhabitants had been
11:117 virtuous.

Had your Lord willed, He would have created mankind a single nation. But they continue to differ, save for those to whom God has shown mercy. It is for this reason that He created them. The Word of your Lord is fulfilled: 'I shall fill hell to the brim with
11:119 both *Jinn* and humans!'

All that We narrate to you from the tales of messengers is such wherewith We fortify your heart. To you thereby has come the Truth, a Lesson and a Remembrance to the believers.

Say to those who do not believe: 'Do the best you can, and we shall do likewise. And watch and wait; we too are watching
11:122 and waiting.'

To God belongs the Unseen in the heavens and earth.
To Him all matters revert.
Worship Him;
Trust in Him;
11:123 Nor is your Lord heedless of what you do.

Joseph

In the name of God,
Merciful to all,
Compassionate to each!

Alif Lam Ra'

Behold the revelations of the Manifest Book!
We have sent it down as an Arabic Qur'an; perhaps you will
understand.
We narrate to you the fairest of narratives, through what We
revealed to you – this Qur'an.
And yet before it you were heedless.   12:3

Remember when Joseph said to his father: 'O father, I dreamt
of eleven stars, and of the sun and moon. I dreamt they were
bowing down before me.'
   He said: 'My son, do not relate your dream to your brothers,
else they will contrive and plot against you. Satan to man is a
manifest enemy. Thus will your Lord choose you and teach you
the interpretation of reports, and perfect His grace upon you
and upon the family of Jacob, as He perfected it upon your
ancestors before you, Abraham and Isaac. Your Lord is
Omniscient, All-Wise.'   12:6

In the story of Joseph and his brothers there were clear signs to
those who seek answers.   12:7

Remember when they said: 'Joseph and his brother are more
dear to our father than we are, though we are a band. Our
father is in manifest error. So kill Joseph or drive him away to
some land, and the face of your father shall be wholly yours,
and after him you shall be a virtuous community.'

One of them said: 'Do not kill Joseph but throw him into the darkness of the well, where some travellers will pick him up – that is, if you carry through that deed.'

They said: 'O father, why is it that you do not trust us with Joseph, though we care for him? Send him with us tomorrow to roam and play, and we will surely guard him well.'

He said: 'It grieves me that you take him away, and I fear the wolf might eat him when you are not minding him.'

12:14 They said: 'Were a wolf to eat him, we being a band, we would most surely be good for nothing!'

12:15 When they set out with him, and all agreed they would hurl him into the darkness of the well, We revealed to him: 'You shall acquaint them with this act of theirs at a time when they shall recall it not.'

So they came to their father in the evening, weeping.

They said: 'O father, we went off to race each other and left Joseph near our baggage, so the wolf ate him. But you will not believe us even though we speak the truth.'

And they brought forth his shirt with fake blood upon it.

He said: 'Rather, your souls have tempted you to some act.
12:18 O seemly patience! God's help against that which you describe!'

A band of travellers passed by. They sent off their water carrier and he lowered his bucket.

He said: 'Glad tidings! Here is a young man!'

And they hid him inside their baggage, and God knew full well what they did.

And they sold him for a paltry sum, a few *dirham*s, for they had little regard for him.

The man who bought him, from Egypt, said to his wife: 'Treat him hospitably, for he might be of use to us, or else we might adopt him as a son.'

Thus did We establish Joseph firmly on earth, in order that We might teach him the interpretation of reports. God's decree will prevail, but most people do not know. 12:21

When he grew to full manhood, We granted him sound judgement and knowledge – thus do We reward those who act righteously. 12:22

The woman in whose house he dwelt sought to seduce him and shut firm the doors upon them. She said: 'Come to me!' He said: 'God forbid! He is my lord and has treated me hospitably. Sinners do not prevail.' For she was about to possess him, and he to possess her, were it not that he saw the proof of his Lord.

Thus did it turn out, so that We might avert from him sin and debauchery. He was one of Our faithful worshippers. 12:24

They raced to the door, and she tore his shirt from behind. They found her master by the door.

She said: 'What is the punishment for one who intended evil against your wife except to be imprisoned or suffer painful torment?'

He said: 'It was she who attempted to seduce me.'

A witness from her family witnessed as follows: 'If his shirt is torn from the front, then she is telling the truth and he is lying. But if his shirt is torn from behind, then she is lying and he is telling the truth.'

When he saw that his shirt was torn from behind, he said: 'This is women's cunning; indeed, your cunning is great. O Joseph, mention this matter to no one; and you, woman, ask forgiveness for your offence, for you have truly been sinful.' 12:29

Now some women in the city said: 'The governor's wife is attempting to seduce her youthful servant, who has infatuated her with ardent passion. We find her to be in manifest error.'

When she heard their sly gossip, she invited them, preparing for them a banquet on couches, and gave each of them a knife.

Then she said: 'Come out and appear before them.' When they saw him, they admired him so much that they cut their hands, saying: 'God forbid! He is no human being! He is nothing but a noble angel!'

She said: 'Here he is, the one you reproached me with! I attempted to seduce him but he resisted my seduction. And yet, if he does not do what I order him, he will assuredly be imprisoned and suffer humiliation.'

He said: 'My Lord, prison is dearer to me than what they invite me to do. If You do not ward off their guile from me, I shall long for them, and so become a man of base desires.'

His Lord answered his call and averted their guile from him
12:34 – He is All-Hearing, Omniscient.

Thereafter, it occurred to them, having witnessed these wonders, that they should imprison him for a while. Entering the prison with him were two young men.

One of them said: 'I dreamt I was pressing grapes.'

The other said: 'I dreamt I was carrying on my head bread from which the birds were eating. Tell us its interpretation, for
12:36 we see you are a virtuous man.'

He said: 'No food, with which you will be served, shall come to you but I shall inform you of its interpretation – before it has come to you. This is part of what my Lord taught me.

'I have forsaken the religion of a people who do not believe in God and who blaspheme against the hereafter. I follow the religion of my forefathers, Abraham, Isaac and Jacob. We were not meant to associate anything with God, this being part of God's grace upon us and upon mankind. But most of mankind do not render thanks.

'My fellow prisoners, are many and diverse gods better, or is the One Omnipotent God? What you worship instead of Him are merely names that you and your ancestors coined, and for which no authority has come from God. Sovereignty belongs solely to God. He commands that you worship none but Him.

This is the upright religion, but most mankind have no understanding.

'My fellow prisoners, as for one of you, he shall serve his
master wine to drink; as for the other, he shall be crucified and
the birds shall eat from his head. The issue is settled upon which
you seek my opinion.'   12:41

To the man he imagined was about to be released from the two
of them, he said: 'Mention me to your master.' But Satan caused
him to forget the mention of this to his master, and he languished
in jail for several years.   12:42

The king said: 'I saw in a dream seven fat cows being eaten by
seven thin; seven green ears of corn, and others seared. O council, give me your opinion of my dream if you can interpret
visions.'

They said: 'A meaningless medley of visions! But we are no
experts in the interpretation of dreams.'

Said he who had been saved from the two of them, now
having, after the passage of time, remembered: 'I will inform
you of its interpretation, so send me out.'   12:45

'Joseph, you who are worthy of all trust, give us your opinion
of seven fat cows being eaten by seven thin and of seven green
ears of corn, and others seared, so I may return to the people
and let them know.'

He said: 'You will sow for seven years, as is your custom.
What you harvest you are to leave on the ear, save a little
for you to eat from. Thereafter shall come seven years of
hardship which will consume what you had laid up before,
save a little for you to store. Afterwards shall come a year
when people are sent rain and in which they will work at the
press.'   12:49

The king said: 'Bring him to me.' When the messenger came to
Joseph he said: 'Go back to your master and ask him about the

matter of the women who cut their hands. My Lord knows full
well their cunning.'

He said: 'What drove you women to seduce Joseph?'

They answered: 'God forbid! We know no sin of which he is
guilty.'

The governor's wife said: 'Now the truth has come to light!
It was I who attempted to seduce him but he is indeed a man of
true faith. This I avow in order that my husband may know
that I did not betray him in secret, and that God guides not the
scheming of betrayers. I do not declare my soul innocent: the
soul ever urges to evil, except when my Lord shows mercy. My
12:53 Lord is All-Forgiving, Compassionate to each.'

The king said: 'Bring him to me, so that I may make him my
personal attendant.'

When he had talked to him, he said: 'Today you are secure
in our favour, worthy of our trust.'

He said: 'Appoint me to oversee the treasures of the land, for
12:55 I am a careful guardian and well qualified.'

This is how We established Joseph firmly in that land, to live
therein wherever he wished. We cast Our mercy upon whomsoever We wish, and We do not neglect the reward of the righteous.
But the reward of the hereafter is better for those who believe
12:57 and are pious.

And the brothers of Joseph arrived and came into his presence.
He recognized them but they knew him not. When he had
provided them with their provisions he said: 'Bring me a brother
of yours, born of your father. Do you not see that I fill the
measure with fairness and that I am the best of hosts? If you do
not bring him to me, there will be no measure for you with me,
and you are not to come near me again.'

They said: 'We will try to lure his father to let him go, and
we will succeed.'

He said to his retainers: 'Place their merchandise in their

saddlebags; hopefully they will recognize it when they head back
to their people, and hopefully they will return.'   12:62

When they returned to their father they said: 'Father, measuring
has been forbidden to us, so send with us our brother and we
shall be given the measure again. We shall take good care of
him.'

He said: 'Am I to trust you with him as I trusted you with his
brother before? God is the best of guardians, the most merciful
of the merciful.'

When they opened their baggage, they found that their merchandise had been returned to them. They said: 'Father, what
more can we want? Here is our own merchandise returned to
us. We shall provision our families, take good care of our
brother and increase our wealth by a camel's load – this indeed
is easy commerce.'   12:65

He said: 'I shall not send him with you until you swear to me
an oath from God that you will bring him back to me; unless,
that is, you are overwhelmed.' When they swore him their oath,
he said: 'God oversees what we say.'

Again he said: 'My sons, do not enter through one gate but
enter through different gates. I find that nothing whatever will
avail you save God. Judgement belongs to God alone; in Him I
place my trust, and in Him let all trust who place their trust.'   12:67

When they entered from where their father had commanded
them, nothing would have availed them against God, were it
not for a certain desire in the soul of Jacob that he satisfied. He
was indeed possessed of a knowledge We had taught him, but
most people have no understanding.   12:68

When they entered upon Joseph he embraced his brother, saying: 'I am your brother, so do not grieve for what they have
done.' When he had provided them with their provisions, he
placed his drinking cup in his brother's saddlebag.

Then a herald called out: 'O caravan, you are thieves!'

Turning towards them, they asked: 'What is it that you find missing?'

They said: 'We are missing the king's drinking cup. Whoever hands it in will receive a camel load; this I warrant.'

They said: 'By God, you know well that we came not to do corruption on earth, nor are we thieves.'

They said: 'What is his punishment if you are lying?'

12:75 They said: 'His punishment is that if it is found in anyone's saddlebag, he will suffer due penalty – thus do we reward wrongdoers.'

So he commenced with their sacks before his brother's sack, until finally he extricated it from his brother's sack – thus did We work this stratagem for Joseph. He was not about to submit his brother to the king's punishment, unless God had willed it.

We elevate whomever We will in rank.

12:76 Above every person possessed of knowledge is One All-Knowing.

They said: 'If he is a thief, a brother of his had stolen before.' Said Joseph to himself, revealing it not to them: 'You are worse in moral standing, and God knows best what tale you are spinning.'

They said: 'O governor, he has a father, a very old man. So take one of us in his place, for we see you are a man of virtue.'

12:79 He said: 'God forbid that we arrest anyone except him with whom we found our property. Otherwise, we would be unjust.'

When they despaired of him, they retired to consult among themselves. The eldest among them said: 'Do you not know that your father made you swear an oath from God and, before that, you had been remiss with Joseph? I shall not move from this spot until my father gives me leave or else God reveals His judgement to me; He is the fairest of judges. So go back to your

father and tell him: "Father, your son is a thief. We merely bear
witness to that which we know for sure. Nor are we privy to
the Unseen. Make inquiries in the city where we were or among
the caravan in which we returned, for we speak the truth." '   12:82

He said: 'Rather, your souls have tempted you to some act. O
seemly patience! It may be that God will bring them all back to
me; He is All-Knowing, All-Wise.'

So he turned his face away from them, saying: 'How I mourn
Joseph!' His eyes turned white from sorrow, but he restrained
himself.   12:84

They said: 'By God, you will never cease from mentioning
Joseph until you waste away or perish.'

He said: 'To God alone do I complain of my heartache and
my sorrow. I know from God what you do not know. My sons,
go and search about for news of Joseph and his brother. Despair
not from the solace of God. Only the unbelievers despair from
the solace of God.'   12:87

When they entered into his presence, they said: 'O governor,
harm has touched us and our family. We come to you with
inferior merchandise. Fill out our measure and be charitable to
us, for God rewards the charitable.'

He said: 'Do you know what you did to Joseph and his
brother when you were wild and heedless?'

They said: 'Is that you, Joseph?'

He said: 'I am indeed Joseph, and here is my brother. God
has been gracious to us. He who is pious and patient – God
wastes not the reward of the virtuous.'

They said: 'By God, God has preferred you to us, and we
were indeed sinners.'

He said: 'No blame shall fall upon you; today, God forgives
you, for He is the most merciful of those who show mercy. Take
this shirt of mine and throw it over my father's face, and he will
see again, and bring me your family, one and all.'   12:93

When the caravan set off, their father said: 'I detect the scent of Joseph, unless you think I am senile.'

They said: 'By God, you are still in your former dotage.'

But when the bearer of glad tidings arrived and threw it on his face, he recovered his sight and said: 'Did I not tell you that I know from God what you do not know?'

They said: 'Father, ask forgiveness for our sins, for we were sinners.'

He said: 'I shall ask forgiveness for you from my Lord. He it 12:98 is Who is All-Forgiving, Compassionate to each.'

When they entered into Joseph's presence, he embraced his parents and said: 'Enter into Egypt, if God wills, safe and secure.' Then he raised his parents up upon the throne, and they fell prostrate before him.

He said: 'Father, this is the interpretation of my former dream; now my Lord has brought it to pass. He was gracious to me when He delivered me from prison and brought you from the wilderness, after Satan had sowed conflict between me and my brothers. My Lord turns with kindness to whomsoever He wills. He is Omniscient, All-Wise.

'My Lord, You have granted me power and taught me the interpretation of reports. Creator of the heavens and earth!

'You are my Protector in this world and in the hereafter!

'Let me die a Muslim and make me join the company of the 12:101 virtuous!'

These are reports of the Unseen which We reveal to you. You were not present among them when they agreed together and plotted. Nor are most people believers, no matter how hard you try.

You ask them no wage for it: it is merely a Reminder to all mankind.

How many a wonder in the heavens and earth they pass by, taking no notice!

And most of them believe not in God unless they associate other gods with Him.

Are they sure they will not be overwhelmed by a torment from God, or that the Hour will come upon them suddenly, unawares?   12:107

Say: 'This is my way. I call to God, clear-sighted – I and those who follow me.

'Glory be to God! Nor am I one to associate others with Him.'   12:108

Before you, We sent not but city men whom We inspired.

Have they not journeyed on earth?

Have they not noticed the fate of those who came before them?

Surely the abode of the hereafter is better for those who are pious – will you not reason?

Until, when the messengers despaired, and imagined that they had been branded as liars, Our victory came to them for We save whomsoever We will. Our might shall not be turned away from the wicked.   12:110

In their narratives is a lesson to those possessed of minds. This is no tale being spun but a confirmation of what came before it, a clear explication of all things, and a guidance and a mercy to the faithful.   12:111

Thunder

In the name of God,
Merciful to all,
Compassionate to each!

Alif Lam Mim Ra'

Behold the verses of the Book!
13:1 What has been sent down upon you from your Lord is the truth, but most men do not believe.

God is He Who raised up the heavens without any pillars that
  you can see.
Then He settled firmly on the throne.
He made the sun and moon to do His bidding, each running
  for an appointed time.
He governs the world;
He makes clear His revelations;
Perhaps you will be convinced of the encounter with your
  Lord.

He it was Who spread out the earth and placed in it towering
  mountains and rivers.
Of all fruits He planted therein two pairs.
He causes night to envelop day.
13:3 In these are wonders for a people who reflect.

On earth are tracts of land, adjoining one another: gardens of
vines, cultivation, and palm trees, clustered or single. They are
all watered by one stream. Yet some We prefer to others in the
nourishment they yield. Surely in these are signs for a people of
understanding.

Should you wonder, then wondrous indeed is what they say: 'How can it be that once we are turned to dust we find ourselves created anew?' These are people who blaspheme against their Lord. These – chains shall encircle their necks. These are the people of the Fire, in which they shall abide for ever. They ask you to hasten calamity upon them rather than good fortune, though punishments in plenty have passed before them. Your Lord is forgiving towards mankind, despite their wickedness, but your Lord is grievous in torment.   13:6

Those who blaspheme say: 'If only some miracle were sent down upon him from his Lord!' You are but a warner, and for every people there is a guide.

God knows what each female is bearing, which wombs shorten their terms and which they lengthen. With Him, all things have their due measure.

Knower of the Unseen and the Seen, Almighty, Exalted!

It is all the same whether one of you conceals his speech or proclaims it, whether he goes into hiding by night or follows a road by day. With him are attending angels, ahead and behind, guarding him in accordance with God's command.

God alters not what is in a people unless they alter what is in themselves.

If God desires to bring evil to a people, nothing can turn it away, nor, apart from Him, have they any protector.   13:11

He it is Who shows you the lightning, causing both fear and
    expectation;
He it is Who raises heavy-laden clouds.
Thunder glorifies His praise and the angels His awe.
He casts thunderbolts and strikes therewith whomsoever He
    wills.
Yet they dispute regarding God, though Mighty in devising!
To Him belongs the Call to Truth.

As for those whom they worship apart from Him, they answer
not their prayer in any wise, save like one who spreads the
palms of his hands towards water to convey to his mouth, and
the water will not reach it. The prayers of unbelievers are noth-
13:14 ing but illusion.

To God prostrate themselves all who are in the heavens and on
earth, willing or unwilling, as do their shadows, at dawn or at
dusk.
      Say: 'Who is the Lord of the heavens and earth?'
      Say: 'God!'
      Say: 'So have you taken to yourselves as protectors, instead
of Him, such as are powerless to benefit or harm themselves?'
      Say: 'Is the blind man the equal of one who sees? Or is
darkness the equal of light? Or have they fashioned partners to
God who created something similar to His creation, and so
creation became a matter that perplexed them?'
      Say: 'God is the Creator of all things; He is One, Over-
13:16 powering.'

He sent down water from the sky, and the valleys flowed in due
measure.
      The torrent carried away a swell of froth, like the froth they
light a fire upon, seeking to fashion an ornament or an article
of pleasure – upon that too is a similar froth. Thus does God
strike a parable of truth and falsehood.
      As to the froth, it vanishes into the earth, but that which
benefits mankind remains on the ground. Thus does God strike
parables.

To those who answered the call of their Lord a fair reward
awaits. As for those who did not answer His call – were they to
possess all that is on earth, and the double thereof, they would
offer it all up as ransom. To these an evil accounting awaits:
13:18 their refuge shall be hell, and what a wretched place of rest!

Is he who knows that the Truth has indeed been sent down to you from your Lord like one who is blind? Only those possessed of minds remember – they who fulfil the pledge of God and do not violate the covenant,
Who bind the ties of kinship that God commanded to be bound,
Who fear their Lord, and fear an evil reckoning,
Who bore in patience, longing for the face of their Lord,
Who performed the prayer, and expended from that which We bestowed upon them, both secretly and in the open,
Who ward off an evil deed with a good one –
Their destiny shall be the Abode of Bliss,
Gardens of Eden which they will enter,
Along with the virtuous among their parents, spouses and offspring,
With the angels entering upon them from every gate:
'Peace be upon you for what you bore in patience!'
How marvellous a destiny is the Abode of Bliss! 13:24

As for those who violate the pledge of God, after the covenant with Him,
Who sever what God commanded to be joined,
Who do corruption on earth –
Upon these a curse, and an Evil Abode awaits them.

God dispenses His bounty to whomsoever He wills – and with-holds it. They find joy in this present life, but the present life is frivolity compared to the hereafter.

The unbelievers say: 'If only a miracle were sent down upon him from his Lord!'

Say: 'God leads astray whomever He wills and guides to Him whoever repents, they who believe and whose hearts feel secure at the remembrance of God' – indeed, let hearts feel secure at the remembrance of God!

They who believe and perform good deeds – blessings be
13:29 upon them and the Abode of Bliss!

Likewise did We send you to a nation before whom many
nations had passed away, in order to recite to them what We
had revealed to you, when they had blasphemed against the
All-Merciful.
    Say: 'He is my Lord. There is no god but He! In Him I trust
and to Him is my journey's end.'
    If only it had been a Qur'an wherewith mountains are moved
or the earth is cut in pieces or the dead are spoken to!
    But to God belongs dispensation of all matters.
    Do the believers not realize that if God had willed, He would
have guided all mankind? And yet the unbelievers continue to
be stricken by a calamity because of their actions, or else by one
which alights close to their homes, until there shall come the
13:31 promise of God. Surely God fails not His appointed time.

Other messengers before you were met with ridicule. I granted
the unbelievers respite and then I seized them – and what a
punishment it was! Is He Who watches over every soul for what
it earns – and yet they ascribe partners to God!
    Say: 'Name them! Or do you wish to inform Him of what He
knows not on earth? Or is this speech a mere show?'
    Rather, to those who disbelieve, their cunning was made
attractive in their eyes, and they were driven away from the
path of righteousness.
    Whoever God leads astray, no guide has he. Torment awaits
them in this present life but the torment of the hereafter is more
13:34 terrible. From God they can expect no one to shield them.

The likeness of the Garden promised to the pious is one beneath
which rivers flow. Its nourishment is everlasting, and so is its
shade. This is the destiny of the pious, but the destiny of unbelievers is the Fire.

Those to whom We brought the Book are happy with what has been sent down upon you. But among religious sects there are some who reject a portion of it.

Say: 'I was merely commanded to worship God and associate none with Him. I call to Him, and to Him is my final return.'

So also did We send it down as an Arabic code of law.

Had you followed their fancies, after Knowledge had come to you, you would have found no protector or shield from God.   13:37

We sent messengers before you to whom We gave spouses and progeny. But no messenger could have worked any miracle except by God's leave.

For every matter decided there is a Register:

God erases what He wills, and ratifies.

With Him is the Archetype of the Book.

Whether We show you part of what We promised them or whether we cause you to die, it is your duty to convey the message, but Ours is the accounting. Do they not see how We descend upon their territory, causing it to shrink from its margins? It is God Who judges, and nothing can hold back His judgement. He is quick to settle accounts.   13:41

Those before them also practised their cunning, but to God belongs all cunning. He knows what each soul earns, and the unbelievers shall surely know to whom belongs the destiny of the Abode.

Those who blaspheme say: 'You are no Messenger.'

Say: 'Let God suffice as witness between me and you – He Who has knowledge of the Book.'

Abraham

In the name of God,
Merciful to all,
Compassionate to each!

Alif Lam Ra'

Behold this Book We have sent down upon you, that you may lead mankind from darkness to light, by leave of their Lord, and onto the path of the Almighty, All-Praiseworthy – God, to Whom belongs all that is in the heavens and on earth.

14:2   Woe to the unbelievers from a terrible torment!

They who fondly embrace this present life in preference to the
     hereafter,
Who obstruct the path to God, seeking to turn it crooked –
These are plunged deep in error.

We sent no Messenger except with the language of his people, that he may enlighten them. Then God leads astray whom He
14:4   wills and guides whom He wills. He is Almighty, All-Wise.

We sent Moses with Our revelations: 'Bring your people out from darkness to light, and remind them of the Days of God. In this are signs for every truly patient and thankful person.'
     Remember when Moses said to his people: 'Recall the blessing of God upon you when He delivered you from Pharaoh's people, who were making you taste evil punishment, slaughtering your children, debauching your women, in all of which was great
14:6   calamity from your Lord.'

Remember too when your Lord promised: 'If you render thanks for blessings I shall multiply them upon you, but if you disbelieve, my torment is indeed terrible.'

Moses said: 'Even if you and everyone else on earth were to disbelieve, God is Self-Sufficient, Praiseworthy.'   14:8

Has there not come to you news of those who were before you, the people of Noah, 'Ad and Thamud, and of those who came after them? None knows them save God. Their messengers came to them with clear proofs, but they bent their fingers back into their mouths and said: 'We disbelieve in what you have been sent with, and we are in doubt concerning that to which you call us, a doubt perplexing.'

Their messengers said: 'Can there be any doubt regarding God, Creator of the heavens and earth? He calls you in order to forgive your sins and to defer you until a stated term.'
They said: 'You are merely human, like us. Do you intend to turn us aside from what our forefathers worshipped? Bring us then a manifest proof.'   14:10

Their messengers said to them: 'We are merely human, like you, but God shows His grace to whomever He wills from among His servants. It is not up to us to bring you proof except with God's leave. In God let the faithful trust. We have no recourse but to trust in God when He has guided us to our paths. We shall indeed be patient in the face of the harm you did us. In God let the faithful trust.'

The unbelievers said to their messengers: 'We will surely drive you out of our land unless you revert to our religion.'
To them their Lord revealed: 'We will assuredly destroy the wicked, and cause you to inhabit the earth after them – and this, to him who fears My station and fears My threat.'

So they prayed for victory, and every obstinate tyrant came to grief – beyond him lies hell, where he will be given pus to drink. He will swallow it but will barely endure its taste, and death will come to him from every direction, though he himself is not dead – beyond lies torment most harsh.   14:17

The likeness of those who blaspheme their Lord – their works are like ash upon which the wind blows hard on a stormy day. They have no power whatever over that which they earned, and this indeed is the most perverse of errors. Do you not see that God created the heavens and earth in justice? If He wishes, He can do away with you and bring forth a new creation. Nor will 14:20 this be a thing onerous to God.

And they shall all rise from the dead before God. The weak shall say to the mighty: 'We were once your attendants, so will you protect us in any wise from the torment of God?'

They shall respond: 'Had God guided us we would have guided you. It is all the same to us whether we mourn or bear with patience; for us there is no escape.'

Satan shall say, when judgement has been passed: 'God made you a promise of truth, and I too promised you, but I let you down. I had no power over you except that I called to you and you responded to me. Do not blame me but blame yourselves. I cannot come to your aid, nor you to mine. I have abjured what you once associated me with, and upon the wicked shall fall a 14:22 torment most painful.'

Those who believed and performed righteous deeds shall be ushered into Gardens beneath which rivers flow, abiding therein for ever with their Lord's leave. Their greeting therein shall be 'Peace!'

Do you not see how God draws a parable:

A goodly word is like a goodly tree; its roots are firm and its branches reach to the sky.

It brings forth its nourishment at every turn, by its Lord's leave.

And God draws parables for mankind; perhaps they will reflect.

And the likeness of an evil word is like an evil tree uprooted from the ground; no bed has she.

God gives strength to the faithful with speech unchanging in the present life and in the hereafter, and He leads the wicked astray. God does what He wills.   14:27

Have you considered those who exchanged the bounty of God for blasphemy, and how they made their people settle in the Abode of Desolation? Hell it is they shall be scorched with! And what a wretched place of rest!

And yet they set up equals to God, to lead astray from His path!
    Say: 'Enjoy yourselves. Your destination is the Fire.' Tell My believing worshippers to perform the prayer and expend from what We bestowed upon them, secretly and in the open, before there comes a Day when there shall be neither commerce nor intimacy.   14:31

God it is Who created the heavens and the earth,
Who made water descend from the sky,
From which He brought forth nourishment, a bounty upon
    you;
Who made ships to serve you,
Running in the sea, by His command,
And made rivers to serve you;
Who made the sun and moon to serve you, alternating,
And made night and day to serve you;
Who granted you all you asked Him.
Were you to count the bounties of God, you could not take
    stock of them.
Man is indeed wicked and most ungrateful.   14:34

Remember when Abraham said: 'My Lord, make this land safe, and avert from me and my offspring the worship of idols.
    'My Lord, they have led astray so many people. Whoso follows me is of my number; whoso disobeys me, You are All-Forgiving, Compassionate to each.
    'Our Lord, I have settled some of my progeny in a valley

where no vegetation grows, near your Sacred House, our Lord, that they may perform the prayers. So turn the hearts of some towards them, and grant them some nourishment; perhaps they will render thanks.

'Our Lord, you know what we conceal and what we proclaim. Nor is anything concealed from God on earth or in heaven.

'Praise be to God Who granted me, though old, Ishmael and Isaac! My Lord hears full well all supplications.

'My Lord, make me perform the prayer with constancy, as also some of my progeny.

'Our Lord, accept my supplication.

'Our Lord, forgive me and my parents, and the believers, on 14:41 the Day when the reckoning shall come to pass.'

Do not imagine that God is indifferent to what the wicked are doing; He is merely deferring them to a Day when their eyes shall be fixed in consternation, their necks outstretched, their heads upraised, unblinking, their hearts a mere void. Warn people of the Day when torment shall overcome them, when the wicked shall say: 'Our Lord, defer us for a little while and we will answer Your call and follow the messengers.'

But did you not swear in times past that no change of abode shall befall you?

Did you not inhabit the homes of those who wronged themselves, and was it not perfectly clear to you what We did to them? 14:45 And did We not strike parables for you?

They did indeed work their cunning, and their cunning was known to God, though their cunning was such as mountains would tumble thereat. So do not imagine that God shall fail His 14:47 promise to His messengers – God is Almighty, Avenging.

A Day shall come when the earth is recast into other than earth and heavens, when they shall all rise from the dead before God, the One, the Victorious. And you shall then see the sinners fettered head and neck in chains, their shirts of copper made, their faces all scorched by fire – that God may reward each soul with what it had earned. God is swift in reckoning.

This is a proclamation to mankind. Let them be warned thereby, and let them know that He is but One God, and let those possessed of minds remember.   14:52

Al-Hijr*

In the name of God,
Merciful to all,
Compassionate to each!

Alif Lam Ra'

Behold the verses of the Book, and a Manifest Qur'an!

It may be that unbelievers wish they were Muslims.
    Leave them alone, to eat, to enjoy themselves, and be lulled by hope, for they will surely know.
    We destroyed not any town but it had already received a well-known verdict. No nation can forestall its appointed span of time, nor can it procrastinate.   15:5

They say: 'O you upon whom the Remembrance has been sent down, you are possessed by *Jinn*! If only you could bring us the angels, if you speak the truth.'
    We only send the angels down in justice, and then they will not be held back.
    It is We Who have sent down the Remembrance, and We Who shall preserve it.
    And We have sent others before you to various groups of ancient peoples, but never did a messenger come to them except they mocked him. It is thus that We thread the matter in the

hearts of sinners: they do not believe him, and the example of
15:13 ancient nations has come and gone.

Even if We open to them a gate from heaven, and they keep
ascending through it, they will still say: 'Ah, our eyes have been
blurred, or rather we are a people bewitched.'

We set up constellations in the heavens, and made them
attractive to onlookers, and We protected them against every
execrable demon, except one who eavesdrops, and whom a
15:18 visible shooting star pursues.

We spread out the earth, and cast upon it mountains firmly
anchored, and caused vegetation to grow therein, balanced in
all its kinds.

In it We created livelihoods for you, as also for those for
whom you do not provide.

There is not anything but We have its treasures with Us, and
We send it down only in well-known proportion.

We send forth the winds, heavy laden, and We bring down
water from the sky, and give you to drink thereof, but you are
not its keepers. It is We Who give life and cause to die, We Who
shall be the inheritors.

We know those of you who came before, and We know who
shall come after.

It is your Lord Who shall muster them – He is All-Wise,
15:25 Omniscient.

We created man from dried clay, from fetid mud. The *Jinn* We
created beforehand, from the fiery wind.

Remember when your Lord said to the angels: 'I shall create
a human being from dry clay, from fetid mud. When I give him
the proper shape and breathe into him from My spirit, you are
to fall down prostrate before him.'

All the angels then bowed down before him except for Satan,
who refused to be among the prostrate.

He said: 'O Satan, why are you not among those who prostrate themselves?'

He said: 'I am not willing to prostrate myself before a human being You fashioned from dried clay, from fetid mud.'

He said: 'Depart therefrom! You are ever to be stoned. Upon you shall fall a curse until the Day of Judgement.'

He said: 'My Lord, defer me until the Day they are resurrected.'

He said: 'You shall be so deferred, until the Day of the Occurrence, well known.'

He said: 'My Lord, inasmuch as You have lured me away, I shall make the earth attractive to them, and lure them all away, except for Your sincere servants among them.'

He said: 'This is a path that lies straight before Me. Over My servants you shall have no authority except those who follow you, lured away.'   15:42

Hell is their appointed place, all of them. It has seven gates, each gate having its apportioned share of them.

But the pious are amidst gardens and springs – 'Enter therein in peace and security.'

We shall uproot all malice from their hearts, so that they become brothers, reclining on couches, face to face. No toil shall touch them, nor will they be made to leave it.

Proclaim to my servants: 'It is I Who am All-Forgiving, Compassionate to each; that My torment is the most painful.'   15:50

Proclaim to them too concerning the guests of Abraham, when they entered upon him and said: 'Peace!'

He said: 'We are wary of you.'

They said: 'Be not wary of us. We bring you tidings of a boy most knowledgeable.'

He said: 'Do you give me these tidings now that old age has touched me? What glad tidings are you giving me?'

They said: 'We brought you glad tidings in truth, so do not despair.'

He said: 'Who despairs from the mercy of his Lord except the lost?'

He said: 'So what is your business, O envoys?'

They said: 'We are sent to a sinning people, except for the family of Lot, all of whom we shall save, except his wife, for we reckon that she will be among those remaining in tor-
15:60 ment.'

When the envoys came to the family of Lot, he said: 'You are unfamiliar to me.'

They said: 'Rather, we come to you with that regarding which they doubted. We brought you the truth and we are assuredly trustworthy. So set out with your family in the course of the night, and follow in their tracks, and let none of you turn their heads back, and head towards where you have been com-manded.' And We decreed to him the verdict that the last remnant of these shall be extirpated in the morning.

And there came to him the people of that town, looking for pleasure.

He said: 'These are my guests, so do not bring scandal upon me. And fear God, and do not shame me.'

They said: 'Did we not forbid you contact with all mankind?'
15:71 He said: 'Here are my daughters, if you insist on your deed.'

By your life, they are reeling in their stupor!

So the Scream seized them at dawn, and We turned it upside down, and rained down upon it stones of baked clay. In this are signs for those who scrutinize and reflect. That town lies on a
15:77 road still in use. In this is a sign for those who have faith.

The People of the Thicket* had also been wicked. So We took revenge upon them, and both towns lie on a well-known road.

The inhabitants of al-Hijr cried lies to messengers.
And We brought them Our revelations but they turned away
    from them.

They would sculpt their habitations from rocks, living
  securely.
But the Scream seized them in the morning,
And there availed them not what once they had earned.   15:84

We created not the heavens and earth and what lies in
  between except in justice.
The Hour is sure to come, so forgive – a gracious forgiveness.
Your Lord is Author of all being, Omniscient.

We brought you the seven, oft-repeated, opening verses, and
  the Glorious Qur'an.
Cast not your eyes in longing upon what We bestowed on
  some groups among them for enjoyment.
Do not grieve for them, and lower the wing of humility to the
  believers,
And say: 'I am in truth a manifest warner.'   15:89

Likewise did We send it down upon those who apportioned
  the Book among themselves,
Who splintered the Qur'an into diverse parts.
By your Lord, We shall question them all,
Regarding what they used to do!   15:93

So let your voice resound with what you have been
  commanded,
And turn away from those who ascribe partners to God.
We have made you immune from those who mock you,
Those who associate another god with God:
They will surely know!
We know that your heart is stricken by what they say,
So glorify the praise of your Lord,
And be among those who prostrate themselves;
And worship your Lord until Certainty comes to you.   15:99

The Bees

In the name of God,
Merciful to all,
Compassionate to each!

God's edict shall come, so do not seek to hasten it.

Glory to Him, far above what they associate with Him!

He sends down the angels with the Spirit, by His command, upon whomever He wishes of His worshippers: 'Be warned! 16:2 There is no god but I, so fear Me.'

He created the heavens and earth in justice – may He be far above what they associate with Him!

He created man from a sperm drop and, behold, he becomes a manifest foe. And cattle He created, from which you derive warmth and other uses, and from which you eat. And there is beauty in them for you, when you rest them or you send them out to pasture. They carry your loads to a land you would not have reached except after much hardship. Your Lord is surely All-Gracious, Compassionate to each. Horses, mules, donkeys are there for you to ride, and an adornment. And He creates 16:8 what you know not.

It is for God to point out the right way, some of which is aslant.

Had He wished He would have guided you all.

He it is Who made water descend from the sky, of which some is for you to drink and some for trees from which you eat. With it He causes vegetation to sprout for your benefit: olives, palms and vines, and all types of fruit.

16:11   In this is a sign for a people who reflect.

He made the night to serve you as also the day, the sun, the
moon and the stars – all are made to serve by His command.

In these are signs for a people who understand.

Behold what He created for you on earth, diverse in colour.

In this is a sign for a people who remember.   16:13

It is He Who made the sea to serve you so that you may eat
from it soft flesh and extract from it jewellery for you to
wear.

Therein you can see ships ploughing through the waves, that
you may seek of His bounty – perchance you will give thanks.

He cast upon the earth towering mountains, lest it should
shake you violently, and rivers and highways – perhaps you will
be guided aright – and signposts; with the star they shall be
guided.   16:16

So then, is He Who creates the equal of one who does not? Will
you not ponder and reflect? If you were to count God's blessings,
you could not take stock of them.

God is All-Forgiving, Compassionate to each.

God knows what you conceal in your hearts and what you
declare in the open.

Those whom they worship instead of God create nothing; it
is they who are created.

Dead, not living, are they; they know not when they shall be
resurrected.   16:21

Your God is One God. Those who believe not in the hereafter,
their hearts are in denial and they grow arrogant. To be sure,
God knows what they conceal in their hearts and what they
declare in the open. He loves not the arrogant.   16:23

And if it is said to them: 'What has your Lord sent down?' they
answer: 'Fables of the ancients.' So let them shoulder their

burdens in full on the Day of Resurrection, as also the burdens of those whom they lead astray, without knowledge. Wretched
16:25   indeed is the burden they carry!

Those before them had also practised their guile but God seized their edifice from its foundations. The roof above them collapsed upon them, and the torment seized them from where they had not expected. Then, on the Day of Resurrection, He shall humiliate them and ask: 'Where are My associates concerning whom you used to dispute?' Those granted knowledge shall say: 'Today humiliation and evil are the lot of the unbelievers.'

They whom the angels carry away in death, wronging themselves – their salute shall be 'Peace!' and they shall say: 'We worked no evil.'

'Yes indeed! And God knows only too well what you used to do. So enter through the gates of hell, dwelling therein eternally.
16:29   Wretched is the resting place of the arrogant!'

Of the pious it shall be asked: 'What has your Lord sent down?' and they shall respond: 'All that is good to those who in this world performed good deeds, but the Abode of the Hereafter is better.'

Happy is the Abode of the pious: the Gardens of Eden that they enter, beneath which rivers flow, in which they shall find all that they desire. Thus does God reward the pious. It is they whom the angels carry away in death, being pure. They tell them: 'Peace be upon you! Enter the Garden in recompense for
16:32   your deeds.'

What can they expect save that the angels shall seize them, or else the decree of your Lord shall pass upon them? This too was what those before them had done. Nor did God wrong them; rather, it was themselves they wronged. The sins they committed shall assail them, and engulfing them shall be that which before
16:34   they used to mock!

Those who associate others with God say: 'Had God willed, we would not have worshipped anything apart from Him, neither us nor our ancestors, nor would we have sanctified anything apart from Him.'

This too is how men before them used to act. Are messengers enjoined to do anything other than deliver a manifest message?

To every nation We sent a messenger: 'Worship God and keep away from idol worship.' Some of them God guided aright; some deserved to be led astray. So journey in the land and observe how the fate of the deniers turned out. Even though you may be concerned that they be guided aright, God guides not whomever He leads astray, nor shall they have any advocate. 16:37

They swore a mighty oath that God does not resurrect the dead.

Yes indeed! Truly a promise He shall keep!

But most of mankind do not understand.

He shall make clear to them what once they argued about, and so the unbelievers will come to admit that they are liars. 16:39

In truth, it is merely Our saying to something, if We wish it to happen, to say to it: 'Be!' and it is.

As for those who emigrated in the cause of God, after they had been wronged, We shall settle them in this world in a good abode, but the reward of the hereafter is greater, if only they knew; so too those who are patient and who put their trust in their Lord. 16:42

We sent not before you save men to whom We revealed – ask the People who possess the Remembrance, if you yourselves do not know – clear signs and the Psalms. Upon you We sent down the Remembrance, to make clear to mankind what has been sent down to them – perhaps they will reflect. 16:44

Those who work their cunning in evil deeds – do they feel secure that God will not make the earth cave in upon them? Nor that a torment will seize them from where they had not expected? Nor seize them as they travel to and fro? They cannot escape Him. Or might He seize them while in a state of fearful expectancy?

16:47   Your Lord is All-Tender, Compassionate to each.

Have they not observed all the things God has created?
    How they cast their shadows left and right, bowing to God in humility?
    To God bow what are in the heavens and earth of things that tread the ground, as also the angels, who display no arrogance.
    They fear their Lord above them, and carry out what they are
16:50 commanded.

God said: 'Take not to yourselves two gods; there is but One God. It is Me you must fear.'
To Him belongs whatever is in the heavens or on earth,
His is the religion eternal.
Is it other than God that you fear?
Whatever blessings you possess come from God.
And then, when harm touches you, to Him you howl in
    prayer.
    But then, when He sweeps away that harm, behold, a group among you associate others with your Lord, to blaspheme against what We bestowed upon them.
16:55   So go and enjoy yourselves, for you shall surely know!

And yet they dedicate to what they know not a portion of what We bestowed upon them! By God, you shall be questioned concerning the lies you fabricated!

And they ascribe daughters to God! Glory be to Him! But they shall have what they desire!

Yet, when one of them is brought tidings of an infant girl, his face turns dark, suppressing his vexation. He keeps out of people's sight, because of the evil news he was greeted with. Will he retain the infant, in disgrace, or will he bury it in haste in the ground? Wretched indeed is their decision!   16:59

To those who do not believe in the hereafter belongs the evil attribute; to God belongs the loftiest of attributes. He is Almighty, All-Wise.

If God were to hold mankind to account for their wrongdoing, He would not leave alive one single creature that treads the earth. He merely defers them until a stated time. When their time arrives they can neither delay it nor bring it forward, even by an instant.   16:61

They ascribe to God what they themselves dislike, and their tongues recount the falsehood that theirs is the best inheritance.
  No indeed! The Fire is theirs by right, and they shall be abandoned and forgotten!
  By God, We sent to nations before you, but Satan embellished their deeds in their eyes; so now he is their patron, and there awaits them a painful torment.   16:63

We sent down the Book upon you only to make clear to them what they disputed about, as a Guidance and a mercy to a people who have faith. And God sends down water from the sky by which He revives the earth after it has died.
  In this is a sign to a people who listen.
  In cattle too there is a lesson for you. We give you to drink from their entrails, in between the filth and the blood, pure milk, tasty to those who drink.
  And from the fruit of palm trees and vines you derive intoxicants as well as a goodly provision.
  In this is a sign for a people who understand.   16:67

Your Lord inspired the bees: 'Take the mountains for your habitation, as also the trees and what they erect on a trellis. Then eat of all fruits and follow the paths of your Lord, made easy for you.' From their entrails comes a drink, of diverse colours, in which there is a remedy for mankind.

16:69   In this is a sign for a people who reflect.

And it is God Who created you and then causes you to die.

Among you is one who shall be reduced to a degrading old age so that, once having known, he comes to know nothing. God is Omniscient, Omnipotent.

God has preferred some of you over others in bounty. Those granted preference will not turn over their bounty to their bondsmen, so as to share it in equity. Do they repudiate the

16:71   blessing of God?

And it is God Who assigned to you, from your own number, spouses, and reared for you from spouses children and grandchildren, and provided you with goodly provisions. Will they then believe in falsehood, and blaspheme against God's blessings?

And yet they worship, instead of God, that which has no provision whatever to grant them, in heaven or on earth! Nor are they able to do so!

So do not strike similes for God; He knows and you do not

16:74   know.

God strikes a simile: a bonded slave who has no power over anything, and a person whom We granted a goodly provision, from which he expends in secret and in the open. Are these two equal? Praise be to God! But most of them have no knowledge.

God strikes a simile of two men: one is dumb with no power over anything, and is a burden to his guardian. Wherever he sends him, he brings back nothing good. Is such the equal of one who commands justice and is set upon a straight path? 16:76

To God belongs the Unseen of the heavens and the earth. The Hour, in reality, is like the blink of an eye, or even closer. God has power over all things.

It is God Who brought you forth from the bellies of your mothers, knowing nothing. And it is He Who created your hearing, your sight and your hearts. Perhaps you will render thanks. 16:78

Have they not observed the birds, made subservient in the sphere of the sky, whom only God can control? In this are signs for a people of faith.

It is God Who made your homes to be places of rest, Who made for you of cattle-skins tents you find light to carry when you travel and where you put up; and from their wool, furs, and hair furnishings and enjoyment, for a while. 16:80

It is God Who made for you, among what He created, the shades, and made the mountains for you places wherein to hide, and made for you shirts to protect you from the heat, and other shirts to protect you in battle. Thus does He complete His bounty upon you; perhaps you will submit to Him.

If they turn away, yours is only to convey a manifest message. They recognize the blessings of God and then repudiate them, and most of them are unbelievers. 16:83

A Day shall come when We resurrect from every nation a witness – and then the unbelievers shall not be permitted to repent, nor be allowed to return to God's favour. When wrongdoers catch sight of the torment, this will not be lessened for them, nor will they be kept waiting. When those who associate catch sight of their associates, they shall say: 'Our Lord, these are our associates whom we used to worship instead of You.' And these shall retort: 'You are indeed liars.' On that Day, they shall 16:87 submit to God, and that which they fabricated will desert them.

And those who blasphemed and obstructed the path to God – We shall multiply for them torment upon torment because of the corruption they worked.

A Day shall come when We resurrect from every nation a witness from their number. And you We shall summon as a witness for these people. We have made the Book to descend upon you, a clear explanation for all things, a Guidance, a mercy and glad 16:89 tidings to the Muslims.

God commands justice, virtue and generosity to kin.
    He forbids debauchery, abomination and injustice.
    He counsels you; perhaps you will remember.

Fulfil the compact of God if you enter into a compact, and do not renege on your oaths once affirmed: you have made God a surety for you. God knows what you do. And do not be like the woman who unravels her weaving, once made fast, into shreds. You consider the oaths you swear among yourselves as trickery, whenever one party is more numerous than another. But God will assuredly put you to the test because of this, and on the Day of Resurrection He will make fully clear to you what you 16:92 once disputed about.

Had God willed, He would have made you a single nation. But He leads astray whom He wills and guides whom He wills, and you will surely be questioned concerning that which you used to do. Do not consider the oaths you swear among yourselves as trickery, lest a foot should slip once it has been firmly set, and you come to taste evil because you obstructed the way to 16:94 God. Great torment awaits you.

Do not barter the covenant of God for a paltry sum. What is with God is better for you, if only you knew.

What is with you comes to an end; what is with God remains for ever.

Indeed, We shall recompense the patient with their wages, in accordance with the best of their deeds. Whoever does good, male or female, while having faith, We shall make him live a decent life, and We shall recompense them with their wages, in accordance with the best of their deeds.   16:97

When you read the Qur'an, seek refuge in God against Satan, ever to be stoned. He has no power over those who believe and place their trust in God. His power is solely over those who take him for their master, and who, because of him, associate others with God. And when We substitute one verse in place of another – and God knows best what He reveals – they say: 'You are simply lying.' But most of them have no understanding. Say: 'It is the Holy Spirit that sends it down from your Lord with the Truth, to confirm the believers, and as guidance and glad tidings to the Muslims.'   16:102

We know that they say: 'A mere human is teaching him.'

The speech of him to whom they allude is foreign, but this is clear Arabic speech.

As for those who do not believe in the revelations of God, God guides them not, and painful torment awaits them. Indeed, it is only those who do not believe in God's revelations who fabricate lies; they are the real liars. Whoso disbelieves in God after his belief – except for one forced to recant though his heart is firm of faith – or else whoever expands his heart with unbelief, upon them shall fall the wrath of God, and a mighty torment awaits them. This is because they fancied the present life above the hereafter; but God guides not the unbelievers. It is they whom God has put a seal upon their hearts, their hearing and their sight. They are the heedless. No doubt about it: in the hereafter

16:109 they shall be the losers.

And then your Lord – to those who emigrated following the ordeal they suffered, then exerted themselves and bore with patience – to them your Lord shall henceforth be All-Forgiving, Compassionate to each. That shall be upon a Day when every soul shall come forward to argue its own case, and every soul shall receive its proper reward for what it did. Nor shall they be

16:111 wronged.

God strikes a simile: a town, once secure and content, its livelihood coming to it in plenty from all directions, which then blasphemes the blessings of God. He made it taste the raiment of hunger and fear because of what they did. A messenger came to them, of their own number, but they called him a liar, so torment seized them as they sinned.

Therefore, eat from what God provided you with, licit and tasty, and give thanks for God's blessings if it is Him you worship. In truth, He forbade you carrion, blood and the flesh of swine, and whatever is consecrated to what is other than God. But if one is compelled, and is not deliberately sinning, nor transgressing, then God is All-Forgiving, Compassionate to each.

And do not say, when your tongues utter lies: 'This is licit and this is illicit,' seeking to fabricate lies from God. Those who fabricate lies from God shall not succeed. A little enjoyment

16:117 they shall have, but painful torment awaits them.

For the Jews We pronounced illicit what We related to you beforehand. We wronged them not; it was their own selves they wronged. But then your Lord – to those who committed evil unknowingly and later repented and made good – your Lord

16:119 shall thereafter be All-Forgiving, Compassionate to each.

Abraham was himself a nation, devoted to God, of pristine faith, and was not an idol worshipper. He rendered thanks for God's blessings, and God chose him and guided him to a straight path. And We brought him in this life much good, and in the hereafter he is among the righteous. Then We revealed to you: follow the religion of Abraham, of pristine faith, who was not an idol worshipper. The Sabbath was merely appointed for those who disputed concerning it, and your Lord shall pass judgement on the Day of Resurrection concerning that over which they used to dispute. 16:124

Call to the way of your Lord with wisdom and fair counsel, and debate with them in the fairest manner. Your Lord knows best who has strayed from His path; He knows best who are guided aright.

And if you punish, you are to punish with the like of what you were punished; but if you bear with patience, then best it is for the patient. 16:126

Bear with patience, for your patience comes solely from God.

Sorrow not for them, nor be vexed by the guile they practise.

Gods stands with the pious and with those who are virtuous.

The Journey by Night

In the name of God,
Merciful to all,
Compassionate to each!

Glory be to Him Who carried His servant by night from the Sacred Mosque to the Furthest Mosque,* whose precincts We have blessed, to show him of Our wonders! He it is Who is All-Hearing, All-Seeing! 17:1

We brought Moses the Book and made it a guidance to the Children of Israel: 'Take none for protector instead of Me.' They were the progeny of those We made to embark with Noah. 17:3 He was in truth a thankful servant.

And We decreed to the Children of Israel in the Book: 'You shall corrupt the earth twice, and shall soar to a great height. When the time came for the first of two promises, We sent against you servants of Ours, of great might, and they marched across your habitations, shedding blood – a promise fulfilled. Then We granted you the counter-attack against them and provided you with wealth and progeny, and made you more numerous as a troop. If you do good, you do good to your own selves, and if you do evil, likewise. When the second promise arrived, We sent against you servants of Ours, to abase your faces, to break into the temple as they did once before and to destroy utterly whatever they laid their hands upon. Perhaps your Lord will show you mercy; but if you begin again, We too shall begin 17:8 again. We have made hell a dungeon for the unbelievers.'

This Qur'an guides to a path most straight, and proclaims glad tidings to believers who do righteous deeds that theirs is a reward surpassing; that for them who believe not in the hereafter We have prepared a torment most painful.

Man prays for evil as he prays for good;
17:11 Man has ever been impatient.

We made night and day to be two wonders, and We erase the wonder of night and cause the wonder of day to appear to the eyes, so that you may seek bounty from your Lord, and learn the computation of years and accounts. All things have We clarified most clearly.
     Upon each human being We have fastened his bird around his neck, and on the Day of Resurrection We bring out for him 17:13 a book which he finds spread out before him.

Read your Book. Let your own soul suffice you now as
    accountant.
He who is guided, is guided solely for his own well-being;
And he who strays, strays only for his own loss.
No soul burdened with sin can carry the burden of another;
Nor do We inflict torment before We have sent a messenger.

If We desire to destroy a town, We order its men of luxury,
and they indulge in sin, so Our just decree comes to pass upon
it, and We destroy it utterly.   17:16

How many a generation We destroyed after Noah!

Let your Lord suffice as One All-Versed, All-Seeing, as to the
sins of His servants!

He who desires this fleeting world, We fleetingly grant him
therein whatever We please, to whomever We desire, and then
We consign him to hell – there to be scorched, disgraced,
confuted!

And he who desires the hereafter, and pursues it as it should
be pursued, being a man of faith, these – their pursuit shall be
worthy of all praise.

To both this group and that We provide from the bounty of
your Lord; nor is the bounty of your Lord ever held back.

Consider how We preferred some to others; but the hereafter
is assuredly higher in degree, and greatly to be preferred.

Take not with God another deity, or you will end up disgraced, thwarted.   17:22

Your Lord decrees: that you worship none but Him, and
graciousness to parents.

If they attain old age with you, either or both, say not to
them: 'Phew!' and do not scold them but speak to them words
of kindness.

And lower to them the wing of humility, out of compassion,
and say: 'My Lord, grant them mercy, as they raised me up
when I was young.'   17:24

Your Lord knows best what lies in your souls; if you are virtuous, He is All-Forgiving to those who turn back to Him.

Give kinsmen their due, as also the poor and the wayfarer. But do not squander and dissipate, for squanderers are the brothers of devils. And Satan has ever been ungrateful to his Lord.

And if you turn away from them, seeking a mercy from your Lord which you hope for, speak to them words of comfort.

17:28

Let not your hand be chained to your neck, nor spread it out as far as it extends, or else you will end up worthy of blame, regretful. Your Lord spreads out His bounty to whomever He wills – and withholds it. In respect of His servants, He is All-Versed, All-Seeing.

17:30

And do not kill your infants for fear of poverty; it is We Who provide for them as well as you. Killing them is a mighty sin.

Do not come near to adultery; it is debauchery and a wretched path to follow.

Do not kill the soul which God declares hallowed except in justice. Whoever is killed unjustly, We have granted authority to his guardian. But he should not exceed the limit in killing, for he has already obtained divine support.

17:33

Do not come near the property of orphans, except in the fairest manner, until the orphan attains manhood. Be faithful to your compacts, for a compact shall be a thing questioned about. Be fair in measures when you measure out, and weigh with a balance that is true: that would be better and more rewarding.

17:35

Follow not what you have no knowledge of: hearing, sight and the heart – all of these a person shall be questioned about.

Do not stride forth jauntily on earth: you will not thereby traverse the earth, nor reach up to the mountains in height.

All these are a sin in God's sight, and hateful.

This is part of what your Lord has revealed to you of Wisdom.

Take not with God another deity, else you will be cast in hell, blameworthy and thwarted. Did God favour you with boys and made the angels female? You are uttering an enormity!   17:40

We have detailed in this Qur'an all manner of things, that they might ponder and remember, but it only increases them in their distaste of it.

Say: 'Had there been with Him other gods, as they allege, then they would have sought access to the Master of the throne.'

Glory be to Him! May He be far, far above what they utter!

The seven heavens and the earth sing His praises, and all who are therein. There is nothing that does not sing His praise, but you do not understand their songs of praise. Surely He is All-Forbearing, All-Forgiving.   17:44

When you recite the Qur'an, We place between you and those who do not believe in the hereafter an impenetrable screen. Upon their hearts We draped veils lest they understand it, and in their ears heaviness. Should you happen to mention in the Qur'an that your Lord is One, they turn tail, and withdraw in aversion.   17:46

We know best what they listen to, when they listen to you, conspiring together, and when the wicked say: 'You are merely following a man bewitched.'

Look how they strike similes for you and go astray, unable to find the right path.

They say: 'Are we, having turned into bones and dust, to be resurrected as a new creation?'

Say: 'Whether you be stones or iron, or any other created thing which looms large in your minds!'

They will say: 'Who shall bring us back to life?'

Say: 'He Who created you in the first place.'

They will shake their heads at you in disbelief, and say: 'When will this be?'

Say: 'Perhaps it will be soon; upon a Day when He will call out to you and you will respond by praising Him, imagining 17:52 that you lasted but a short span on earth.'

Tell My servants to say only what is right and proper, for Satan stirs dissension among them; assuredly Satan is to man a manifest enemy. Your Lord knows you best: if He wishes, He will show you mercy, or if He wishes, He will torment you. We sent you not as guardian over them. Your Lord knows best who is in the heavens and on earth. We preferred some prophets over 17:55 others and brought David the Psalms.

Say: 'Call upon those you allege are gods apart from God, but they shall have no power to remove harm from you, nor turn it away.' Those whom they worship are themselves seeking a path to God as to who shall be nearest to Him. They hope for His mercy and fear His torment; the torment of your Lord is truly 17:57 to be feared.

No town there is but We shall destroy it before the Day of Resurrection, or else torment it with a grievous torment. For this is inscribed in the Book. Nothing prevented us from sending down miracles except that the ancients called them lies. We brought Thamud the she-camel, an evident miracle, but they 17:59 repudiated it. We send down miracles only to inspire awe.

Remember when We said to you that your Lord encompasses mankind in His knowledge. Nor did We make the vision We showed you except as a test to people, as also the accursed tree in the Qur'an.

We frighten them, but this renders them ever more arrogant.

Remember when We said to the angels: 'Bow down before Adam,' so they bowed, all but Iblis,* who said: 'Am I to bow to what You created of clay?'

He said: 'Do You see this creature You honoured above me? If You defer me till the Day of Resurrection, I will chew up his progeny, except for a few.'

He said: 'Depart! Whoso follows you of their number, hell will be your reward, a reward unstinted. And dazzle whomever you can of them with your voice, and yell out to them with your cavalry and footmen. Share with them their property and their progeny, and give them hope – but Satan's hope is mere illusion. Over My servants you shall have no dominion: let your Lord suffice as guardian.'

It is your Lord Who drives on ships at sea for your sake, that you may seek of His bounty. To you He has ever been Compassionate. When calamity touches you at sea, they are nowhere to be found – those you call upon instead of Him. And if He should deliver you safely to shore, you turn away from Him. Man is truly ungrateful.

Are you so confident He will not, when on land, make the earth cave in beneath you, or send you a fire storm from which you will find no protector?

Or are you so sure He will not, once more, send you back to sea, where He will unleash upon you a devastating hurricane, drowning you for your ingratitude, whereupon you will find none to plead your case before Us?

We honoured the progeny of Adam and carried them on land and sea.

We provisioned them with delicacies and preferred them far above many whom We had created.

A Day shall come when We shall call each community through

its Book of Guidance. He who is given his record-book with his right hand – these shall read their record-book, and shall not be wronged one jot. Whoso is blind in this world, in the hereafter 17:72 he shall be even more blind and more astray from the path.

There was a time when they almost beguiled you away from what We had revealed to you, to falsely ascribe to Us something different, whereupon they would have taken you for a friend. Had We not made you stand firm, you were about to lean a little towards them. Had you done so, We would have made you taste a double torment in this world, and double after death, and then you would have found no one to help you against Us. Again, they were about to provoke you so as to drive you away from the land; but had they succeeded, they would not have lasted after you except for a short while. Such was the precedent among those of Our messengers We sent before you – and never 17:77 will you find Our precedent to vary!

Perform the prayer at the setting of the sun and until darkness of night and the Recitation of dawn – the Recitation of dawn is always witnessed from on high. For part of the night, wake up and recite – an act of supererogation for you. Perhaps your Lord will resurrect you in a commendable station.

And say: 'My Lord, lead me in through a gate of truth, and lead me out through a gate of truth, and grant me, from where You are, power and support.'

And say: 'The Truth has come and falsehood is stifled – 17:81 falsehood shall ever be stifled.'

We send down from the Qur'an what is a remedy and a mercy to the faithful, but it only increases sinners in perdition.

When We send down Our blessings upon man, he turns away, and moves to the side, but when evil touches him he becomes despondent.

Say: 'Each person acts according to what befits him, but your 17:84 Lord knows best who is better guided on the way.'

They ask you about the soul.

Say: 'The soul belongs to the realm of my Lord, and of knowledge you have been granted but little.'

If We wish, We can do away with what We revealed to you, whereupon you will find none to champion you before Us in this matter, unless it be a mercy from your Lord. His grace towards you has indeed been abundant.

Say: 'Were humans and *Jinn* to band together to produce a semblance of this Qur'an, they could not do so, even if they back one another up.'   17:88

In this Qur'an, We have elucidated to mankind every sort of parable, but most people will assent to nothing but blasphemy.

They say: 'We will not trust you unless you cause a spring to gush forth for us from the ground; or else you come to own a garden of palm trees and vines, and you cause rivers to gush forth in torrents through it all; or you make the sky fall upon us in bits and pieces, as you allege; or you summon God and the angels in our presence; or else you come to own a house made of gold; or you ascend to the sky – nor will we trust your ascent unless you bring down upon us a book we can read.'

Say: 'Glory be to my Lord! Am I anything other than a human being, a Messenger?'   17:93

Nothing prevented mankind from believing, when Guidance came to them, except their saying: 'Did God really send a mere human as Messenger?'

Say: 'Had earth been peopled by angels, walking about, their minds at ease, We would have sent down upon them from heaven an angel as messenger.'

Say: 'Let God suffice as witness between me and you – with His worshippers He is All-Versed, All-Seeing.'   17:96

He whom God guides is truly guided; he whom He leads astray, for him you shall find no protectors apart from Him. We shall herd them, tumbled upon their faces, on the Day of Resurrection

– blind, dumb and deaf. Their refuge will be hell; whenever its flames subside, We intensify the blaze upon them. This shall be their punishment for having blasphemed against Our revelations, and their saying: 'Can it really be, when we are bones and 17:98   dust, that we shall be resurrected as a new creation?'

Do they not realize that God, Who created the heavens and the earth, is capable of creating their like, and appointing for them a term of life, of which there is no doubt? And yet the wicked will assent to nothing but blasphemy.

Say: 'Had you possessed the treasures of my Lord's mercy, you would have held them back, for fear of spending; man has 17:100   always been miserly.'

To Moses We brought nine clear wonders – ask the Children of Israel. When he came to them, Pharaoh said to him: 'O Moses, I believe you are a man bewitched.'

He said: 'You know well that what brought down these wonders is none other than the Lord of the heavens and earth – thereby to open all eyes. O Pharaoh, I believe you are a man lost to virtue.'

So he planned to drive them out of the land, but We drowned him, he and all who were with him. Thereafter, We said to the Children of Israel: 'Inhabit the land, and when the promise of the hereafter is fulfilled, We shall summon you forth, all in a 17:104   swarm.'

With the Truth We sent it down, and with the Truth it
    descended.
We sent you only as a herald of glad tidings, and a warner.
    And a Qur'an We divided in distinct parts, so that you may 17:106   recite it to people, unhurriedly. And We revealed it in succession.

Say: 'Whether you believe in it or you do not, those to whom Knowledge was sent before it, when it is recited to them, sink down to their faces in prostration, saying: "Glory be to our

Lord! The promise of our Lord will surely come about."' They
sink down to their faces, weeping, and it increases them in piety.   17:109

Say: 'Call upon God or call upon the All-Merciful: whichever
you call upon, to Him belong the names most glorious.'

Do not raise your voice in prayer, nor whisper it, but seek a
middle way between. And say: 'Praise be to God, Who took no
child to Himself, nor has a partner in His dominion, nor ever
had a protector against humiliation.'

And magnify Him – magnify Him above all else!   17:111

The Cave

In the name of God,
Merciful to all,
Compassionate to each!

Praise be to God, Who brought down the Book upon His
  servant, and rendered it free from distortion, unswerving,
To give warning of grievous wrath from on high,
And announce glad tidings to the faithful who perform good
  deeds, that a fair reward awaits them, therein dwelling for
  ever,
And to warn those who claim that God took a child to
  Himself.
Of this matter they have no knowledge, neither did their
  forefathers.
Blasphemous indeed is the word that issues from their mouths!
  They utter a mere falsehood.
And will you, perchance, torture yourself by following in their
  footsteps, if they do not believe in this discourse, in grief
  for them?   18:6

We fashioned what lies upon the earth as an ornament for it, to test them as to who shall be the best in works. And We shall turn all that lies upon it into a desolate plain.

Or did you imagine that the People of the Cave and al-Raqim* were a unique wonder among Our revelations?

Remember when the youths took refuge in a cave, saying: 'Our Lord, bring down upon us mercy from on high, and make it easy for us to find the right way to follow in this matter.'

So We sealed their ears in the cave for a number of years, then We brought them forth in order to learn which of the two 18:12   groups was more accurate as to the time they spent.

We shall now narrate to you their story, in truth.

They were youths who believed in their Lord, and whom We increased in guidance. And We strengthened their hearts when they rose up, saying: 'Our Lord, Lord of the heavens and earth! We shall call upon no other god besides Him, else we utter a falsehood. These our people have taken to themselves gods apart from Him. If only they could show some manifest proof for them! But who is more wicked than he who fabricates lies from God? And now, having abandoned them and what they worship other than God, let us take refuge in a cave, and God will spread out His mercy and make it easy for you to find the prudent path 18:16   to follow in this matter.'

And you would have seen the sun, as it arose, veering away from their cave on the right, and, as it set, cutting them out of its path on the left, they being in a cavity therein.

That was a wonder of God.

He whom God guides is truly guided; he whom He leads astray, for him you shall find no protector, no mentor.

And you would have imagined them to be awake as they slept on. And We would turn them from right side to left, as their dog spread its paws across the entrance. If only you had seen them, you would have turned and fled from them, filled with terror of them. Thus did We make them rise up again, to question one another.

Said one of them: 'How long did you remain thus?'

They said: 'We remained for a day, or a part thereof.'

He said: 'Your Lord knows best how long you remained. So send out one of you, with this your silver money, to the city, and let him find out which is the tastiest of food, and let him bring back to you a provision of it. Let him be discreet, and let no one know of your presence. For, if they catch sight of you, they will stone you or force you back into their religion, and thus you will never prevail.'

18:20

Nevertheless, We divulged their presence, that they might know that God's promise is true and that the Hour shall come, no doubt about it.

Remember when they argued among themselves, saying: 'Build on top of them a structure – their Lord knows best about them.' Those who won the argument said: 'Let us build on top of them a house of prayer.'

They shall say: 'They were three in number, their dog a fourth.' Others will say: 'They were five in number, their dog a sixth' – predicting the Unseen. Yet others will say: 'Seven, their dog an eighth.'

Say: 'My Lord knows best what their number was, and none knows it but a few.' So do not dispute this issue with them except in a superficial manner, and do not solicit the opinion of any of them concerning their number.

18:22

And do not say of anything: 'I shall do this tomorrow' unless you add: 'If God wills.' And remember your Lord if you forget, and say: 'Perhaps my Lord will guide me to a path nearer than this in righteousness.'

18:24

They remained in their cave for three hundred years, to which were added nine.

Say: 'God knows how long they remained. To Him belongs the Unseen in the heavens and earth. How He sees all! How He hears all! Apart from Him they have no protector, nor does He associate anyone with Him in His judgement.'

And recite what has been revealed to you from the Book of your Lord; no change shall come over His words, nor will you ever find a berth, apart from Him. And confine yourself to those who call upon their Lord, morning and evening, seeking His face. Let not your eyes wander beyond them, seeking the luxuries of this present life. And do not obey him whose heart We have sealed from the mention of Our name, and who followed his whims. His cause is lost.

Say: 'The truth has come from your Lord. Whoso wishes, let him believe; whoso wishes, let him blaspheme.' To the wicked We have prepared a Fire, with its wall surrounding it. When they cry out for help, they are helped to water resembling molten metal, scorching their faces. Wretched that drink and wretched
18:29 that place of rest!

As for those who believed and performed good deeds – We waste not the wage of one righteous in works. To them belong the Gardens of Eden, beneath which rivers flow, and in which they shall be decked with bracelets of gold, and shall wear green raiment of silk and brocade, reclining therein on couches. Happy
18:31 that reward and happy that place of rest!

Strike for them a parable of two men. To one of them We allotted two gardens of vine, which We surrounded with palms, and We placed a cultivated field in between. Both gardens produced their harvest in full, diminishing it not one bit. Through them both We caused a river to gush forth.

One of them gathered his fruit and said to his companion, in conversation: 'I am greater in wealth than you are and more powerful in kin.' So he entered his garden, having wronged himself, and said: 'I imagine that this will never become desolate. I doubt that the Hour shall come. And if I am ever returned to my Lord, I shall find something even better than it as a final destination.'

His companion said to him, in conversation: 'Are you blaspheming against Him Who created you from clay, then from a sperm, then fashioned you into a man? Assuredly, it is God my Lord, and I associate none with Him. If only you had entered your garden and said: "This is the will of God! There is no strength save in God!" If you see me inferior to you in wealth and offspring, perhaps my Lord will bring me what is better than your garden. Or perhaps He will cast down upon it thunderbolts from the sky, and it will become a slippery plain. Or perhaps its waters will sink into the earth, and you will not be able to make use of them.'

18:41

So his fruit was utterly consumed. And he began to wring his hands for what he had spent upon it, while it lay bereft of its trestles. And he said: 'If only I had never associated anyone with my Lord!' He had no band to support him, apart from God, nor could he escape God's might. It is there where the dominion of the true God is seen: He is greater in reward and more beneficent in destiny.

18:44

Strike for them a parable of this present life. It is like water We caused to descend from the sky, with which the vegetation of the earth was mingled. But it turned into chaff, scattered by the winds. God has power over all things.

Property and progeny are the ornament of this present life, but those things that abide, virtuous deeds, are better in reward with your Lord, and better in prospect.

A Day shall come when We shall cause mountains to heave, when you shall see the earth flattened. And We shall herd them all, and shall not overlook any of them. They shall be passed in

review before your Lord, in line: 'So now you come to Us just
as We created you the first time. Or do you claim that We have
18:48   not assigned an appointed time for you?'

The Book shall be laid out, and you will see sinners afraid of
what it contains. They shall say: 'Alas for us! What is it with
this Book that neglects no matter, trivial or weighty, but it
records in detail?' They shall find what they committed displayed before them, and your Lord shall wrong no one.

And remember when God said to the angels: 'Kneel before
Adam'; they knelt, all except Iblis, for he was from the *Jinn*. He
defied the command of his Lord: 'Will you then take him and
his progeny as protectors instead of Me, when they are your
enemies? Wretched for sinners is this barter!'

I did not make them witness the creation of the heavens and
earth, nor witness their own creation. Nor would I ever take
18:51   those who lead astray to be My supporters.

Upon that Day, He shall say: 'Call on My associates, those that
you allege.' They will call on them, but they will not respond to
them. Between them We have set a valley of destruction. The
evil ones shall see the Fire, and will know for sure that they are
18:53   about to tumble into it, but from it they shall find no deliverance.

In this Qur'an, We have elucidated to mankind every sort of
parable, and man is, of all beings, the most argumentative.
    What prevents mankind from believing, now that Guidance
has come to them, or from seeking the forgiveness of their Lord,
unless it be the example of the ancients that will overwhelm
them, or else they be overwhelmed by imminent torment? We
send messengers only as heralds of glad tidings and warners.
But those who disbelieve use false arguments in order to refute
the truth. They have taken My verses, and the warnings they
18:56   received, as a laughing matter.

Who is more wicked than he who, when reminded of the wonders of his Lord, turns his face away from them, and forgets what his hands had committed beforehand? Upon their hearts We draped veils lest they understand it, and in their ears heaviness. And were you to call them to right guidance, they will never be guided.

Your Lord, All-Forgiving, Abounding in mercy – were He to hold them to account for what they earned, He would hasten torment upon them. Indeed, an appointed time is set for them, and they shall find no escape from it.

These cities We destroyed when they sinned, and set an appointed time for their destruction.   18:59

Remember when Moses said to his youthful attendant: 'I shall not pause until I reach the place where two seas meet, even if I journey for years to come.'

When they arrived at the place where two seas meet, they forgot their fish, which headed for the sea, slinking away.

When they had passed beyond, Moses said to his attendant: 'Bring us our food, for we have met with much toil on our journey.'

He said: 'Do you recall when we sheltered by the rock? I forgot the fish and none but Satan made me forget it. And so it headed into the sea, a wonder to behold.'

He said: 'This is just what we were seeking.'

So they turned back, retracing their steps.   18:64

And they came upon one of Our servants, to whom We had shown mercy, and to whom We from on high had brought knowledge.

Moses said to him: 'What if I follow you, provided you teach me what you have been taught, as a way to truth?'

He said: 'My company you cannot endure.

'How can you endure a knowledge not granted to you?'

He said: 'You will find me, God willing, a man of endurance; nor will I ever disobey your command.'

He said: 'If you follow me, you are not to ask me about
18;70 anything until I make mention of it to you.'

So they set off, and once aboard a ship, he scuttled it.

He said: 'Do you scuttle it to drown its passengers? You have
done a terrible deed!'

He said: 'Did I not tell you that you cannot endure my
company?'

He said: 'Take me not to task for what I forgot, and do not
18;73 overburden me with difficulties.'

So they set off until, meeting with a youth, he killed him.

He said: 'Did you kill an innocent soul, and not in revenge
for another? You have done an execrable deed!'

He said: 'Did I not tell you that you cannot endure my
company?'

He said: 'If I ask you about anything hereafter, deny me
your company, for you have reached the limit of forgiveness
18;76 with me.'

So they set off until, reaching the people of a town, they begged
its people for food, but they refused to offer them hospitality.
In it they found a wall about to collapse and he repaired it.

He said: 'Had you wished, you could have obtained a wage
for it.'

He said: 'Here then is the parting of ways between me and
you. I shall tell you the interpretation of what you could not
endure.

'Regarding the ship, it belonged to poor people working in
the sea, and I wanted to make it defective; beyond them was a
king who seized every ship, unlawfully.

'As to the youth, his parents were believers, and we feared he
might overburden them with his arrogance and blasphemy. So
we wished that their Lord would give them in exchange one
more pure than him in character, and more caring towards
his kin.

'As to the wall, it belonged to two young orphans in the city. Beneath it was a treasure belonging to them. Their father was a man of virtue. So your Lord wished that they attain to maturity and extract the treasure, as a mercy from your Lord. I did not do it of my own free will.

'This then is the interpretation of what you could not endure.'   18:82

They ask you about the two-horned, Dhu'l Qarnayn.*

Say: 'I shall recite to you some mention of him.'

We had established him firmly on earth, and granted him a path to the knowledge of all things.

So he followed a path.

Until, when he reached the place of the sun's setting, he found it setting in a pool of hot water, and there he found a people.

We said: 'O Dhu'l Qarnayn, either you torment them or you follow with them the way of virtue.'

He said: 'Whoso is wicked we shall torment. Then he will be turned over to his Lord, Who will torment him with grievous torment. Whoso is faithful and does good deeds, to him belongs a reward most fair, and to him we shall teach some of what we know.'   18:88

Then he followed a path.

Until, when he reached the rising of the sun, he found it to rise on a people for whom We had provided no shelter from it. Thus did We encompass in our knowledge all that he achieved.   18:91

Then he followed a path.

Until, when he reached between two towering barriers, he found nearby a people barely able to understand human speech.

They said: 'O Dhu'l Qarnayn, Gog and Magog are working corruption on earth. Shall we pay you a wage in return for your building us a barrier between us and them?'

He said: 'What my Lord enables me to do is of His bounty. So help me with all your might and I will construct a dam between you and them. Bring me large lumps of iron.'

Until, when he made the two sides equal, he said: 'Blow hard upon it.' When he turned it into something like fire, he said: 'Bring me molten brass to pour on it.' They could not climb over it, nor were they able to tunnel through it.

He said: 'This is an act of grace from my Lord, but when the promise of my Lord is fulfilled, He shall level it to the ground –
18:98 my Lord's promise is ever true.'

On that Day, We shall abandon them, to swarm one against another. And the Trumpet shall be sounded, and We shall herd them all together.

On that Day, We shall open hell to the unbelievers' view, all in one view. It is they whose eyes were veiled from My remembrance, and who were incapable of hearing.

Did they who disbelieved imagine that they could adopt My servants as protectors instead of Me? To the unbelievers, We
18:102 have prepared hell as a resting place.

Say: 'Shall We inform you who are the greatest losers in works?

'It is they whose manner of living in this present world has strayed far, while all the time imagining that they are acting righteously.

'It is they who blasphemed against the revelations of their Lord, and the encounter with Him. Their works are voided and on the Day of Resurrection We shall consider them of no weight. Thus, their reward is hell for their blasphemy, and for having taken My revelations and messengers as a laughing matter.

'But they who believed and performed good deeds, to them the Gardens of Paradise shall be a resting place. There they will
18:108 remain for ever, seeking no departure from it.'

Say: 'If the sea were ink for the words of my Lord, the sea itself would run dry before the words of my Lord had run dry, even if We provided its like to replenish it.'

Say: 'I am but a human being like you, to whom inspiration

is sent. Your God is in truth One God. Whoso hopes to meet
his Lord, let him perform deeds of righteousness, and associate
none with the worship of his Lord.'   18:110

Mary

In the name of God,
Merciful to all,
Compassionate to each!

Kaf Ha' Ya' 'Ayn Sad

A mention of your Lord's mercy towards His servant
    Zachariah,
When he called out to his Lord, calling in seclusion.

He said: 'My Lord, here I am.
    'My bones have grown soft, and my head is aflame with grey
hair.
    'Nor was I ever chagrined when calling out to you, my Lord.
    'I fear my kinsmen after I am gone, and my wife is barren.
    'So grant me a kinsman from on high to be my heir and the
heir of the House of Jacob, and make him, my Lord, acceptable
to You.'   19:6

'O Zachariah, We bring you glad tidings of a son, whose name
is John. Upon none before him have We bestowed this name.'
    He said: 'My Lord, how can I have a son when my wife is
barren and I have reached the age of impotence?'
    He said: 'Thus spoke your Lord. It is a matter easy for Me,
and I created you before, when you had been nothing.'
    He said: 'My Lord, grant me a sign.'
    He said: 'Your sign shall be not to speak to people for three
full nights.'

So he came out from the sanctuary to his people and gestured
19:11   to them to magnify God, morning and evening.

'O John, take firm hold of the Book.'
And We granted him sound judgement, when still a child,
And tenderness, from on high, and purity. He was truly a
     pious man,
Dutiful towards his parents, and was not arrogant or
     disobedient.
Peace be upon him the day he was born, the day he dies and
19:15   the day he is resurrected, alive!

And mention in the Book Mary, when she withdrew from her
people to an eastern place.
     She set up a screen to veil her from them.
     And We sent her Our Spirit, which appeared before her as an
immaculate human.
     She said: 'I take refuge in the All-Merciful from you, if you
fear God.'
     He said: 'I am but a messenger from your Lord, to bestow
upon you a son most pure.'
     She said: 'How can I have a son when no man has ever
touched me, nor am I an adulteress?'
     He said: 'Thus did your Lord speak: "It is a matter easy for
Me. We shall make him a wonder to mankind and a mercy from
19:21   Us – a decree ordained."'

So she conceived him and withdrew with him to a distant place.
And labour pains came upon her by the trunk of a palm tree.
     She said: 'I wish I had died before this and become a thing
utterly forgotten!'
     He called out to her from beneath her: 'Do not grieve. Your
Lord has made a brook to flow beneath you. So shake towards
you the trunk of the palm and it will drop down on you dates
soft and ripe. Eat and drink and be of good cheer. And if you
happen to see any human being, tell him: "I have vowed to the

All-Merciful a fast, and will not speak a word today to any human being.'"

And she came to her people, carrying him.

They said: 'O Mary, you have committed a monstrous act! Sister of Aaron, your father was not an evildoer, nor was your mother an adulteress.'

She pointed to him.

They said: 'How do we speak to an infant in his cradle?'

He said: 'I am the servant of God. He brought me the Book and made me a prophet, and made me blessed wherever I may be. He charged me with prayer and alms-giving as long as I live, and to be dutiful to my mother. And He did not make me arrogant and wicked. Peace be upon me the day I was born, the day I die, and the day I am resurrected, alive!'

This is Jesus, son of Mary: a statement of truth, concerning which they are in doubt.

It is not for God to take a child – Glory to Him! When He determines any matter, He merely says to it: 'Be!' and it is.

God is my Lord and your Lord, so worship Him.

This is a straight path.

But sects fell into dispute among themselves. Woe to those who blaspheme against the spectacle of a terrifying Day!

How well they shall hear, how well they shall see, upon that Day when they come before Us! But the wicked today are plunged in manifest delusion.

Warn them of the Day of Regret, when judgement is passed, while yet they remain inattentive, and have no faith.

It is We Who shall inherit the earth and all that is upon it, and it is to Us that they shall be returned.

And mention in the Book Abraham; he was a man of deepest faith, a prophet.

Remember when he said to his father: 'My father, why do you worship what does not hear, what does not see, what is of no use to you whatsoever?

'My father, there has come to me of Knowledge what did not come to you, so follow me and I shall guide you to a level path.

'My father, do not worship Satan: Satan has always been disobedient to the All-Merciful.

'My father, I fear a torment will touch you from the All-Merciful, and you become a follower of Satan.'

He said: 'Are you renouncing my gods, O Abraham? If you do not desist, I shall curse you. Leave me alone for a while.'

He said: 'Peace be upon you! I shall ask my Lord forgiveness for you, for He has always been kind to me. I shall keep aloof from you and from what you worship instead of God, and I shall call upon my Lord; perhaps by calling Him I will not be

19:48   amiss.'

When he abandoned them and what they worshipped instead of God, We bestowed on him Isaac and Jacob, and each We made a prophet. And We granted them of Our mercy, and

19:50   conferred upon them the highest praise on tongues of truth.

And mention in the Book Moses; he was a man of sincerity, a messenger, a prophet. We called out to him from the right side of the mountain, and We drew him near to Us, intimately conversing. And We granted him from Our mercy his brother

19:53   Aaron, a prophet.

And mention in the Book Ishmael; he was a man true to his word, a messenger, a prophet. He would command prayer and

19:55   alms-giving to his kin, and was a man favoured by his Lord.

And mention in the Book Idris;* he was a man of deepest faith,

19:57   a prophet. And We raised him up to an elevated rank.

These are, of prophets, the ones on whom God bestowed His blessings from among the progeny of Adam, from those We carried with Noah, from the progeny of Abraham and Israel, and from those whom We guided and elected. When the verses of the All-Merciful are recited to them, they fall down in prostration, weeping.

After them there followed successors who forsook prayer, and pursued their base desires. They shall meet with evil – except for those who repent, and believe, and do good deeds. These shall enter the Garden and not be wronged in any wise.

The Gardens of Eden! They are what the All-Merciful has promised His worshippers in the realm of the Unseen. His promise will surely come to pass. In it they hear no empty talk, but only 'Peace!' In it they shall receive their provisions, morning and evening. Such is the Garden We shall bequeath to the pious among Our worshippers.   19:63

We are not made to descend except by command of your Lord. To Him belongs what lies ahead of us and what lies behind, and all that is in between. Nor is your Lord forgetful.

Lord of the heavens and earth and what is in between! So worship Him, and bear His worship with patience. Do you know His like?   19:65

Man says: 'Once I die, am I really to be brought back, alive?'
But does man not remember that We created him beforehand,
    when he was nothing?
By your Lord, We shall herd them along with the demons!
And then We shall force them to come to the precincts of hell,
    upon their knees.
And then We shall snatch from every sect whoever among
    them was the most obdurate against the All-Merciful,
And We know best those who most deserve to be scorched
    therein.   19:70

None of you there are but shall come to it: a decree destined from your Lord.

Then We save those who were pious, and in it We abandon the wicked, upon their knees.

And when Our revelations, manifestly clear, are recited to them, those who disbelieve say to the believers: 'Which of the two groups is better in station, or more glittering in company?'

But how many a generation We exterminated before them! And they were more splendid in trappings and in outward appearance.

Say: 'Whoso is in error, the All-Merciful shall drag him further and further into error until, when they behold what they were promised, either the torment or the Hour, they will surely know
19:75 who is worse in station and weaker in warriors!'

God increases in guidance those who are guided.
And those things that abide, virtuous deeds, are better in
    reward with your Lord, and better in outcome.
Did you heed him who, blaspheming against Our revelations,
    said: 'I shall be endowed with wealth and progeny?'
Did he light upon a knowledge of the Unseen?
Or did he conclude a compact with the All-Merciful?
No indeed! We shall record what he says and drag him further
    and further in torment!
We shall inherit what he speaks about, and he shall appear
19:80   before Us, all by himself!

And yet they take to themselves gods apart from God, to be a power that sustains them!

No indeed! They shall forswear their worship, and shall be enemies to them!

Have you not seen how We dispatched devils against the unbelievers, distressing and beguiling them with sin?

So be not in haste concerning them; We are in truth making things ready for them!

Upon a Day when We muster the pious towards the All-Merciful, all in one delegation, and We drive on the sinners to hell, thirsty.

They shall have no intercession, except one who compacted with the All-Merciful.   19:87

And yet they say: 'The All-Merciful has taken to Himself a
    son!'
You have uttered a thing most terrible!
The heavens well nigh convulse at the mention of it,
The earth is split asunder,
The mountains stagger and collapse,
That they ascribe a son to the All-Merciful!
It is not fit for the All-Merciful to take to Himself a son.
All who are in the heavens and earth – none but shall appear
    before the All-Merciful, as a servant.
He has counted them all, and numbered every one!
And all shall appear before Him on the Day of Resurrection,
    singly, alone.
But those who believed and did good deeds, the All-Merciful
    shall show them affection.   19:96

We made it easy upon your tongue, to give glad tidings to the pious, and to warn a people who harbour much malice.

How many a generation We destroyed before them! But do you perceive any of them? Or do you hear a whisper from them?   19:98

Ta' Ha'

In the name of God,
Merciful to all,
Compassionate to each!

Ta' Ha'

We did not bring down the Qur'an upon you to make you suffer; rather, it is a Remembrance to him who fears God. It is a revelation from Him Who created the earth and highest heavens.

The All-Merciful is seated firmly upon the throne:

To Him belongs whatsoever is in the heavens and on earth, and what is in between, and what lies beneath the ground.

And if you are loud in speech, He knows what is kept secret, or even more deeply concealed.

God! There is no god but He! To Him belong the names most glorious!

20:8

Has there come to you the narrative of Moses?

When he saw a fire, he said to his family: 'Stay behind. I have glimpsed a fire; perhaps I will bring you a brand from it, or find at the fire guidance.'

When he drew near it, a voice called out to him: 'O Moses! It is Me, your Lord. Remove your sandals. You are in the sacred valley, Tuwa.* I have chosen you, so listen to what is being revealed.

'It is Me, God: there is no god but I. So worship Me and perform the prayer for My remembrance.

'The Hour is coming – I am about to reveal it – so that every soul is rewarded for what it has achieved.

'Let him not turn you away from it, he who does not believe in it and follows his base desires, else you will perish.'

20:16

'And what is that in your right hand, O Moses?'

He said: 'It is my staff; I lean upon it, and tend my sheep with it, and I have other uses for it.'

He said: 'Throw it down, O Moses.'

He threw it down, and behold, it turned into a serpent, swiftly crawling.

He said: 'Pick it up and fear not; We shall return it to its former state.

And tuck your hand into your armpit and it shall come out white, but without harm – another miracle. Thus will We show you some of Our greatest wonders.

'Go to Pharaoh: he has grown tyrannical.'   20:24

He said: 'My Lord, open my breast, make my mission easy for me, and untie the knot in my tongue, so that they may understand my speech.

'And appoint for me one to share my burden, from my family, Aaron my brother, that through him I may brace my strength, and make him a partner in my mission.

'Thus will we glorify You often, and remember You often. You have ever been mindful of us.'   20:35

He said: 'Your request has been granted, O Moses.
We had favoured you once before;
Remember when We revealed to your mother what was revealed:
"Throw him into a basket and fling him into the river,
And let the river deliver him to the bank,
Where an enemy of Mine and his will pick him up.
I have cast upon you a love from Me, and you shall be
    brought up under My caring eye."
'That was when your sister went about saying: "Shall I point out to you one who will take charge of him?"

'We then returned you to your mother so that she may be of good cheer and not sorrow.

'And you once killed a soul but We delivered you from distress, and subjected you to an ordeal most severe.

'For years you remained with the people of Midian,
And then you came back at a time appointed, O Moses.
And I made you My very own.
So go forth, you and your brother, with My signs, and do not
    neglect My remembrance.
Go to Pharaoh: he has grown tyrannical,
And speak gently to him; perhaps he will remember or be in
20:44   awe of Me.'

They said: 'We fear he might fly into a rage against us, or grow tyrannical.'

He said: 'Fear not. I am with you, listening and seeing. Go to him and say: "We are the messengers of your Lord. Send out with us the Children of Israel, and do not torment them. We bring you a wonder from your Lord, and peace be upon him who follows right guidance. To us has been revealed that tor-
20:48 ment shall fall upon him who denies and turns away."'

He said: 'Who is your Lord, O Moses?'

He said: 'Our Lord is He Who gave each thing its likeness in form, and then guided it.'

He said: 'What of earlier ages?'

He said: 'Knowledge of them is with my Lord in a Book. My
20:52 Lord neglects nothing, nor does He forget.'

It is He Who made the earth level for you, and marked out in it highways for you, and made water descend from the sky, through which We caused to come forth pairs of diverse plants. Eat, and pasture your animals – in this are signs for those possessed of reason.

    From it We created you, to it We shall return you, and from
20:55 it We shall once more resurrect you.

And We showed him all Our wonders, but he called them lies, and disbelieved.

He said: 'Did you come to drive us out of our land, through your magic, O Moses?

'We will indeed bring you magic to match it.

'So set a date for us and you, not to be missed by us or you, at a place midmost between us.'

He said: 'Your appointment is on the Feast of the Pageant, and all people must be gathered there, in the morning.'   20:59

Pharaoh retired, gathered together all his cunning and came back.

Moses said to them: 'Wretches! Do not lie in God's name, or He will ravage you with a torment; liars shall surely fail.'

So they argued among themselves over their plan of action, and consulted in secret.

They said: 'These two are sorcerers who intend to drive you out of your land by their sorcery, and do away with your customary practice. So muster your cunning and go forth in single file. Today, whoso comes out on top will surely prosper.'   20:64

They said: 'O Moses, either you cast, or we cast first.'

He said: 'No, you cast first.'

And it was as if their ropes and staffs appeared to him, through their sorcery, to be swiftly crawling.

In his heart Moses sensed fear.

We said: 'Fear not; you shall indeed be the victor. Cast down what is in your right hand and it shall swallow what they devised. They merely devised a sorcerer's deception, but the sorcerer shall not prosper, wherever he may be.'   20:69

The sorcerers were hurled to the ground, prostrate.

They said: 'We believe in the Lord of Aaron and Moses.'

He said: 'You believe in him before I grant you leave? He is merely the greatest among you, the one who taught you sorcery. I shall cut your hands and feet, alternately, and I shall crucify you on the trunks of palm trees. And you will surely know which of us is more grievous in torment and more lasting!'

They said: 'We will not prefer you to what has come to us by way of clear proofs, nor to Him Who created us. Decree what you wish to decree: your decree runs only in this present life.

'We believe in our Lord that He may pardon our sins, and what you forced upon us of sorcery. God is better and more abiding.

'Whoso comes to his Lord a sinner, hell shall be his lot, where he is neither dead nor alive.

'Whoso comes to his Lord a believer, having done righteous deeds, to these belong the highest of ranks: the Gardens of Eden, beneath which rivers flow, abiding therein for ever. Such is the
20:76   reward of one who purifies his soul.'

We revealed to Moses: 'March out at night with My worshippers, and stake out a dry path for them through the sea. Fear not pursuit, and be not anxious.'

Pharaoh pursued them with his troops, and there flowed over them from the sea what flowed.
20:79   And Pharaoh led his nation astray, and guided them not.

O Children of Israel, We delivered you from your enemy and promised you the right side of the mountain. We caused manna and quail to descend on you.

Eat of the good things We provided you, but do not transgress, or My wrath shall fall upon you. He upon whom My wrath falls will sink to the depths.

And yet I am All-Forgiving towards him who repents, and
20:82   believes, and does good deeds, and then is guided aright.

And what made you hurry forward, away from your people, O Moses?

He said: 'These others are pursuing my tracks, and I hurried on to you, my Lord, that You may be content with me.'

He said: 'We beguiled your people, after you left them, and
the Samaritan has led them astray.'   20:85

Moses returned to his people, angry and in sorrow.

He said: 'My people, did not your Lord make you a fine
promise? Has time stretched too long for you, or did you wish
your Lord's anger to blaze upon you, and so broke my
appointment?'

They said: 'We did not break your appointment through any
wish of ours, but we were weighed down with the ornaments
of these people, and we cast them, as did the Samaritan, into
the pit of fire.'   20:87

He brought out to them a calf, with a body that lowed.

They said: 'Here is your god and the god of Moses whom
Moses forgot.'

Can they not see that it gives them back no response, and
cannot bring them either harm or benefit?

Aaron had already said to them: 'O people, you are merely
enchanted with it. Your Lord is the All-Merciful, so follow me
and obey my command.'

They said: 'We shall continue to minister to it until Moses
returns to us.'   20:91

He said: 'O Aaron, what held you back, when you saw they had
erred, from following me? Or did you disobey my command?'

He said: 'Son of my mother, seize me not by beard or head! I
feared you would say: "You have divided the Children of Israel
and paid no heed to my word."'

He said: 'What then is the matter with you, O Samaritan?'

He said: 'I was aware of something they were not aware of.
So I picked up a handful from the traces of the messenger and
flung it away. Thus did my soul tempt me to do.'

He said: 'Depart! Your lot in life is to say: "No touching!"
You shall have an appointed time which you will not miss. Look
at your god, near which you remained, ministering to it! We

shall burn it all up, and then shall blow it away into the sea,
like powder. Your god is but God, and there is no god but He.
20:98 His knowledge encompasses all things.'

Thus do We narrate to you reports of times gone by.
And from on high We brought you a Remembrance.
   Whoso turns away from it shall carry on the Day of Resurrec-
tion a heavy burden, abiding in it for ever. Wretched is their
load on the Day of Resurrection!
A Day shall come when the Trumpet shall be blown,
And We herd sinners that Day, blinded.
   They shall whisper to each other: 'We remained in the world
a mere ten!'
   We know best what they say, for the most just among them
20:104 will say: 'You remained in the world a mere day!'

And they ask you about the mountains.
   Say: 'My Lord shall shatter them utterly, leaving them level
20:107 and desolate; nor will you see in them any slope or loftiness.'

On that Day they shall follow the Caller, in whom there is no
      crookedness,
And all voices shall fade in the presence of the All-Merciful,
And you will hear nothing but whispers.
On that Day, intercession shall be of no avail,
Except for him to whom the All-Merciful grants leave, and
      with whose word He is content.
He knows their present affairs and their past,
And they do not comprehend Him in knowledge.
Faces shall grow humble before the Ever-Living, Ever-
      Lasting,
And whoso bears a burden of sin shall not prosper.
Whoso does good deeds, and is faithful, need fear no injustice
20:112   ˙or grievance.

Hence We sent it down, an Arabic Qur'an, and We detailed in it all manner of threat; perhaps they will turn pious, or else it may inspire them to remembrance.

Exalted is God, the true King!

And do not hasten along with the Qur'an before its revelation to you is ended, and say: 'My Lord, increase me in knowledge.' 20:114

We entrusted Our revelation to Adam in days gone by, but he forgot, and We found in him no steadfastness.

Remember when We said to the angels: 'Bow down to Adam,' and they bowed down, all except Satan, who refused.

We said: 'O Adam, this person is an enemy to you and your wife. Let him not drive you both out of the Garden, else you will be wretched. It is granted to you that you will not go hungry therein, nor naked. Nor will you be thirsty therein, nor swelter.' 20:119

But Satan whispered to him and said: 'O Adam, shall I indicate to you the Tree of Eternity, and kingship that grows not old?'

So they ate from it, and their shame became visible to them, and they went about sewing leaves of the Garden upon themselves.

And Adam disobeyed his Lord, and went astray. 20:121

Then His Lord elected him, pardoned him, and guided him.
He said: 'Descend from it, both of you, an enemy one to
    another.
When guidance comes to you from Me,
Whoso follows My guidance shall neither stray nor be
    wretched.
Whoso turns away from remembrance of Me
Shall live a life of hardship,
And We shall herd him on the Day of Resurrection, blind.'

He shall say: 'My Lord, why do you herd me blind when before I could see?'

He said: 'Because My revelations came to you and you forgot
20:126 them, and because even today you forget.'

Thus do We reward him who transgresses, and believes not in
the revelations of his Lord. For the torment of the hereafter is
more grievous and longer-lasting.

Was it not obvious to them how many generations We destroyed
before them, people walking about inside their homes? In this
are signs for people possessed of reason.

Were it not for a prior Word from your Lord, judgement
would have been passed and a set term appointed.

So bear with patience what they say, and glorify the praise of
your Lord before sunrise and before sunset. And during some
hours of the night and the edges of day, glorify Him too; perhaps
you will find contentment.

And cast not your eyes in longing upon what We bestowed
on some of them for enjoyment – the luxury of this present life.
This We do to tempt them with it, but the bounty of your Lord
is better and more abiding.

And command your family to pray, and be constant in per-
forming it.

We seek no sustenance from you: it is We Who sustain you.
20:132 Piety shall ultimately prevail.

They say: 'If only he would bring us some proof from his Lord!'
    But has not such proof come to them, as in earlier Scriptures?
    Had We destroyed them with a torment before its revelation,
they would have said: 'Our Lord, if only You had sent us a
messenger, so we could follow Your revelations before we are
humbled and disgraced!'
    Say: 'Everyone is waiting in suspense, so wait, and you will
surely know who are travelling on the level path, and who have
20:135 been guided aright.'

The Prophets

In the name of God,
Merciful to all,
Compassionate to each!

Nearer to mankind their reckoning draws,
And yet in heedlessness they turn away.
There comes to them no remembrance from their Lord, new to
      their ears,
But they listen to it while amusing themselves, their hearts
      distracted.
They converse in secret, those who are wicked, saying:
'Is he not a human like you? Will you then accept sorcery with
      open eyes?'
Say: 'My Lord knows all speech of heaven and earth: He is
      All-Hearing, Omniscient.'   21:4

Or else they say: 'Muddled dreams!' or else: 'He fabricated it'
or else: 'He is a poet. Let him bring us a wonder such as earlier
messengers were sent.'
   No town before them which We destroyed had believed; will
they believe?
   We sent not before you except men whom We inspired.
   Ask the people of Remembrance if you do not know.   21:7

We created them not as bodies that eat no food, nor were they
immortal.
   Then We were true to Our promise to them, and saved them,
together with anyone We wished, and We destroyed the dissolute.
   We have sent down on you a Book in which there is renown
for you: will you not be reasonable?

How many a wicked town We crushed, and reared thereafter another people!

But no sooner did they sense Our might than they ran away from it.

Do not run! Turn back to the luxuries you wallow in!

Turn back to your houses and perhaps you will be held to account!

21:13

They said: 'Alas for us, we were indeed wicked.'

Such was their plaint until We turned them into parched stubble.

We created not the sky and earth, and what is in between, in jest.

Had We wanted to take up some amusement, We would have done so from on high – if indeed We were set on doing it.

Rather, We hurl truth against falsehood, dealing it a mighty blow – and there it lies, expired!

Woe to you for what you recount!

21:18

To Him belongs whosoever is in the heavens and on earth.

They who are with Him disdain not to worship Him, nor do they grow weary.

They magnify Him night and day, and slacken not.

21:20

Or have they indeed taken to themselves earthly gods? And is it indeed these gods who resurrect the dead?

Had there been many gods, instead of God, in the heavens and earth, they would have been corrupted.

Exalted is God, Lord of the throne, far above what they recount!

He cannot be questioned about what He does. It is they who are questioned.

21:23

But have they truly taken to themselves gods other than Him?

Say: 'Show me your proof. This is a Remembrance of those

now with me, and of those who came before me. But most of them do not know the Truth, and turn away.'

We sent not a messenger before you except that We revealed to him that there is no god but I, so worship Me.

Yet they say that the All-Merciful has taken to Himself a son! Exalted is He! Rather, they are honoured servants.

They forestall Him not in speech, and act according to His command.

He knows their present affairs and their past, and they do not intercede except for him with whom God is well pleased.

From awe of Him they are faint-hearted.

Whoso among them says: 'I am a god, instead of Him,' him We reward with hell. Thus do We reward the impious.   21:29

Do the unbelievers not realize that the heavens and earth were sewn together, but We ripped them apart, and from water created every living thing? Will they not believe? On earth We fixed towering mountains lest the earth should shake them violently, and in them We fixed signposts and paths, that they may find their way. The sky We made as a well-protected canopy, but they avert their eyes from its wonders.   21:32

It is He Who created the night and day, the sun and moon – each in its orbit floating.

On no human being before you did We confer immortality. If you were to die, will they be immortal?

Every soul shall taste death.

We put you to the test, with evil and good, as an ordeal, And to Us you shall return.   21:35

And when the blasphemers see you, they take you only for jesting: 'Is this the fellow who makes mention of your gods?'

And they, at the mention of the All-Merciful – they blaspheme.

Man was created hasty;

21:37   And I shall show you My wonders, so do not be in haste.

They say: 'When will this promise be fulfilled if you speak the truth?'
   If only the unbelievers knew of a time when they cannot ward off the fire from their faces or from their backs, nor will they find anyone to help them!
   In truth, it shall come upon them suddenly, and bewilder them, and they will not be able to hold it off, nor will they be
21:40   kept waiting.

Messengers before you were mocked. But those who mocked them were overwhelmed by that which they used to mock.
   Say: 'Who shall keep you safe from the All-Merciful, by night or day?'
21:42   Instead, they turn away from remembrance of their Lord.

Or do they have gods that protect them, apart from Us?
   They cannot come to their own aid, nor will We give them the safe conduct of neighbours.
   Rather, We gave these people enjoyment of life, they and their ancestors, until time grew long upon them.
   Do they not see how We descend upon their territory, causing
21:44   it to shrink from its margins? Will they be the victors?

Say: 'I merely warn you through Revelation, but the deaf cannot hear the Call when they are being warned.'
   And if there should touch them a dole of your Lord's torment, they will say: 'Woe to us! We were truly wicked!'
   We shall set up fair balances on the Day of Resurrection, and a soul shall not be wronged in anything, even if they had committed the like of the weight of a mustard seed.
21:47   Let Us suffice as keepers of account.

We brought Moses and Aaron the Criterion:
A shaft of light and a Remembrance to the pious,

To those who fear their Lord in the Unseen,
And tremble at the Hour.
This is a Blessed Remembrance which We have sent down:
Will you then deny it?   21:50

Before, We had bestowed right guidance on Abraham, and knew
him well.

   This was when he said to his father and his people:
'What are these idols that you keep ministering to?'
They said: 'We found our ancestors had worshipped them.'
He said: 'You and your ancestors are in manifest error.'
They said: 'Do you come to us with the truth, or are you
   jesting?'
He said: 'Rather, it is your Lord, Lord of the heavens and
   earth, Who created them.
Of this I am witness.
By God, I shall confute your idols, once you depart and turn
   your backs.'   21:57

So he smashed them into fragments, all but their greatest, hoping
they would turn back to God.
They said: 'Who did this to our gods? He must truly be
   wicked.'
They said: 'We heard a young man make mention of them,
   called Abraham.'
They said: 'Bring him out in full view of people, and perhaps
   they will give witness.'
They said: 'Is it you who did this to our gods, O Abraham?'
He said: 'Rather, it was this greatest among them who did it.
   Ask them, if they can speak.'
   They reconsidered within themselves, and said: 'It is you who
are the wicked ones.'
   But then – head over heels they were made to turn: 'You
know these do not speak.'
   He said: 'Do you indeed worship, apart from God, that which
has no power to benefit you in anything, nor harm you?

'Shame on you and on what you worship instead of God!
21:67 Will you not come to your senses?'

They said: 'Burn him, and uphold your gods, if ready to act
    thus.'
We said: 'O fire, be cool and comforting to Abraham.'
And they intended him malice, but We made them the
    losers,
And We delivered him and Lot to the land We blessed for all
    mankind.
And We bestowed on him Isaac and Jacob, as an added
    bounty from Us,
And all We created righteous.
And We made them leaders, guiding to Our commands.
And We inspired them to do righteous deeds,
To perform the prayer, and hand out alms,
21:73 And they were Our worshippers.

To Lot We granted sound judgement and knowledge, and
delivered him from a town that committed foul deeds.
    They were indeed an evil people, and dissolute.
    And We admitted him into Our mercy: he was a man of
virtue.

Remember Noah, before that, when he called out in supplication, and how We answered his call, and delivered him and
his family from great anguish; how We stood by him against a
people who cried lies to Our signs.
21:77   They were an evil people, and We drowned them all.

Remember David and Solomon, as they judged in the matter of
the orchards, when a people's flock pastured therein.
    We were there to witness their judgement.
    We instructed Solomon as to that judgement, and upon all
bestowed right counsel and knowledge.

With David We prevailed on mountains and birds to glorify –
indeed We did!

And We taught him the craft of breastplate-making, for your
sake, to protect you in battle.

Will you then render thanks? 21:80

For Solomon's sake, We prevailed on the winds, hard blowing,
to run at his command to the land which We had blessed. And
of all things We were fully cognizant.

And demons there were who dived deep at his command,
and performed other, lesser tasks. Of them We took good
care. 21:82

Remember Job, when he cried out to his Lord: 'Evil has
touched me, and You are the most merciful of those who show
mercy.'

We answered his prayer, drew away his distress, and restored
his family to him, and as many besides: a mercy from Us, and a
remembrance to worshippers. 21:84

Remember Ishmael, Idris and Dhu'l Kifl:* all were men of
patience.

We admitted them into Our mercy, and they were righteous
men. 21:86

Remember the Man in the Whale, when he departed in fury.

He imagined We had no power over him, and cried out from
the depths of darkness: 'There is no god but You! Glory to You!
I have been wicked.'

We answered his call and delivered him from his grief: thus
do We deliver the faithful. 21:88

And Zachariah too, when he cried out to his Lord: 'My Lord,
leave me not all alone, for You are the best of inheritors.'

We answered his prayer, bestowed upon him John, and made

his wife fertile: for they had always hastened to do good deeds, and to pray to Us, in hope as well as in fear. They were ever
21:90   humble before Us.

Remember also she who preserved her virginity, and We breathed into her of Our Spirit, and made her and her son to be a wonder for mankind.

This then is your community, a single community, and I am
21:92   your Lord, So worship Me.

But they splintered their religion among themselves, though all shall return to Us.

Whoso does good deeds, while believing, there shall be no denial of his endeavour, and We shall inscribe it for him.

But such is forbidden to a town We destroyed: its people shall not repent.

Until, when Gog and Magog are flung open, and they descend from every height, and the Promise of Truth draws near, behold how the eyes of blasphemers stare: 'Woe to us! We were heedless of all this! Indeed, we were wicked!'

You and what you worship instead of God shall be timber for hell, and you will surely come to it.

Had these been true gods, they would not have come to it. All shall abide in it for ever.
21:100   In it they shall wail; in it they do not hear.

As for those on whom Our grace was bestowed beforehand,
        they are kept far from it.
They do not hear it sizzle.
They live amidst what their souls desired, eternally.
The Great Fear grieves them not,
And the angels are there to receive them:
21:103   'This is your Day, the one you were promised.'

That will be the Day when We roll up the sky,
As a scroll rolls up books.

As We began the first creation, so shall We renew it:
A promise We pledge – and We shall carry it out.

In the Psalms We wrote, following the Remembrance, that the
earth shall be inherited by my righteous servants.
   In this is admonition enough for a people of true worship.   21:106

We sent you not but as a mercy to mankind.
Say: 'I am only one upon whom revelation descends. Your
   God is but One God. Will you submit to Him?'
If they turn away, say: 'I delivered the message to all alike.
   I know not if what you are promised is near at hand, or
   far.
He knows speech that is loud, and He knows what you
   conceal.
I know not whether this is a temptation set before you,
Or else enjoyment for a little while.'

Say: 'My Lord, judge with the Truth.
Our Lord, the All-Merciful, is our source of help against what
   you recount.'   21:112

The Pilgrimage

In the name of God,
Merciful to all,
Compassionate to each!

O mankind, fear your Lord!
The Quake of the Hour is a thing terrible!
On the Day you witness it, every nursing woman shall be
   distracted from what she nurses;
Every pregnant woman shall deliver what she carries;
And you shall see mankind drunk,

But they are not drunk.

22:2   Rather, God's punishment is so grievous!

Among people is one who argues about God, without knowledge, and follows thereby every obdurate demon.

It has been decreed upon him: whoever takes him for master, he shall lead him astray and guide him to the torment of the

22:4   raging Fire.

O mankind, if you are in doubt about the resurrection,

We created you from dust, then from a sperm, then from a
   blood clot, then from a morsel, formed and unformed, to
   make it plain to you.

And We plant in the wombs whatever We desire, for a stated
   term,

Then We bring you forth, a child,

And then to reach full maturity.

Some of you die, some are held over to the most degrading old
   age,

So that, once having known, he comes to know nothing.

And you will see the earth lifeless,

But when We send down the rain upon it, it vibrates, and
   doubles its yield,

22:5   And comes out in plants, of every kind, a joy to behold.

This is so because God is the Truth.

It is He Who revives the dead, and has power over all
   things.

The Hour is coming, no doubt about it,

22:7   And God shall resurrect all who are now in their graves.

Among people is one who argues about God, without knowledge, without guidance, without a Luminous Book.

He twists his neck in arrogance, to lead astray from the path of God.

In this world he shall meet with disgrace, and on the Day of Resurrection We shall make him taste the torment of the Blaze.

And this because of what your hands committed before; but God is not unjust to His servants. 22:10

Among people is one who worships God – on condition.
If good befalls him, he grows content with it.
But if an ordeal befalls him, he turns his face about,
Losing this world and the next.
This is the most manifest bereavement!

He calls, instead of God, on that which harms him not, nor
    benefits him:
This is error, far gone.
He prays to one whose harm is nearer to hand than his
    benefit.
Wretched is that master, and wretched his company! 22:13

God admits those who believed and did good deeds into Gardens beneath which rivers flow. God does what He pleases.

Whoever imagines that God shall not champion him, in this world and the next, let him extend a rope to the ceiling, then let him hang himself, and see whether this trick will curtail his exasperation! 22:15

Thus did We send it down – manifest revelations. And God guides whomever He pleases.

As for the believers, the Jews, the Sabeans, the Christians, the Magians and the polytheists – God shall judge between them on the Day of Resurrection.

God is a witness of all things.

Do you not see how to God bows down all who are in the heavens and on earth, and the sun and moon, the stars, the mountains, the trees and animals, and many people too?

But many are also justly deserving of punishment.

Whom God abases, none will there be to honour him.

22:18   God does what He pleases.

Here are two rivals who disputed about their Lord.

For those who blasphemed, garments of fire have been tailored,

And over their heads is poured scalding water,

Melting therewith their innards and their skins.

Upon them shall be clasps of iron;

Whenever they seek to escape their torment, they are driven back to it:

22:22   'Taste the agony of the raging Fire!'

God admits those who believe and do good deeds into Gardens beneath which rivers flow.

They are decked out in golden bracelets and pearls, and their garments are made of silk.

They are guided to decorous speech,

They are guided to a praiseworthy path.

As for the unbelievers, it is they who obstruct the way to God and to the Sacred Mosque, which We have dedicated to all mankind, whether residing therein or passing through.

Whoso commits sacrilege therein, or sin, We shall make him

22:25   taste a painful torment.

Remember when We prepared for Abraham the site of the House:

'You are not to associate anything with Me, and to purify My House for those who circumambulate and those who stand and pray, and for those who kneel down, prostrate. And call out to people to go on pilgrimage, and they shall come to you on foot, and on every skinny riding animal they shall come, from every distant valley, there to meet with much profit to themselves, and to mention the name of God, on certain well-known days, in thanks to Him for providing them with cattle. So eat from them and feed the wretched and the poor.'

22:28

So let them carry out their ritual of cleansing, fulfil their vows and circumambulate the Ancient House. For whoso exalts the sacred commands of God, this is best for him with his Lord.

And cattle are pronounced licit for you, except as recited to you.

So keep away from the defilement of idols, and avoid perjury.

Be pristine in your faith in God, ascribing no partners to Him. Whoso ascribes partners to God is like one who falls from the sky, and the birds of the air tear him apart, or else the wind sweeps him away into a distant abyss.

But whoso exalts the sacred rites of God, these shall inhere in the piety of hearts.

22:32

From them you derive profit for a certain time; thereafter to be sacrificed by the Ancient House.

For every nation We have assigned a place of sacrifice, where they mention the name of God in thanks for what He provided them of cattle.

Your God is One God, so submit to Him and give glad tidings to those who find rest in God; they who, when God is mentioned, their hearts grow pious; they who bear with patience that which befalls them; who persevere in prayer and who expend of what We bestowed upon them.

22:35

Livestock We have assigned for you to be part of the rituals of God. In them there is good for you. So mention the name of God upon them as they are tied up for sacrifice. When fallen upon their sides, eat thereof and feed the beggar, humble or importunate. Thus did We create them to serve you, that you

might give thanks. Their flesh and their blood shall not reach
up to God; rather, it is your piety that will reach Him.

22:37 Thus did He create them to serve you in order that you magnify
God for His guidance. And give glad tidings to the charitable.

God safeguards the believers; God loves not every treacherous
renegade.

Leave is granted to those who are being attacked, for they
were wronged, and God is assuredly capable of sending them
victory. They are those who were driven out of their homes
without just cause, only because they said: 'Our Lord is God.'

Had God not caused people to restrain one another, destruction would have fallen upon monasteries, churches, oratories
and places of prayer, where the name of God is often mentioned.

God will assuredly uphold those who uphold Him. God is
All-Powerful, Almighty. They are those who, when We em-
power them in the land, perform the prayer, hand out alms,
command the good and forbid evil. To God is the outcome of

22:41 all matters.

And if they call you a liar, so also before them did the people
of Noah, of 'Ad and of Thamud call their prophets liars, as did
the people of Abraham and the people of Lot, and, too, the
people of Midian. And Moses was called a liar. I granted the
blasphemers respite, and then I seized them – behold the reversal

22:44 of their fortunes!

How many a town We destroyed for its wrongdoing!

Desolate its habitations, its wells abandoned, its towering
palaces in ruin!

Have they not journeyed in the land, and had minds to appre-
hend with, or ears to listen with? It is not their eyes that are

22:46 blind; rather, it is the hearts in their breasts.

They ask you to hasten the torment! God shall not fail to
keep His promise. A day with your Lord is like a thousand

years of your reckoning. How many a town I granted respite, though sinning, and then I seized it! To Me is the journey's end.

22:48

Say: 'O people, to you I am but a manifest warner. To them who believe and do good deeds there is ample pardon and a noble bounty. But those who challenge Our revelations, seeking to undermine them – these are the denizens of hell.'

22:51

We sent not any messenger or prophet before you but one who, when prophesying, Satan intrudes into his prophecies. God then abrogates Satan's intrusions, and God enshrines His revelations, and God is Omniscient, All-Wise. And this, in order to make what Satan interpolates a seduction to those in whose hearts lies sickness, or whose hearts are hard. Wrongdoers are at rift with God, and far from the truth.

22:53

Let those endowed with knowledge know that it is the Truth from your Lord, and let them believe in it, so that their hearts can find peace therein. God shall surely guide the believers onto a straight path.

But the unbelievers will remain in doubt of it until the Hour comes to them suddenly, or there comes to them the torment of a matchless Day. On that Day, sovereignty belongs to God, Who shall judge between them. Those who believed and did good deeds are in the Gardens of Bliss. Those who disbelieved and cried lies to Our revelations, these shall receive a humiliating punishment. And those who emigrated in the cause of God, and were then killed or died, God shall provide them with a splendid provision, and God is the best of Providers. He shall admit them through a portal that they shall be content with: God is Omniscient, All-Forbearing.

22:59

Furthermore, whoso exacts a punishment equal to that with which he was punished, and is then unjustly assailed, God shall come to his aid – God is All-Pardoning, All-Forgiving.

For it is God Who entwines night with day, and day with night. God is All-Hearing, All-Seeing.

For God is the Truth, and that which they worship instead of Him is falsehood. God is the All-Exalted, All-Supreme.

Do you not see how God brings down water from the sky and the earth turns green? God is All-Benign, All-Experienced.

To Him belongs whatsoever is in the heavens and on earth, and God is All-Sufficient, All-Praiseworthy.

Do you not see how God placed what is on earth to serve you, how ships run in the sea by His command, how He holds up the sky lest it fall on earth, save by His leave? With mankind God is All-Clement, Compassionate to each.

He it is Who gave you life and will cause you to die, and then
22:66   revives you – Man is truly ungrateful.

For every nation We established a ritual that they follow, so do not allow them to dispute this matter with you. And call to your Lord, for you are upon a path of right guidance.

And if they argue with you, say: 'God knows best what you do.'

God shall judge between you on the Day of Resurrection concerning that in which you used to dispute. Do you not know that God knows whatever is in the heavens and on earth? It is
22:70   all in a Book; it is all easy for God.

And yet they worship, instead of God, that for which He revealed no authority, and of which they have no knowledge. Wrongdoers shall have none to champion them.

When Our revelations are recited to them, manifestly clear, you detect in the faces of unbelievers disapproval; they could almost do violence to those who are reciting Our verses to them!

Say: 'Shall I inform you of what is more evil than this? It is the Fire that God promised to unbelievers – and what a wretched
22:72   outcome!'

O mankind, a parable is struck, so listen to it. Those whom you worship instead of God cannot create a fly, even if they join forces to do so. And if flies were to rob them of something, they could not retrieve it from them: weak is the seeker and weak the thing sought! They did not esteem God as He must rightly be esteemed. God is All-Powerful, Almighty.   22:74

God chooses messengers from among the angels and from among mankind. God is All-Hearing, All-Seeing. He knows their future and their past, and to God shall all matters revert.   22:76

O Believers, bend down and prostrate yourselves and worship your Lord. And perform good works; perhaps you shall prosper.

   And strive in the cause of God as He must rightly be striven for. He chose you and did not burden you in religion; it is the religion of your father Abraham, and it was he who before now called you Muslims, in order that the Prophet might witness on your behalf, and that you be witnesses for mankind.

So perform the prayer and hand out alms, and seek refuge with God, your Protector – what an excellent Protector! What an excellent Champion!   22:78

The Believers

In the name of God,
Merciful to all,
Compassionate to each!

The believers have prevailed!
They who in prayer are humble;
Who abstain from idle chatter;
Who constantly fulfil the obligation of alms-giving;

Who guard their chastity, except with spouses or what their
    right hands own,
For then they are not to blame –
But whoso covets what lies beyond this,
These are transgressors –
Who are faithful in their trusts and contracts;
Who persevere in prayer.
These are the inheritors,

23:11 Who shall inherit Paradise, abiding therein for ever.

We created man from the essence of clay,
Then made him a sperm in a well-guarded cavity,
The sperm We turned into a blood clot, the blood clot into a
    morsel,
The morsel into bones,
The bones We clothed with flesh,
And then We reared him into another creation.

23:14 Blessed is God, the most excellent of Creators!

Thereafter you will surely die,
And on the Day of Resurrection you will surely be brought
    out, alive.
Above you We created seven heavens; nor were We heedless of
    creation.
We made water descend from the sky, in measure,
And settled it on earth,
But We are in truth capable of blotting it out.
For you We reared therewith gardens of palms and vines,
From which you garner much fruit, and from which you eat.
A tree too We reared, sprouting on Mount Sinai,
Which brings forth oil and flavouring to those who eat

23:20   from it.

In livestock you have a lesson:
From their bellies We give you to drink;
In them are many benefits to you;

From them you eat.

Upon them, and aboard ships, you are carried. 23:22

We sent Noah to his people.

He said: 'My people, worship God. You have no other god but He. Will you not turn to piety?'

The chieftains of his people who disbelieved said: 'This fellow is nothing but a human being, like you, who seeks preferment over you. Had God willed, He would have sent down angels. We never heard the like of it among our ancient forefathers. He is but a man in whom there is madness. So watch him closely for a while.'

He said: 'My Lord, help me against their lies about me.'

So We inspired him: 'Build the Ark where We can watch over you, and with Our inspiration.'

And when Our command went forth, and water gushed up to the surface, We said: 'Load up on board two of every kind, and your family – except for those foretold – and do not plead with Me regarding those who are wicked. They shall be drowned. When you and your followers are safely settled aboard the Ark, say: "Praise be to God, Who delivered us from an evil people," and say: "My Lord, grant me a blessed resting place: You are the best of those who grant a place of rest."' 23:29

In this are signs. We brought upon them a true calamity.

Then, after them, We reared another generation. And We sent them a messenger, from their number, saying: 'Worship God. You have no other god but He. Will you not be pious?'

The chieftains of his people, who blasphemed and denied the encounter of the hereafter – We had granted them a life of luxury in this present world – said: 'This fellow is nothing but a human being like you, who eats what you eat and drinks what you drink. If you obey a mere human like you, you would truly be the losers. Does he promise you that, once dead and turned into dust and bones, you will again be brought forth? How far-fetched, how far-fetched that which you are promised! There is nothing but our present life: we die and we live and we shall not be resurrected. He is merely a man who fabricates lies from God, and we do not believe in him.'

He said: 'My Lord, support me, seeing that they called me a liar.'

He said: 'In a short while, they will wake up and be truly repentant.'

The Scream seized them in truth, and We turned them into 23:41 flotsam. Away with a wicked people!

Then, after them, We reared other generations.

No nation can bring forward its appointed span of time, nor can they delay it.

Then We sent Our messengers, one after the other. Whenever a messenger came to a nation, they called him a liar. So We made them follow one another into destruction, and made them 23:44 into moral examples – away with a people who do not believe!

Thereafter We sent Moses and his brother Aaron, with Our revelations and manifest proof, to Pharaoh and his chieftains. But they grew arrogant and were a haughty people.

They said: 'Are we to believe in two humans, like us, while their own people are serving us?'

So they called them liars and were among those condemned 23:48 to perish.

To Moses We brought the Book, that they may find guidance.

And We made the Son of Mary and his mother a wonder.

We caused them to retire to a high place, with level ground 23:50 and a fountain.

O messengers, eat what is licit and wholesome, and perform righteous deeds; I know full well what you do.

This, your nation, is a single nation, and I am your Lord. So 23:52 fear Me.

Mankind, however, rent the true faith into books, each sect content with what they have. So leave them in their depths of ignorance – for a while.

Do they suppose that, in furnishing them with wealth and progeny, We are ever ready to bring them favours? In truth, they are oblivious.   23:56

Those who, from awe of their Lord, are fearful;
Those who have faith in their Lord's revelations;
Those who associate no partners with their Lord;
Those who expend what they expend with hearts anxious for
    acceptance,
Knowing that they will surely return to their Lord;
These outstrip one another to do righteous deeds,
And, because of this, they shall have precedence.   23:61

We charge not a soul except with what it can bear.
With Us is a Book that utters the Truth, and they shall not be
    wronged.
Rather, their hearts are sunk in ignorance of it.
Their works are inferior to those who have faith,
And they persist in their acts of sin.
Until, when We seize the decadent among them with torment,
See how they shriek for help!
Do not shriek Today! You shall have no support from Us.   23:65

My verses used to be recited to you, and you used to turn heel,
    recoiling,
Too arrogant to give heed, and would spend your evenings
    defaming it.
Did they not reflect on what was said?
Or has something come to them that did not come to their
    ancient forefathers?
Or did they fail to recognize their Messenger, and so denied
    him?
Or do they say there is madness in him?

Rather, he brought them the Truth, but most of them detest
23:70   the Truth.

Had the God of Truth indulged their whims, the heavens and
earth, and all therein, would have been corrupted. Instead, We
brought them their renown, but they turn away from it.

Or do you ask them for a wage for it? But your Lord's wage
is better, and He is the best of Providers.

You are calling them to a straight path, but those who believe
not in the hereafter are surely wandering off that path.

If We show them mercy and draw away the hardship they
suffer, they would persist in their outrage, groping in blindness.

We had seized them with torment, but they neither submitted
to their Lord, nor entreated Him.

Until, when We open wide to them a gate of terrible torment,
23:77   behold how they despair!

It is He Who devised your hearing, eyesight and hearts, but
        little thanks do you offer.

It is He Who created you upon the earth, and to Him you
        shall be mustered.

It is He Who gives life and deals death,

And He Who contrived the alternation of night and day:
23:80   Will you not consider?

Instead, they spoke as did the ancients.

They said: 'Are we, once dead and become dust and bones, to
        be resurrected?

We and our forefathers had been promised this before.
23:83   This is nothing but fables of the ancients.'

Say: 'To whom does the earth and all upon it belong, if you
happen to know?'

And they shall respond: 'To God.'

Say: 'Will you not reflect?'

Say: 'Who is the Lord of the seven heavens, the Lord of the great throne?'

And they shall respond: 'God.'

Say: 'Will you not be pious?'

Say: 'Who holds in His hand sovereignty over all things, who shelters but cannot be sheltered from, if you happen to know?'

And they shall respond: 'God.'

Say: 'How then can you be so beguiled?' 23:89

Indeed, We brought them the Truth, but they are liars.

God did not take to Himself a son, nor has He another god with Him, or else every god would have appropriated his own creation, and some would be superior to others.

May God be exalted far above what they recount!

Knower of the Unseen and the Seen:

May He be far above what they associate with Him! 23:92

Say: 'My Lord, if only You could show me what they have been promised! My Lord, place me not among the wicked!'

And We are surely able to show you what We promised them! 23:95

Ward off insolence with what is more seemly: we know best what they recount. And say: 'My Lord, I seek Your protection against the whisperings of devils. I seek Your protection, my Lord, from any harm they may do me.' 23:98

Until, when death comes to one of them, he says: 'My Lord, bring me back to life. Perhaps I will perform a virtuous deed among others I neglected.'

Oh no! It is a mere word that he utters, but behind them lies a rampart, until the Day they are resurrected.

But when the Trumpet is blown, no ties of kinship between them shall there be on that Day, nor will they question each other about them.

They whose scales are weighed down – these shall prevail.

They whose scales are light – these have lost their souls, and in hell shall abide for ever.

The fire shall scorch their faces, and in it their visage shall
23:104   be grim.

Were not My revelations recited to you, and you cried lies to them?

They said: 'Our Lord, our wickedness gained mastery over us, and we were a people in error.

'Our Lord, remove us hence, and if we relapse we would truly be evil.'

He said: 'Cower in it, and speak not to Me.

'Once there was a group of My worshippers who would call out: "Our Lord, we believe, so pardon us and have mercy upon us, for You are the best of those who show mercy."

'But you took them for mockery until they made you forget My remembrance. And you would laugh at them. I have rewarded them this Day for what they bore with patience, and
23:111   it is they who are the victors.'

He shall say: 'How long did you remain on earth, in number of years?'

They will respond: 'We remained for a day or a part thereof. Ask those who count.'

He will say: 'You remained only a short while, if only you
23:114   knew.'

Do you imagine that We created you in vain? That you will
         not return to Us?

Exalted is God, the True King!

There is no god but He, Lord of the noble throne!

Whoso calls upon another god with God, and has no proof thereof, his account is with his Lord, and the blasphemers shall not prevail.

Say: 'My Lord, forgive, and be merciful! You are the best of
23:118   the merciful.'

Light

In the name of God,
Merciful to all,
Compassionate to each!

Here is a *sura* that We have sent down, and made distinct, and sent down in it verses manifest, that you might remember.   24:1

The adulteress and the adulterer: flog each of them a hundred lashes. And let not pity for them overcome you in regard to the law of God, provided you believe in God and the Last Day. And let their punishment be witnessed by a group of believers.

The adulterer shall marry none but an adulteress or an idolatress; and the adulteress shall marry none but an adulterer or an idolater. But this is forbidden to believers.   24:3

Those who falsely accuse married women of adultery, and fail to produce four witnesses, flog them eighty lashes and never thereafter accept their witness. These are the dissolute.

Except for those who later repent and reform their ways, for God is All-Forgiving, Compassionate to each.   24:5

Those who accuse their wives of adultery, and have no witnesses but themselves, let each of them witness four times by God that he is telling the truth, and a fifth time that the curse of God shall fall upon him if he is a liar. They are then to ward off punishment from her if she testifies four times by God that he is a liar, and a fifth time that God's wrath shall fall upon her if he is telling the truth.   24:9

Were it not for God's favour upon you and His mercy – and that God is All-Forgiving, All-Wise!

Those who made up that libel were a gang among you. Count it not as an evil that befell you, but rather as something good. To every one of them is due what he earned of sin, and to him among them who had most to do with magnifying that libel, there awaits a terrible torment.

Why is it that, when you heard it, the believers, men and women, did not think well of each other, and say: 'This is a manifest libel'? If only they had produced four witnesses! But since they did not produce witnesses, these people, in God's sight, are indeed liars.

Were it not for God's favour and mercy upon you, in this world and the next, terrible torment would have touched you in regard to the libel that you spread about. You would lap it up with your tongues, and utter with your mouths what you had no knowledge of. You imagined it was a simple matter, but it is momentous with God.

Why is that, when you heard it, you did not say: 'It is not fitting for us to speak of such matters. Glory be to You! This is a dreadful falsehood?'

God admonishes you never to return to its like again if you are true believers.

And God makes clear His revelations to you, and God is
24:18   Omniscient, All-Wise.

As for those who enjoy spreading obscenities about the believers, painful torment awaits them in this world and the next. God knows and you do not.

Were it not for God's favour upon you and His mercy – and that God is All-Tender, Compassionate to each!

O believers, follow not in the footsteps of Satan. Whoso follows in Satan's footsteps, let him know that Satan commands obscenity and immorality. Were it not for God's favour upon you and His mercy, none of you would ever have been guided aright. It is God, rather, Who grants guidance to whom He pleases. And
24:21   God is All-Hearing, Omniscient.

Let not those among you, virtuous and affluent, forswear from giving to kinsmen, to the poor and to emigrants in the cause of God. Let them pardon, and let them forgive. Do you not want God to pardon you? God is All-Forgiving, Compassionate to each!

Those who falsely accuse women who are chaste, innocent of sin and possessed of faith shall be cursed in this world and the next. Awaiting them is a terrible torment. On that Day, there shall testify against them their own tongues, hands and feet concerning what they used to do. On that Day, God shall pay them in full their just reward, and they shall know that God is the Manifest Truth.   24:25

Unchaste women for unchaste men,
Unchaste men for unchaste women,
Chaste women for chaste men,
Chaste men for chaste women –
They are declared innocent of what they impute to them.
For them there is forgiveness, and a generous provision.

O believers, do not enter houses other than your own until you make your presence known and greet their inhabitants. This is better for you; perhaps you will remember. If you find no one therein, do not enter unless granted leave. If you are asked to leave, then leave; this would be more seemly for you, and God knows best what you do. But no blame attaches to you if you enter uninhabited houses for which you might find some use. And God knows best what you reveal and what you hide.   24:29

Tell believing men to avert their eyes, and safeguard their private parts; this is more decent for them, and God is All-Experienced with what they do.
    Tell believing women to avert their eyes, and safeguard their private parts, and not to expose their attractions except what is visible. And let them wrap their shawls around their breast

lines, and reveal their attractions only before their husbands or fathers, or fathers-in-law, or sons, or sons of their husbands, or brothers, or sons of brothers, or sons of sisters, or their womenfolk, or slaves, or male attendants with no sexual desire, or children with no intimate knowledge of the private parts of women. And let them not stamp their feet to reveal what they hide of their ornaments.

24:31   Believers all! Repent before God that you might succeed.

Marry the unwed among you and the virtuous among your slaves, male and female. If they are poor, yet God shall enrich them from His bounty, and God is All-Encompassing, Omniscient. And let those who find not the means to marry have recourse to chastity until God enriches them from His bounty.

Whoso from among your slaves seeks a contract of manumission, contract with them accordingly, if you know of any talent in them, and grant them of the wealth that God has granted you. Do not force your female slaves into prostitution, if they desire chastity, in order to gain some advantage in this present world. If forced, God, once they are forced, is towards them All-Forgiving, Compassionate to each. To you We sent down edifying revelations and examples, drawn from those who
24:34   passed away before you, and a homily to the pious.

God is the light of the heavens and the earth.
His light is like a niche in which is a lantern,
The lantern in a glass,
The glass like a shimmering star,
Kindled from a blessed tree,
An olive, neither of the East nor of the West,
Its oil almost aglow, though untouched by fire.
Light upon light!
God guides to His light whomever He wills,
And strikes parables for mankind.
24:35   God has knowledge of all things.

In houses which God permits to be raised,
And His name to be mentioned therein,
There He is glorified, morning and evening,
By men whom neither commerce nor trade
Distracts from the remembrance of God,
From constant prayer, and from giving alms.
They fear a Day when hearts and eyes will turn and turn
    again,
When God shall reward them for their best deeds,
And multiply His favours upon them.
And God bestows His bounty, uncountable,
Upon whomsoever He wills.   24:38

As for the unbelievers, their works are like a mirage in a
    far-flung plain,
That a thirsty man imagines to be water,
Until, when he arrives thereto, he finds it to be nothing,
But there he finds God, Who pays him his account in full,
And God is swift to settle accounts.

Or else they are like shades obscure over a vast ocean,
Enveloped by the waves,
Above which are waves,
Above which is fog;
Darkest shades, piled one upon the other.
If he stretches forth his hand, he can scarcely see it.
He on whom God sheds no light, no light has he.   24:40

Do you not see how all that is in the heavens and earth
    glorifies God,
And the birds with wings outspread?
Each has learnt his prayer and his glorification.
And God knows full well what they do.

To God belongs the kingdom of the heavens and the earth,
And to God is the journey's end.   24:42

Do you not see how God drives the clouds,
Then blends them together,
Then turns them into billowing masses, and you can see the
    rain coming down from their crevices?
How He sends from the sky, from mountains therein,
    hailstones, with which He strikes whomever He wishes,
    and averts it from whomever He wishes?
The flash of its lightning almost blinds the eyes. God alternates
24:44   night with day; in this is a lesson to people of insight.

God created every creature from water. Some crawl on their
bellies, some on two legs, some on four. God creates what He
pleases, and God is Omnipotent.

We sent down revelations fully elucidated.

24:46   God guides whomsoever He wishes onto a straight path.

They say: 'We believe in God and in the Messenger, and we
obey.' But a band of them turns away thereafter, and these
are not believers. If summoned to God and His Messenger in
order to judge between them, a band of them will suddenly
refuse. If they have right on their side, they come to him in a
hurry. Is there sickness in their hearts? Or did they have second
thoughts? Or were they afraid that God and His Messenger
would do them an injustice? Rather, it is they who are unjust.
The believers, in contrast, when summoned to God and His
Messenger to judge between them, will merely say: 'We hear
and obey.' These are the prosperous. Whoso obeys God and
His Messenger, and fears God and is pious before Him – these
24:52   are the victors.

They swore by God a mighty oath that if you ordered them,
they would march out. Say: 'Do not swear by God – simple
obedience is best!' God is All-Experienced as to what you do.

Say: 'Obey God and obey the Messenger.' If they turn and
go, upon him rests his burden, and upon you your own. If you

obey Him, you will be guided aright. The Messenger is enjoined
only to deliver the clear message.   24:54

God has promised those among you who believed and did
righteous deeds to make them inherit the earth, as He caused
those before them to inherit, and to establish their religion on
firm foundations – the religion He sanctioned for them – and to
instil peace of mind following their fear. And let them worship
Me, and associate nothing with Me. Thereafter, whoso disbelieves, these are the dissolute.

Perform the prayer constantly, and pay alms, and obey the
Messenger – perhaps you will be shown mercy. Do not imagine
that the unbelievers can evade the power of God on earth. Their
refuge is hell, and a wretched destiny it is.   24:57

O believers, your slaves are to ask your permission, as also the
minors among you, on three occasions: before the dawn prayer,
when you remove your clothes at noon, and after the evening
prayer. These are times of your nakedness. But no blame
attaches to you or them thereafter, as they go to and fro, each
to each. Thus does God clarify His revelations to you, and God
is Omniscient, All-Wise. When your children reach the age of
puberty they are to ask permission as did others before them.
Thus does God clarify His revelations to you, and God is
Omniscient, All-Wise.   24:59

Women past the age of child-bearing, who do not look forward
to marriage – to them no blame attaches if they remove their
cloaks, but do not display any ornament. If they behave with
modesty this would be better for them. God is All-Hearing,
Omniscient.

No blame attaches to the blind; no blame attaches to the lame;
no blame attaches to the sick; and no blame attaches to you if
you eat at your own houses, or at the houses of your fathers

and your mothers, your brothers or your sisters, or the houses of your paternal uncles or aunts, or your maternal uncles and aunts, or any house whose keys you own, or at the house of a friend.

No blame attaches to you if you eat all together or scattered in groups. When entering a house, greet each other with the greeting of peace, a greeting blessed and seemly from God. Thus does God clarify His revelations to you; perhaps you will 24:61 understand.

The believers are those who believe in God and His Messenger. If they are with him on some common endeavour, they should not depart until they ask his permission. Those who ask your permission are the ones who believe in God and His Messenger. If they ask your permission to attend to some affair of theirs, grant permission to whomever of them you wish, and ask God's forgiveness for them. God is All-Forgiving, Compassionate to each.

Do not address the Messenger in your midst as you address one another. God knows those of you who slink away, hiding behind each other. Let those who defy his orders beware lest some ordeal should befall them, or else a painful torment. In truth, to God belongs what is in the heavens and on earth. He knows what you are about, and on the Day they are returned to Him, He shall inform them of what they did. And God has knowledge 24:64 of all things.

The Criterion

In the name of God,
Merciful to all,
Compassionate to each!

Blessed is He Who sent down the Criterion upon His servant,
    to be a warning to mankind!
He to Whom belongs the kingdom of the heavens and earth,
Who took to Himself no son,
Who never had a partner in His kingship,
Who created all things in perfect order.   25:2

And yet, instead of Him, they procure for themselves gods that
create nothing, but are themselves created, that have no power
to do themselves harm or benefit, and no power over life, death
or resurrection.

Those who blaspheme say: 'This is but falsehood which he
contrived, and other people have helped him with it. They have
committed iniquity and perjury.'
    They say: 'These are legends of the ancients that he has had writ-
ten down, and they are read out to him, morning and evening.'
    Say: 'He sent it down, Who knows the secret of the heavens
and earth. He is Ever-Forgiving, Compassionate to each.'
    They say: 'What is it with this Messenger who eats food and
wanders in the market-place? If only an angel were sent down
to be alongside him as a warner! Or if only a treasure were
dropped down upon him or he had an orchard from which he
could eat!'
    The wicked say: 'You are merely following a man bewitched.'   25:8

Behold how they draw parables for you and how they go astray,
and cannot find the right way. Blessed is He Who, if He so

wishes, can provide you with better than this: Gardens beneath
25:10 which rivers flow – and provide you with palaces.

They even denied the Hour!
    For he who denies the Hour We have prepared a raging Flame.
When it sees them from afar, they hear its rumbling and sighing.
When flung in chains into some narrow corner of it, they pray
there for extinction.
    Pray not for one extinction today; pray rather for many!
    Say: 'Is this better or the Garden of Eternity, promised to the
pious as reward and final destination? In it they obtain what
they desire, abiding for ever. This is a promise of your Lord, to
25:16 be asked of Him.'

There comes a Day when He shall herd them and what they
worship instead of God, and He shall say to them: 'Was it you
who led these My worshippers astray, or did they themselves
stray from the path?'
    And they shall answer: 'Glory to You! We ought not to have
adopted protectors other than You. But You gave them and
their forefathers enjoyment to the point where they forgot the
Remembrance and became a people utterly lost.'
    Thus, they shall refute what you claim, and you are powerless
to escape or be aided. If any of you commits such sin, We shall
25:19 make him taste a mighty torment.

We sent not before you any messengers but they ate food and
wandered in the market-place. Some of you We appointed as a
temptation to others. Will you bear this in patience? Your Lord
is All-Seeing.

Those who do not look forward to Our encounter say: 'If only
the angels were sent down upon him, or else we could see our
Lord!'
    Their souls have grown haughty, and they are exceedingly
insolent. The Day they see the angels is a day of no glad tidings

to the wicked; and these shall say: 'We beseech you not to harm
us!'

And We shall attend to their deeds, and turn them into drifting
specks of dust. The denizens of the Garden shall, on that Day,
be happier in abode, and more tranquil in repose.   25:24

A Day shall come when the sky is torn apart by clouds, and the
angels are sent down, in numbers vast. True sovereignty on that
Day shall belong to the All-Merciful, a Day that shall indeed be
arduous for unbelievers. That will be the Day when the sinner
shall bite his fingers and say: 'If only I had followed the Messenger on the path! Alas for me! I wish I had never taken so-and-so
as an intimate friend! He made me stray from the Remembrance
after it had come to me. Satan will always let man down.'

The Messenger shall say: 'My Lord, my people have decided
to forsake this Qur'an.'

Likewise, to every prophet We assigned an enemy from among
the reprobate. But let your Lord suffice as Guide and Champion.   25:31

Those who blaspheme say: 'If only the Qur'an had been sent
down upon him whole and undivided!'

Rather, to confirm your heart with it! And We made it to be
chanted, a sublime chant!

They bring you no simile without Us bringing you the Truth,
superior in sense.

Those herded to hell upon their faces – these are more evil in
abode and furthest in straying from the path.   25:34

We brought Moses the Book and appointed Aaron his brother
with him to be his deputy. And We said: 'Go to the people who
cried lies to Our revelations.' And We destroyed them utterly.
As for the people of Noah, when they had cried lies to the
messengers, We drowned them, and made of them a wonder to
mankind. For sinners We have prepared a torment most painful.
So too with 'Ad, Thamud and the people of al-Rass,* and many
generations in between.

25:39   To each We struck parables, and each We utterly devastated.

They have surely passed by that town upon which was rained a baneful rain. Did they not see it? Rather, they had no hope of resurrection. When they see you, they simply take you for mockery: 'Is this the fellow God sent as Messenger? He was about to lead us astray from our gods, had we not stood fast by them.'

25:42   They will surely know, when they witness the torment, which one strayed further from the way!

Have you observed him who took his own caprice as his god? Are you to act as his warden? Or do you imagine that most of them listen or understand?

25:44   They are just like cattle! Indeed, more lost in their ways!

Have you not seen how your Lord has stretched the shadow? Had He willed, He could have stood it still. The sun We made as a pointer to it. Then We draw it in to Ourselves, a little at a time.
It is He Who made the night to cloak you, sleep a time of rest, and the day a time of stirring.
It is He Who sent the winds as harbingers ahead of His mercy.
From the sky We pour down pure water, therewith to revive a region that was dead,
And to give to drink, among what We created, many cattle and humans.
And We divided it among them, in order that they remember, but most mankind persist in their denial.

Had We wished, We could have sent a warner to every town. So do not obey the blasphemers and, with It, exert yourself
25:52   against them, surpassingly.

It is He Who merged the two seas,
This one fresh and sweet water,

That one salty and bitter.
Between them He erected a barrier, an impassable boundary.
It is He Who, from water, created man,
Conferring on him kinship, of blood and of marriage.
Your Lord is Ever-Powerful.   25:54

And yet, instead of God, they worship what benefits them not,
nor harms them!
   The unbeliever has ever been ready to challenge his Lord.
   But you We sent only as a herald of glad tidings and a warner.

Say: 'I ask you no wage for it, except one who desires to follow
the way to his Lord.'

Place your trust in the Ever-Living, Who dies not,
And magnify His praise.
Let Him suffice as One All-Experienced as to the sins of His
   servants.
It is He Who created the heavens and the earth, and what is
   between them, in six days,
Then sat firmly on the throne.
All-Merciful is He! Ask about Him one who knows.   25:59

And if they are told: 'Bow down before the All-Merciful,' they
respond: 'What is the All-Merciful? Are we to bow down to
whatever you command us?' And it increases them in revulsion.

Blessed is He Who set up constellations in the sky,
And fixed therein a lamp, and a resplendent moon.
   It is He Who made night and day to succeed one another for
him who wishes to remember or wishes to offer thanks.   25:62

The true servants of the All-Merciful are those who walk the
   earth in humility,
And when the vicious address them their only word is: 'Peace!'
They are those who pray to their Lord, bowing or standing,

Those who say: 'Our Lord, avert from us the torment of hell;
      its torment is an eternal penalty. Wretched is it as
      residence and abode!'
Those who, when they spend, are neither wasteful nor
      niggardly,
But something reasonable in between.
Those who pray to no other god with God,
Who do not kill the soul which God declares hallowed except
      in justice,
Who fornicate not – he who does so shall undergo
      punishment,
And torment shall be multiplied upon him on the Day of
      Resurrection,
And he shall abide therein for ever, in disgrace;
Except one who repents, has faith and does good deeds,
These – God shall replace their sins with favours.
25:70 And God is All-Forgiving, Compassionate to each.

Whoso repents and does good deeds must repent to God in all
      sincerity.
And those who do not bear false witness,
Who, when passing by idle gossip, pass on in dignity;
Those who, when reminded of the verses of their Lord, do not
      bow down, dumb and blind;
Those who say: 'Our Lord, grant that from our spouses and
      our offspring comes that which comforts our eyes, and
25:74   make us as guides to the pious.'

It is these who shall be rewarded with the heavenly Chamber
for their patience, and where they shall encounter salutation
and peace, abiding therein for ever – glorious is it as final
residence and abode!
      Say: 'My Lord would pay you no heed were it not for your
25:77 prayer. For you consider it a lie, and this shall shackle you.'

The Poets

In the name of God,
Merciful to all,
Compassionate to each!

Ta' Sin Mim

Behold the Revelations of the Manifest Book!
And will you perchance torture yourself because they are not
   believers?
If We so wish, We could send down upon them from heaven a
   wonder,
At which their necks would remain bowed in humility.

There comes not to them any remembrance, inspired from
the All-Merciful, but they turn away from it.

They have cried lies! But there shall come to them the true
import of what they used to mock.

Have they not observed the earth and how many We planted
therein of every beauteous species?
In this is a wonder, but most of them are not believers.
It is your Lord Who is Almighty, Compassionate to each.   26:9

Remember when your Lord called out to Moses: 'Go forth to
that wicked people, the people of Pharaoh – will they not fear
Me?'

He said: 'My Lord, I fear they will call me a liar, that my
heart will grow impatient, and my tongue will not flow freely.
So send to Aaron. Besides, they hold me accountable for a crime,
and I fear they will kill me.'

He said: 'No, they shall not, so go forth, you two, with Our
revelations, and We shall be with you, listening. Go to Pharaoh
and say to him: "We are the messenger of the Lord of the
Worlds. So send out with us the Children of Israel."'   26:17

He said: 'Did we not raise you up among us as an infant? Did you not remain with us some years of your life? And then you went and committed your crime! You are indeed an ingrate!'

He said: 'I committed that crime when I was straying in error. So I fled from you in fear of you. But My Lord has granted me right judgement and made me a messenger. And is this the favour you reproach me with: that you enslaved the Children of Israel?'

Pharaoh said: 'What is the Lord of the Worlds?'

He said: 'He is Lord of the heavens and the earth, if you are true believers.'

To those around him he said: 'Are you listening?'

He said: 'He is your Lord and the Lord of your ancient forefathers.'

He said: 'This, your messenger who has been sent to you, is mad.'

He said: 'Lord of the East and the West, if you possess understanding.'

He said: 'If you take for god any other than me, I shall throw you in prison.'

He said: 'What if I bring you a manifest miracle?'

26:31   He said: 'Bring it on if you speak the truth.'

So he threw down his staff and, behold, it turned into a real serpent. And he pulled his hand out and, behold, it turned white for all to see.

To the chieftains round about he said: 'This fellow is a most experienced sorcerer. He intends to drive you out of your land with his sorcery. What do you advise?'

They said: 'Put him off, him and his brother, and send mar-
26:37   shals out to all cities to bring you every expert sorcerer.'

The sorcerers were then summoned for an appointment on a day made known.

To the people it was said: 'Are you all assembled? We might follow the sorcerers if they are the victors.'

When the sorcerers arrived, they said to Pharaoh: 'Are we to have our wage if we are the victors?'

He said: 'Yes, indeed, you will be among my intimates.' 26:42

Moses said to them: 'Throw down whatever you wish to throw.'

So they threw down their ropes and staffs and said: 'By the majesty of Pharaoh, we shall be the victors.'

Moses threw down his staff, whereupon it swallowed their deceits.

The sorcerers were thrown to the ground, prostrate.

They said: 'We believe in the Lord of the Worlds, the Lord of Moses and Aaron.' 26:48

He said: 'You believe in Him before I grant you leave? He is merely the greatest among you, who taught you sorcery. You will surely know! I shall cut off your hands and legs, on opposite sides, and then crucify you all.'

They said: 'No harm in that, for we shall return to our Lord. We hold out hope that our Lord will forgive us our sins, for we are the first to believe in Him.' 26:51

To Moses We revealed: 'March out at night with My servants, and you shall be followed.'

Pharaoh sent out marshals to all the cities: 'They are but a few stragglers, but they are a nuisance to us. We are all to be as one, and on alert.' 26:56

So We led them out of a land of gardens and springs, of treasures and a noble habitation. Thus did We bequeath them upon the Children of Israel.

But they followed them, heading eastward. When the two hosts were within sight of one another, the companions of Moses said: 'We will surely be overtaken.' He said: 'No. I have my Lord with me, Who shall guide me.' 26:62

We inspired Moses: 'Strike the sea with your staff,' and it split open, each side like a towering mountain. Then We brought the others near, and We saved Moses and all who were with him, and We drowned the others.

In this was a wonder, but most of them were not believers.

26:68 It is your Lord Who is Almighty, Compassionate to each.

And recite to them the story of Abraham, when he said to his father and people: 'What is it that you worship?'

They said: 'We worship idols and minister diligently to them.'

He said: 'Do they hear you when you pray? Do they benefit or harm you?'

They said: 'Rather, we found our forefathers so doing.'

He said: 'Do you realize what you have been worshipping, you and your ancient forefathers? They are an enemy to me, all except the Lord of the Worlds.

'He it was Who created me, and He it is Who guides me;

He feeds me and gives me to drink;

When I am sick He cures me;

He shall cause me to die and He shall resurrect me;

He, I hope, will forgive my sins on the Day of Judgement.

My Lord, grant me right reason, and make me follow the path of the virtuous,

And confer upon me a reputation for truth among later generations.

Admit me among those who shall inherit the Garden of Bliss,

And forgive my father – he was one of those who went astray.

Do not disgrace me the Day they are resurrected,

A Day when neither wealth nor progeny shall be of any worth,

26:89 Except one who approaches God with a pure heart.'

The Garden shall be drawn near to the pious,

And hell shall be revealed to the fiendish.

And it shall be said to them: 'Where now is what you once worshipped, instead of God? Will they come to your aid, or can they themselves prevail?'

Into it they shall be bundled, they and the fiendish,
As also the troops of Satan, outright.

They shall say, as they bicker therein: 'By God, we were
indeed in manifest error, when we held you equal to the Lord
of the Worlds. None led us astray but the wicked, and there is
none to plead for us, nor have we an intimate friend. If only we
could have a second chance, we would join the faithful.'   26:102

In this was a sign, but most of them were not believers.
    It is your Lord Who is Almighty, Compassionate to each.

Noah's people cried lies to the messengers.
    This is when their fellow tribesman Noah said to them: 'Will
you not fear God? To you I am a trustworthy messenger, so
fear God and obey me. I ask you no wage for it; my wage falls
solely upon the Lord of the Worlds. So fear God and obey me.'   26:110

They said: 'Are we to trust you when only the riff-raff have
followed you?'
    He said: 'How should I know what they do? Their account
rests only with my Lord, if only you knew. I am not one who
drives away believers. I am solely a manifest warner.'
    They said: 'If you do not desist, O Noah, you shall be
stoned.'
    He said: 'My Lord, my people are liars. So pronounce between
me and them a judgement, and deliver me and those with me
among the believers.'
So We delivered him and those with him in the teeming Ark,
And thereafter drowned the others.   26:120

In this was a sign, but most of them were not believers.
It is your Lord Who is Almighty, Compassionate to each.

'Ad cried lies to the messengers.
    This is when their fellow tribesman Hud said to them: 'Will
you not fear God? To you I am a trustworthy messenger, so

fear God and obey me. I ask you no wage for it; my wage falls solely upon the Lord of the Worlds. Do you build on every height a marvellous mansion for your revelry? And erect palaces, trusting to win immortality? When you rage, you rage like tyrants.

'So fear God and obey me.

'Fear Him Who provided you with what you well know: with cattle and progeny, gardens and fountains. I fear for you the

26:135 torment of a mighty Day.'

They said: 'It is all the same to us whether you admonish or do not admonish. This is nothing but fabrication, familiar among ancestors. Nor shall we be tormented.'

So they called him a liar and We destroyed them.

In this was a sign, but most of them were not believers.

26:140 It is your Lord Who is Almighty, Compassionate to each.

Thamud cried lies to the messengers.

This is when their fellow tribesman Salih said to them: 'Will you not fear God? To you I am a trustworthy Messenger, so fear God and obey me. I ask you no wage for it; my wage falls solely upon the Lord of the Worlds. Are you to be left in peace in this spot, amidst gardens and fountains, plantations and palms, their fruits full-ripe? And do you carve your homes from the mountains, exulting in them?

'But fear God and obey me.

'Do not obey the commands of the prodigal, those who cor-

26:152 rupt the earth and do not mend their ways.'

They said: 'You are but a man who succumbed to sorcery. You are merely a human being, like us, so produce a miracle if you are truthful.'

He said: 'Here is a she-camel. For her there is a draught of water, and for you a draught, on a certain day. Do her no violence, or else there shall seize you the torment of a mighty Day.'

But they hamstrung her and rose the following morning, repentant.

And the torment seized them.

In this was a sign, but most of them were not believers.

It is your Lord Who is Almighty, Compassionate to each.   26:159

The people of Lot cried lies to the messengers.

This is when their fellow tribesman Lot said to them: 'Will you not fear God? To you I am a trustworthy messenger, so fear God and obey me. I ask you no wage for it; my wage falls solely upon the Lord of the Worlds. Do you cohabit only with males among mankind, and abandon what your Lord created for you of wives? You are a people who have truly overstepped the limit.'   26:166

They said: 'If you do not desist, O Lot, you will be driven out.'

He said: 'I detest your practice. My Lord, deliver me and my family from what they do.'

So We delivered him and all his family, except for an old woman, who remained behind.

Then We destroyed the others, pouring down upon them rain – and what a frightful rain it was to a people already warned!   26:173

In this was a sign, but most of them were not believers.

It is your Lord Who is Almighty, Compassionate to each.

The People of the Thicket cried lies to the messengers.

This is when Shu'ayb said to them: 'Will you not fear God? To you I am a trustworthy messenger, so fear God and obey me. I ask you no wage for it; my wage falls solely upon the Lord of the Worlds. Be fair in weights and measures, and do not shortchange, but weigh with a balance that is true. Do not cheat people in the value of their goods, and do not cause havoc on

earth, corrupting it. Fear Him Who created you, as He created
26:184 earlier generations.'

They said: 'You are but a man who succumbed to sorcery. You
are merely a human being, like us, and we reckon you are a liar.
So make the sky fall upon us in fragments, if you speak the
truth.'

He said: 'My Lord knows best what you do.'

They called him a liar, and there seized them the torment of
the Day of the Shadow – it was indeed the torment of a mighty
26:189 Day!

In this was a sign, but most of them were not believers.
It is your Lord Who is Almighty, Compassionate to each.

It is indeed a Revelation from the Lord of the Worlds, brought
down by the Trustworthy Spirit, upon your heart, so that you
may be a warner, in manifest Arabic speech; it is also in the
26:196 Books of the ancients.

Is it not a proof to them that it is recognized by the scholars of
the Children of Israel?

Had We sent it down upon a foreigner, and he recited it to
them, they would still not believe in it.

Thus did We make it permeate the hearts of sinners: they do
not believe in it until they witness the painful torment. It comes
upon them suddenly, unawares.

They say: 'Will we be granted some respite?'

Do they wish to hasten Our punishment?

But consider this. If We grant them enjoyment for a number
of years, and there comes to them what they had been threatened
with, what use will it be to them – that which they were granted
26:207 to enjoy?

We destroyed no town except it had warners, as a remembrance,
and We were not unjust.

It was not the demons who brought it down: it befits them not, nor are they able to do so. They are barred from hearing it.

Do not pray to another god with God, else you will be among those tormented; and warn your closest relatives.

Lower the wing of your humility to those who have followed you from among the faithful; and if they disobey you, say: 'I am quit of what you do.'

And put your trust in the Almighty, the Compassionate to each, Who sees you when you rise to pray, and at your devotions amidst those who bow in worship. He is All-Hearing, Omniscient.

26:220

Shall I tell you upon whom the demons descend?
They descend upon every lying villain
Who gives ear but most of whom are liars.
And the poets – the tempters follow them.
Do you not see how they wander in every valley,
Boasting of things they have not done?
Except for those who believe and do good deeds,
Who mention the name of God often,
And who win through, after being wronged.
Wrongdoers will surely know what adversity they shall fall
    upon!

26:227

The Ants

In the name of God,
Merciful to all,
Compassionate to each!

Ta' Sad

Behold the verses of the Qur'an, and a Manifest Book!
A Guidance and glad tidings to the faithful,
Who perform the prayer, hand out alms and are certain of the
    hereafter.
As for those who do not believe in the hereafter, We have
    made their deeds appear attractive in their sight, so they
    stumble aimlessly in their error.
It is they whom an evil torment awaits, who shall be the
    greatest losers in the hereafter.

You are being taught the Qur'an from on high,
27:6 From One All-Wise, Omniscient.

Remember when Moses said to his family: 'I have glimpsed a
fire, and shall bring you news of it, or else a flaming brand, to
warm yourselves thereby.'

    When he drew near it, a voice called out to him: 'Blessed be
He Who is in the fire and around it! Glory be to God, Lord of
the Worlds! O Moses, it is I, God, Almighty, All-Wise. Throw
down your staff.'

    When he saw it twitching like a serpent he turned and fled,
and did not return.

    'O Moses, fear not. With Me, messengers have no cause to
fear, except one who did wrong, then exchanged good for evil.
I am All-Forgiving, Compassionate to each. Put your hand inside
your sleeve and it will come out white, but without harm.' This

was among nine other wonders done before Pharaoh and his people – they were indeed a people depraved.

When Our wonders came to them, for all to see, they said: 'This is sorcery manifest.' And they rejected them, though in their hearts they were convinced, out of wickedness and arrogance. See what fate came upon the debauched! 27:14

We bestowed knowledge on David and Solomon.

They said: 'Praise be to God Who preferred us above many of His believing worshippers.' And Solomon inherited David. He said: 'O people, we have been taught the language of birds, and granted of all gifts. This is truly a favour most conspicuous.' To Solomon were mustered his troops of *Jinn*, humans and birds, all held in strict order. Until, when they arrived at the Valley of Ants, an ant said: 'O ants, enter your dwellings lest Solomon and his troops should crush you unawares.' 27:18

He smiled in amusement at its words and said: 'My Lord, inspire me to offer thanks for the bounty You bestowed upon me and upon my parents, and to do a good deed of which You will approve, and admit me, through Your mercy, into the company of your virtuous servants.'

And he inspected the birds.

He said: 'Why do I not see the hoopoe? Or is he among the absent? I shall punish him most harshly or even slit his throat, unless he brings me a clear justification.' 27:21

But the bird was not absent for long.

He said: 'I have learnt what you have not. I come to you from Saba',* with a sure report. I found a woman ruling over them, and one granted of all gifts, with a magnificent throne. I found her and her people bowing in worship to the sun, instead of God. Satan has made their works appear attractive to them, and barred them from the way; thus they are not guided aright. If only they would bow in worship to God, Who reveals whatever is hidden in the heavens and on earth, Who knows what you

conceal and what you openly declare! God, there is no god but
27:26 He, Lord of the mighty throne!'

He said: 'We shall wait and see if you speak the truth or you
are a liar. Take this letter of mine and deliver it to them, then
turn aside and observe what answer they return.'

She said: 'O council, a noble letter has been delivered to me.
It is from Solomon and begins "In the name of God, Merciful
to all, Compassionate to each." It says: "Hold not your head
high against me, and come to me as Muslims."'

She said: 'O council, give me your considered opinion on this
matter, for I am not accustomed to decide a matter unless you
are present before me.'

They said: 'We are men of might and great courage, but the
decision is up to you. So consider what you wish to command.'

She said: 'When kings enter a city they corrupt it, and reduce
its grandees to abject misery. This is how they act. I am sending
27:35 them a gift, and will see what the messengers bring back.'

When the messenger came to Solomon, he said: 'Are you really
handing out money to me? What God has provided me with is
better than what He provided you. Indeed, you seem happy
with your gift! Go back to them and tell them that we shall
advance against them with troops they cannot resist, and shall
27:37 drive them out, abject and humbled.'

He said: 'O council, which one of you can bring me her throne
before they come to me as Muslims?' A giant *jinni* said: 'I shall
bring it to you, before you rise from your seat. I am powerful
and trusty enough to do it.'

Said one who had knowledge of the Book: 'I shall bring it to
you before you blink your eye.'

When he saw it set up firmly in his presence, he said: 'This is
a favour from my Lord, in order to test me whether I shall give
thanks or be ungrateful. Whoso gives thanks, gives thanks only

for his own good. Whoso is ungrateful, my Lord is All-Sufficient, All-Forgiving.'

27:40

He said: 'Disguise her throne and let us see whether she will be guided to it, or unguided.'

When she arrived, she was asked: 'Is this what your throne looks like?'

She said: 'It is nearly so.'

He said: 'We were granted Knowledge before her, and became Muslims. Barring her from right guidance is that which she worships instead of God. She belongs to a disbelieving nation.'

27:43

It was said to her: 'Enter the roofed terrace.' When she saw it, she thought it was a large body of water, and exposed her legs.

He said: 'This is a terrace burnished with glass.'

She said: 'My Lord, I have wronged myself and I have submitted, along with Solomon, to God, Lord of the Worlds.'

We sent to Thamud their fellow tribesman Salih, to call them to the worship of God, whereupon they became two contending groups.

He said: 'My people, why are you quick to do evil rather than good? If only you would ask for God's forgiveness, you may be shown mercy.'

They said: 'We hold you and those with you to be an evil omen.'

He said: 'Your omen comes from God. In truth, you are a people in thrall to sin.'

Inside the city was a band of nine who corrupted the land and did no good. They said: 'Let us swear by God to murder him and his family by night, then tell his avenger that we did not witness the murder of his family, and that we speak the truth.'

27:49

And they worked their cunning, and We worked Our cunning, of which they were unaware. Behold the outcome of their

cunning! We destroyed them and their people, outright. There stand their habitations, desolate because of their wickedness. In this is a sign to a people who understand. And We saved those
27:53 who believed and were pious.

And remember Lot, when he said to his people: 'Do you commit debauchery with open eyes? Do you really lust after men instead of women? You are indeed a vicious people.'
    No answer did his people give but to say: 'Drive out Lot's family from your town, for they are a people determined to be chaste.'
    So We delivered him and his family, except for his wife, whom We destined to remain behind. And We rained upon them a rain – baleful the rain that fell upon those who had been
27:58 warned!

Say: 'Praise be to God, and peace be upon His servants whom He elected! Is God better or is it what they associate with Him?
    'Is it not He Who created the heavens and the earth?
    'Who brought down water for you from the sky, from which We caused to sprout gardens most pleasing, whose trees you could not have planted?'
    Is there to be another god with God? Indeed, they are a people who set up equals to God!

Is it not He Who made the earth be at rest, and made rivers run through it, and erected mountains therein, and built a barrier between the two seas? Is there to be another god with God?
27:61 Truly, most of them have no understanding.

Is it not He Who answers the one in need when he prays to Him, Who draws away evil and makes you inherit the earth? Is there to be another god with God? Little do you remember!

Is it not He Who guides you in the darknesses of land and sea, Who sends the winds as glad tidings ahead of His mercy? Is

there to be another god with God? May God be exalted far
above what they associate with Him!   27:63

Is it not He Who originates creation then restores it? Who
grants you a livelihood from sky or earth? Is there to be
another god with God? Say: 'Show me your proof if you speak
the truth.'

Say: 'None in the heavens or on earth know the Unseen save
God.' They know not when they shall be resurrected. Indeed,
they have no knowledge of the hereafter; or rather they are in
doubt thereof; or rather they are blind to it.
   The blasphemers say: 'How can it be that when we and our
forefathers have turned to dust, we shall once again be brought
forth? We were promised this before, we and our forefathers.
This is nothing but legends of the ancients.'
   Say: 'Journey on earth and observe the fate of sinners.'
   Do not grieve for them, nor be anxious about that which they
are plotting.   27:70

They say: 'When will this promise come about if you people
speak the truth?'
   Say: 'Perhaps there comes near to you some of what you wish
to hasten.'
   Your Lord is gracious to mankind, but most do not offer
thanks.
   Your Lord knows what their hearts conceal and what they
declare.
   There is no hidden matter in heaven or on earth except it be
in a Manifest Book.   27:75

This Qur'an narrates to the Children of Israel most of what they
dispute about. It is a guidance and a mercy to the faithful. Your
Lord shall judge between them with His decree. He is Almighty,
Omniscient.

Put your trust in God, for you are upon a manifest truth. You cannot make the dead hear, nor make the deaf hear the call if they turn their backs and depart. Nor can you guide the blind away from their error. Only him can you make hear who 27:81 believes in Our revelations; and these are Muslims.

When the Decree falls upon them, We shall bring up a beast from the earth who will speak to them. But mankind is not convinced by Our signs.

A Day shall come when We shall herd from every nation a group who cried lies to Our revelations, all held in strict order. When they arrive, He will say: 'Did you cry lies to My revelations, and were unable to comprehend them? Or what else were you doing?' But the Decree shall be handed down to them because of their wickedness, and they shall become 27:85 speechless.

Have they not observed that We created the night for them to rest therein, and created the luminous day? In this surely are signs for a people of faith.

A Day shall come when the Trumpet shall be blown, and all who are in the heavens and earth shall be filled with fright, save 27:87 those whom God wills. But all shall come to it, grovelling.

And you will see the mountains, and imagine them standing still, as they flit by like clouds – God's devising, Who does all things to perfection. He is All-Experienced with what you do.

Whoso brings with him a righteous deed shall receive one better than it. That Day they shall be secure from fright. Whoso brings with him an evil deed – their faces shall be tumbled into 27:90 the Fire. Will you be rewarded other than how you acted?

I have only been commanded to worship the Lord of this city which God has sanctified. To Him all things belong. And

I have been commanded to be a Muslim, and to recite the Qur'an.

Whoso is guided, is guided for his own good. Whoso strays into error, say: 'I am merely a warner.'

Praise be to God! He shall show you His wonders, and you shall recognize them; nor is your Lord heedless of what you do. 27:93

The Narrative

In the name of God,
Merciful to all,
Compassionate to each!

Ta' Sin Mim

Behold the revelations of the Manifest Book!

We are reciting to you some reports of Moses and Pharaoh, the very truth to a people who believe. 28:3

Pharaoh had grown high and mighty on earth. He had turned its inhabitants into diverse classes, holding a group among them to be weak, slaughtering their progeny and debauching their womenfolk. He truly was a corrupter.

We, however, wish to bestow Our favour on those held to be weak on earth. We intend to make them guides to mankind, and make them the inheritors. We intend to establish them firmly on earth, and to make Pharaoh, Haman* and their troops witness at their hands what once they feared. 28:6

To the mother of Moses We revealed: 'Give him to suck. Then, if you fear for him, cast him into the river and fear not, nor grieve. We shall restore him to you and make him a messenger.'

The family of Pharaoh picked him up, to be for them an enemy and a source of grief.

28:8 Pharaoh, Haman and their troops were indeed in error.

The wife of Pharaoh said: 'May he be a comfort to the eye, for me and you. Do not kill him; perhaps he might benefit us, or we adopt him as a son' – all unawares.

The following day, the heart of Moses' mother was bereft of sense. She was on the point of revealing the truth about him had We not steadied her heart that she might become a believer. She said to her sister: 'Follow his tracks.' Her sister espied him from a distance, while they were unaware. We had already forbidden him suckling by wet-nurses, so she said: 'Shall I point out to you a household who would look after him for you and

28:12 raise him well?'

So We returned him to his mother, that her eye might be comforted and not grieve, and that she might know that God's promise is true.

But most of them do not understand.

When he reached full maturity, consummate in form, We endowed him with right judgement and knowledge. Thus do

28:14 We reward those who do good.

He entered the city, when its people were not paying notice, and found therein two men engaged in combat, this one belonging to his sect and that one to his enemies. The man from his own sect called out to him for help against the other, the enemy, and Moses punched and killed him.

He said: 'This is the work of Satan, for he is an enemy that leads astray, no doubt about it.'

He said: 'My Lord, I have wronged myself, so forgive me.' And He forgave him – He is All-Forgiving, Compassionate to

28:16 each.

He said: 'My Lord, because of Your favours to me, I shall never make common cause with criminals.'

The following day, he went about the city in fear and looking about him, when the man who the day before had called out to him for assistance was now screaming for his help. Moses said to him: 'You are clearly unregenerate.' When he was about to strike down the man who was an enemy to them both, he said: 'O Moses, do you intend to kill me as you killed a soul yesterday? You only want to be a despot in the land, and have no desire to do good.'

A man came running from the other end of the city, saying: 'O Moses, the council are planning to kill you, so depart. I give you good counsel.'   28:20

So he left the city, fearful and looking about him. He said: 'My Lord, deliver me from a wicked people.' When he set out in the direction of Midian, he said: 'Perchance my Lord will guide me to a straight path.'

Arriving at the waters of Midian, he found thereat a concourse of people drawing water and, to one side of them, two women tending flocks. He said: 'What is the matter with the two of you?' They said: 'We cannot give to drink until the shepherds have departed, and our father is an old man.' So he drew water for them and retired to the shade, saying: 'My Lord, I am in dire need of some act of goodness that You might send down upon me.'   28:24

One of the two women approached him, walking shyly, and said: 'My father invites you in order to reward you with a wage for drawing us water.' When he came to him and narrated to him the story of his life, he said: 'Fear not; you have been saved from an evil people.' One of the women said: 'Father, hire him; the best person to hire is one strong and trustworthy.'   28:26

He said: 'I wish to marry you to one of these two daughters of mine, provided you hire yourself to me for eight years. If you complete ten years, that would be a charitable act on your part. I do not wish to overburden you. And, God willing, you shall find me a man of righteousness.'

He said: 'Let this be the understanding between you and me. Whichever of the two terms I fulfil, let me suffer no injustice, 28:28 and may God be a witness of what we speak.'

When Moses fulfilled the allotted term, he departed with his family. He espied a fire upon the side of the mountain and said to his family: 'Stay behind. I have glimpsed a fire; perhaps I will bring you news of it or a brand from it, to warm yourselves thereby.'

Arriving at the fire, a voice called out to him from the right side of the valley, at a blessed spot, and coming from the tree: 'O Moses, it is I, God, Lord of the Worlds. Throw down your staff!'

When he saw it twitching like a serpent he turned and fled, and did not look back.

'O Moses, come near and be not afraid; you are safe from harm. Put your hand inside your sleeve and it shall come out white, but without harm. And press tight your hand to yourself to ward off fear. These are two wonders from your Lord to Pharaoh and his council – a people depraved.'

He said: 'My Lord, I killed one of them and fear they might kill me. My brother Aaron is more eloquent in tongue than me, so send him with me to back me up and verify my words. I fear they will call me a liar.'

He said: 'We shall grant you added strength, through your brother, and give power and authority to you both, so that they will not be able to come close to you because of Our wonders. 28:35 And those who follow you both shall be victorious.'

When Moses came to them with Our conspicuous wonders, they said: 'This is nothing but sorcery, artfully contrived. We never heard its like among our ancient forefathers.'

Moses said: 'My Lord knows best who comes with guidance

from Him, and who shall inherit the Final Abode. The wicked
shall not prosper.'

28:37

Pharaoh said: 'O council, I know no other god for you than me.
O Haman, fire some clay for me, and build me a tower that I
may climb up to the god of Moses. I consider him a liar.'

And he and his troops grew arrogant in the land, unjustly,
imagining they would not be restored to Us. So We seized him
and his troops and flung them into the sea – behold what end
they met, those evildoers! And We turned them into guides who
summon to the Fire. On the Day of Resurrection, they shall find
no support. In this life We pursued them with a curse, and on
the Day of Resurrection they shall be among the damned.

28:42

To Moses We brought the Book, after having destroyed earlier
generations, as an illumination to mankind, a guidance and a
mercy, that they might remember.

You yourself were not present at the western side of the mountain when We decreed the matter for Moses, nor were you a
witness to that event. Rather, We reared many generations,
upon whom time grew long.

Nor did you live among the people of Midian, reciting to
them Our verses. We, however, were sending the messengers.

Nor were you by the side of the mountain when We called
out. Rather, it was a mercy from your Lord, so that you may
warn a people to whom no warner before you had been sent;
perhaps they will ponder and reflect.

28:46

If some calamity befalls them for their past misdeeds, they
would say: 'Our Lord, if only You had sent us a messenger,
so we could abide by Your revelations and be among the
faithful.' And yet, when the Truth comes to them from Us,
they say: 'If only he was granted the like of what Moses was
granted!'

But did they not in fact repudiate what Moses was brought in the past?

Did they not say: 'Here are two sorceries, reinforcing each other'?

Did they not say: 'We spurn them both'?

Say: 'Bring a Book from God, more conducive to guidance than both, and I shall follow it, if you speak the truth.'

If they do not respond to you, know that they merely follow their caprice – and who is more lost than he who follows his caprice, without guidance from God? God guides not those who
28:50 are wicked.

We revealed to them Our Speech, without interruption, that they might remember – they to whom We brought the Book, and who believed in it before this present Revelation. And when it is recited to them, they say: 'We believe in it. It is the Truth from our Lord. We had indeed been Muslims before it.' These shall be paid their wages twice for their steadfastness; they ward off evil by doing good, and expend from what We provided them. If they hear idle talk they turn away from it and say: 'We have our deeds and you have your deeds. Peace be upon you!
28:55 We have no truck with the vicious.'

You do not guide those whom you love; rather, God guides whom He wishes, and He knows best who are guided aright.

They say: 'If we follow guidance with you we will be up-rooted from our land.' Did We not establish them firmly in a safe and sacred place, to which are conveyed crops of all varieties, as a provision from Us on high? But most of them are ignorant.

How many a town, grown excessively luxurious in manner of life, have We destroyed! Behold their habitations, uninhabited after them except for a few! It was We Who were their heirs.

Nor would your Lord have destroyed these towns unless He

had first sent a messenger to their capital city, reciting Our revelations.

Nor would We have destroyed these towns had not their inhabitants been wicked.   28:59

Whatever you have been granted are merely the joys of this present life and its adornments, but what is with God is better and more lasting. Will you not understand? Is he to whom We made a wonderful promise, which he will surely attain, the equal of one whom We allowed to savour the joys of this present life and then, on the Day of Resurrection, is among those summoned to judgement?   28:61

A Day shall come when He shall call out to them and say: 'Where are My associates whom you falsely avowed?'

Said they upon whom sentence was justly pronounced: 'Our Lord, here are the ones whom we tempted to unbelief. We tempted them as we too were tempted. We beg Your forgiveness. It was not us they worshipped.'

It was said: 'Summon your partners.'

They summoned them but they did not answer their call. And then they caught sight of the torment! If only they had followed the path of guidance!   28:64

A Day shall come when He shall call out to them and say: 'What answer did you give to the messengers?' All discourse shall be indistinct to them that Day, and they cannot question one another.

But he who repents, has faith and does a good deed might perhaps be among the prosperous. It is your Lord Who creates what He wills, and it is He Who chooses – the choice is not theirs. May God be glorified and exalted far above what they associate with Him!   28:68

Your Lord knows what their breasts conceal and what they
    openly declare.

He is God: there is no god but He.

To Him be praise in this life and the hereafter!

28:70 To Him is the final judgement. To Him you shall be returned.

Say: 'Consider. Had God made the night descend upon you without cease, and up to the Day of Resurrection, which god other than God can bring you light? Can you not hear?'

Say: 'Consider. Had God made the day shine upon you without cease, and up to the Day of Resurrection, which god other than God can bring you the night in which you may find rest? Can you not see?'

It is a mercy from Him that He created for you the night and the day, in which you may find rest or seek His bounty; perhaps

28:73 you will give thanks.

A Day shall come when He shall call out to them and say: 'Where are My associates whom you falsely avowed?'

From every nation We shall select a witness and say: 'Produce your proof.' They will then know that the Truth is God's. And

28:75 that which they fabricated shall stray far from them.

Korah* was from the nation of Moses, but he oppressed them. We had brought him treasures, the keys to which would have weighed down a band of stalwarts.

Remember when his people said to him: 'Do not exult in joy: God loves not those who exult. Among what God has brought you, seek too the Abode of the Afterlife but do not forget your share of good fortune in this life. Be generous, as God was generous with you, and do not intend corruption on earth: God loves not the corrupters.'

He said: 'I was granted all this because of a knowledge I possessed.'

Is that so? Did he not know that God destroyed many generations before him, men more powerful than he, more heaped with

28:78 wealth? But the guilty shall not be questioned about their sins.

So he came out to his people in all his finery. Said those who preferred this present life: 'If only we possessed what Korah was granted! He is assuredly a man of immense good fortune.'

Those granted knowledge said: 'You wretches! God's reward is better for one who believes and does good deeds. Only the steadfast shall encounter it.'   28:80

Then We caused the earth to cave in upon him and his house, and no group came to his rescue, apart from God, nor was he among those who won through. And those who, the day before, had coveted his position, rose up and said: 'Alas for us! It is God Who spreads forth His bounty to whom He wills among His servants, and He Who holds it back. Had God not shown us His favour, He would have caused the earth to cave in beneath us. Alas! The unbelievers shall not win through.'   28:82

There stands the Abode of the Hereafter, which We have assigned to those who do not seek exaltation on earth, nor corruption. The final outcome belongs to the pious.

Whoso comes forth with a good deed shall obtain one better than it.

Whoso comes forth with an evil deed, the evildoers shall be recompensed only in accordance with what they committed.   28:84

He Who ordained the Qur'an upon you shall bring you back to the place of origin.

Say: 'My Lord knows best who brings guidance and who is in manifest error.'

You had not expected the Book to be delivered to you, were it not for a mercy from your Lord.

So do not give aid to the blasphemers.

Let them not distract you from the revelations of God, now that they have been sent down upon you.

And call to the way of your Lord and be not among those who associate others with Him.

Do not pray to any other god with God: there is no god but He! All things shall pass away, except His face.

To Him belongs judgement.

28:88   To Him you shall be returned.

The Spider

In the name of God,
Merciful to all,
Compassionate to each!

Alif Lam Mim

Do people imagine they will be left alone if they simply say 'We believe', and are not put to the test? We put to the test those who came before them, that God may know who were sincere 29:3   and who were lying.

Or do those who commit sin imagine they can escape Us? Wretched is their opinion! Whoso desires the encounter with God, God's final destiny shall arrive. He is All-Hearing, 29:5   Omniscient.

Whoso exerts himself does so for his own benefit. And God has no need of mankind. As for those who believe and perform righteous deeds, We shall grant remission for their sinful deeds 29:7   and reward them for the best of their acts.

Upon man We enjoined charity towards father and mother. And yet, should they press you to associate with Me that of which you have no knowledge, do not obey them. To Me is your return, when I shall inform you of what you used to do.

And those who believe and perform righteous deeds, these We shall admit among the virtuous. There are people who say: 'We believe in God.' If he meets with harm in the cause of God, he considers harm done by other people as the equal of God's punishment. If, however, a victory comes from God, he would say: 'We were always on your side.' Does not God know best what lies in the breasts of mankind? God shall surely know those who truly believe and those who are hypocrites.   29:11

The unbelievers tell the believers: 'Follow our way and we shall shoulder your sins.' But they cannot shoulder their sins in any wise. Indeed, they are liars. They shall shoulder their own burdens – and burdens atop their burdens! On the Day of Resurrection they shall be questioned about the lies they fabricated.   29:13

We sent Noah to his people, and he remained among them for a thousand years, less fifty. And the Deluge swept them away, being wicked. But him We saved, as also the passengers in the Ark, making it a wonder to mankind.   29:15

Remember Abraham too, when he said to his people: 'Worship God and fear Him; that would be best for you if only you knew. It is mere idols you worship, instead of God, thereby engendering falsehood. Those you worship, instead of God, cannot provide you with livelihood; so seek your livelihood with God. Worship Him and give thanks to Him, for to Him you shall return. If you deny the truth, other nations before you also denied it. The Messenger is bound only to deliver the message with total clarity.'   29:18

Have they not observed how God originates creation and then revives it? Such is an easy matter for God.

Say: 'Journey in the land and observe how He began His creation, and how God then brings into being the life hereafter.

God has power over all things. He punishes whom He wills, and shows mercy to whom He wills, and to Him you shall be restored. Nor can you escape His power, on earth or in heaven. Apart from God, you have no protector, no champion.'

Those who deny God's revelations and the encounter with Him – these have despaired of My mercy, and there waits them
29:23 a painful torment.

No answer did his people give but to say: 'Kill him, or burn him!' But God delivered him from the fire. In this are signs for a people who believe.

He said: 'You took up the worship of idols, instead of God, only to please one another in this present life. However, on the Day of Resurrection, you shall charge one another with unbelief, and shall curse one another, and your refuge shall be the Fire. None shall come to your aid.'

Lot, following his example, said: 'I shall emigrate to my Lord.
29:26 He is Almighty, All-Wise.'

We bestowed on him Isaac and Jacob, and made prophecy and the Book descend in his progeny, and granted him his reward in this life while in the hereafter he shall be among the righteous.

Remember Lot, when he said to his people: 'You are committing a disgraceful act, unprecedented before you among mankind. You fornicate with men, you do violence to passersby and you commit foul deeds in your own assembly.'

No answer did his people give but to say: 'Bring on us the torment of God if you speak the truth.'

He said: 'My Lord, help me against a people who work
29:30 corruption.'

When Our heralds brought Abraham the good news, they said: 'We are about to destroy the inhabitants of this town, for its people are wicked.'

He said: 'But Lot lives there.'

They said: 'We know best who lives therein. We shall deliver him and his family, all but his wife, who shall remain behind.'

When Our heralds came to Lot, he was distressed and grew impatient with them.

They said: 'Fear not, and do not grieve. We are about to save you and your family, except for your wife who shall remain behind. We are about to send down on the inhabitants of this town a terrible torment from heaven because of their depravity.'

We left behind a clear trace of it to a people who understand.   29:35

To Midian was sent their fellow tribesman, Shu'ayb.

He said: 'My people, worship God and keep the Last Day in view, and do not work corruption on earth.' They called him a liar, and a great quake seized them and, on the morrow, they lay dead in their houses. So also with 'Ad and Thamud: you can see this clearly in their habitations. Satan had made their deeds attractive in their eyes, and barred them from the right path, even though they were a discerning nation. So also with Korah, Pharaoh and Haman: Moses had brought them manifest signs, but they grew arrogant on earth, and could not escape torment.   29:39

Each We seized for his sin: upon some We sent down a fire storm; some were seized by the Scream; some We caused the earth to cave in beneath them, and some We drowned. Nor would God have wronged them; rather, it was themselves they wronged.

The likeness of those who took to themselves patrons instead of God is like the spider that builds a house for itself. But surely the most fragile of houses is the spider's house, if only they knew! God knows what thing they worship instead of Him. He is Almighty, All-Wise.   29:42

These parables We strike for mankind, and only the wise understand them.

God created the heavens and earth in truth. In this is a sign to people who have faith.

Recite what has been revealed to you, and perform the prayer constantly: prayer repels debauchery and vice. The remembrance of God is the greatest of devotions; and God knows what 29:45 you do.

Do not argue with the People of the Book except in the best manner, save the wicked among them, and say: 'We believe in what has been sent down upon us, and sent down upon you. Our God and yours is One God, and to Him we submit.'

So too did We send down the Book upon you. Those to whom We brought the Book believe in it, as do some of them here present. None but the unbelievers repudiate Our revelations.

You never recited any Book before it, nor ever wrote it down with your right hand. Otherwise, the impious would have had their doubts. Rather, it contains revelations most clear in the hearts of those granted knowledge, and none repudiates Our 29:49 revelations save the wicked.

They say: 'If only some wonders had been sent down on him from his Lord!'

Say: 'Wonders are with God. I am only a manifest warner.'

Was it not enough for them that We sent down the Book on you to be recited to them? In this is a mercy and a remembrance to a people who have faith.

Say: 'God suffices as witness between you and me. He knows what is in the heavens and on earth. And those who believe in 29:52 falsehood and repudiate God – these are truly the losers.'

They ask you to hasten the torment upon them. Were it not for a stated term, the torment would have befallen them. It will indeed fall upon them suddenly, unawares.

They ask you to hasten the torment upon them, but hell shall

THE SPIDER 325

surely engulf the blasphemers. A Day shall come when the torment overshadows them from above them and from below their feet, and He shall say: 'Taste that which you used to commit!'

29:55

O worshippers of Mine who believe, My earth is wide.

It is Me you must worship.

Every soul shall taste death and then to Us you shall revert.

And those who believe and do good deeds – We shall lodge them in the Garden, in lofty chambers, beneath which rivers flow, abiding therein for ever. Excellent indeed is the wage of those who do good, those who stand fast, and who put their trust in their Lord!

29:59

How many a beast of burden there is that stores not its provisions. Rather, it is God Who provides for it – and for you. He is All-Hearing, Omniscient.

And if you ask them: 'Who created the heavens and the earth, and who made the sun and moon to do His bidding?' They will answer: 'It is God.'

How then can they possibly be so deluded?

29:61

God spreads wide His bounty to whomever He wishes among His servants, but He also withholds it. God has knowledge of all things.

And if you ask them: 'Who brings water down from the sky and therewith revives the earth after it is dead?' They will answer: 'It is God.' Say: 'Thanks be to God!' But most of them have no understanding.

29:63

This present life is nothing but frivolity and amusement. But the Abode of the Hereafter is the real life, if only they knew!

Embarked on a ship, they pray to God, sincere of faith. Once He delivers them safely to shore, behold, they ascribe partners to Him!

Let them blaspheme against what We brought them, and let
29:66   them enjoy themselves – they will surely know!

Do they not see that We established a peaceful sanctuary while
all around them people are rent by violence? And yet they believe
in falsehood and disown the bounty of God!

Who is more wicked than he who fabricates lies from God,
or calls the Truth a lie once it has come to him? Is not hell the
final berth of blasphemers?

But those who exerted themselves in Our cause – these We
shall guide to Our ways. God will assuredly stand with the
29:69   righteous.

The Byzantines

In the name of God,
Merciful to all,
Compassionate to each!

Alif Lam Mim

The Byzantines have been defeated in the nearer part of the
land, and yet, after their defeat, they shall be victorious – in a
few years.

It is God Who decides – as it was in the past, so it shall be in
future.

That day the believers shall rejoice at God's victory, for He
grants victory to whomever He wishes. He is Almighty, Com-
30:5   passionate to each.

This is God's promise, and God does not renege on His promise.
But most people are ignorant. They know only the externals of
30:7   this present life, but as for the hereafter they are totally heedless.

Have they not pondered within themselves? God did not create the heavens and earth, and what lies between, except in truth, and for a stated term.

And yet many there are who disavow the encounter with their Lord.

Have they not journeyed in the land and observed the final end of those who preceded them? They were greater than them in might. They ploughed the land and made it prosper to an extent greater than they have done. Their messengers came to them with clear signs. God did not wrong them: it was themselves they wronged. There then followed the punishment of those who had done the greatest evil, for they had repudiated the revelations of God and would mock them.   30:10

God originates creation, then restores it, and then to Him you shall be returned.

When the Hour arrives, sinners shall despair. Among their associates they shall find none to intercede for them, and they shall repudiate their associates. When the Hour arrives, it is then that they shall divide into groups.

Those who believed and did good deeds – these are in a Garden, overjoyed.

But those who blasphemed and cried lies to Our revelations and to My encounter in the hereafter – these shall be summoned to torment.   30:16

Glory be to God, when you retire at night and when you
   awake!
Praise be to Him in the heavens and on earth,
At night, and when you approach midday!
He brings forth the living from the dead and the dead from the
   living;
He revives the earth after its death, and thus will you too be
   brought forth.   30:19

Among His wonders is that He created you from clay and behold, you are human beings pervading the earth.

Among His wonders is that He created for you, from among yourselves, spouses with whom to find comfort, and instilled between you love and mercy. In these are signs for a people who ponder and reflect.

Among His wonders is the creation of the heavens and the earth, and the diversity of your languages and colours. In these are signs for mankind.

Among His wonders is your sleep by night and day, and your pursuit of His bounty. In these are signs for a people who can hear.

Among His wonders is that He displays the lightning to you, causing both fear and hope, and sends down from the heavens water wherewith He revives the earth after its death. In these are signs for a people who understand.

Among His wonders is that the heavens and earth are formed in accordance with His command. Then, when He sends out a call to you from beneath the earth, behold, you come forth.

To Him belongs whoever is in the heavens and on earth: all are obedient to Him.

It is He Who originates creation and then restores it, a matter easy for Him.

Highest in attributes is He, in the heavens and on earth.

30:27   He is Almighty, All-Wise.

He has struck a parable for you, drawn from yourselves. Are you partners with your slaves in what We bestowed upon you? Do you share equally in this bounty, and fear them as you fear one another? Thus do We make plain Our revelations to a people who understand.

Instead, the wicked pursued their caprice, in ignorance. Who can guide one whom God has led astray? None shall come to their rescue. So set your face to the true religion, in pristine faith.

This is the primordial nature that God implanted in mankind – there can be no change in God's creation.

This is the religion unswerving, but most people know it not.   30:30

Turn back to Him and fear Him. Perform the prayer constantly, and do not be among those who associate other gods with Him, those who have sundered their religion and turned into sects, each sect happy with what they have.

And if harm touches people, they pray to their Lord, turning penitently towards Him. Then, if He makes them taste a mercy from Him, behold, a party among them ascribe partners to their Lord, disowning what We conferred upon them.

Enjoy yourselves, for you will surely know!   30:34

Or is it that We sent down upon them some proof, whereby it tells them to ascribe partners to God?

If we make mankind taste mercy, they are happy with it, but if some affliction befalls them for their past misdeeds, behold, they despair. Do they not observe that God spreads forth His bounty to whomever He wills – and withholds it? In this are signs for a people who have faith.   30:37

So render to kinsmen what is their due, as also to the poor and the needy wayfarer. This is best for those who seek the face of God, and they shall prevail. What usury you practise, seeking thereby to multiply the wealth of people, shall not multiply with God. But the alms you render, seeking the face of God – these shall multiply their reward.   30:39

It is God Who created you, then provides for you, then causes you to die, then resurrects you. Are any of your partners capable of any of this? Glory to Him! May He be exalted above what they associate with Him!

Corruption has appeared on land and sea because of what

people's hands have earned. He will make them taste part of what they have committed; perhaps they will turn back.

Say: 'Journey in the land and observe the fate of those who 30:42 came before' – most had been polytheists.

So set your face towards the true religion, before a Day arrives from God, inevitable.

On that Day they shall be torn asunder.

Whoso disbelieved, upon him falls his disbelief. Whoso has done a righteous deed, it is for themselves that they prepare their berth, so that He may recompense, from His bounty, those who believed and did righteous deeds. God loves not the 30:45 unbelievers.

Among His signs is that He sends forth the winds bearing glad tidings, to make you taste His mercy, and that ships may run at His command, for you to seek His bounty; perhaps you will offer thanks. We sent before you messengers to their peoples, bringing them clear signs, and We took vengeance upon those who sinned, just as it was right and proper for Us to aid the 30:47 faithful.

God it is Who sends forth the winds, agitating clouds, which He then spreads across the sky in any manner He pleases. He turns it into billowing masses and you can see the rain coming forth from its crevices; and if He causes it to fall down on whomever He pleases of His servants, behold, they rejoice even though, before it was sent down upon them, they had been 30:49 despondent.

Behold the traces of God's mercy, how He revives the earth after its death! He it is Who will surely raise the dead to life, and He is Omnipotent.

And if We send forth a wind and they find it to have turned their harvest yellow, they remain thereafter blaspheming. You

cannot make the dead hear, nor make the deaf hear the call, if
they turn and walk away. Nor can you guide the blind away
from their error. It is only they who believe in Our revelations
whom you can make hear, and they are Muslims.   30:53

God it is Who created you from weakness then, following weakness, created strength then, following strength, created weakness and grey hairs. He creates what He wills. He is Omniscient,
Omnipotent.

The Day the Hour arrives, sinners shall swear they remained a
mere hour on earth; thus too did they fabricate lies.
    Said those granted knowledge and faith: 'You remained in
the Book of God until the Day of Resurrection. Here now is the
Day of Resurrection, but you were without understanding.'
    On that Day, the pleas of the wicked shall be in vain, nor
shall they be allowed to redeem themselves.   30:57

In this Qur'an, We have struck for mankind every sort of
parable. And if you bring them a proof, those who blaspheme
will say: 'You are merely dabbling in falsehood.' Thus does God
stamp the hearts of those who do not understand.

So bear with patience. God's promise is true; and be not dis-
heartened by those who have no conviction.   30:60

Luqman*

In the name of God,
Merciful to all,
Compassionate to each!

Alif Lam Mim

Behold the revelations of the Wise Book!
   A Guidance and a mercy to the righteous, who perform the prayer, pay the alms and are certain of the hereafter. These are 31:5 rightly guided by their Lord; these shall prevail.

Among people is one who trades in idle chatter, to lead astray from the path of God, without knowledge, and treats it as a pastime. To them there awaits a humiliating punishment. When Our revelations are recited to him, he turns away in arrogance, as if he had not heard them, or as if there is heaviness in his 31:7 ears. So give him tidings of a painful torment.

Those who believe and do righteous deeds shall attain the Gardens of Bliss, abiding therein eternally – a true promise from God. He is Almighty, All-Wise.

He raised up the heavens without pillars that you can see, and cast upon the earth towering mountains, lest it should shake you violently, and He set loose in it every sort of animal. From the heavens We sent down water and caused to grow therein of every noble species.
   This is God's creation – now show Me what they created, 31:11 those other than Him! Indeed, the wicked are in manifest error.

We endowed Luqman with wisdom: 'Give thanks to God, for whoso renders thanks does so to his own benefit but whoso blasphemes, God is All-Sufficient, All-Praiseworthy.'

And remember when Luqman said to his son, admonishing him: 'My son, do not ascribe partners to God for such is a terrible sin.'   31:13

And We enjoined upon man to care for his parents – his mother carried him in hardship upon hardship, and his weaning lasts two years – and to say: 'Give thanks to Me and to your parents, and to Me is your homecoming.' And yet, should they press you to associate with Me that of which you have no knowledge, do not obey them, but befriend them in this life, in kindness. And follow the path of one who has turned in repentance to Me. Then to Me is your final return and I will inform you of what you used to do.   31:15

'My son, even if it were the weight of a mustard seed upon a rock, or in the heavens, or on earth, God shall bring it to light. God is All-Perceptive, All-Experienced.

'My son, perform the prayer, command to virtue and forbid evil, and bear with patience whatever befalls you. This is a course of action upright and prudent.

'Do not turn your cheek away from people in contempt, and do not walk merrily upon the earth: God loves not every swaggering snob. Let your walk be modest and keep your voice low: the ugliest of sounds is the braying of an ass.'   31:19

Have you not observed how God placed at your service all that is in the heavens and on earth? How He showered His blessings upon you, visible and invisible? And yet there are people who argue about God without any knowledge, any guidance or any Luminous Book. And if it is said to them: 'Follow what God has sent down,' they answer: 'Rather we shall follow what we find our forefathers had followed.' Even if Satan is calling them to the torment of a raging Fire?   31:21

Whoso surrenders his face to God, and acts righteously, has held fast to a handle most secure. To God belongs the outcome of all affairs.

Whoso blasphemes, let not his blasphemy grieve you.

To Us is their return, whereupon We shall inform them of what they used to do.

God knows best what lies within breasts.

We allow them a little enjoyment, then We drive them on to
31:24 a harsh torment.

And if you ask them: 'Who created the heavens and earth?' They answer: 'God.' Say: 'Praise be to God!', but most of them have no understanding. To God belongs all that is in the heavens and on earth. God is All-Sufficient, All-Praiseworthy.

If every tree on earth was a pen refilled by the sea, and by seven more seas besides, the words of God would not be exhausted.
31:27 God is Almighty, All-Wise.

He created you not, nor shall He resurrect you, save as if you were a single soul. God is All-Hearing, All-Seeing.

Have you not seen how God entwines night with day and day with night? How He made the sun and moon to do His bidding, each running for an appointed time?

God is All-Experienced with what you do.

That is because God is Truth, and that to whom they pray,
31:30 instead of Him, is falsehood. God is All-Exalted, All-Surpassing.

Have you not seen that ships run in the sea by God's blessing, to make you see His wonders? In this are signs for every long-suffering, much-thankful person.

And if the waves cover them like arching shadows, they pray to God, sincere in faith. But when He delivers them safely to shore, some retain a little faith. But none repudiates Our signs save the treacherous blasphemer.

Mankind, fear your Lord.

Dread a Day when no parent will answer for his child,

Nor any child for their parent, in any way.
God's promise is true.
So let not this present life deceive you,
And let not the Tempter tempt you regarding God.   31:33

With God rests knowledge of the Hour.
He sends down the sustaining rain,
And knows what wombs enfold.
And no soul can know what it might earn tomorrow;
And no soul can know in what land it shall die.

God is Omniscient, All-Experienced.   31:34

The Prostration

In the name of God,
Merciful to all,
Compassionate to each!

Alif Lam Mim

The revelation of the Book, of which there is no doubt,
From the Lord of the Worlds!   32:2

Or do they say: 'He forged it?'
   Rather, it is the Truth from your Lord, to warn a people to
whom no warner had been sent before you, that they may be
guided.

It is God Who created the heavens and the earth, and everything
in between, in six days, then sat firmly on the throne.
   Apart from Him, you have no patron and no intercessor. Will
you not reflect?
   He governs creation from the heavens to the earth, and it

ascends back to Him in one day, the length of which is a
32:5   thousand years by your reckoning.

Such is the Knower of the Unseen and the Seen, Almighty,
    Compassionate to each!
He Who perfected everything He created, and fashioned man's
    creation from clay,
Then made his progeny to issue from a sordid fluid,
Then gave him shape and breathed into him of His spirit,
Then granted you hearing, eyesight and hearts – but little
32:9   thanks do you give in return.

They say: 'So then, once consigned to earth, are we to be created
anew?'
    In fact, they disavow the encounter with their Lord.
    Say: 'The angel of death, entrusted with you, shall cause you
to die and then to your Lord you shall be returned.'
    If only you could see the sinners that Day, their heads bowed
before their Lord, saying: 'Our Lord, look down upon us and
hear us. Restore us to life and we shall act righteously. We are
firm of faith.'
    Had We wished, We could have granted each soul its right
guidance. But My decree is binding: I shall fill hell with both
Jinn and humans.
    So taste it – and since you forgot the encounter of this your
Day, We have forgotten you – taste the punishment of eternity
32:14   for what you have committed.

They only believe in Our revelations who, when reminded of
them, fall down in prostration, glorifying the praise of their
Lord; nor are they too proud to do so. Their limbs shun their
beds, as they pray to their Lord in fear and expectation, and
expend of what We provided them. No soul knows what lies in
wait for them to comfort the eye, as a reward for what they did.
Is he who was faithful to be the equal of one who was dissolute?
32:18   They are indeed unequal.

As for those who believed and did righteous deeds, to them belong the Gardens of Refuge as abodes, as a reward for their works. The dissolute, however, shall have the Fire as their refuge: each time they purpose to leave it, they are turned back to it, and it is said to them: 'Taste the torment of the Fire, which once you disowned.' We shall make them taste the lesser torment rather than the greater – perchance they might return. Who is more wicked than he who, when reminded of his Lord's revelations, turns away from them? We shall surely take vengeance upon sinners.   32:22

We brought Moses the Book – so do not be in doubt regarding His encounter – and We made him a guide to the Children of Israel. And of their number We appointed leaders who guided by Our command, for they had borne with patience, and believed firmly in Our revelations.   32:24

Your Lord shall decide between them on the Day of Resurrection as to that over which they differed. Did He not make amply clear to them how many generations We destroyed before them, as they walked about in their homes? In this are signs: will they not hear?

Do they not observe how We drive water to a land without vegetation, and bring forth therewith crops on which their cattle and they themselves feed? Can they not see?   32:27

They say: 'When will this Verdict come to pass if you speak the truth?'

Say: 'On the Day of the Verdict the faith of blasphemers shall be of no use to them, nor will they be granted respite.'

So turn away from them and wait – and they too will be waiting.   32:30

The Confederate Troops

In the name of God,
Merciful to all,
Compassionate to each!

O Prophet, fear God and do not obey the unbelievers and Hypocrites. God is Omniscient, All-Wise. Follow what is revealed to you by your Lord; God is All-Experienced as to what you do. Put your trust in God – let God suffice as worthy 33:3 of all trust.

God did not place two hearts inside a man's chest.

God has not made the wives you cast out by saying 'You are to me like my mother's back'* to be truly your mothers, nor has He made your adopted children to be like your true children. This is merely something you utter with your mouths, but God speaks the truth and guides to the right path. So call them by their fathers' names: this is more fair with God. If you do not know who their fathers are, then they are your brothers in faith or your clients. But no blame attaches to you if you make a mistake – save only in what your hearts premeditate. God is 33:5 All-Forgiving, Compassionate to each.

The Prophet is more caring of the believers than they are of themselves, and his wives are their mothers. Kinsmen by blood are more caring for one another in the Book of God than the believers and Emigrants, unless you wish to bestow some act of kindness upon your clients. This is inscribed in 33:6 the Book.

Remember when We received from prophets their pledges: from you and Noah, Abraham and Moses and Jesus son of Mary. From them We received a most solemn pledge, so that He may

question the sincere regarding their sincerity. To unbelievers He
has prepared a most painful torment.

33:8

O believers, remember the blessing of God upon you when
enemy troops attacked you and We sent against them a wind,
and troops invisible to you. And God is All-Aware of what
you do.

Remember when they attacked you from higher ground and
lower, when eyes were transfixed, and hearts reached up to
throats, and you thought evil thoughts of God.

It was there that the believers were tested, and convulsed a
mighty convulsion.

It was then that the Hypocrites and those sick in heart said:
'God and His Prophet promised us nothing but delusion.'

It was then that a party of them said: 'People of Yathrib,*
this is no place for you to linger in, so fall back.' And a group
of them asked the Prophet's permission saying: 'Our homes are
totally exposed' – nor were they really exposed, for they merely
intended to flee. Had their homes been invaded from every side,
and they were asked to renege on their faith, they would have
accepted, and would not have clung to it for long. They had
previously given their solemn word before God that they would
not turn their backs in flight, and the Word of God shall be held
accountable.

Say: 'Flight will do you no good when you flee death or
slaughter, for you will only be granted enjoyment for a little
while.'

Say: 'Who shall protect you against God if He intends you
evil or intends you mercy?' They shall not find, apart from God,
any patron nor any champion.

33:17

God must surely know who among you discourage others and
who are the ones who say to their brothers: 'Come quickly to
us' – for they seldom march to war. Chary are they towards
you. For, when terror approaches, you see them staring at you,
their eyes rolling like one swooning in death. But when the

terror recedes, they bruise you with sharp tongues and are chary
with good fortune. These men have not believed, and God shall
33:19   render their works futile – a matter easy for God.

They imagine the Confederates* have not really withdrawn, but
if the Confederates return, they wish they could escape into the
wilderness with the Bedouins, there to inquire about your news;
but had they been among you, they would have done little
fighting.

In the Prophet of God you have an excellent example to follow
for one who seeks God and the Last Day, and who remembers
33:21   God often.

When the believers saw the Confederates they said: 'This is what
God and His Prophet promised us, and God and His Prophet
have spoken the truth.' This only increased them in faith and
submission.

Among the believers are men who are true to their word with
God: some have fulfilled it through death, and some are waiting,
never wavering in their constancy.
      This is so in order that God may reward the sincere for their
sincerity and punish the Hypocrites if He wills, or else pardon
33:24   them. God is All-Forgiving, Compassionate to each.

God repelled the unbelievers, bitterly angry, and having gained
nothing, and He spared the believers combat. God is All-
Powerful, Almighty.
      He compelled those who aided them from among the People
of the Book to come down from their strongholds, and cast
terror into their hearts – some of them you killed, others you
took prisoner. And He made you inherit their lands, their homes
and their wealth, as well as a region you had never set foot in
33:27   before. And God has power over all things.

O Prophet, tell your wives: 'If you desire this present life and its adornments, come let me provide for you and part with you amicably. But if you choose God and His Prophet and the Abode of the Hereafter, God has made ready for the righteous among you a most glorious reward.'

33:29

O wives of the Prophet, if any of you commits a proven indecency, torment shall be multiplied upon her twice over, a matter easy for God. And if any of you devoutly obeys God and His Prophet, and does good deeds, We shall pay her reward twice over, and We have made ready for her a noble provision.

33:31

O wives of the Prophet, you are not like other women if you are pious. So do not speak enticingly lest he who has sickness in his heart lust after you, but be chaste in your speech. Remain in your homes, and do not display your adornments, as was the case with the earlier Age of Barbarism.* Perform the prayer and pay the alms, and obey God and His Prophet – God wishes only to drive away pollution from you, members of the household, and to purify you, purify you completely. And mention what is recited in your homes of God's revelations and wisdom. God is All-Tender, All-Experienced.

33:34

Muslim men and Muslim women,
Believing men and believing women,
Devout men and devout women,
Sincere men and sincere women,
Patient men and patient women,
Humble men and humble women,
Charitable men and charitable women,
Fasting men and fasting women,
Men who guard their chastity, and women who guard their
    chastity,
Men who often remember God, and women who often
    remember God,

To all of them God has made ready a pardon and a glorious
33:35   reward.

It is not for any believer, man or woman, if God and His Prophet
decide some matter, to have liberty of choice in action. Whoso
disobeys God and His Prophet has strayed far in manifest error.

Remember when you said to him to whom God had been generous, and you had been generous: 'Retain your wife, and be pious
before God' – all the while hiding within yourself what God
was to reveal, and fearing people, though God is more worthy
of your fear.
    Thus, when Zayd* had satisfied his desire for her, We gave
her in marriage to you in order that no blame might attach to
the believers regarding wives of their adopted children, once
they have satisfied their desire for them. God's command shall
be enforced. No blame attaches to the Prophet in what God has
ordained for him – such has been the precedent of God regarding
those who came before. The command of God is fate decreed.
Such also was the case with those who transmit the messages of
God and fear Him, fearing none but God. And God suffices as
33:39   Appraiser.

Muhammad is not the father of any man among you, but he is
the Prophet of God and the Seal of Prophets. God has knowledge
of all things.

O believers, remember God frequently and glorify Him morning
and evening. It is He Who blesses you, along with His angels,
in order to lead you out of the darkness and into the light. He
is Ever-Merciful to the believers. Their greeting, the Day they
encounter Him, is 'Peace!' For them He has made ready a noble
33:44   reward.

O Prophet, We have sent you as a witness, a herald of glad
tidings and a warner, one who calls to God, and a luminous

lamp. Give glad tidings to the believers that they shall obtain from God a marvellous favour. Do not obey the blasphemers and Hypocrites, and disregard their harm. Put your trust in God and let God suffice as Protector.   33:48

O believers, if you marry believing women and then divorce them before you have touched them, you are not to count for them any waiting period. Provide for them and part with them amicably.

O Prophet, We have made licit for you the wives to whom you have given their bridal money, as also the slaves that God assigned you as war booty, the daughters of your paternal uncles and aunts, the daughters of your maternal uncles and aunts, who emigrated with you, and also a believing woman if she offers herself to the Prophet, provided the Prophet wishes to marry her, as a special dispensation to you only, but not to the believers. We know what We ordained upon them regarding their wives and slaves so that no blame might attach to you. God is All-Forgiving, Compassionate to each.   33:50

You may defer any of them you wish, and take in any of them you wish. And should you desire any of those you had deferred, no blame attaches to you – that is more likely to give them contentment, prevent them from sorrowing, and be well pleased with what you have granted all of them. God knows what is in your hearts, and God is Omniscient, All-Forbearing. Henceforth it is not licit for you to take more wives, nor to exchange them for other wives even if you admire their beauty – except for slaves. God watches closely over all things.   33:52

O believers, do not enter the chambers of the Prophet for a meal unless given leave, and do not wait around for it to be well cooked. Rather, if invited enter, and when fed disperse, not lingering for conversation. This behaviour irritates the Prophet, who is embarrassed to tell you, but God is not embarrassed by the truth. And if you ask his wives for some favour, do so from behind a screen; this is more chaste for both your hearts and theirs. You must not offend the Prophet, nor must you ever marry his wives after him, for such would be a mighty sin in the sight of God. Whether you reveal a thing or whether you conceal 33:54 it, God has perfect knowledge of all things.

No blame attaches to the Prophet's wives if they unveil before their fathers, their sons, their brothers, their nephews and nieces, paternal or maternal, their female visitors or their slaves. And let them fear God: God is a witness of all things.

God and His angels bless the Prophet. O believers, bless him and greet him with the full greeting of peace. Those who offend the Prophet are cursed by God in this life and in the hereafter. 33:57 To them He has made ready an abasing torment.

Those who offend the believers, men or women, for acts they did not commit, shall bear a burden of perjury and manifest sin.

O Prophet, tell your wives, your daughters and women believers to wrap their outer garments closely around them, for this makes it more likely that they will be recognized and not be 33:59 harassed. God is All-Forgiving, Compassionate to each.

If the Hypocrites, and the sick in heart, and those who spread panic in the city, do not desist, We will give you sway over them, and then they will no longer be your neighbours therein, except for a short while. Accursed they shall be; wherever they are found they shall be captured and killed outright. Such has been the precedent of God with those who came before, and you 33:62 shall not find God's precedent to vary.

People ask you about the Hour.
   Say: 'Knowledge of it rests with God.' Who knows? Perhaps the Hour has drawn near.

God has cursed the unbelievers and made ready for them a raging Flame, abiding therein for ever. They shall find no patron and no champion, upon a Day when their faces are twisting and turning in the Fire. And they shall say: 'If only we had obeyed God and His Messenger!' adding: 'Our Lord, we obeyed our chieftains and grandees, and they led us astray from the path. Our Lord, double their torment and curse them with a mighty curse!'   33:68

O believers, do not be like those who taunted Moses but God declared him free of what they charged him with, and he was found honourable in God's sight.

O believers, fear God and speak in a forthright manner, and He will set straight your works and forgive your misdeeds. Whoso obeys God and His Messenger has won a mighty victory.   33:71

We offered the Trust to the heavens, the earth and the mountains, but they declined to carry it and were afraid of it, but man carried it – and he has ever been unjust, intemperate.

God shall punish the Hypocrites, male and female, and the idolaters, male and female, and shall forgive the believers, male and female. God is All-Forgiving, Compassionate to each.   33:73

Sheba

In the name of God,
Merciful to all,
Compassionate to each!

Praise be to God to Whom belongs all that is in the heavens
    and earth!
And praise to Him in the hereafter!
He is All-Wise, All-Experienced.

He knows what enters into the earth and what comes out of it,
What descends from heaven and what ascends to it;
34:2 He is Compassionate to each, All-Forgiving.

The unbelievers say: 'The Hour shall not come upon us.'
Say: 'Yes indeed, by my Lord, it shall come upon you, through Him Who knows the Unseen! There escapes Him not even the weight of an atom in the heavens or on earth, nor is there anything smaller or larger but is inscribed in a Manifest Book. He shall recompense those who believe and do righteous deeds: they shall receive an ample pardon and a noble provision. But they who challenge Our revelations, thinking to refute them –
34:5 these shall receive a torment of a most painful agony.'

Those granted knowledge, such as was sent down upon you from your Lord, consider it to be true, and to guide to the path of the Almighty and All-Praiseworthy.
Those who blaspheme say: 'Shall we point out to you a man who prophesies to you that, once torn to shreds, you shall be created anew? Has he forged a lie upon God or does he have a touch of madness?'
It is they rather who believe not in the hereafter – it is they who shall be in torment and are far astray. Do they not reflect on what lies before and behind them of the heaven and earth? If We wish, We can make the earth cave in beneath them, or hurl down upon them missiles from heaven. In this is a sign for
34:9 every devout servant.

Upon David We bestowed of Our grace: 'O mountains, join him in glorifying God, as too the birds.' And We made iron soft for his benefit, and said to him: 'Make coats of mail and fashion their links in right measure. And you all, do good deeds for I
34:11 see full well what you do.'

To Solomon We granted power over the winds, blowing for a month in one direction and a month in another. And We made the fountain of brass to flow for him, and the *Jinn* to labour in his presence by his Lord's leave. Whoso among them strayed from Our command, We would make him taste some of the torment of the raging Flame.

They fashioned for him whatever he wished: temples, statues, bowls as large as water troughs, and cauldrons firmly fixed. 'O House of David, offer thanks' – but only a few of My servants are thankful.

34:13

When We decreed his death, it was but a crawling creature of earth which indicated to them he was dead, as it gnawed his staff. When he fell, the *Jinn* realized that, had they known the Unseen, they would not have lasted in their abasing torment.

In the homelands of Sheba there was a wonder: two gardens to right and left. 'Eat from the bounty of your Lord and give thanks to Him' – a goodly town and a Lord All-Forgiving.

But they took no notice, so We let loose upon them the flood of 'Arim and, in exchange for the two gardens, We substituted two other gardens bearing bitter fruit, tamarisk bushes and a scattering of lote-trees. This is how We requited them, for they had blasphemed – and do We requite any but the blasphemer?

34:17

Between them and the towns We had blessed, We placed towns in a row, and We made them easy of access: 'Travel therein by night or day, in safety.'

Instead, they said: 'Our Lord, make far and distant the journeys between us and them.'

They wronged themselves, so We turned them into topics of legend, and scattered them utterly. In these are signs for every steadfast and thankful person.

Satan thus vindicated his low opinion of them, and they followed him, all but a band of believers. And he would not have held sway over them except in order for Us to know who

believes in the hereafter and who is in doubt thereof – your
34:21 Lord is Guardian over all things.

Say: 'Call on those you claim to worship instead of God. They
possess not even an atom's weight of power in the heavens or
on earth. In neither place do they have any share, nor is any of
them of any use to Him.'

Intercession is of no value in His sight except for one to whom
He grants leave – until, when terror is removed from their
hearts, they shall ask: 'What did your Lord say?' and they shall
34:23 answer: 'The truth!' He is All-Exalted, All-Supreme.

Say: 'Who provides for you from the heavens and earth?'
    Say: 'It is God. And either we or you are rightly guided, or
else astray in manifest error.'
    Say: 'You shall not be questioned as to what we committed,
nor will we be questioned as to what you did.'
    Say: 'Our Lord shall bring us together and shall then decide
between us in truth. He is the All-Decider, All-Knower.'
    Say: 'Show me those you joined to Him as partners. No
34:27 indeed! Rather, He is God, Almighty, All-Wise!'

We sent you not but to all of mankind – a herald of glad tidings
and a warner.
    But most of mankind has no understanding.
    They say: 'When is this promise due, if you people are speak-
ing the truth?'
    Say: 'There awaits you an appointment on a Day which you
34:30 can neither postpone, nor yet bring forward, by one instant.'

The blasphemers say: 'We shall not believe in this Qur'an or in
what came before it.' If only you could see the sinners then,
captive before their Lord, and arguing back and forth with one
another!
    Those considered weak shall say to the arrogant: 'Were it not

for you, we would have been believers,' and the arrogant shall answer the weak: 'Was it really us who barred you from right guidance, once it had come to you? No indeed! You yourselves were sinful.'

The weak shall answer: 'It was rather your plotting against us, day and night, as you commanded us to blaspheme against God and to contrive peers for Him.'

They shall repent in secret when they see the torment. And We shall place chains around the necks of unbelievers – will they be rewarded for anything other than what they used to do?   34:33

We sent no warner to any town without its men of luxury saying: 'We disown what you have been sent with,' adding: 'We have ampler wealth and more progeny, and we shall not be tormented.'

Say: 'My Lord spreads out His bounty to whomever He pleases, or withholds it. But most people have no understanding.'

Your wealth and progeny will not be the things that bring you close to Us, save for him who believes and does good deeds – these shall obtain a doubled reward for their works, and shall rest in Celestial Chambers, free of all cares.

But they who challenge Our revelations, seeking to undermine them – they shall be summoned to the torment.   34:38

Say: 'My Lord spreads out His bounty to whomever He pleases among His servants, or withholds it. Whatever you spend He shall make it up for you, and He is the best of providers.'

A Day shall come when He shall muster them all, and then say to the angels: 'Was it you these people worshipped?' and they shall answer: 'Glory be to you! You are our Master, not them! Rather, they worshipped the *Jinn*, and most believed in them.'

This Day you can do each other neither profit nor harm, and We shall say to those who sinned: 'Taste the torment of the Fire in which you disbelieved.'   34:42

And when Our manifest revelations are recited to them, they say: 'He is nothing but a human being who intends to dissuade you from what your forefathers worshipped,' adding: 'This is merely fabricated falsehood.'

When the Truth came to them, the blasphemers said: 'This is nothing but manifest sorcery.'

We had not sent them Scriptures to study, nor had We sent them a warner before you. Those who came before them had also cried lies – and these people here have not attained a tenth of the power We had granted the former. But they too had cried 34:45 lies to My messengers – behold how I reversed their fortune!

Say: 'I offer you a single counsel: draw close to God, in twos and ones, and then reflect. There is no touch of madness in your fellow townsman. He is merely a warner to you that great suffering is imminent.'

Say: 'If ever I ask you for a wage, here, it is yours! My wage falls only on God, and He is a witness of all things.'

Say: 'My Lord casts down the Truth – Knower of the Unseen is He.'

Say: 'The Truth is come, and falsehood can neither create nor bring back to life.'

Say: 'If I have strayed into error, it is only my own soul I have led astray, and if I am rightly guided, it is because of what my 34:50 Lord reveals to me. He is All-Hearing, Ever Close.'

If only you could see them when gripped by terror, and there is no escape!

They shall be seized from a place close to hand.

They will say: 'We believe in Him.' But how can they acquire faith from such a distant place? For they had spurned it before, while now they offend against the Unseen from a distant place.

A bar shall be set between them and what they desire, as was done with their like in times past. They are plunged in perplexing 34:54 doubt.

The Creator

In the name of God,
Merciful to all,
Compassionate to each!

Praise be to God, Creator of the heavens and earth!
It is He Who appoints the angels as envoys, having two, three,
    four wings –
He adds to His creation what He wills.
God has power over all things.   35:1

Whatever blessings God spreads forth to mankind, none can
    hold back;
Whatever He holds back, none can confer after Him.
He is Almighty, All-Wise.

O mankind, remember the grace of God upon you. Is there any
other creator save God who provides for you from heaven and
earth? There is no god but He, so how can you be so deceived?
If they call you a liar, messengers before you were called liars,
and to God all matters revert.   35:4

O mankind, God's promise is true, so let not this present life
seduce you, and let not the Tempter tempt you away from God.
Satan is your enemy, so treat him as an enemy. He merely invites
his gang of followers to be denizens of the raging Flame! They
who blasphemed shall receive a terrible punishment, but they
who believe and do righteous deeds shall obtain forgiveness and
a great reward.   35:7

Consider a person whose evil deed is made attractive to him,
and he regards it as good. God leads astray whomever He
pleases and guides whomever He pleases. So let not your

soul perish with grief over them: God knows full well what they do.

God it is Who sends forth the winds, agitating clouds, which We drive forth to a parched land, and thereby revive the ground after it has died.

Likewise is the resurrection.

Whoso desires grandeur, all grandeur belongs to God. To Him ascends speech that is pure, and righteous deeds He elevates. As for those who contrive evil, terrible punishment awaits

35:10   them, and their contriving itself shall be in vain.

God it was Who created you from dust, then from a sperm, then fashioned you into two genders. No female bears or delivers save by His knowledge; no person who attains old age shall attain it, nor will his life be curtailed, except it be in a Book – a thing easy for God.

The two seas are not alike: this one is fresh and sweet water, tasty to drink, that one salty and bitter. From both you eat flesh that is soft, and you extract jewellery to wear. Therein you can see ships ploughing through the waves, that you may seek of His bounty – perchance you will give thanks. He entwines night with day and day with night, and made the sun and moon to do His bidding, each running for an appointed time. Such indeed is God your Lord! To Him belongs sovereignty.

As for those to whom you pray instead of Him, they cannot command even the skin of a date! When you pray to them, they do not hear your prayers. Even if they could hear them, they would not respond to you. On the Day of Resurrection, they shall repudiate your idolatry – there is none like the All-

35:14   Experienced who can give you certain news.

O mankind, it is you who stand in need of God – God is All-Sufficient, All-Praiseworthy.

If He wishes, He can make you vanish and bring forth a new creation, a thing not difficult for God. No soul burdened can carry the burden of another. If a soul heavy-laden calls for help with its load, not a speck of it shall be carried, not even by a relative.

You are to warn those who fear their Lord in the realm of the Unseen, and who perform the prayer. Whoso is pure in soul, his purity rebounds to his own benefit, and to God is the final destination.

35:18

Unequal are the blind and those who see;
Darkness and light;
Pleasant shade and scorching wind;
Unequal are the living and the dead.
God hears whom He pleases, but you cannot make them hear, those who are in their graves.
You are but a warner.
We sent you with the Truth, a herald of glad tidings and a warner, and there is no nation but a warner had passed it by.
If they call you a liar, so too did those who came before them cry lies; their messengers had come to them with wonders, with the Psalms and the Luminous Book.
Then I seized the blasphemers – behold how I reversed their fortunes!

35:26

Have you not seen how God causes water to descend from the sky with which We bring forth fruits diverse in colours?
And mountain-tracks, white and red, diverse in colours,
And other pathways, dark and obscure?
So also humans, beasts of burden and cattle of diverse
    colours?

From among His worshippers, only the learned fear God.
God is Almighty, All-Forgiving.

35:28

Those who recite the Book of God, who perform the prayer, who expend of what We provided them, secretly and in the open – these can expect a commerce that will never fail. He shall pay them their wages in full and increase His favours upon 35:30 them. He is All-Forgiving, All-Praiseworthy.

What We inspired you with from the Book is the Truth, confirming what came before. Regarding His servants God is All-Experienced, All-Seeing.

Then We bequeathed the Book to those of Our servants whom We chose: some wronged themselves, some mixed good with evil, and some were quick to do righteous deeds, by God's leave. And that is the greatest of favours.

The Gardens of Eden shall they enter.
　　They shall be decked therein in bracelets of gold and pearls, and their garments shall be of silk. They shall say: 'Thanks be to God Who caused all sorrows to depart from us.
'Our Lord is All-Forgiving, All-Praiseworthy.
It is He Who lodged us in the Eternal Abode, by His favour,
Where no pain can touch us,
35:35 No fatigue can touch us.'

As for the unbelievers, theirs is the fire of hell. They shall not be judged and thus die, nor shall they be spared any of its torment. Thus do We reward every single unbeliever. In it they shall scream: 'Our Lord, take us out and we will act righteously, otherwise than what we used to do!'
　　Did We not grant you span of life enough for one who remembers, to have remembered? The warner came to you, so taste 35:37 your torment. The wrongdoers shall have none to support them.

God is knower of the Unseen in the heavens and earth,
He knows full well what lies within breasts.
It is He Who made you deputies on earth.

Whoso blasphemes, his blasphemy shall rebound upon him,
And blasphemy will only increase the blasphemers in
    repugnance with their Lord;
And blasphemy will only increase the blasphemers in abject
    loss.   35:39

Say: 'Have you considered those partners of yours that you
worship instead of God? Show me what they created on this
earth! Or do they have a partnership with heaven?'

Or have We brought them a Book and they understand it well?
In truth, the wicked promise each other nothing but illusion.

God grasps firmly the heavens and earth lest they pass away. If
they were to pass away, none after Him can grasp them firmly.
God is All-Forbearing, All-Forgiving.   35:41

They swore by God a mighty oath that if a warner would come
to them, they would be more rightly guided than any nation.
But when a warner did come to them, this merely increased them
in aversion, as they grew arrogant on earth and in their plotting
of evil. But evil plotting engulfs only those who work it.
    Can they look forward to anything other than the precedent
of the ancients?
You shall not find the precedent of God to change in the least;
You shall not find the precedent of God to vary in the least.
    Have they not journeyed in the land and observed the final
end of those who preceded them? They were greater than them
in might. Nor can anything escape God's power in the heavens
or on earth. He is Omniscient, Omnipotent.   35:44

Had God taken mankind to task for what they earned, He
would not have left a crawling creature on the face of the earth.
    Instead, He postpones them to a stated term.
    When their final end arrives, God, in regard to His servants,
is All-Seeing.   35:45

Ya Sin *

In the name of God,
Merciful to all,
Compassionate to each!

Ya Sin

By the All-Wise Qur'an! You are indeed one of the
    messengers,
Upon a straight path.
This is the Revelation of the Almighty, Compassionate to each,
In order that you warn a people whose ancestors were not warned,
36:6 And thus are heedless.

Upon most of them the divine Word has come true, and they
do not believe.
   We have placed collars on their necks, reaching to their chins,
so their heads are upraised.
   We fixed before them a barrier and behind them a barrier,
turning them blind, so they cannot see.
   It is all the same to them whether you warn or do not warn
them – they have no faith.
   You only warn him who follows the Remembrance and fears
the All-Merciful in the Unseen. To him give glad tidings of
36:11 forgiveness and a noble wage.

It is We Who revive the dead,
We Who register what deeds they committed,
What traces they left behind.
All things have We tallied in a Manifest Record.

Strike for them the parable of the people of the town, when
messengers arrived.

We had sent them two but they called them liars, so We backed them with a third, and they said: 'We are messengers to you.'

They said: 'You are merely human beings like us. The All-Merciful has revealed nothing. You are nothing but liars.'

They said: 'Our Lord knows that we are sent as messengers to you. Ours is only to convey a manifest declaration.'

They said: 'We hold you to be an evil omen. If you do not desist, we will stone you and a most painful torment will touch you from us.'

They said: 'Your evil omen is upon you. Is it because you have been reminded of God? You are indeed a people far gone in sin.'

36:19

A man came running from the other end of the city, saying: 'O people, follow the messengers. Follow him who asks you no wage. These men are guided aright. How can I not worship Him Who created me, and to Whom you shall return? Am I to take other gods instead of Him? If the All-Merciful wishes me ill, their intercession will not benefit me in the least, nor will they be able to save me. I would then be in manifest error. I believe in your Lord, so listen to me.'

It was said to him: 'Enter the Garden.'

He said: 'If only my people knew how my Lord forgave me and placed me among the honoured!'

36:27

After him, We sent no troops from heaven against his people, nor did We intend to do so. It was but a single Scream and, behold, they were lifeless.

Alas for humanity! No messenger comes to them but they mock him.

Have they not observed how many generations We destroyed before them, and that they do not return to them? That all of them, every single one, shall be summoned before Us?

36:32

Here is a sign for them: a dead land which We revive, and from which We sprout grains for them to eat. In it We planted gardens of palms and vines, and caused fountains to burst forth, that they may eat of its fruits and the work of their hands – will they 36:35 not render thanks?

Glory be to Him Who created all kinds of what the earth produces, as also of themselves, and of what they know not!

A sign for them is the night, from which We strip the day and, behold, they are plunged in darkness.

And the sun runs its own course, unchanging.

Such is the disposition of the Almighty, the Omniscient.

And the moon We disposed in phases until it comes back like a withered stalk of palm.

Neither the sun may outstrip the moon nor the night the day: each plies its own orbit.

A sign for them is that We carried their progeny in the laden Ark, and fashioned its like of ships, for them to embark therein.

If We wish We can drown them – no screaming to be heard from them, nor can they be saved, unless it be a mercy from Us 36:44 and a brief enjoyment of life.

And when it is said to them: 'Beware of the present and the future that you may obtain mercy,' there comes to them no sign from the signs of their Lord but they turn their back upon it.

And when it is said to them: 'Expend from what God in His bounty has provided you,' the unbelievers say to the believers: 'Are we to feed one whom God can feed if He so wishes?' In truth you have strayed far in error.

They say: 'When will this promise be fulfilled if you speak the truth?'

All they can expect is a single Scream, which shall seize them while they dispute so that they have no time to make a bequest, 36:50 nor return home to their families.

And the Trumpet shall be sounded and, behold, from their graves and to their Lord they shall hurry.

They shall say: 'Alas for us! Who resurrected us from our resting place?' This is what the All-Merciful promised, and the messengers spoke the truth. It shall be but a single Scream and, behold, they will all be conducted before Us.

Today no soul shall be wronged one jot, and you will be recompensed only for the deeds you committed.

Today the denizens of the Garden are preoccupied with joy, they and their spouses, reclining on cushions under the shade. There they shall have fruits, and all that they wish for. 'Peace' shall be the word from a Compassionate Lord.

Today, O sinners, keep yourselves apart!   36:59

Children of Adam, did I not enjoin upon you not to worship Satan? To you he is an enemy, undisguised. And to worship Me? This is the path that is straight.

He has led astray so many of you! Were you incapable of reasoning?

Here is the hell you were promised: today let it scorch you for what you blasphemed!

Today We shall seal their mouths and it will be their hands that shall speak to Us and their feet that shall testify as to what they earned.

If We wish, We can blind their eyes as they pursue the Path – but how will they see?

If We wish, We can cripple them where they sit, so they cannot move forward or backward.

Whomever We grant old age, We cause to droop in figure: will they not be reasonable?   36:68

We did not teach him poetry, nor does this befit him.
It is nothing but a Remembrance, and a Manifest Qur'an,
Therewith to warn him who is living,
And to fulfil the Word against the unbelievers.   36:70

Have they not observed that We created for them, from Our handiwork, cattle which they come to possess? That We tamed them for their benefit, that upon them they ride and from them they eat? That they have other uses for them, and draughts to
36:73 drink? Will they not render thanks?

And yet, instead of God, they take to themselves gods, hoping for success. These cannot grant them success, though they possess troops massed in their service. Therefore, let not their speech
36:76 sadden you: We know what they conceal and what declare.

Has not man observed that We created him from a sperm drop but, behold, he becomes a determined adversary? He coins a parable for Us but forgets his own creation, when he says: 'Who shall revive bones when turned to dust?'

Say: 'He Who created them in the first place shall revive them – He knows full well all His creation.'

It is He Who procured fire for you from green trees, from which you kindle a flame. Is He Who created the heavens and earth not able to create their like? Yes indeed! He is the All-
36:81 Creator, the Omniscient.

His wont, if He desires anything, is but to say to it: 'Be!' and it is.

So glory be to Him, Who holds in His hand sovereignty over
36:83 all things! To Him you shall be returned.

Arrayed in Ranks

In the name of God,
Merciful to all,
Compassionate to each!

By those arrayed in ranks!
By those who loudly clamour!
By those who recite the Remembrance!
Your God is One,
Lord of the heavens and earth and what is in between,
Lord of all sunrises!
We adorned the lower sky with the adornment of stars,
A protection against every rebellious demon.
They cannot eavesdrop on the Highest Assembly,*
And are pelted from every side,
Thrown back, and theirs is an eternal punishment;
Except for one who happens to catch a scrap,
And is then pursued by a shooting star.   37:10

So sound them out: 'Are they more difficult to create, or those
    others We created?'
We created them from viscous clay.
You are filled with wonder but they mock,
And when reminded they do not remember.
If they see a sign, they gather around to mock.
    They say: 'This is nothing but flagrant sorcery. When we are
dead and turned into dust and bones, are we to be resurrected?
Our forefathers too?'
Say: 'Yes indeed, and utterly humbled.'
It is but a single Cry of Rebuke and, behold, their eyes are
    opened!
They shall say: 'Alas for us! This is the Day of Judgement.'
This indeed is the Day of Division, which you used to impugn.   37:21

Herd them, those evildoers, together with their spouses and what they worshipped instead of God! And guide them on the path to hell! Seize them, for they are accountable!

What is the matter with you? Why are you not helping each other?

37:26   Ah, but Today they are in total surrender.

And they shall approach each other and begin to argue, some saying: 'You used the right arm of power to lord it over us,' and others answering: 'Not at all; you were unbelievers. We held no sway over you. Rather, you yourselves were a rebellious people. The Word of our Lord has come true upon us, and we shall

37:32   taste it. We seduced you, for we were indeed seducers.'

On that Day they shall be partners in torment. Thus do We deal with wrongdoers.

Time was when, if told 'there is no god but God', they would
        grow arrogant.
They would say: 'Are we to abandon our gods for a crazed
        poet?'
Rather, he came with the Truth, corroborating the messengers.
You shall surely taste the most painful torment,

37:39   Nor will you be recompensed except for what you used to do.

Except for the worshippers of God in all sincerity – these shall
receive a notable bounty, and fruits, and they shall be highly
honoured,
In Gardens of Bliss,
On couches, face to face.
There shall pass among them a cup from a fountain,
Crystal clear, a delight to those who drink it;
In it there is neither delirium nor are they intoxicated.
With them are women, chaste of glance, large-eyed,

37:49   Egg-like, well-guarded.

And they shall approach each other and begin to question.

And one of them shall say: 'I had a close friend who used to say: "Are you really a firm believer? When we are dead and turned into dust and bones, will we be held to account?"'

He will then say: 'Will you look down?' And he will look down and see him in the pit of hell.

And he will say: 'By God, you were about to destroy me! Were it not for the grace of my Lord, I would have been among those summoned to damnation. So then, are we not to die after our first death? Are we not to suffer torment? This is truly the greatest of triumphs!'

For such a reward let labourers labour.   37:61

Is this a better welcome or the tree of Zaqqum, which We set
    as an ordeal for the wicked?
It is a tree which grows in the pit of hell, with fruit like heads
    of demons.
They shall eat from it and fill their bellies;
Then, in addition, they shall have a scalding drink,
Then will they be returned to hell.   37:68

They find their forefathers erring,
And rush along in their footsteps.
Before them erred most of the ancients.
To them We sent warners: behold the end of those who were
    warned!
Except for those who worshipped God in all devotion.   37:74

Noah called out to Us: how excellent were Those who
    answered!
And We delivered him and his family from a mighty
    calamity,
Making his progeny the only survivors,
And conferred honour upon him among later generations.
Peace be upon Noah, among all mankind!

Thus do We reward the virtuous – he is truly one of our
    believing servants.

37:82   Then We drowned the others.

Of his party was Abraham, when he approached his Lord with
    a devout heart.
Remember when he said to his father and his people:
'What is it that you worship? A delusion? Is it gods you desire
    rather than God?
37:87   How then do you regard the Lord of the Worlds?'

So he cast a glance at the stars and said: 'I am diseased.'
They turned from him and fled.
    He then secretly approached their gods and asked: 'Will you
not eat? What is it with you that you do not speak?'
37:93   And he turned upon them, smiting them with his right hand.

His people came to him in a hurry.
    He said: 'Do you worship what you sculpt with your own
hands when it is God Who created you and all that you do?'
    They said: 'Build him a structure and hurl him into the raging
flame.'
37:98   They intended him mischief but We brought them low.

He said: 'I shall go to my Lord and He shall guide me. My Lord,
grant me a virtuous progeny.'
    And We gave him glad tidings of a wise and forbearing son.
    When the son was old enough to accompany him, he said:
'My son, I saw in a dream that I was sacrificing you, so reflect
and give me your opinion.'
    He said: 'Father, do as you are commanded and you shall
find me, God willing, steadfast.'
    When both submitted to the will of God, he bent his head
down and on its side.
    And We called out to him: 'O Abraham, you have made your
vision come true.'

Thus do We reward the virtuous.
That was indeed a conspicuous ordeal.
And We ransomed him with a mighty sacrifice,
And conferred honour upon him among later generations. 37:108

Peace be upon Abraham! Thus do We reward the virtuous.
He was one of our faithful worshippers.
And We gave him glad tidings of Isaac, a prophet and man of
  virtue.
And We blessed him and Isaac. And of their progeny, some
  were virtuous and some manifestly self-wronging. 37:113

And We were gracious to Moses and Aaron,
Delivering them and their people from terrible distress.
And We came to their aid, and they were the victors.
And We brought them both the Lucid Book,
Guiding them to the straight path,
Conferring honour on both among later generations.
Peace be upon Moses and Aaron! Thus do We reward the
  virtuous.
Both were among our faithful worshippers. 37:122

Elias* too was a messenger.
Remember when he said to his people: 'Will you not fear
  God?
Do you worship Baal and forsake the best of Creators?
God is your Lord and the Lord of your ancient forefathers.'
But they called him a liar – and will be summoned to
  damnation,
All except the sincere worshippers of God.
And We conferred honour upon him among later
  generations.
Peace be upon the House of Elias! Thus do We reward the
  virtuous.
He was one of our faithful worshippers. 37:132

Lot too was a messenger.
Remember when We delivered him and all his household,
Except for an old woman, who was left behind.
Then We destroyed the others.
You pass by them morning and night; will you not
37:138   understand?

Jonah too was a messenger.
Remember when he fled on a laden ship.
He cast lots and was bested.
A great fish swallowed him: he was to blame.
Had he not been one who glorified God,
He would have stayed in its belly till the Day that mankind is
      resurrected.
We then cast him out into the wilderness, ailing.
And We caused to sprout over him a tree of gourd,
And sent him to a hundred thousand, or more.
They believed, so We granted them enjoyment of life for a
37:148   while.

So sound them out: 'To your Lord daughters are born, and to
      them sons?
Or did We create the angels female, in their presence?'
It is only their deceit that makes them say that God begat
      progeny;
They are indeed lying.
So He preferred girls to boys?
What is it with you and your judgements?
Will you not remember? Or do you possess some obvious
      proof?
37:157 Go bring your book then, if you speak the truth!

And they set up a kinship between Him and the *Jinn*,
Even though the *Jinn* know that they shall be summoned to
      judgement –
May God be glorified far above what they allege! –

Save for the devout worshippers of God.
You, and what you worship, shall not lead any astray from
    Him,
Save those to be scorched in hell.   37:163

'None of us there is but has a well-known station.
We are indeed arrayed in ranks;
We are indeed the glorifiers.'   37:166

Once they would have said: 'If only we had a Remembrance
from the ancients, we would be devout servants of God.'
But they blasphemed against it, and they will surely know!
Our Word has already passed to Our servants the messengers,
That they shall be granted victory,
That Our troops shall prevail.   37:173

So leave them alone for a while,
And observe them, and their eyes shall be opened.
Is it Our torment they wish to hasten?
When it descends upon their vicinity, grievous shall be the
    dawn of those who were warned!
So leave them alone for a while,
And observe, and their eyes shall be opened.
May your Lord, Lord of Might, be glorified far above what
    they allege!
Peace be upon the messengers!
Praise be to God, Lord of the Worlds.   37:182

Sad *

In the name of God,
Merciful to all,
Compassionate to each!

Sad

By the Qur'an of Remembrance!

It is the unbelievers who are plunged in arrogance and schism.

How many a generation We destroyed before them! They 38:3 cried for help, but there was no time for escape.

They find it strange that a warner has come to them, of their number; and the blasphemers say: 'He is a lying sorcerer. Does he reduce the gods to One God? This is surely a thing most bizarre!'

And their council breaks up, saying: 'Depart, and remain faithful to your gods, for this is a cause to be cherished. We never heard of this in the latest religion. This is nothing but fabrication. Was the Remembrance sent down on him – from among us all?'

No indeed! Rather, they are in doubt regarding My Remem- 38:8 brance. Or rather, they have yet to taste torment!

Or is it that they possess the treasures of your Lord's mercy,
    Almighty and All-Giving?
Or do they hold sovereignty over heaven and earth, and what
    is in between?
Let them then ascend the ropes!
An army of Confederates will therein be put to rout!
Before them lied the people of Noah, of 'Ad, and of Pharaoh,
    he of the pegs, *

As too Thamud, the people of Lot and the People of the
    Thicket – these are the Confederates.   38:13

In truth, none there were but called the messengers liars, and
    torment was deserved.
These can only expect a single Scream, from which there is no
    recovery.
They say: 'Our Lord, hasten Your writ upon us, before the
    Day of Reckoning.'
Be patient with what they say,
And remember Our servant David, a man of great power, a
    man of constant penitence.
We made the mountains submit and, with him, glorify God at
    evening and dawn,
And the birds too, mustered from all sides – all turn in
    penitence to Him.
And We buttressed his rule, and granted him wisdom and
    overpowering eloquence.   38:20

Has there come to you news of the disputants, when they
climbed up the entrance gate?

    Remember how they entered upon David, and he was fright-
ened of them.

    They said: 'Be not afraid. Two disputants are we, and one
has done the other wrong. So judge between us in justice, and
do not be biased, but guide us to an upright path. This, my
brother, has ninety-nine ewes and I have but one. And yet he
says to me: "Place her in my charge," and he overcomes me in
argument.'   38:23

He said: 'He has done you wrong by badgering you to add your
ewe to his. Indeed, many who own in common transgress against
one another – save those who believe and do good deeds, and
they are few in number.'

    And David imagined that We had put him to the test. So he
sought his Lord's forgiveness, fell in prostration and repented.

And We forgave him that act; to Us he shall be drawn near, and
38:25 shall have a goodly place to rest.

O David, We appointed you a deputy on earth, so judge between
people in truth, and follow not your caprice, for this will lead
you astray from the path of God. Those who stray from the
path of God shall meet with terrible torment, for they forget the
Day of Reckoning.

We did not create the heavens and earth, and what is in between,
in vain. This is the fantasy of unbelievers – alas for the
unbelievers from the Fire!
   Or are We to treat those who believed and did righteous deeds
like those who do corruption on earth? Are We to treat the
pious like the impious?
   Here is a Book We brought down upon you, blessed, that
they might ponder its verses and that men possessed of mind
38:29 might remember.

And on David We bestowed Solomon – excellent was he as
servant, and ever repentant!
   Remember when, on an evening, were displayed before him
horses frisky and fleet.
   He said: 'I have a love of horses that makes me forget my
Lord till the sun hides behind its veil. Bring them back to me.'
38:33 And he proceeded to stroke their shanks and necks.

And We tested Solomon by placing on his throne a physical
likeness. Then he repented and said: 'My Lord, forgive me, and
grant me a kingship which no one after me shall possess; it is
You Who are All-Giving.'
   We placed the wind at his service to blow at his command,
mildly, and wherever he pleased; so too the demons, every
builder and diver, and others bound in chains.
   'This is Our bounty: grant or withhold it, without reckoning.'
   To Us he shall be drawn near, and shall have a goodly place
38:40 to rest.

And mention too Our servant Job, when he called out to his
Lord: 'Satan has touched me with hardship and torment.'

'Kick with your foot: this is a place for washing, cool, and
for drinking.'

And We restored to him his family, and their like with them,
as a mercy from Us, and a remembrance to men possessed of
minds.

'Clasp a bunch of grass with your hand, and strike with it,
and do not break your oath.'

We found him to be patient – excellent was he as servant, and
ever repentant.   38:44

And mention too Our servants, Abraham and Isaac and Jacob,
men of strength and perspicacity. We made them pure because
of their purity in remembering the Final Abode. With Us they
shall be among the most virtuous of the elect.   38:47

And mention too Ishmael, Elisha and Dhu'l Kifl: all most
    worthy.
This is a Remembrance,
And the pious shall have a goodly place of rest:
Gardens of Eden, with their gates flung open to them.
They shall recline therein, and shall call therein for fruits in
    abundance, and drink.
With them shall be maidens chaste of glance, of equal age.
This is what you are promised on the Day of Reckoning.
Such is Our bounty, inexhaustible.   38:54

But then, the worst homecoming awaits transgressors:
Hell, with which they shall be scorched – wretched is that
    berth!
That is so. Let them taste it: scalding water and pus,
And similar torments of diverse kinds.   38:58

'Here is a batch of people plunging into it with you!
No "Welcome" to them: they shall be scorched by the Fire.'

They will say: 'It is you rather who are not welcome. It is you who led us to it – wretched is this destination!'

They will say: 'Our Lord, whoever led us into this, multiply his torment in the Fire.'

They will say: 'Why is it that we do not see men we used to regard as evil, and took for objects of mockery? Have we overlooked them?'

38:63

Such shall in truth be the mutual recrimination of the people of the Fire.

Say: 'I am but a warner, and there is no god but the One, All-Conquering God; Lord of the heavens and earth and what is in between, Almighty, Ever-Forgiving.'

Say: 'It is a message of great import, but you turn your backs upon it. I had no knowledge of the Highest Assembly as they disputed one against another. I am merely one who receives inspiration, merely a clear warner.'

38:70

Remember when your Lord said to the angels: 'I am creating a human being from clay. When I give him the right shape and breathe into him of My spirit, bow down prostrate before him.'

The angels bowed, all in a body, except Iblis, who became proud and was an unbeliever.

He said: 'O Iblis, what prevented you from bowing to what I created with My hands? Are you too proud or are you too exalted?'

He said: 'I am better than him; You created me of fire, but him You created of clay.'

He said: 'Depart from this place, ever to be stoned! My curse shall be upon you until the Day of Judgement.'

He said: 'My Lord, defer me till the Day they are resurrected.'

He said: 'You shall be deferred until that well-known moment.'

He said: 'I swear by Your Might, I shall seduce them all, except for Your devout worshippers.'

He said: 'In truth, in very truth, I say to you: I shall fill hell to the brim with you and all who follow you of their number.'

38:85

Say: 'I ask you no wage for it, nor am I one who dissembles. This is but a Remembrance to mankind. And, in a while, you will surely come to know its true import.'

38:88

The Groups

In the name of God,
Merciful to all,
Compassionate to each!

Behold the revelation of the Book from God, Almighty, All-Wise!

We sent down on you the Book with the Truth,
So worship God, sincere in your faith.
It is to God that pure faith belongs.
    As for those who take up masters instead of Him, saying 'We only worship them to bring us close in nearness to God,' God shall judge between them as to what they disputed about. God guides not the lying blasphemer.
    Had God wanted to take a child He would have selected whom He wished from His creation. Glory be to Him! He is God, One, All-Conquering.

39:4

He created the heavens and earth in truth.
He wraps night around day and day around night.
He made the sun and moon subservient – each runs in a
    predetermined course.
He is Almighty, Ever-Forgiving.

He created you from a single soul, then from it fashioned its
     counterpart.
And He sent down on you of cattle eight pairs.
He created you in your mothers' wombs, form following form,
     in three darknesses.
Such is God, your Lord, to Whom belongs sovereignty.
39:6   There is no god but He: how then can you veer away?

If you disbelieve, God has no need of you, yet He approves not
of unbelief from His servants. And if you render thanks, He will
be well pleased with you.

No soul burdened can carry the burden of another.

Then to your Lord is your return and He will acquaint you
with your deeds – He knows full well what lies within breasts.

If harm touches a man, he calls on his Lord in penitence, but if
He favours him with an act of grace, he forgets what he had
called upon before, and sets up rivals to God, to lead astray
from His path.

Say: 'Enjoy your blasphemy for a little while, for you shall be
an inhabitant of the Fire.'

And what of one who bows or stands in devotion through
the watches of the night, fearing the hereafter and hoping for
his Lord's mercy?

Say: 'Are those who know the equal of those who do not
know? They only remember who are possessed of minds.'

Say: 'My faithful worshippers, fear your Lord. For those who
do good in this present life there is a goodly reward. God's earth
is wide. The steadfast shall be paid their wages in full, without
reckoning.'

Say: 'I have been commanded to worship God, sincere of faith
in Him. And I have been commanded to be the first Muslim.'

Say: 'If I disobey my Lord, I fear the torment of a mighty
Day.'

Say: 'It is God I worship, sincere in my faith in Him. But you
can worship what you will instead of Him.'

Say: 'The real losers are those who lose themselves and their families on the Day of Resurrection. That, assuredly, is the most glaring loss. They shall have sheets of fire above them, and sheets of fire below them.'

With this God strikes fear into His servants – 'My servants, fear Me.'   39:16

As for those who avoided the worship of idols, and turned in faith to God, they shall obtain glad tidings, so announce glad tidings to My servants. They are those who give heed to speech and follow the best part thereof, those whom God has guided, and it is they who are possessed of minds.

As for him upon whom the decree of torment has been justly passed, is it you who can save those in the Fire?

But those who fear their Lord shall have chambers, above which are chambers, rising high, and beneath which rivers flow – this is God's promise, and God fails not His appointed time.   39:20

Have you not observed how God causes water to descend from the sky, making it flow as springs on the ground, then through it causes crops of diverse colours to sprout forth, then the crops dry out and you see them yellowing, then He turns it all into stubble? In this surely is a remembrance to men possessed of minds.

Consider therefore where stands one whose breast God spreads open to Islam. He is surely walking in the light of his Lord. But alas for the hard of heart for abandoning the remembrance of God! These are in flagrant error.   39:22

God has sent down the most perfect discourse: a Book concordant and recapitulating. At the mention of it the skins of those who fear their Lord shudder, but then their skins and hearts grow soft at the remembrance of God. Such is God's guidance: through it God guides whomever He pleases. And whom God leads astray, no guide has he.

Consider therefore one who covers his face against the baneful torment on the Day of Resurrection. To the wicked it shall be said: 'Taste what you earned.'

Those who came before them cried lies, so the torment fell upon them unawares. And God made them taste humiliation in this present life, though the torment of the hereafter is more 39:26 grievous, if only they knew.

In this Qur'an, We have struck for mankind every sort of parable; perhaps they will remember.

An Arabic Qur'an, unequivocal; perhaps they will grow 39:27 pious.

God strikes a parable: a man shared by partners at loggerheads, and a man belonging wholly to another man – can the two be equal in likeness?

God be praised! In truth, most of them are ignorant.

You shall die, and they shall die. Then, on the Day of Resur-39:31 rection, you shall dispute with one another before your Lord.

Who is more wicked than he who lies in God's name, and cries lies to Truth when it comes to him? Is not hell the cradle of blasphemers? But he who came with the Truth and believed in it – these are the pious. They shall have whatever they please with their Lord: such is the reward of the virtuous. God shall pardon them the worst of their deeds, and reward them with 39:35 wages for the best of their past deeds.

Will not God suffice for His servant? And yet they scare you with these idols, instead of Him! Whom God leads astray, no guide has he; whom God guides, none there are to lead him 39:37 astray. Is not God Almighty capable of revenge?

If you ask them who created the heavens and earth, they answer: 'God.'

Say: 'Consider that which you worship instead of God. If

God wills me harm, are these idols able to efface His harm? Or else, if He wills me mercy, can they hold back His mercy?'

Say: 'God suffices me, and in Him let all trust who place their trust.'

Say: 'O people, do the best you can, and I too shall do likewise, and you will surely know who shall meet with a torment that abases him, and on whom shall fall eternal punishment.'   39:40

We sent down on you the Book for mankind, in truth. Whoso follows guidance does so for the good of his soul; whoso strays in error does so to its detriment. You are not their guardian.

God takes the souls to Him at death, and takes souls that have not died, in their sleep. He retains the soul on which He has decreed death and releases the others, until a stated term. In this are signs for people who ponder and reflect.   39:42

Or is it that they have adopted intercessors other than God?

Say: 'Even if they own nothing and are devoid of reason?'

Say: 'All intercession rests with God. To Him belongs sovereignty over the heavens and earth, and to Him you shall revert.'   39:44

When God alone is mentioned, the hearts of those who do not believe in the hereafter are scandalized. But when those apart from Him are mentioned, behold, they take heart.

Say: 'God is the Creator of the heavens and earth, Knower of the Invisible and the Visible. It is You Who shall judge among Your servants concerning their disputes.'   39:46

If the wicked possessed all that is on earth, and the same besides, they would offer it up as ransom from the grievous torment on the Day of Resurrection. They shall then witness from God what they had not reckoned with; the vices of what they earned shall be revealed to them, and there shall engulf them what once they mocked.   39:48

If harm touches a man, he calls upon Us, but if We favour him with an act of grace from Us, He says: 'I was granted this only because of God's knowledge of my merit.' No indeed! It is but a test, but most of them are ignorant. This was said by people before them, but that which they earned availed them not. Therefore, the vices of what they earned caught up with them, and the wicked among them – their vices too shall catch up with 39:51 them; nor can they escape God's power.

Do they not know that God spreads out His bounty to whomever He wills – and withholds it? In this are signs for a people who have faith.

Say: 'O My servants who have transgressed against themselves, do not despair of God's mercy. God forgives all sins: He is All-Forgiving, Compassionate to each. Turn in penitence towards your Lord, and submit to Him before the torment 39:54 overtakes you, when you shall have none to support you.'

Follow the best of what has been sent down to you from your Lord before the torment overtakes you suddenly and unawares, lest a soul should say: 'Woe to me for the blunders I committed against God, for the fact that I mocked.' Or lest it should say: 'Had God guided me, I would have been pious.' Or lest it should say, when facing torment: 'If only I could have my life again, I 39:58 would be virtuous.'

And yet, My revelations did come to you but you called them lies, grew arrogant and were a blasphemer. On the Day of Resurrection you shall see those who cried lies to God with blackened faces.
Is there not in hell a berth for the arrogant?
As for the pious, God shall deliver them for their having won
    through;
No harm shall touch them, nor shall they grieve.
God is the Creator of all things, the Guardian of all things.
    To Him belong the reins of the heavens and earth. But those

who blasphemed against God's revelations – they are the
losers.   39:63

Say: 'Is it other than God you command me to worship, you
lawless crowd? It was revealed to you and to those before you
that if you ascribe partners to Him, He will frustrate your
endeavours, and you will end up a loser. Rather, it is God you
must worship, and be one who offers thanks.' Nor have they
esteemed God as He ought to be esteemed, when the whole
earth shall be in His grasp the Day of Resurrection, and when
the heavens shall be rolled up in His right hand. Glory be to
Him, and may He be exalted far above what they associate
with Him!   39:67

The Trumpet shall be sounded, and everyone in the heavens and
earth shall fall down dead, except for whomever God wills; it
shall be sounded again and, behold, they shall rise up and see.
    And the earth shall shine with the light of its Lord, the Book
shall be spread out, prophets and witnesses shall be summoned,
and judgement will be passed among them in truth, nor will
they be wronged.
    Each soul shall be paid in full for what it did, and they shall
know best what they used to do. The unbelievers shall be herded
to hell in groups. Once they come to it, its gates shall be opened,
and its guards shall say to them: 'Did not messengers come to
you, from among your number, who recited to you the revelations of your Lord, and warned you of meeting a day like this?'
They shall answer: 'Yes.' But the verdict of torment will have
come true for blasphemers.
    It shall be said to them: 'Enter through the gates of hell, there
to abide eternally.' Wretched is the berth of the arrogant!   39:72

But those who feared their Lord in piety shall be herded to the
Garden in groups. Once they come to it, its gates shall be
opened, and its guards shall say to them: 'Peace be upon you!
You were pure in heart, so enter it, there to abide eternally.'

They shall answer: 'Praise be to God, Who fulfilled His promise to us, and gave us the earth in inheritance, that we may make our dwelling in any part of the Garden we please. How 39:74 excellent is the reward of those who do good!'

And you shall see the angels hovering around the throne, glorifying the praises of their Lord. The judgement of truth will have been passed on them, and it shall be said: 'Praise be to God, 39:75 Lord of the Worlds!'

Forgiver

In the name of God,
Merciful to all,
Compassionate to each!

Ha Mim

Behold the revelation of the Book from God, Almighty, Omniscient!

Forgiver of sins,
Accepter of repentance,
Grievous in punishment,
Boundless in bounty;
40:3 There is no god but He, and to Him is the final return.

None disputes the revelations of God save the unbelievers, so do not be taken in by their hustle and bustle in the land. Before them the people of Noah cried lies, as did the Confederates after them. Each nation planned to seize their messenger, and used false arguments to rebut the truth, but I seized them – and what a punishment it was! Thus did the Word of your Lord come

true against those who blasphemed, that they are the denizens
of the Fire. 40:6

Those who carry the throne, and those around it, glorify the
praises of their Lord and believe in Him. They ask His forgive-
ness for the believers:
'Our Lord, You encompass all things in Your mercy and
    knowledge.
Forgive those who repent and follow Your way,
And spare them the torment of hell.
Our Lord, admit them into the Gardens of Eternal Abode
    which you promised them,
As also the virtuous from among their parents, spouses and
    progeny,
For You are in truth Almighty, All-Wise.
Protect them from sin, for he whom You protect from sin on
    that Day
Shall be one to whom You have shown mercy,
And this is the greatest of triumphs.' 40:9

The unbelievers will be addressed thus: 'The anger of God is
greater than your anger with yourselves when you were once
called to faith and you disbelieved.' And they shall answer: 'Our
Lord, You caused us to die two deaths and to live two lives. We
acknowledge our sins, so is there any way to escape?' 40:11

But that is because when God alone was called upon, you would
blaspheme, and when other gods were associated with Him,
you would believe. Judgement belongs to God, Exalted and
Great. He shows you His signs, and brings down to you from
the sky a livelihood, but only He remembers who turns in piety
to Him. 40:13

So call on God, sincere in faith, even though the unbelievers
    are averse.

Exalted in degree,
Possessor of the throne.

He casts down the Spirit, by His command, upon whomever He wishes of His servants, to warn against the Day of Encounter, a Day when they shall come out of their graves, when nothing about them shall be hidden from God.
To whom does sovereignty belong this Day?
To God, One, All-Conquering!
Today each soul shall be rewarded for what it earned.
Today there is no injustice.
40:17   God is quick to settle accounts.

Warn them of the Day, soon to come, when hearts shall reach up to throats, convulsed in agony. The wicked shall have no intimate friend, and no intercessor whose word is obeyed.

He knows what eyes betray, and what breasts conceal.

God shall judge in justice, while they, whom they worshipped instead of Him, can judge nothing. God is All-Hearing, All-
40:20   Seeing.

Have they not journeyed in the land and observed the final end of those who preceded them? They were greater than them in might, and left behind more landmarks on earth. And yet God seized them for their sins, and they had none to shield them from God. That is because their messengers would come to them with signs, but they disbelieved, so God seized them – for
40:22   He is Mighty, grievous in punishment.

We sent Moses with Our signs and clear authority to Pharaoh, Haman and Korah, but they called him a sorcerer and liar. When he brought them the Truth from Us, they said: 'Slaughter the sons of those who believed with him, and debauch their
40:25   women.' But the guile of unbelievers can only go astray.

Pharaoh said: 'Let me kill Moses, and let him call on his Lord. I fear he may change your religion, or may unleash corruption in the land.'

Moses said: 'I seek refuge in my Lord and your Lord from every arrogant person who believes not in the Day of Reckoning.'   40:27

A believer from Pharaoh's household, who kept his faith secret, said: 'Will you kill a man merely because he says: "My Lord is God"? He has brought you signs from your Lord. If he is a liar, his lying shall rebound upon him. If he is truthful, some of what he promises you will befall you. God guides not the outrageous and deceitful. My people, today you hold sovereignty and mastery over the earth, but who will come to our help against the might of God should it fall upon us?'

Pharaoh said: 'I merely inform you of what I myself can see, and I merely guide you on the path of prudence.'

The believer said: 'My people, I fear for you a day like that of the Confederates, or like the example of the people of Noah, 'Ad and Thamud, and those who came after them. God desires no injustice to His servants. My people, I fear for you the Day of Clamouring, a day when you shall turn your backs and flee, with no one to shelter you from God. Whom God leads astray no guide has he. In times past Joseph came to you with signs, but you continued to be in doubt about what he brought you. When he died, you said that God will not send a messenger after him. Thus does God lead astray the outrageous and the doubting, who argue over God's revelations without receiving authority: a heinous sin in God's sight and with those who believe. God seals the heart of every arrogant tyrant.'   40:35

Pharaoh said to Haman: 'Build me a tower that I may ascend to the gates, the gates of heaven, and climb up to the god of Moses, for I think him a liar.' Thus was Pharaoh's evil act made to appear attractive to him, and he was diverted from the right way. But Pharaoh's guile could only end in perdition.   40:37

The believer said: 'My people, follow me and I shall guide you to the path of prudence. My people, this present life is but a passing frivolity, but the hereafter is the Abode of Permanence. Whoso commits a sin shall only be rewarded with its like; whoso does a righteous deed, be they male or female, while believing, these shall enter the Garden, where they shall be provided for without reckoning.

'My people, why do I call you to salvation and you call me to the Fire? And you call me to blaspheme against God and to associate with Him what I have no knowledge of, while I call you to the Almighty, the All-Forgiving? There is no doubt that what you call me to is unworthy of being called upon either in this life or in the hereafter, that God is our ultimate destination, that the shameless shall be the denizens of the Fire. You shall indeed remember what I have told you. I entrust my fate to 40:44 God: God is ever attentive to His worshippers.'

So God protected him from their evil designs, and engulfed Pharaoh's people with terrible torment – the Fire, to which they are exposed morning and evening. And when the Hour arrives, 'Enter, O Pharaoh's people, into the most grievous torment.'

They will then dispute with one another in the Fire, and the weak shall say to the arrogant: 'We were your dependants, so can you spare us a portion of the Fire?'

And the arrogant shall reply: 'We are all in it together, for God has judged His servants.'

And those in the Fire shall say to the guardians of hell: 'Call on your Lord to mitigate for us the torment of a single day.'

And these shall ask: 'Did not your messengers come to you with clear signs?'

'Yes,' they shall answer.

They shall say: 'Call out then, but the prayer of blasphemers 40:50 will only be in vain.'

We will assuredly come to the aid of Our messengers, and of those who believed in this present life, and on the Day when the

witnesses shall rise up, a Day when the excuses of the wicked
shall be worthless. A curse shall fall upon them and an Evil
Abode awaits them. 40:52

We brought Moses guidance and bequeathed the Book to the
Children of Israel, a Guidance and Remembrance to those pos-
sessed of minds.
   Therefore, be patient, for the promise of God shall come true,
and ask forgiveness for your sins, and glorify the praise of your
Lord, at evening and dawn. 40:55

As for those who argue about the revelations of God, no authority having come to them – there is nothing in their hearts save
a pride which they can never satisfy. Seek refuge in God, for He
is All-Hearing, All-Seeing.

The creation of the heavens and earth is far greater than the
creation of humanity, but most humans are ignorant.
Unequal is the blind man and the one who sees,
Unequal too are those who believe and do good deeds, and
   those who are wicked.
But little do you remember!
The Hour shall come, no doubt about it, but most people do
   not believe. 40:59

Your Lord says: 'Call upon Me and I shall answer you. Those
too proud to worship Me shall enter hell in humiliation.'
It is God Who made the night a time of rest for you,
And made the luminous day.
God has shown favours to mankind,
But most of mankind does not render thanks. 40:61

Such is God, your Lord, Creator of all things; there is no god
but He, so how can you turn away?
   So also did turn away those who repudiated the revelations
of God.

It is God Who made the earth your place of habitation and the heavens an edifice, He Who gave you form, and made your form attractive, and provided you with pure things.
Such is God, your Lord – blessed be God, Lord of the Worlds!
He is the Ever-Living,
There is no god but He!
So pray to Him in sincerity of faith.

40:65 Praise be to God, Lord of the Worlds!

Say: 'I have been forbidden to worship what you call upon other than God, now that clear revelations have come to me from my Lord. I have been commanded to submit to the Lord of the Worlds.'

It is He Who created you from dust, then from a sperm, then
    from a blood clot,
Then He brings you forth, a child,
And then to reach full maturity,
And then to grow old.
Some of you die beforehand,
Attaining a stated term of life.

40:67 Would that you come to reason!

It is He Who gives life and deals death.
    Once He decides a matter, He merely says to it 'Be!' and it is.
    Have you not observed those who argue about God's revelations, and how they are turned away?
    They who called the Book a lie, as too what We sent Our messengers with – they shall surely know, when fetters are upon their necks and they are dragged in chains, when in boiling water, then in fire, they are tossed.
    It shall then be said to them: 'Where now are those you once worshipped instead of God?'
    And they shall answer: 'They have vanished from our sight. Indeed we did not before now call on anything at all.'
    Thus does God lead unbelievers astray. That is because you

used to make merry on earth, without justice, and because of
your revelry.

So enter the gates of hell, to remain therein for ever – wretched
is the berth of the arrogant!   40:76

Therefore, be patient, for the promise of God shall come true.

Whether We show you part of what We promised them or
We cause you to die, to Us they shall be returned.

We sent messengers before you, some of whose stories We
narrated to you, and some We have not. No messenger can
work a wonder except by God's leave. But when the command
of God arrives, fair judgement shall be passed, and the repudi-
ators will then come to grief.   40:78

It is God Who created cattle for you upon which you ride, and
from which you eat. From them you derive other benefits, or
else fulfil some desire of your hearts. Upon them, and upon
ships too, are you carried.

He shows you His wonders: which of God's wonders do you
deny?   40:81

Have they not journeyed in the land and observed the final end
of those who preceded them? They were more numerous, and
greater than them in might, and left behind more landmarks
on earth, but what they earned availed them not. When their
messengers came to them with wonders, they grew elated with
the knowledge they had, and that which they mocked engulfed
them. But when they witnessed Our might, they said: 'We believe
in the One God and repudiate what we associated with Him.'
But their belief shall profit them not when they witness Our
        might.
Such has been the precedent of God with His servants,
And the unbelievers will then come to grief.   40:85

Made Distinct

In the name of God,
Merciful to all,
Compassionate to each!

Ha Mim

A Revelation from the All-Merciful, Compassionate to
    each!
Behold a Book whose verses are made distinct:
An Arabic Qur'an, to a people who have knowledge,
A Herald of glad tidings and a Warner.
41:4 But most have turned away, for they cannot hear.

They say: 'Our hearts are veiled from what you call us to, and
in our ears is heaviness. Between us and you there stands a
curtain. So do what you will, and we shall do likewise.'

Say: 'I am but a human being like you, to whom inspiration
is sent. Your God is in truth One God. Act righteously in His
sight and seek His forgiveness. And woe to the polytheists, who
do not pay alms and who, moreover, repudiate the hereafter.
But those who believe and do righteous deeds shall receive a
wage unstinted.'

Say: 'You are blaspheming against Him Who created the earth
in two days, and you set up rivals to Him – He Who is Lord of
41:9 the Worlds!'

Above the earth He erected towering mountains, and He blessed
it, and appraised its provisions in four days, in equal measure
to those who need them.

Then He ascended to heaven, while yet smoke, and said to it
and to the earth: 'Come forth, willing or unwilling!'

And both responded: 'We come willingly.'

Then He ordained seven heavens in two days, and inspired each heaven with its disposition.

And We adorned the lowest heaven with lanterns, and for protection. Such was the devising of the Almighty, All-Knowing. 41:12

If they turn away, say: 'I warn you of a thunderbolt like the thunderbolt of 'Ad and Thamud.'

Remember when messengers came to them, back and forth, saying: 'You must not worship any but God.' But they replied: 'Had our Lord wished, He would have sent down angels. So we spurn what you have been sent with.'

As regards the people of 'Ad, they grew arrogant on earth, unjustly, saying: 'Who is mightier than us?'

Did they not observe that God Who created them is mightier than them?

And they reviled Our revelations.

So We hurled at them a howling wind in ill-omened days, to make them taste the torment of humiliation in this present life. Yet the torment of the hereafter is more humiliating – nor shall they find any to support them.

As regards Thamud, We conferred guidance upon them, but they chose blindness over guidance, and there seized them a thunderbolt of abasing torment because of what they earned. And We delivered those who believed and were pious. 41:18

A Day shall come when the enemies of God shall be herded into the Fire, all held in tight order, until, arriving there, their own ears, eyes and skins shall testify as to what they used to do.

They shall say to their skins: 'Why did you testify against us?'

And these shall answer: 'God gave us speech, He Who gave speech to all things. It was He Who created you the first time, and to Him you have been returned. Nor were you discreet lest your ears and eyes and skins might testify against you; instead, you imagined that God does not know most of what you do.' 41:22

Such were the fantasies you fantasized about your Lord! He struck you down, and you ended up as losers. If they bear patiently, the Fire will nonetheless be their home; and if they ask to be granted grace, they will not be among those granted it.

To them We had assigned accomplices who embellished their actions, present and past, in their eyes. So the Word of God came true upon them, as among other nations past, of humans 41:25 and *Jinn*, that they were the losers.

The unbelievers say: 'Do not listen to this Qur'an, and trifle with it; perhaps you will win the dispute.'

We shall force the blasphemers to taste a grievous torment, and shall requite them for the worst of their deeds. Such shall be the reward of God's enemies: the Fire, which to them shall be the Abode of Eternity, as a reward for repudiating Our 41:28 revelations.

The unbelievers shall say: 'Our Lord, show us those who led us astray, humans or *Jinn*, so that we may trample them under our feet, and they become the lowest of the low.'

As for those who say 'Our Lord is God' and are upright in deed, angels shall be made to descend upon them:

'Fear not, and do not grieve. Here are glad tidings of the Garden which you were promised. We are your guardians in this life and the next. In it you shall have all that your souls desire, all that you pray for, hospitably received by One All-41:32 Forgiving, Compassionate to each.'

Who is more admirable in speech than one who calls upon God, acts righteously and says: 'I am a Muslim'?

A virtuous deed is not the equal of a sinful deed.

Repay injury with conduct more becoming and, behold, the person with whom you are at enmity becomes like an intimate friend.

But none can attain this except the steadfast;
None can attain it except the most fortunate.
If a surge of anger that issues from Satan sweeps over you,
　　seek refuge with God;
He is All-Hearing, Omniscient.　　41:36

Among His signs are the night and day, the sun and moon. Bow
not to the sun or moon, but bow to God Who created them, if
it is Him you worship.
　　If they are too proud to do so, yet those who are with your
Lord glorify Him night and day, and do not grow weary.　　41:38

Among His signs is that you will see the earth arid and
　　lifeless,
But when We send down the rain upon it, it vibrates, and
　　doubles its yield.
He Who revives it will surely revive the dead: He has power
　　over all things.

Those who blaspheme Our signs cannot hide from Us.
　　Is he who is hurled into the Fire better off than one who
comes to the Day of Resurrection, secure? Do what you please:
He knows full well what you do.　　41:40

As for those who blaspheme the Remembrance when it comes
to them – a Book Exalted, which no falsehood can blemish,
adding or subtracting, a Revelation from the All-Wise, All-
Praiseworthy – remember that nothing is being said to you that
was not said to messengers before you. Your Lord is forgiving,
yet grievous in punishment.　　41:43

Had We revealed the Qur'an in a foreign tongue, they would
have said: 'If only its verses were made clear! What? Foreign
and Arabic?'
　　Say: 'To those who believe, it is Guidance and Remedy. But

those who do not believe have heaviness in their ears, and to them it is blinding. These shall be called as though from a remote place.'

We brought Moses the Book, but disputes arose concerning it. Were it not that a Word had already passed from your Lord, judgement would have been pronounced between them. And 41:45 yet they are in perplexing doubt about it.

Whoso does a good deed does himself good. Whoso does an evil deed does himself evil. And your Lord is never unjust to His servants. To Him must knowledge of the Hour be referred.

No fruits issue from their sheaths, and no female bears or delivers except with His knowledge.

A Day shall come when He shall call out to them: 'Where are My partners?' and they shall answer: 'We declare to You that none of us can testify to this.' And there shall stray far from them what once they worshipped, and they shall conclude that 41:48 they have nowhere to escape.

Man wearies not from praying for good, but if evil touches him he grows desperate and dismayed. And if We make him taste a mercy from Us, after harm had touched him, he is wont to say: 'This is mine to claim, and I do not think the Hour is coming. But if I am returned to my Lord, I shall have a rich recompense with him.'

But We will assuredly inform the unbelievers of what they 41:50 did, and will assuredly make them taste a harsh punishment.

And if We show Our favour to a man, he spurns it and turns aside, but if evil touches him, he is much in prayer.

Say: 'Consider. If it is from God and you then scorn it, who can be more lost than one sunk deep in discord?'

We shall show them Our wonders on all horizons and in their very souls, until it becomes obvious to them that it is the Truth. Does it not suffice that your Lord is a witness of all things? And yet they are in doubt about the encounter with their Lord, though it is He Who encompasses all things.   41:54

Deliberation

In the name of God,
Merciful to all,
Compassionate to each!

Ha Mim
'Ayn Sin Qaf

Thus are you being inspired, as were those before you.
God, Almighty, All-Wise:
To Him belongs what is in the heavens and on earth,
Exalted, All-Supreme.
The heavens above them are all but split asunder,
While the angels glorify the praises of their Lord and ask
     forgiveness for those on earth.
But God is assuredly All-Forgiving, Compassionate to each.
     As for those who adopted masters other than Him, God is their custodian, and you are not a guardian over them.   42:6

Thus We revealed to you an Arabic Qur'an, in order that you warn Mecca, the Mother of Cities, and its surroundings, and warn of the Day of Assembly, of which there is no doubt: a party in the Garden, a party in the raging Furnace.
     Had God willed, He would have made them a single community, but He admits into His mercy whomever He pleases and the wicked shall have no protector and no ally.   42:8

Or have they truly had recourse to other protectors than Him?
    God is the only Protector.
It is He Who revives the dead and has power over all things.
If there be anything over which you differ, the verdict is
    God's.
This then is God, my Lord: in Him I place my trust, and to
    Him I turn in repentance.
Creator of the heavens and earth!

It is He Who assigned to you, from your own number,
    spouses, and from cattle, pairs, wherewith to multiply you.
Nothing resembles Him. He is All-Hearing, All-Seeing.
To Him belong the reins of the heavens and earth.
He spreads out His bounty to whomever He wills – and
    withholds it.
42:12 He is Omniscient.

He prescribed to you of religion what He once enjoined upon
Noah, as also what We revealed to you and what We enjoined
upon Abraham, Moses and Jesus: to follow the right religion
and not be in dispute over it.

    For the idolaters, what you call them to seems excessive. But
God chooses to His side whom He wills, and guides to Himself
whoever turns in repentance to Him.

They differed not concerning it except when Knowledge had
come to them, out of mutual envy. Were it not for a prior Word
from your Lord which set a stated term, judgement would have
been passed on them. And those bequeathed the Book after
42:14 them are in perplexing doubt about it.

Therefore, call to the faith, and persevere, as you have been
commanded. Do not follow their caprice, but say:
'I believe in any Book sent down by God;
I was commanded to judge with fairness among you;

God is our Lord and your Lord;
We have our works and you have your works;
There is no quarrel between us and you;
God shall gather us together, and to Him is our homecoming.'

As for those who continue to dispute about God after having
answered His call, their arguments hold no value with their
Lord. Upon them shall fall wrath, and grievous torment awaits. 42:16

It is God Who sent down the Book, in truth and balanced
measure. Who knows? Perhaps the Hour is near. Those who
have no faith in it wish to hasten it, but the faithful are in awe
of it, and know it is the truth, while they who question the Hour
are far gone in error.

God is gracious towards His worshippers;
He provides to whomever He pleases;
He is All-Powerful, Almighty.   42:19

Whoso desires the tillage of the hereafter, We double his tillage;
Whoso desires the tillage of this world, We provide him of it,
    but he has no share in the hereafter.

Or is it that they have partners who instituted for them a religion
for which God granted no authority? Were it not for a prior
Word of Decision, judgement would have been passed among
them, and the wicked will have a punishment most painful.
    You shall see the wicked in fear of what they had earned as
torment falls upon them, but the faithful and righteous in deeds
you shall see in the meadows of the Gardens. They shall have
whatever they please from their Lord, and that is the greatest of
favours.
    These are the glad tidings that God conveys to His wor-
shippers, to them who are faithful and righteous in deeds.

Say: 'I ask you no wage for it save amity of kinship. Whoso performs a goodly deed, to him We shall increase it in goodness. God is All-Forgiving, All-Thankful.'

Or do they say he fabricated a lie from God? If God wishes, he can seal your heart. God erases falsehood, and enforces the truth 42:24   with His Word. He knows full well what lies within breasts.

It is He Who accepts repentance from His worshippers, forgives sins and knows full well what you do. He answers the prayers of those who have faith and do righteous deeds, and multiplies His favours upon them, but the unbelievers shall meet with 42:26   grievous torment.

Had God spread out His bounty to His servants, they would have grown shameless on earth. Rather, He dispenses it in any measure He wills. Regarding His servants, He is All-Experienced, All-Seeing. It is He Who brings down rain after they have despaired, He Who spreads forth His mercy. He is 42:28   the Protector, the All-Praiseworthy.

Among His signs is the creation of the heavens and earth, and what He dispersed therein of creatures that crawl; and He is capable of gathering them together whenever He pleases.

Any calamity that befalls you is due to what your own hands have earned – but He forgives much. You cannot escape His power on earth and, apart from God, you have no guardian and 42:31   no champion.

Among His signs are ships that run in the sea like mountain-tops. If He wills, He can still the wind and they remain motionless on its surface. In this are signs for every one who is truly patient, ever thankful. Or else He drowns them through shipwreck for 42:34   what they earned – but He forgives much.

Those who argue against Our revelations know there is no escape for them. For all that you have been granted is but a

fleeting enjoyment in this present life, but what is with God is
better and more lasting:
For those who believe and place their trust in God;
Those who refrain from major sins and debaucheries, and
    forgive when wrathful;
Those who answer the call of their Lord and perform the
    prayers;
Those who settle their affairs through common deliberation;
Those who expend from what We provided them;
Those who, when aggression assails them, show a bold
    front. 42:39

Harm is requited by a similar harm. But whoso forgives and
makes peace, his reward shall be with God, for He loves not the
unjust.

Whoso retaliates in kind after being wronged – these are not
held to account. Rather, account is demanded of those who
oppress people and commit transgression on earth, unjustly. To
them there is painful torment. But he who bears with patience
and forgives, this would be a course of action upright and
prudent. 42:43

Whom God leads astray, no guide has he apart from Him.

And you shall witness how the wicked, when they behold the
torment, will say: 'Is there any way of going back to life?'

You shall see them being paraded before it, heads bowed in
humility, and casting furtive glances.

And the believers shall say: 'The real losers are those who
have lost themselves and their families on the Day of Resurrection.' The wicked will truly be in everlasting torment. No allies
will they have to come to their help, apart from God.

Whom God leads astray, no path to truth has he. 42:46

Answer the call of your Lord before a Day arrives which cannot
be staved off from God. On that Day, you will have no refuge,
nor is any denial possible.

If they turn away, it is not as their guardian that We sent you: yours is but to convey the message.

And We – if We make man taste a mercy from Us, he is delighted with it. But if harm befalls them for what their hands 42:48 wrought beforehand, man turns blasphemous.

To God belongs sovereignty of the heavens and earth.
He creates what He wills.
He bestows females on whomever He wills,
And bestows males on whomever He wills,
Or joins them together, male and female,
Or makes barren whom He wills.
42:50 He is Omniscient, All-Powerful.

It is not vouchsafed for any human being that God should address him except through inspiration or from behind a veil, or else He sends a messenger who reveals what he wills, by His leave. He is Exalted, All-Wise.

So too did We inspire you with a spirit, by Our command.

Time was when you knew not what the Book was, nor faith, but We brought it forth as a light by which We guide whomever We will of Our servants.

And you are assuredly guiding to a straight path, the path of God, to Whom belongs all that is in the heavens and earth.
42:53 In truth, all matters shall revert to God.

Ornament

In the name of God,
Merciful to all,
Compassionate to each!

Ha Mim

By the Manifest Book!
We have revealed it as an Arabic Qur'an: perhaps you will
    understand.
It is in the Mother of the Book, with Us, Exalted, All-Wise.
    Shall We hold back the Remembrance from you because you
are a dissolute people?
    How many a prophet We sent to the ancients! But no prophet
came to them except they would mock him.
    We destroyed men more violent than them, and the example
of the ancients is a thing of the past.   43:8

And if you were to ask them who created the heavens and earth,
they would answer: 'The Almighty and All-Knowing created
them.'
    It is He Who made the earth level for you, and marked out
in it highways for you, that you may be guided; He Who sent
down water from the sky in measure, therewith to revive a dead
region. So too will you be brought forth from the dead.
    It is He Who created all kinds of creatures, and provided you
with ships and cattle which you ride, that you may sit on their
backs, and then remember the grace of God when firmly seated,
saying: 'Glory be to God Who placed all this at our service, a
thing we could not ourselves undertake. To Our Lord we shall
assuredly revert.'   43:14

And yet they turn one of His servants into a part of Him!

Man is so evidently blasphemous!

Or did He take to Himself, from what He created, daughters, and privileged you with sons? If one of them receives tidings of the birth of that which he likens to the All-Merciful, his face turns dark, suppressing his vexation. And yet they attribute to God beings brought up in luxury but are indistinct in argument?

43:18

And the angels, servants of the All-Merciful, they turn into females!

Did they witness their creation? Their word of witness shall be recorded, and they shall answer for it.

They say: 'Had the All-Merciful willed it, we would not have worshipped them.'

They have no knowledge of this; they are merely lying.

Or is it that We brought them a Book before it, and they hold fast to it?

Instead, they say: 'We found our forefathers set on this course, and are guided in their footsteps.'

Likewise, We sent no warner before you to any city but its men of luxury would say: 'We found our forefathers set on this course, and are following in their footsteps.'

Say: 'What if I bring you guidance greater than what your forefathers had followed?'

They say: 'We abjure the message you have been sent with.'

So We took revenge on them. Consider the end to which these liars came!

43:25

Remember when Abraham said to his father and people: 'I am quit of what you worship, except for Him Who created me, for it is He Who shall guide me.' This was a saying which he made to endure among his progeny, in order that they may turn back to God.

Instead, I gave these people and their forefathers enjoyment of life till the Truth came to them, and an indisputable Messenger.

But when the Truth came to them, they said: 'This is sorcery and we refuse to believe it.'

43:30

They say: 'If only this Qur'an was sent down on some grandee in the two cities!'

Is it they who hand out the mercy of your Lord?

We distributed their livelihoods among them in this present life, and raised some above others in rank, that some might take others into their service. But the mercy of your Lord is better than what they amass. Were it not that mankind would have become a single disbelieving community, We would have provided the houses of those who disavow the All-Merciful with roofs of silver, and grandiose stairs on which to mount, with magnificent entrance gates and sumptuous couches on which to recline, and fine adornments.

All these are merely the delights of this present life, but the hereafter belongs to the pious in your Lord's sight.

43:35

Whoso wilfully ignores the mention of the All-Merciful, We will set upon him a demon who will be his intimate companion. They shall bar them from the Way though they themselves imagine they are rightly guided till, when he comes before Us, he will say: 'Would that between you and me were the distance between East and West' – wretched is that companion!

Today it profits you not, if you are wicked, that you are all in torment together.

43:39

Do you think you can make the deaf hear, or guide the blind and those who have strayed far in sin? If We cause you to die, We will take revenge upon them, or else We will make you witness what We promised them, for We hold total power over them.

Therefore, hold fast to what you were inspired with, for you are set on a straight path.

This is a Remembrance to you and your people, and you will surely be questioned.

Question the messengers We sent before you: did We appoint
43:45 gods for them to worship other than the All-Merciful?

We sent Moses with Our revelations to Pharaoh and his court,
saying: 'I am the messenger of the Lord of the Worlds.' When
he came to them with Our wonders, there they were, laughing
at them. Each wonder We showed them was more marvellous
than the last, so We seized them with torment that they might
turn back in repentance.

They said: 'O sorcerer, call on your Lord as He covenanted
with you – we shall follow right guidance.'

When We drew away the torment from them, behold, they
reneged, and Pharaoh called out to his people: 'My people, do
I not hold kingship in Egypt? And what of these rivers flowing
beneath my feet? Can you not see? Am I not better than this
pitiful person, who can barely make himself understood? If only
he were decked with golden bracelets, or else the angels had
43:53 come with him, as intimate allies!'

So he carried his people with him, and they obeyed him – they
were indeed a dissolute people. When they provoked Our wrath,
We took vengeance on them and caused them all to drown.
Forerunners We made them, and an example to later gener-
43:56 ations.

And when the Son of Mary is adduced as an example, behold,
your people are loud in protest, and say: 'What! Are our gods
better or is he?' They adduce his example to you only for
argument's sake. Indeed they are a people very fond of dispu-
tation.

He is but a servant on whom We conferred Our grace, and
43:59 We made him a model for the Children of Israel.

Had We willed We could have created you as angels, to take
your place on earth.

Jesus is a portent of the Hour, so be in no doubt regarding it, and follow Me, for this is a straight path.

Let not Satan bar your way: to you he is a manifest enemy.   43:62

When Jesus came with evident signs, he said: 'I come to you with Wisdom, and to make clear to you some of what you differ about. Be pious before God and obey me. God is my Lord and your Lord, so worship Him, for this is the straight path.'

But the sects among them fell into dispute – woe to the wicked from the torment of a painful Day!

Can they expect anything other than the Hour which will come upon them suddenly and unawares? On that Day, intimates will become enemies one to another – except for the pious.   43:67

My worshippers, this Day no fear shall fall upon you, nor shall you grieve – they who believed in Our revelations and submitted to the true faith:

'Enter the Garden, you and your spouses, rejoicing.'

There shall pass among them trays of gold and cups, and in it shall be all that souls desire or eyes delight in, and you shall abide therein eternally.

Such is the Garden bequeathed to you in return for your
    deeds.

In it you shall have much fruit from which to eat.   43:73

The wicked shall abide in the torment of hell, eternally,

A torment never subsiding for them, wherein they are bereft of
    hope.

We wronged them not, but it was they who were wrongdoers.

They shall cry out: 'O Malik,* let your Lord deprive us of
    life!'

And he shall answer: 'You shall remain as you are.'

We brought you the Truth, but most of you detest the Truth.   43:78

Or have they devised some plan? We too shall devise.

Or do they imagine that we do not hear their secret and intimate conversations? Yes indeed, and Our envoys are by their 43:80 side, recording.

Say: 'If the All-Merciful had a child, I would be the first to worship.'

Glory be to the Lord of the heavens and earth, Lord of the throne, above what they assert!

So leave them to sink further in falsehood, and amuse themselves, till they encounter the Day they have been promised.

He it is Who in heaven is God and on earth is God – All-Wise, Omniscient.

Blessed is He to Whom belongs sovereignty of the heavens and earth, and what lies between! With Him is knowledge of 43:85 the Hour, and to Him you shall be returned.

Those who call on what is other than Him cannot intercede, unless it be one who witnesses to the Truth, in full knowledge.

If you were to ask them who created them, they would say: 'God' – so how can they contradict themselves?

And as for his saying: 'My Lord, these are a people who do not believe,' you are to turn away from them and say: 'Peace!' 43:89 – for they will surely know.

Smoke

In the name of God,
Merciful to all,
Compassionate to each!

Ha Mim

By the Manifest Book!
We sent it down on a blessed night – We have warned!
During that night all matters are wisely apportioned,
At Our command – We have sent a messenger!
A mercy from your Lord – All-Hearing, All-Knowing is He!
Lord of the heavens and earth and what lies between, if your
    faith is firm.
There is no god but He,
He gives life and deals death,
Your Lord is He, and Lord of your ancient forebears.   44:8

And yet, in their doubt, they dally.

So look out for a Day when heaven exhales smoke, for all to
see, that envelops mankind – a painful torment that!

'Our Lord, draw away this torment from us, for we are
believers.'

But how will remembering help them when a messenger,
undeniable, had already come to them, and they had turned
their backs on him, saying: 'He is tutored and crazed'?

If We draw away the torment a little, and you revert to
unbelief, a Day shall come when We shall deliver the Great
Blow – We shall exact vengeance.   44:16

Before them We had tested the people of Pharaoh, when a noble
messenger came to them saying:

'Deliver God's worshippers into my hands, for I am a

trustworthy messenger to you. Do not uplift yourselves above God for I come to you with clear authority. I take refuge in my Lord and yours lest you stone me. If you do not believe me, keep away from me.'

So he prayed to his Lord: 'These are a wicked people.'

'Set out at night with My worshippers, but you will surely be pursued. And leave the sea behind you calm and still, for they 44:24 are a troop that will surely be drowned.'

How many a garden they left behind them,
How many a spring,
How many crops,
How many a noble dwelling,
44:27 How many a blessing which once they enjoyed!

And so it was that We bequeathed it all to another nation.
Neither sky nor earth shed a tear for them,
Nor were they kept waiting.

And We delivered the Children of Israel from the humiliating
    torment of Pharaoh,
A man of towering arrogance, and excessively wicked.
And We chose them, knowingly, above all mankind,
44:33 And We brought them wonders, in which was a clear ordeal.

But now these people say: 'There is nothing but our first death, and we shall not be resurrected. Bring back to us our forebears, if you speak the truth.'

Are they better than the people of Tubba'* and those We destroyed before them? They were indeed sinners.

We created not the heavens and earth, and what is in between, in order to play a game.

We created them not except in justice, but most of them are ignorant.

The Day of Decision shall be their appointed time, all of them: a Day when no patron can avail his client in any wise, nor will

they be succoured, except such as God has shown mercy to, for
He is Almighty, Compassionate to each.   44:42

The Zaqqum-tree shall be the food of the grave sinner,
Like molten brass, boiling in stomachs like boiling water.
'Seize him, and hurl him into the pit of hell
Then pour over his head a torment of boiling water.
Taste it, you who are mighty and noble!
Here it is, that which you used to doubt!'   44:50

But the pious shall be in a dwelling secure,
Amidst gardens and springs,
Clothed in silk and brocade, face to face.
And, too, We married them to spouses with dark and large
    eyes.
Therein they call for every kind of fruit, in peace of mind.
Therein they do not taste death, except for the first death,
And He has spared them the torment of hell – a favour from
    your Lord.
This in truth is the greatest of triumphs.   44:57

We have indeed made it easy by your tongue; perhaps they
    will remember.
So watch and wait, and they too shall watch and wait.   44:59

Kneeling

In the name of God,
Merciful to all,
Compassionate to each!

Ha Mim

Behold the revelation of the Book from God, Almighty,
    All-Wise!
In the heavens and earth are signs for those who believe,
As also in your creation, and in creatures He dispersed
Are signs for a people of firm faith.

So too in the alternation of night and day, and in what God
has sent down from heaven of livelihood whereby He revived
the earth after its death, and in varying the winds, are signs for
45:5   a people who understand.

These are the revelations of God We recite to you in truth. So
what discourse, coming after God and His revelations, do they
believe in?

Woe to every lying sinner!

He hears the revelations of God being recited to him, then
clings to his pride, as though he had not heard them. Give him
tidings of a painful torment!

And if he knows a little of Our revelations, he takes them in
jest. These shall have an abasing punishment. Beyond them lies
hell, and what they earned shall avail them nothing, nor what
they adopted as lords instead of God. A mighty torment awaits
them.

This is Guidance, and they who blaspheme the revelations
of their Lord shall receive a punishment of the most painful
45:11   torment.

It is God Who placed the sea at your service, that ships may run therein by His command, and that you may seek of His bounty – perhaps you will render thanks. And He placed at your service what is in the heavens and the earth – all of it from Him. In this are signs for a people who reflect.   45:13

Tell the believers to forgive those who do not fear the battle-days of God, that He may reward a people for what they have earned. Whoso does a good deed does himself good. Whoso does an evil deed does himself evil. Then to your Lord you will be returned.   45:15

To the Children of Israel We gave the Book, the Law and Prophecy. We provided them with the good things of life and preferred them above mankind. And We gave them precise rulings, but they fell into dispute only after Knowledge had come to them, out of mutual envy. Your Lord shall judge between them on the Day of Resurrection concerning that over which they differed.   45:17

Then We set you upon a Pathway of faith. So follow it, and do not follow the whims of those who have no understanding. They will in no wise avail you against God. The wicked are patrons one of another, and God is the Patron of the pious. This Qur'an is an enlightenment to mankind, and a Guidance and a mercy to a people of firm faith.   45:20

Do those who commit evil deeds imagine that We shall treat them like those who believe and do good deeds, that they are equal in life and death? How badly they judge!

God created the heavens and earth in justice, so that each soul shall be rewarded for what it earned, nor will they be wronged.   45:22

Have you considered him who takes his own caprice as his god? God, in His foreknowledge, has led him astray. He sealed his hearing and heart, and shrouded his vision. Who can guide him other than God? Will you not remember?

They say: 'There is nothing but our present life. We die, we live, and only Time destroys us.' Of this they have no knowledge. They are merely guessing.

And when Our revelations are recited to them, plain and clear, their only argument is to respond: 'Bring back our forefathers if you speak the truth!'

Say: 'It is God Who gives you life, then causes you to die, then gathers you together on the Day of Resurrection, of which 45:26 there is no doubt.' But most people have no understanding.

To God belongs sovereignty of the heavens and earth. When the Hour arrives, on that Day the falsifiers shall fail.

And you will witness how every nation will be on its knees, how every nation will be called back to its own Book: 'Today you shall be recompensed for what you did. Here is Our Book, speaking about you with truth. Therein We have had inscribed 45:29 all you have done.'

As for those who believed and did righteous deeds, their Lord shall admit them into His mercy – that is the most conspicuous of triumphs.

But as for those who blasphemed: 'Were not My revelations recited to you? But you stood upon your pride and were a people steeped in sin.'

When you were told: 'God's promise is true and the Hour is beyond all doubt,' you answered: 'We know not what the Hour 45:32 is. We are merely guessing, but are not certain.'

The evil they committed shall be fully revealed to them, and that which they once would mock shall now engulf them.

They will be told: 'Today We shall forget you, as you once forgot the encounter of this your Day. The Fire will be your refuge and none shall come to help you. That is because you took the revelations of God in jest, while the present life seduced you.'

Today they shall not emerge from it, nor shall they be permitted to repent.   45:35

Praise be to God, Lord of the heavens and earth, Lord of
 mankind!
To Him be exaltation in the heavens and earth!
He is Almighty, All-Wise.   45:37

Rolling Sands

In the name of God,
Merciful to all,
Compassionate to each!

Ha Mim

Behold the revelation of the Book from God, Almighty, All-Wise!

We created not the heavens and earth and what lies between except in truth, and for a stated term. But the blasphemers continue to ignore the warnings they receive.   46:3

Say: 'Consider that which you worship instead of God. Show me which portion of the earth they have created. Or do they own a share of the heavens? Bring me a Book prior to this one, or even a smattering of Knowledge, if you speak the truth.'

Who is more sunk in error than one who worships, instead of God, someone that answers him not till the Day of Resurrection? They pay no heed to their prayers. And when mankind are

mustered, they shall be their enemies, and shall renounce their
46:6   worship of them.

And when Our revelations are recited to them, plain and clear,
they who renounced the Truth when it came to them, say: 'This
is manifest sorcery.'

Or do they say: 'He fabricated it?'

Say: 'If I have fabricated it, you can do me no good at all
against God. He knows best your constant haranguing concerning it. Let it suffice as witness between me and you.' He is
46:8   All-Forgiving, Compassionate to each.

Say: 'I am not a novelty among messengers. I know not what is
to be done to me or you. I merely follow what is revealed to
me. I am nothing but a manifest warner.'

Say: 'Consider if it be from God and you blasphemed against
it; and then someone from the Children of Israel witnesses to
its like, and believes, while you stand on your pride.' God guides
46:10 not wrongdoers.

The blasphemers say to the believers: 'Had it been anything
good, they would not have preceded us to it.' But since they
have not gained guidance from it, they say: 'This is an age-old
falsehood.'

Before it there was the Book of Moses, a guide and a mercy;
and this is a Book that confirms it, in the Arabic tongue, to warn
46:12 the wicked and bring glad tidings to the righteous.

Those who say: 'Our Lord is God,' and are upright,
No fear shall come upon them,
Nor shall they grieve.
They are the inhabitants of the Garden,
Dwelling therein for ever,
46:14 As a reward for their deeds.

We enjoined upon man to be kind to his parents.
His mother bore him in hardship,
And delivered him in hardship;
His bearing and his weaning are thirty months.
Until, when he is fully grown and reaches forty years, he says:
'My Lord, inspire me to be thankful for Your blessings,
Which You bestowed on me and my parents,
And that I act in virtue, pleasing to You.
Grant me a virtuous progeny;
I have sincerely repented before You,
And I have sincerely embraced Islam.'

These shall be the ones whose best deeds We shall accept, and whose sins We shall disregard. They shall be among the denizens of the Garden: a true promise which they have been vouchsafed.

46:16

And remember him who said to his parents: 'How you exasperate me! You promise me that I shall be resurrected when centuries have passed before me?' while they were imploring God and saying to him: 'Believe, you wretch, for the promise of God is true,' and he replied: 'These are but fables of the ancients.'

Upon such people shall the Word come true, as it did among nations before them of both *Jinn* and humans. They were indeed lost.

For all there are stations, in accordance with their deeds. He will pay them in full for their works, and they shall not be wronged.

46:19

A Day shall come when the unbelievers shall be paraded before the Fire: 'You wasted the good things in your present life and had full enjoyment of them. Today, you shall be rewarded with an abasing torment because you grew arrogant on earth, unjustly, and because of your debauchery.'

Remember the man from 'Ad, when he warned his people, amidst the rolling sands, and when warners had passed away before and after him: 'Worship none but God. I fear for you the torment of a mighty Day.'

They answered: 'Have you come to lure us away from our gods? Bring upon us what you threaten, if you speak the truth.'

He said: 'Knowledge belongs solely to God. I proclaim to you what I have been sent with, but I see you are a vicious people.'

When they saw a cloud on the horizon, heading towards their valleys, they said: 'This cloud shall bring us rain.'

'Rather, it is what you brought quickly upon yourselves – a wind in which lies painful punishment. It shall destroy everything, by command of its Lord.'

46:25   When morning came upon them, only their houses could be seen. Thus do We reward a wicked people.

We had granted them such power as We had not granted you, giving them ears, eyes and hearts; but neither their ears, eyes nor hearts availed them in any way, for they blasphemed against God's signs, and there engulfed them what once they mocked.

We destroyed the towns that surround you, and displayed all manner of wonders that they might turn back to God. If only they had come to their aid – those whom they had adopted as gods, instead of God, in order to bring them close to Him! But no! They strayed far from them.

46:28   Such was their falsehood and what they used to fabricate.

Remember when We steered towards you a small band of *Jinn* to listen to the Qur'an. When they arrived, they said: 'Listen!' When it was finished, they returned to their people, carrying a warning.

They said: 'Our people, we heard a Book, sent down after Moses, that confirms what came before it. It guides to the Truth and to a path that is straight. Our people, answer him who calls to God, and believe in Him, and God shall forgive you your sins and save you from a painful punishment. Whoso answers not him who calls to God cannot escape His power on earth, nor

has he any patrons apart from Him. Such people are in manifest
error.'

46:32

Do they not realize that God, Who created the heavens and
earth, and did not grow weary from their creation, is capable
of reviving the dead? Yes indeed, He has power over all things.

A Day shall come when blasphemers are paraded before the
Fire.
'Is this real?'
'Yes, by our Lord,' they shall reply.
And He shall say: 'Then taste the torment for your blas-
phemy!'

46:34

So remain steadfast, as other resolute messengers had stood
    fast.
Seek not to bring it quickly upon them.
It will be as if, when they witness the Day they are promised,
They had been on earth a mere hour of a day.
That is the message!
Will any be destroyed but the dissolute?

46:35

Muhammad

In the name of God,
Merciful to all,
Compassionate to each!

Those who disbelieve and bar the way to God – He shall cause
their works to founder.
But those who believe and do righteous deeds and believe in
what was sent down on Muhammad, which is the Truth from
their Lord, those – He shall expiate their sins, and set their
affairs in order.

47:2

That is because those who disbelieved followed falsehood, while those who believed followed the Truth from their Lord. Thus does God strike to mankind their parables.

When you encounter the unbelievers, blows to necks it shall be until, once you have routed them, you are to tighten their fetters. Thereafter, it is either gracious bestowal of freedom or holding them to ransom, until war has laid down its burdens. Yet, had God willed, He could Himself have vanquished them, but it was so in order that He might test some of you through others. And those who were killed in the cause of God – He shall not cause their works to founder. He shall guide them, and set their affairs in order, and admit them into the Garden He made known to 47:6 them.

O believers, if you help God, He will help you and make firm your feet. As for the unbelievers, wretched is their lot! He shall cause their works to founder. That is because they despised what God has sent down, so He caused their works to come to 47:9 grief.

Have they not journeyed on earth? Have they not observed the fate of those who came before them? God brought utter destruction upon them, and the unbelievers shall suffer likewise. This is because God is the Patron of the believers, and the unbelievers have no patron. God shall admit those who believe and do good deeds into Gardens beneath which rivers flow, while the unbelievers frolic and eat like cattle, and the Fire shall 47:12 be their berth.

How many a town, more mighty than your own which drove you out, have We destroyed! No champion did they have.

So is he who is certain of his Lord like one to whom his misdeeds are made to appear attractive, and who pursue their whims?

The likeness of the Garden promised to the pious is this: in it are rivers of water, not brackish, and rivers of milk, unchanging in taste, and rivers of wine, delicious to them who drink it, and rivers of honey, pure and limpid. Therein they shall enjoy all kinds of fruits, and forgiveness from their Lord.

Can this be compared to one abiding eternally in the Fire, where they are given boiling water to drink, which rends their innards?

47:15

Among them are some who listen to you but when they leave your presence, they say to those granted knowledge: 'What did he just say?' These are the ones whose hearts God has sealed and who pursue their whims.

But those who are rightly guided He shall increase in guidance, and reward them for their piety. Can they expect anything other than the Hour, which shall come upon them suddenly? Its portents are already here. How will remembering avail them when it comes upon them?

47:18

Know that there is no god but God.
Seek forgiveness for your sins, and for the believers, male and
    female.
God knows all your active pursuits and all your times of rest.

The believers say: 'If only a *sura* were revealed!' But when a *sura* is revealed, unambiguous, in which fighting is mentioned, you notice those in whose heart is sickness looking at you like one swooning from fear of death. More seemly for them is obedience and gracious consent. When matters are grave, it would be best for them to have faith in God. If you run away, might you not go on to work corruption on earth and sever your ties of kinship? These are the ones whom God has cursed, making them deaf and blinding their sight. Will they not weigh and consider the Qur'an, or are there padlocks on their minds?

47:24

They who turned tail and fled after Guidance had become fully apparent to them – Satan it was who tempted them and gave them false hope. For they had said to those who disliked what God had revealed: 'We will obey you in certain matters only.' And God knows full well their secret thoughts. How will it be when angels have caused them to die and are striking their faces and backs? For they had followed a path displeasing to God, and 47:28 eschewed His good-will, so He caused their works to founder.

Could it be that those with sickness in their hearts imagine that God will not unearth their secret spite? If We wish to do so, We can point them out to you and you will recognize them by their outward visage; and you will indeed recognize them by the 47:30 allusive manner of their speech. God knows all your deeds.

We shall put you to the test, to know who are truly exerting themselves for God and are standing firm, and We shall put to the test your secret thoughts.

Those who disbelieve and bar the way of God, and who defy the Messenger after Guidance has become fully apparent to them – they shall not harm God in any wise, and He shall cause 47:32 their works to founder.

O believers, obey God and obey the Messenger, and let not your works go to waste. Those who disbelieve and bar the way of God, then die as unbelievers – God shall not forgive them.

Be not faint-hearted and call for peace when you have the upper hand. God is on your side and will not diminish the reward of your deeds.

The present life is mere play and frivolity. If you believe and are pious, He shall pay your wages in full and will not ask you to surrender your property. Were He to ask you for it, and insist, you would begrudge it, and thus He would expose your 47:37 malice.

Here you are, called upon to expend your wealth in the cause of God. Some of you begrudge this, and whoso begrudges it is merely begrudging himself! God is All-Sufficient, and it is you

who are poor. And if you turn away, He will substitute another
community for you, and they shall not be like you.   47:38

Victory

In the name of God,
Merciful to all,
Compassionate to each!

We have granted you a conspicuous victory,
That God may forgive your sins, past and to come,
And complete His favour upon you,
And guide you to a straight path,
And lend you His mighty aid.   48:3

It is He Who sent down the spirit of serenity into the hearts of
the believers, that they may increase in faith, over and above
their faith.
To God belong the troops of the heavens and the earth.
God is All-Knowing, All-Wise.   48:4

He will admit the believers, male and female, into Gardens
beneath which rivers flow, abiding therein for ever, and He shall
pardon their sins – this is the greatest triumph in God's sight.
    And He shall punish the Hypocrites, male and female, and
the idolaters, male and female, those who entertain evil thoughts
of God. Upon them shall turn the wheel of misfortune. God
shall be wrathful towards them, curse them and prepare hell for
them – a wretched destiny!
To God belong the troops of the heavens and the earth.
God is Almighty, All-Wise.   48:7

We have sent you as a witness, a bearer of glad tidings and a
    warner,

That you may believe in God and His Messenger,
That you may lend Him your aid, be in awe of Him and
    glorify Him, morning and evening.
Those who pay you homage are in fact paying homage to God
    – the hand of God rests above their own.
Whoso breaks his word has only himself to blame for
    breaking it;
Whoso fulfils the obligations that God enjoined upon him,
48:10   God shall bestow on him a glorious wage.

The Bedouins left behind will say to you: 'We have been preoccupied with our properties and our families, so please ask forgiveness for us.' They say with their tongues what lies not in their hearts.

Say: 'Who can do anything against God's will should He intend you harm or intend you benefit?' Rather, God knows perfectly well what you do.

Or did you imagine that the Messenger and the believers will never return home to their families? This notion was made to appear attractive in your hearts, and you entertained evil thoughts, and were a worthless people.

Whoso believes not in God and His Messenger, We have
48:13 prepared a raging Fire for the unbelievers.

To God belongs sovereignty of the heavens and earth.
He forgives whom He wills and punishes whom He wills.
God is All-Forgiving, Compassionate to each.

Those left behind will say, once you have set forth to capture booty: 'May we please follow in your tracks?'
    They merely wish to warp the speech of God.
    Say: 'No, you shall not follow us. God has already spoken.'
    And they shall respond: 'Ah no! You begrudge us this.'
48:15   In fact they are a people of little understanding.

Say to the Bedouins left behind: 'You shall be called up against a people of great might, whom you are to fight, or else they might surrender. If you are obedient, God will grant you a fair wage. But if you turn tail, as you did before, He will punish you most painfully.'

No blame attaches to the blind, the lame or the sick.

Whoso obeys God and His Messenger, He shall admit into Gardens beneath which rivers flow.

Whoso turns tail, He shall punish most painfully.   48:17

God was well pleased with the believers, when they made their pledge to you beneath the tree. He knew what was in their hearts, and sent down the spirit of serenity upon them, and rewarded them with news of an imminent victory, and much booty for them to capture.

God is Almighty, All-Wise.   48:19

God has promised that you will capture much booty, and hastened this present booty for you. He has restrained the hands of people from you, that this may be a sign to the believers, and that He may guide you along a straight path. There was other booty which you could not seize but which God has encompassed in His knowledge, and God has power over all things.   48:21

Had the unbelievers fought you, they would have turned tail and fled, thereafter having none to protect or aid them.

Such has been the precedent of God beforehand, and you shall not find God's precedent to vary.

It was He Who restrained their hands from you and your hands from them, after having granted you victory over them in the vale of Mecca. God knew full well what you were doing.

It is they who blasphemed, and they who kept you away by force from the Sacred Mosque, while sacrificial animals were prevented from reaching their rightful place.

Were it not for the presence of believing men and women, unknown to you, and lest you trample them underfoot and so become guilty of an unintentional crime, and God may admit into His mercy whom He wills, and had believers and unbelievers been clearly separated from one another, We would have
48:25 punished the unbelievers most painfully.

For the unbelievers had planted in their hearts a zealotry, the zealotry of lawlessness, so God sent down the spirit of serenity upon His Messenger and upon the believers, and charged them with the word of piety, of which they were more worthy –
48:26 indeed its true keepers. And God is All-Knowing.

God has confirmed the vision of His Messenger by making it come true: you shall indeed enter the Sacred Mosque, God willing, in security, your heads shaved, your hair cropped short, and having no fear. So He knew what you did not know, and has decreed an imminent victory to precede that entry.

It is He Who sent His Messenger with Guidance and the religion of truth, that He may exalt it above all religions. Let God suffice
48:28 as witness.

Muhammad, the Messenger of God, and those who are with him, are adamant against the unbelievers but merciful towards one another.
     You see them bowing in prostration, seeking God's favour and good-will. Their marks are upon their foreheads from the traces of prostration. Such is their description in the Torah and their description in the Evangel: like a sown field that sends forth its shoots, then braces it so it thickens and rests firmly on its stalk – a sight pleasant to farmers, but thereby to mortify the unbelievers.
     God promises those among them who believe and do right-
48:29 eous deeds forgiveness and a glorious reward.

The Chambers

In the name of God,
Merciful to all,
Compassionate to each!

O believers, do not anticipate the decision of God and His Messenger, and fear God.

God is All-Hearing, All-Knowing.

O believers, raise not your voices above the voice of the Prophet, and do not speak loudly to him, as you speak loudly to one another, lest your works founder, and you are unaware of it. They who lower their voices in the presence of the Messenger of God – these are the ones whose hearts God has tested as to their piety. To them shall come forgiveness and a glorious reward. They who call out to you from behind the chambers – most have no understanding. If only they had been patient until you came out to them, it would have been better for them. God is All-Forgiving, Compassionate to each.   49:5

O believers, if a dissolute person brings you a piece of news, make sure you do not cause harm to people, unwittingly, and so come to regret your action. Know that the Messenger of God is among you; had he heeded your words in many a matter, you would have suffered hardship. But God has endeared faith to you and adorned it in your hearts, and made unbelief, depravity and mutiny hateful to you.

These are rightly guided: a favour from God and a blessing. God is All-Knowing, All-Wise.   49:8

If two groups of believers fight each other, make peace between them. If one group transgresses against the other, fight the transgressing group until it returns to the judgement of God. If it returns, settle the dispute between them in justice and be fair: God loves those who are fair.

The believers are indeed brothers, so make peace among your 49:10 brothers, and fear God – perhaps you will be shown mercy.

O believers, let no group make fun of another, for they may be better than them.

Let no women make fun of other women, for they may be better than them.

Refrain from backbiting one another, and from calling each other by nicknames. Wretched is a depraved name once faith 49:11 has come! But those who are unrepentant are surely wicked.

O believers, avoid undue suspicion, for some suspicions are sinful. Do not spy on one another or speak ill behind one another's back. Would any of you like to consume the flesh of his brother when dead? You would surely find it repulsive. And fear God, for God is All-Pardoning, Compassionate to each.

O mankind, We created you male and female, and made you into nations and tribes that you may come to know one another. The noblest among you in God's sight are the most pious. God 49:13 is All-Knowing, All-Experienced.

The Bedouins say: 'We believe.'

Say: 'You do not believe. Instead you may say: "We surrender," but faith has not entered your hearts. If you obey God and His Messenger, God will not diminish your works in any wise.' God is All-Forgiving, Compassionate to each.

The true believers are those who believe in God and His Messenger, then are free of doubt, and expend their properties and themselves in the cause of God. These are the sincere 49:15 believers.

Say: 'Do you presume to inform God of the sincerity of your religion when God knows all that is in the heavens and earth? God knows all matters full well.'

They make you feel beholden to them for having embraced Islam.

Say: 'Do not make me feel beholden to you for embracing Islam. Rather, it is God Who makes you beholden to Him for having guided you to the faith – provided, that is, you are sincere.'

49:17

God knows the Unseen of the heavens and earth, and of what you do He is All-Seeing.

49:18

Qaf

In the name of God,
Merciful to all,
Compassionate to each!

Qaf, and by the Glorious Qur'an!

Indeed, they are amazed that there came to them a warner from among their number.

The blasphemers say: 'This is an amazing claim! When we are dead and turned to dust, a return to life is surely far-fetched.'

We know what the earth shrivels of their bodies, but with Us is a Book that records all.

In fact, they cried lies to the Truth when it came to them, and are thus in perplexity.

50:5

Have they not observed the sky above them and how We erected it and decked it out, how free of cracks it is?

And the earth, how We spread it out and placed in it towering mountains, and caused it to sprout forth of every lovely species?

An eye-opener is this, and a remembrance to every servant
50:8   turning to God in repentance.

From the sky We sent down blessed water,
Wherewith We caused gardens to flower and grains for the
      harvest,
Soaring palm trees bearing serried clusters – sustenance to
      mankind.
With it We revived a region that was dead.
50:11 Likewise shall be the Resurrection.

Before them the people of Noah, of al-Rass and Thamud had
also cried lies, as too the people of 'Ad, and Pharaoh and the
fellow townsmen of Lot, the People of the Thicket and of
Tubba'. Each had cried lies to messengers, and the divine threat
came true upon them.

Did the first creation make Us weary? And yet they doubt a
50:15 new creation.

We created man and know what his soul murmurs to him,
50:16 But We are nearer to him than his jugular vein.

When the two recording angels begin to record,
Poised one to the right and one to the left,
Not a word escapes him but he has with him a watchman in
50:18   attendance.

And the stupor of death shall come with the Truth – this is
      what you tried to avoid.
And the Trumpet shall be sounded: that shall be the Day of
      Menace.
And every soul shall come forth,
With it an angel that drives it on, and an angel that
50:21   witnesses.

You had been heedless of all this,
But We drew away your veil and now your insight is sharp as
    steel.   50:22

And his demon-comrade shall say: 'This is what I have, ready
    to hand.'
'Hurl into hell, you two, every obstinate blasphemer,
Every persistent denier of virtue, every aggressor, every
    doubter,
As also him who set up another god alongside God.
Hurl him into the terrible torment.'   50:26

And his demon-comrade shall say: 'My Lord, it was not me who
made him impious – he himself was far gone in error.'
    He shall answer: 'Do not squabble in My presence after
having sent you a threat.
    'My word is unchanging, nor am I ever unjust to My ser-
vants.
    'A Day shall come when We shall say to hell: "Are you full?"
and it shall answer: "Can there be more?"'   50:30

And the Garden shall be drawn near to the pious, not far at
    all.
This is what you are promised – to every devout and mindful
    person,
One who fears God in the Unseen and comes forward with a
    penitent heart:
'Enter it in peace, for this is the Day of Eternity.'
In it they shall have whatever they wish – and We have still
    more.
How many a generation We destroyed before them!
    They were greater than them in prowess, and traversed the
earth – but was there any escape?
    In this is a reminder to one possessed of mind, or one who
hears attentively, and bears witness.   50:37

We created the heavens and earth and what lies between in six
  days, and no weariness touched Us.
Bear patiently what they say, and glorify the praises of your
  Lord,
Before sunrise and before sunset.
In the night, glorify Him, as too after prostration.
And listen carefully the Day a caller shall call from a nearby
  place,
A Day when they shall hear the Scream of Truth.
That shall be the Day of Emergence.
It is We Who give life and deal death, and to Us is the
  journey's end.
A Day shall come when the earth shall crack,
And shall reveal them, hurrying forth.
50:43   That is a mustering easy for Us.

We know best what they say,
And you are not a tyrant ruling over them.
50:45   So remind with the Qur'an whoever fears My threat.

The Lashing Gales

In the name of God,
Merciful to all,
Compassionate to each!

By the lashing gales!
By heavy-laden clouds!
By ships plain sailing!
By angels disbursing as commanded!
What you are promised is real,
51:6   And Sentence shall be passed.

By the sky with its wondrous mazes!
Discordant is your speech,
And whoso denies it is living a lie. 51:9

Perish the fanciful liars!
They who are heedless in their shrouded ignorance!
They ask when the Day of Judgement will come.
The Day when they are tested at the Fire:
Taste this ordeal that you wished to hasten! 51:14

But the pious are amidst Gardens and springs,
Receiving what their Lord provided them,
And before that they had been righteous.
Of nights they slept little,
And at dawns they prayed for pardon.
In their wealth beggars and the deprived had a rightful share. 51:19

On earth are signs for people of certain faith,
So too inside yourselves: will you not open your eyes?
In the sky is your livelihood, and what you are promised. 51:22

By the Lord of heaven and earth!
It is as real as the fact that you speak.

Has there come to you the story of Abraham's honoured friends?

When they entered upon him and said: 'Peace!' and he said: 'Peace! But you are unknown to me.'

So he slipped away to his family and brought back a fatted calf. He set it near and asked: 'Will you not eat?' But secretly he was in fear of them.

They said: 'Fear not,' and brought him glad tidings of a prudent son.

His wife came forward, in utter amazement, scratching her face and saying: 'A barren old woman!'

They said: 'Thus spoke your Lord; He is All-Wise, All-Knowing.' 51:30

He said: 'What is your business, O envoys?'

They said: 'We have been sent to a sinful people, to send down upon them stones of baked clay, each bearing its mark from your Lord, and aimed at the profligate.'

And thus We brought out from that town those who believed, and found not in it except one household of Muslims.

And We left it as a sign for those who fear the painful tor-
51:37   ment.

In Moses too was a sign,
When We sent him to Pharaoh with a manifest proof.
But he turned away, he and all who supported him, saying: 'A
        sorcerer, or a mad man!'
So We seized him and his troops and hurled them into the sea,
51:40 And he was fully to blame.

In 'Ad too was a sign,
When We sent them a sterile wind,
51:42 Leaving nothing in its wake but it turned into ruin.

In Thamud too was a sign,
When it was said to them: 'Enjoy your life for a while.'
But they defied the command of their Lord,
So the Thunderbolt struck them as they looked on:
51:45 No defence could they put up, nor could they find support.

And, before that, in the people of Noah was a sign:
They were a dissolute people.

And the sky We built in strength,
And surely We can do so.
The earth We spread out – blessed are They Who levelled it!
From every species We created a pair, that you may ponder
51:49   and reflect.

So flee to the shelter of God: to you I am a manifest warner
    from Him.
And do not set up another god alongside God: I am a manifest
    warner from Him.
And so it has always been: no messenger came to those before
    them but they called him a sorcerer or a mad man.
Did they bequeath this saying to one another?
Rather, they are a rebellious people.   51:53

So turn away from them, for you are not to blame.
And remind – reminding is good for the believers.
I created the *Jinn* and humans but to worship Me.
I wish for no livelihood from them,
Nor do I wish them to feed Me.
It is God Who is the All-Provider, Almighty, Ever-Unyielding.   51:58

To the wicked belongs a share of punishment, like the
    punishment of their comrades,
So let them not hasten it.
Woe to the blasphemers from the Day they have been
    promised!   51:60

The Mountain

In the name of God,
Merciful to all,
Compassionate to each!

By the Mountain!
By a Book inscribed,
In parchment unrolled!
By the populous House!
By the canopy raised high!
By the teeming sea!

Your Lord's torment shall surely fall.

52:8 Nothing can repel it.

The Day when heaven shall heave in turmoil,
And the mountains shall scurry in haste,
Woe is it on that Day to those who cry lies!
They who amuse themselves with idle talk;
That Day they shall be hustled to hell – and what hustling!
Here now is the Fire you used to disavow!
And this too you call sorcery, or are you blind?
Be scorched by it; it is all alike whether you bear it with
     patience or you do not:

52:16 You will only be rewarded for the acts you committed.

But the pious are amidst Gardens and Bliss,
Enjoying what their Lord has given them,
For their Lord has spared them the torment of hell.
Eat and drink in delight for the deeds you have done,
Reclining on couches, lined in rows.
We shall marry them to spouses, with dark and large eyes.
And those who believed, and were followed in their faith by
     their progeny,
We shall join them to their progeny,
And shall not stint their works in any wise.

52:21 Every person is accountable for what he earns.

And We shall supply them with fruits and meat, their hearts'
     desire.
They shall pass a cup from hand to hand,
Wherein there is no drunken uproar, nor any wrongdoing.
And moving among them will be their very own pages,
Looking like well-guarded pearls.
And they shall turn to one another and wonder:
'We had once been fearful for our families,
But God has favoured us, and spared us the torment of the
     scorching wind.

We would once pray to Him – He is All-Generous,
    Compassionate to each.'   52:28

Therefore, remind.
You are not, by grace of your Lord, a soothsayer or a mad
    man.
Or do they say: 'He is a poet, upon whom we await the
    capricious turns of fate'?
Say: 'Wait, and I shall be waiting with you!'
Or is it that their whims command them to this?
Or are they a people obdurate and rebellious?   52:32

Or do they say: 'He himself improvised it'?
Rather, they have no faith.
Let them, if they are telling the truth, bring forth a discourse
    like it.   52:34

Or is it that they were created from nothing?
Or could it be that they are the creators?
Or was it them who created the heavens and earth?
Rather, they possess no certainty.   52:36

Or is it that they possess the treasures of your Lord?
Or are they the ones in supreme control?
Or do they have a ladder they climb upon, to listen?
Let the listener among them come forth with manifest
    proof.   52:38

Or is it that He has daughters while you have sons?
Or do you demand a wage from them, and hence they are
    heavily indebted?
Or is the Unseen at their disposal, and they are writing it
    down?
Or are they intending guile?
It is the blasphemers, rather, who shall suffer guile.   52:42

Or do they have a god other than God?
Glory be to God far above what they associate with Him!

Even if they see missiles raining down from the sky,
52:44   They would say: 'Massed clouds!'

So leave them till they encounter the Day in which they will be
    thunderstruck,
A Day when their guile shall avail them nothing,
52:46   And they shall be without support.

And as for those who were wicked, a torment awaits before
    that Day,
But most of them are without understanding.

Be patient with the decree of your Lord, for you are in Our
    Very Eyes.
And glorify the praises of your Lord when you arise,
52:49   And in the night glorify Him, when stars vanish.

The Star

In the name of God,
Merciful to all,
Compassionate to each!

By the star when it plunged!
Your companion has not veered from the truth, nor is he
    misguided.
Nor is he giving voice to his fancies.
It is but an inspiration, inspired,
Taught him by one immense in power, daunting.
He took his stand, being on the upper horizon,

Then drew near and hung suspended,
And was two bows' length, or nearer.
And He revealed to His servant what He revealed.   53:10

The mind did not question what it saw.
Do you dispute with him what he saw?

And he saw him a second time,
By the lote-tree of the Extremity,
Near which is the Garden of Refuge,
When there covered the lote-tree that which covered it.   53:16

The eye neither veered nor overreached.
He saw some of his Lord's greatest wonders.

Have you considered al-Lat* and al-'Uzza?*
And Manat,* the third, the other?
To you belong males and to Him females?
What a crooked way of sharing!
They are but names that you and your forefathers coined:
Regarding them God sent down no authority.
They merely follow conjecture, and what their souls hanker
    for,
Even though Guidance has come to them from their Lord.   53:23

Or will man obtain what he longs for?
To God belong the Last and the First.

How many an angel there is in heaven whose intercession is of
    no avail,
Save when God permits it to whom He wills, and with whom
    He is well pleased.   53:26

Those who believe not in the hereafter give the angels female
    names,

But of this they have no knowledge,
And merely follow surmise,
53:28   Though surmise avails nothing when compared to truth.

Therefore, shun him who turns away from Our Remembrance,
And desires only the present world.
Such is the extent of their knowledge.
Your Lord knows best who has strayed from His path,
53:30   And knows best who has found guidance.

To God belongs whatever is in the heavens and the earth,
That He may requite the wicked for what they committed,
And reward the good with good.

And they who refrain from major sins and debaucheries, save
      minor misdemeanours –
Towards them your Lord is assuredly expansive in His
      forgiveness.
He knows you best, ever since He created you from the
      earth,
Ever since you were embryos in your mothers' wombs.
Therefore, do not acclaim your own virtue,
53:32   For He knows best who is truly pious.

Have you considered him who turned away?
Who gave a little and then withheld?
Does he possess knowledge of the Unseen, and hence can see
      far?
Or was he not apprised of what is in the scrolls of Moses and
      of Abraham, he who kept faith?
That no soul burdened shall bear the burden of another;
That man shall gain only what he endeavours;
That his endeavour shall be noted;
Then He shall reward him with the most ample reward,
53:42   And to your Lord is the final destination.

That it is He Who causes laughter and weeping;
Who brings about death and life;
Who created pairs, male and female,
From a sperm drop, when discharged;
That it is He Who shall undertake the Second Creation;
And He Who is richest and most bountiful;
That He is Lord of Sirius,
And He Who destroyed ancient 'Ad and Thamud, leaving no
 trace of them,
And before them the people of Noah – assuredly more wicked
 and transgressing.
And it was He Who toppled the towns, now in ruins,
When there enveloped them what enveloped.   53:54

So which of your Lord's bounties do you wish to question?
Here now is a warner, one among others before him.
The Imminent Event is at hand!
It shall have no revealer apart from God.   53:58

So is it this discourse that you find so strange?
And you laugh instead of weeping – lost in your frivolity?

Bow to God and worship!   53:62

The Moon

In the name of God,
Merciful to all,
Compassionate to each!

The Hour has drawn near, and the moon is split!
And if they witness a wonder, they turn aside and say: 'Potent
 sorcery!'

They lie, and follow their whims,

54:3 But every matter shall reach its proper end.

There came to them news in which was remonstrance,
And consummate Wisdom;
But how will warners avail them?
So leave them alone.
A Day shall come when the caller shall call to a thing they
   now deny,
And their eyes shall be downcast,
As they come out of their tombs, like spreading locusts,
And crane their necks in haste to the caller,
And the blasphemers shall say: 'This surely is a most arduous
54:8   Day!'

Before them the people of Noah had cried lies, and called Our
servant a liar, saying he was mad; and he was rebuked.
So he prayed to his Lord: 'I am overpowered, so come to my
   aid.'
And We opened the floodgates of heaven with pouring waters,
And caused earth to gush forth in springs,
And the waters joined together, to conform with a decree that
   was passed.
And We carried him aloft on a craft with planks and nails,
Running under Our eyes – a reward to one who had been
   repudiated.
And We left it behind as a wonder, but is there anyone to
   recall it to mind?
54:16 So how do you find My torment and My warnings?

And We made the Qur'an easy to remember,
But is there anyone to recall it to mind?

And 'Ad cried lies,
So how do you find My torment and My warnings?
We sent upon them a howling gale,

On a day of evil, unending,
Wrenching people away like stumps of palms, uprooted.
So how do you find My torment and My warnings?   54:21

And We made the Qur'an easy to remember,
But is there anyone to recall it to mind?

Thamud cried lies to My warnings, saying:
'Are we to follow a mere human, one of us?
We would surely be in error, or mad.
Was the Remembrance revealed to him – of all people here?
No indeed! He is a puffed-up liar.'
They will know soon enough who is the puffed-up liar!
We shall send them the she-camel, to test them,
So watch them and be patient.
Tell them that water is to be divided among them,
Taking turns to drink.
But they called upon their fellow tribesman
And he drew his sword and hamstrung the she-camel.
So how do you find My torment and My warnings?   54:30

And We let loose upon them a single Scream,
And they became like the straw of the sheep-fold maker.
And We made the Qur'an easy to remember,
But is there anyone to recall it to mind?   54:32

The people of Lot cried lies to My warnings,
And We sent them a hail-storm,
All except the family of Lot,
Whom We saved at dawn, as a favour from Us.
Thus do We reward the thankful.
We had warned them of Our wrath,
But they refused to believe Our warnings,
And tried to seduce his guest,
So We blotted out their eyes.
Taste, then, My torment and My warnings!

The morning that followed brought them a lasting torment.
Taste, then, My torment and My warnings!
And We made the Qur'an easy to remember,
54:40   But is there anyone to recall it to mind?

To the people of Pharaoh came warnings,
But they cried lies to all Our wonders,
So We seized them like the seizure of one Almighty,
54:42   All-Powerful.

Are the blasphemers among you better than all these?
Or do you possess some safe-conduct in ancient Scriptures?
Or do they claim that victory lies in their number?
Their number shall be defeated and turn tail.
Indeed the Hour is their appointed time,
54:46   And the Hour shall be still more calamitous and bitter!

The wicked are sunk in error and madness.
A Day will come when they shall be dragged into the Fire, on
       their faces:
54:48   'Taste the touch of the gate of hell!'

We have created all things in due measure,
And Our command is but a single word,
Like the twinkling of an eye.
We have destroyed your like,
But is there anyone to recall it to mind?

All they have done is in ancient Scriptures,
And all of it, small or great, is recorded.

The pious are amidst Gardens and rivers,
54:55   In an assembly of virtue, and with a mighty King.

The All-Merciful

In the name of God,
Merciful to all,
Compassionate to each!

The All-Merciful!
He taught the Qur'an,
He created man,
He taught him eloquence.   55:4

Sun and moon move in measured order;
Shrubs and trees bow down;
The sky He raised, and established the balance,
So that you do not infringe the balance,
But measure in fairness, and not shortchange the balance.   55:9

The earth He laid out for the living,
Wherein are fruits and palms in clusters,
Grains on stalks, and sweet-scented flowers.   55:12

So which of your Lord's blessings will the two of you deny?

He created man from thin clay, like earthenware,
And created the *Jinn* from shimmering flame.
So which of your Lord's blessings will the two of you deny?

Lord of the two Easts and the two Wests!
So which of your Lord's blessings will the two of you deny?   55:18

He brought the two seas together, but as they meet,
Between them is a barrier they do not overrun.
So which of your Lord's blessings will the two of you deny?

From both come forth pearl and coral.

55:23   So which of your Lord's blessings will the two of you deny?

To Him belong running ships, galleons, ploughing the sea like
    mountain-tops.
So which of your Lord's blessings will the two of you deny?

All who are upon it shall perish,
And there remains the face of your Lord, Majestic and Noble.

55:28   So which of your Lord's blessings will the two of you deny?

All in the heavens and earth beseech Him;
He is ever engaged upon some matter.

55:30   So which of your Lord's blessings will the two of you deny?

We shall apply Ourselves to you, you two great masses of
    creation!
So which of your Lord's blessings will the two of you deny?

Species of *Jinn* and humans, if you can make your escape
From the regions of the heavens and earth, escape!
You shall not escape except by divine authority.

55:34   So which of your Lord's blessings will the two of you deny?

Hurled upon the two of you shall be flames of fire and brass,
And none shall come to your aid.
So which of your Lord's blessings will the two of you deny?

When the sky is split,
Turning rose-coloured like leather;

55:38   So which of your Lord's blessings will the two of you deny?

That Day none shall be questioned regarding their guilt,
Neither human nor *Jinn*.
So which of your Lord's blessings will the two of you deny?

Sinners shall be known by their outward visage,
And they shall be seized by forelocks and feet.
So which of your Lord's blessings will the two of you deny?   55:41

Here is the hell that sinners deny!
They shall wander between it and water, fiercely boiling.
So which of your Lord's blessings will the two of you deny?

But to him who fears the encounter of his Lord are two
        Gardens.
So which of your Lord's blessings will the two of you deny?
Both covered with foliage.
So which of your Lord's blessings will the two of you deny?
In it are two running springs.
So which of your Lord's blessings will the two of you deny?
In it are, of every fruit, two kinds.
So which of your Lord's blessings will the two of you deny?
They recline on couches, their mattresses of brocade,
With the fruit of the two Gardens close to hand.
So which of your Lord's blessings will the two of you deny?
Therein are maidens, chaste of glance,
Undefiled before them by humans or *Jinn*.
So which of your Lord's blessings will the two of you deny?
As if they were rubies or coral.
So which of your Lord's blessings will the two of you deny?
Can the reward of goodness be other than good?
So which of your Lord's blessings will the two of you deny?   55:61

Below these two are two other Gardens.
So which of your Lord's blessings will the two of you deny?
Over-shadowing.
So which of your Lord's blessings will the two of you deny?
In them are two fountains, ever gushing.
So which of your Lord's blessings will the two of you deny?
In these two are fruits, palms and pomegranates.
So which of your Lord's blessings will the two of you deny?

In them are maidens, virtuous and beautiful.
So which of your Lord's blessings will the two of you deny?
Dark-eyed, confined to pavilions.
So which of your Lord's blessings will the two of you deny?
Undefiled before them by humans or *Jinn*.
So which of your Lord's blessings will the two of you deny?
They recline on green cushions, and sumptuous rugs.
So which of your Lord's blessings will the two of you deny?

55:78   Blessed be the name of your Lord, Majestic and Noble!

The Calamity

In the name of God,
Merciful to all,
Compassionate to each!

When the Calamity shall fall,
And there is no denying its fall,
Abasing and exalting;
When the earth is made to tremble and totter,
And the mountains are pulverized,
Turning into scattered dust,
You shall be of three kinds:
The companions of the Right – wondrous are the companions
    of the Right!
The companions of the Left – wondrous are the companions
    of the Left!
And the surpassing, the truly surpassing.
These shall be the nearest,
In the Gardens of Bliss:
A crowd of ancient communities,
56:14   And a few from latter times.

Upon couches studded with jewels
They shall recline, face to face.
Passing among them are youths, ever young,
With chalices and pitchers, and cups of a pure draught,
Causing them neither ache nor intoxication.
And fruits they shall have, whatever they choose,
And flesh of fowl, whatever they desire,
And maidens, eyes large and dark,
Like pearls in their shells,
As a reward for past deeds.
Therein they hear neither chatter nor malediction,
But solely the phrase: 'Peace! Peace!'   56:26

The companions of the Right – wondrous are the companions
    of the Right!
They are among lote-trees without thorns, and acacia in clusters,
And shade outspreading, and waters overflowing,
And fruits in profusion,
Neither ceasing nor forbidden;
And marriage-beds raised high,
For We have created them in perfection,
Making them intact virgins,
Loving spouses, similar of age,
To the companions of the Right.
A crowd of ancient communities,
And a crowd from latter times.   56:40

The companions of the Left – wondrous are the companions
    of the Left!
They are amidst scorching wind and boiling water,
And a shade of black smoke,
Neither cold nor kindly.
Once they had lived in luxury,
Persevering in great sin.
For they would say: 'Once dead and turned into dust and
    bones, are we to be resurrected?

And, too, our ancient forefathers?'
Say: 'First and last shall all be gathered at an appointed time,
56:50   on a familiar Day.'

As for you who have gone astray and cry lies,
You shall assuredly eat from the Zaqqum-tree,
And shall fill your bellies from it,
And shall drink, to boot, boiling water,
And lap it up, like sick camels.
Such shall be the abodes that welcome them on the Day of
56:56   Judgement!

We it was Who created you – will you not believe?
Think of the sperm you discharge – did you create it, or are
        We its creators?
We have apportioned death among you,
And We shall not be forestalled if We substitute your like in
        your place,
56:61 And recreate you in a form you do not recognize.

You know all about the first creation – will you not remember
        and reflect?
And have you given thought to what you plough?
Is it you who sow it, or are We its sowers?
Had We wished We could turn it into stubble, and you would
        then be aghast:
56:67 'We are loaded with debt! Indeed, we are impoverished!'

Have you given thought to the water you drink?
Was it you who poured it down from the rain-clouds, or was
        it Us Who poured it?
If We wish We could turn it into salt water – will you not offer
56:70   thanks?

Have you given thought to the fire you kindle?
Did you create its fire-wood, or are We its creators?

We have made it to be a reminder – and, too, a comfort to
   hungry travellers.
Therefore, glorify the name of your Lord, All-Supreme.   56:74

Yes, indeed!
I swear by the motions of the stars –
And a mighty oath it is, if only you knew!
This is a Glorious Qur'an,
In a Book well-sheltered
That only the pure can touch;
A Revelation from the Lord of the Worlds.   56:80

Is it this Discourse that you take so lightly,
And give thanks for your livelihood by lying?
Wait till your soul reaches your throat – as you yourselves
   look on!
At that moment, We shall be closer to it than you, but you
   will not see this.
And if you are not held to account,
Then bring it back, if you are telling the truth!   56:87

But if it be one who is close to God,
Then ease and fragrance and Gardens of Bliss.
And if it be one who is a Companion of the Right,
Then peace upon you from the Companions of the Right!   56:91

But if it be one who lies and strays in error,
Then welcoming abodes – of boiling water and the roasting of
   hell!   56:94

This is the truth, certain beyond all doubt.
So glorify the name of your Lord, All-Supreme.   56:96

Iron

In the name of God,
Merciful to all,
Compassionate to each!

Glorifying God is all that exists in the heavens and earth –
Almighty, All-Wise!
To Him belongs sovereignty of the heavens and earth.
He grants life and He deals death, and He has power over all
things.
He is the First and the Last, the Apparent and the Hidden,
57:3   And has knowledge of all things.

He it is Who created the heavens and earth in six days, then
sat firmly on the throne.
He knows whatever passes into the earth and whatever comes
out thereof,
What comes down from heaven, and what ascends thereto;
He is with you wherever you may be; He knows full well what
you do.
To Him belongs sovereignty of the heavens and earth, and to
God all matters shall revert.
He it is Who entwines night with day, and day with night, and
57:6   knows full well what lies within breasts.

Believe in God and His Messenger,
And expend of what He caused you to inherit.
Those among you who believe and expend their wealth shall
receive an ample wage.
    Why do you not believe in God when the Messenger calls you
to believe in your Lord, and obtained your solemn word, if you
are true believers?
    It is He Who sends down on His servant revelations plain and

distinct, to lead you out of the darkness and into the light.
Towards you God is All-Kind, Compassionate to each.   57:9

Why do you not expend in the cause of God, when to God
belongs the inheritance of the heavens and earth?
   Unequal are those among you who expended before the Conquest, and took part in the fighting. They are higher in station
than those who expended after, and took part in the fighting.
But God promises both a goodly reward. And God is All-
Experienced with what you do. Whoso loans God a goodly
loan, He shall multiply it for him, and shall receive a noble
wage.   57:11

A Day shall come when you shall observe believing men and
believing women, with their light shimmering before them and
upon their right hands: 'The good news to you today is Gardens
beneath which rivers flow, abiding therein for ever. And this is
the greatest of triumphs.'
   That Day, the Hypocrites, men and women, shall say to those
who believed: 'Please allow us to obtain a ray from your light,'
and it shall be said to them: 'Turn back, and search for a light!'
   A wall shall be erected between them in which there is a gate,
with mercy on its outer and torment on its inner side.
   They shall call out to them: 'Were we not with you?' and the
others shall answer: 'Yes indeed, but you led yourselves into
sin, you plotted, you doubted, and false hopes seduced you,
until the command of God arrived and the Tempter tempted
you away from God. Today no ransom shall be accepted from
you, nor from those who disbelieved. Your refuge is the Fire –
and what a wretched destination!'   57:15

Is it not time for those who believe that their hearts should grow
humble at the mention of God and the Truth that has been
revealed? That they should not act like those to whom the Book
was previously sent? Time itself has grown long upon them, and
their hearts have hardened. Many of them are dissolute.

Know that God revives the earth after its death. We have made
57:17 the revelations plain in order that you may come to reason.

Alms-givers, men and women, who loan God a goodly loan – it
shall be multiplied to them, and they shall receive a noble wage.
    And they who believe in God and His messengers – these are
the sincere in faith. And the martyrs are with their Lord; they
shall have their wage and their light.
    But those who disbelieve and blaspheme Our revelations –
57:19 these are the denizens of hell.

Know that the present life is but amusement, frivolity and
    finery,
And mutual boasting among you and accumulation of wealth
    and progeny.
It is like a rainfall whose vegetation pleases the sowers,
But then goes dry, and you see it yellowed till it becomes
    chaff.
In the hereafter there is grievous torment, but also forgiveness
    from your Lord and His good pleasure.
And this present life is but the rapture of delusion.

Vie with each other to obtain forgiveness from your Lord, and
a Garden as wide as the heavens and the earth, made ready for
those who believe in God and His messengers.
Such is God's favour dispensed to whomsoever He wishes.
57:21 And God's favour is All-Surpassing.

No calamity strikes on earth, or in yourselves, but was recorded
in a Book, before We brought it to pass. Such a matter is easy
for God, in order that you do not regret what eluded you nor
be overjoyed by what came your way. God loves not every
57:23 swaggering snob.

As for those who are stingy, and enjoin others to be stingy, or
those who turn away – God is All-Sufficient, All-Praiseworthy.

We sent Our messengers with evident wonders, and sent down with them the Book and the Balance that mankind may act with fairness. And We sent down iron in which there is great strength and benefits to mankind, that God may know who will come forward to support Him and His messengers, in the Unseen. God is All-Powerful, Almighty.   57:25

We had sent Noah and Abraham and assigned prophecy and the Book to their progeny. Some are guided aright, but many of them are dissolute. Then, following them, We sent Our messengers, and followed them up with Jesus son of Mary, and granted him the Evangel. In the hearts of those who followed him We planted kindness and compassion; and also a monasticism that they invented but which We did not ordain for them except to seek the good pleasure of God. But they did not do it justice. Hence, We granted those among them who believed their reward, but many of them are dissolute.   57:27

O believers, fear God and believe in His Messenger and He will double your share of His compassion, and shine His light upon the path you tread, and forgive you. God is All-Forgiving, Compassionate to each.

Let the People of the Book know that they are not entitled to any bounty from God, and that bounty rests in the hands of God, Who dispenses it to whomsoever He wills. God is surpassing in bounty.   57:29

The Dispute

In the name of God,
Merciful to all,
Compassionate to each!

God has heard the speech of the woman who disputed with you regarding her husband, as she complained to God, while God heard your conversation. God is All-Hearing, All-Seeing.

They who say to their wives: 'You are to me like my mother's back' – even so, they are not their mothers. Their true mothers are those who gave them birth. Their words are reprehensible and specious. God is All-Pardoning, All-Forgiving.

58:2

They who pronounce this formula to their wives and then retract what they said – from them is due the manumission of a slave, before the two of them can touch each other. And this, in order that you may be taught a lesson. God is All-Expert as to what you do.

If he has no slave, then a fast of two consecutive months is due before the two of them can touch each other. If he cannot, then the feeding of sixty poor. And this, in order that you believe in God and His Messenger.

These are the bounds of God, and a painful torment awaits the unbelievers.

58:4

They who contradict God and His Messenger shall be thwarted, as were those who came before them. The revelations We have sent down are plain and distinct, and the unbelievers can expect a humiliating torment.

A Day shall come when God shall resurrect them all and inform them of their deeds, which God has placed on record and they have forgotten. And God is witness to all things.

58:6

Have you not observed that God knows whatsoever is in the heavens and earth? No three people converse in intimacy but God is their fourth, nor five but He is their sixth, nor less than this number, nor more, but He is with them wherever they may be. He shall then inform them of their deeds on the Day of Resurrection. God is Omniscient.

Have you observed those who were forbidden to hold furtive conversations, yet revert to what they have been forbidden? They whisper to each other of sin and crime and defiance of the Messenger, but when they come to you, they greet you in a manner that God did not greet you with. Within themselves they say: 'Why does God not punish us for what we say?' Let hell suffice them for their scorching – and what a wretched destiny!   58:8

O believers, if you converse in secret, do not converse about sin and crime and defiance of the Messenger, but about virtue and piety; and fear God, to Whom you shall be mustered. Such secret conversation comes from Satan, in order to cause sorrow to the believers, but he cannot harm them in any wise save by God's leave. It is in God that the believers should place their trust.   58:10

O believers, if you are told to make room for each other in the assemblies, make room and God shall make room for you. And if you are told to disperse, then disperse. And those among you who believe, and who are granted knowledge, God elevates by several degrees. God is All-Experienced as to what you do.

O believers, if you wish to converse in privacy with the Messenger, offer a gift in charity before your intimate conversation, for this would be better for you and more pure. If unable to do so, God is All-Forgiving, Compassionate to each. Are you reluctant to offer gifts in charity before your private conversation? If you do not do so, and God grants you pardon, then attend to your

prayers, and offer alms, and obey God and His Messenger, for
58:13 God is All-Experienced as to what you do.

Have you observed those who took under their protection a
group with whom God was angry? They are not part of you, nor
of those. They swear false oaths, knowingly. God has readied for
them a most painful torment – wretched is their deed! They
have treated their oath as a cover, and barred the path to God.
58:16 A humiliating punishment awaits them.

Neither their wealth nor their progeny shall avail them one jot
against God. They are the denizens of the Fire, in which they
shall abide eternally. A Day shall come when God shall resurrect
them all, and they shall swear to Him as they swear to you,
imagining that they have gained something. No indeed! They
are themselves the real liars! Satan has gained power over them
and caused them to forget God. They are the party of Satan,
58:19 and the party of Satan are assuredly the losers.

Those who contradict God and His Messenger shall be among
the very lowest, for God has ordained: 'I and My messengers
58:21 shall prevail.' God is All-Powerful, Almighty.

You shall not find any group who believe in God and the Last
Day to be friendly towards those who contradict God and His
Messenger, even if they were their own fathers, sons, brothers
or fellow clansmen. These – He has inscribed faith in their hearts
and aided them with a spirit from Him. He shall admit them
into Gardens beneath which rivers flow, abiding therein for
ever. God shall be well pleased with them, and they with Him.
They are the party of God, and the party of God shall surely
58:22 win through.

The Mustering

In the name of God,
Merciful to all,
Compassionate to each!

Glorifying God is all that exists in the heavens and earth –
Almighty, All-Wise!

He it is Who expelled the unbelievers among the People of
the Book from their homes, to be mustered on the first summons.

You did not think they would depart, while they imagined
that their forts rendered them secure from God. But God came
upon them from where they did not reckon, and threw terror
into their hearts, so they demolished their homes with their own
hands and the hands of the believers – a lesson to ponder, O
people of insight! Had God not ordained expulsion upon them,
He would have tormented them in this life, and in the hereafter
they shall face the torment of the Fire. That is because they
rebelled against God and His Messenger, and whoso rebels
against God, God is grievous in punishment.   59:4

No palm-tree did you cut down, or leave standing on its trunk,
except by God's consent, and that He may shame the insincere.
Whatever booty God has granted His Messenger from their
possessions was not such for the sake of which you rode to war,
on horse or camel. Rather, it is God Who gives mastery to His
messengers over whomsoever He wills, and God has power over
all things.   59:6

Whatever God grants His Messenger in booty from the people
of the towns belongs to God and His Messenger, as also to
kinsmen, the orphans, the poor and the needy wayfarer, in order
that wealth does not circulate solely among those of you who
are rich. Whatever the Messenger bestows upon you, accept it;

whatever he disallows, desist. And fear God, for God is grievous in punishment.

It belongs also to the poor Emigrants, who were driven out of homes and property, as they sought the favour of God and His good pleasure, and came to the aid of God and His Messenger. These are truly sincere.

And those who, before them, had made their home in this city, with faith in their hearts – they love those who emigrated to them, and in their hearts nurse no envy for what others have been granted; who, even when needy, prefer them to themselves. Whoso is guarded against his own soul's avarice – these shall win through.

And those who came afterwards say: 'Our Lord, forgive us and our brothers who preceded us in faith. Do not plant malice in our hearts towards those who believed. Our Lord, you are 59:10 All-Tender, Compassionate to each.'

Have you observed the Hypocrites saying to their comrades, the unbelievers among the People of the Book: 'If you are expelled, we shall leave with you, and shall never obey anyone where you are concerned. If you are attacked, we shall come to your aid,' while God witnesses that they are lying?

If they are expelled, they will not leave with them. If attacked, they will not go to their aid. And if they do go to their aid, they will turn tail and flee, and they shall not be aided. Indeed, you inspire greater terror in their hearts than God, for they are a 59:13 group with no understanding.

They do not fight you when massed together except from fortified towns or from behind walls. Their enmity towards each other is relentless. You imagine them to be united, but their hearts are diverse, for they are a people who do not reason. They are like those who came before them, a little while ago. They tasted the evil consequences of their deeds, and painful torment awaits them. Or they are like Satan when he said to man: 'Blaspheme!' When he blasphemed, he said: 'I have nothing to do with you, for I fear God, Lord of the Worlds.' Both ended up in the Fire, abiding therein for ever. Such is the reward of the wicked.   59:17

O believers, fear God, and let each soul consider what it has laid in stock for the morrow, and be pious before God – God is All-Experienced as to what you do. Be not like those who forgot God, and God made them forget themselves – these are the dissolute. Unequal are the denizens of the Fire and the denizens of the Garden. The denizens of the Garden are the victors.   59:20

Had We sent down this Qur'an upon a mountain,
You would have seen it humbled,
Shattered from the fear of God.
These parables We strike for mankind,
That they may come to reflect.

He is God,
There is no god but He,
Knower of the Unseen and the Seen,
All-Merciful, Compassionate to each.   59:22

He is God,
There is no god but He,
Sovereign, All-Holy, the Bringer of Peace,
The All-Faithful, the All-Preserver,
The Almighty, the All-Compelling,
The All-Sublime!
Glory to Him far above what they associate with Him!

He is God,
The Creator, Originator, Giver of Forms,
To Him belong the Names most beautiful;
All on earth and in heaven magnify Him;
He is the Almighty, the All-Wise!   59:24

The Woman Tested

In the name of God,
Merciful to all,
Compassionate to each!

O believers, do not adopt My enemy and yours as comrades!
You greet them in amity though they have blasphemed against
what came to them of the Truth and drove out the Messenger,
as well as you, because you believed in God, your Lord – provided, that is, you really came forth to exert yourselves on My
behalf and to seek My good pleasure.

And yet, you show them amity in secret, and I know best what
you conceal and what you proclaim. Whoso among you does
this has strayed from the straight path. If they happen to meet
you in battle, they become your enemies, and stretch out their
hands and tongues to harm you, hoping you would blaspheme.
But neither kinships nor progeny shall avail you when He distinguishes between you on the Day of Resurrection, and God sees
60:3 full well what you do.

A good example for you was Abraham and those who were
with him, when they said to their people: 'We abjure you and
what you worship instead of God. We disown you, and the
enmity and hatred between us shall always be manifest, until
you come to believe in the One God' – barring the occasion
when Abraham said to his father:
    'I shall ask forgiveness for you though I cannot be of any help
to you against God.
    'Our Lord, we put our trust in You, and turn in repentance
towards You, and with You is our final destiny.
    'Our Lord, put us not to the test with those who disbelieve,

and pardon us, O Lord, for it is You Who are Almighty, All-Wise.' 60:5

In them you have a good example for him who seeks God and the Last Day. Whoso turns away, God is All-Sufficient, All-Praiseworthy.

Perhaps God will create affection between you and those among them with whom you were at enmity, for God is Omnipotent, and He is All-Forgiving, Compassionate to each.

As for those who have not fought against you over religion, nor expelled you from your homes, God does not forbid you to treat them honourably and act with fairness towards them, for God loves those who act with fairness. God, however, forbids you to ally yourselves with those who fought against you over religion, expelled you from your homes or contributed to your expulsion. Whoso allies himself with them – these are the unjust. 60:9

O believers, if believing women come to you as emigrants, test them. God knows best as to their faith. If you know them to be faithful, do not send them back to the unbelievers: they are not licit to the unbelievers, nor the unbelievers to them. Give their husbands what they paid, and no blame shall attach to you if you marry them, provided you pay them their bridal money. Do not cling to your bonds with unbelieving women; but demand what you spent, and let them demand what they spent. Such is the judgement of God, Who judges among you. God is All-Knowing, All-Wise.

If any of your wives flee to the unbelievers, and you afterwards fall on some booty, pay those whose wives have fled the equal of what they had expended, and fear God in Whom you believe. 60:11

O Prophet, if believing women come to offer you homage on condition that they shall associate nothing with God, shall not steal or commit adultery, kill their infant children or commit perjury as to parenthood, or disobey you in any virtuous deed, accept their homage and ask God's forgiveness for them – God is All-Forgiving, Compassionate to each.

O believers, do not ally yourselves with people on whom God's wrath has fallen. They have abandoned all hope of the hereafter, just as the unbelievers have abandoned all hope of resurrection 60:13 for those who dwell in graves.

The Battle-Line

In the name of God,
Merciful to all,
Compassionate to each!

Glorifying God is all that exists in the heavens and earth – Almighty, All-Wise!

O believers, why do you say what you do not do? It is greatly abhorrent to God that you say what you do not do! God loves those who fight in His cause in a battle-line, like an edifice, 61:4 impenetrable.

Remember when Moses said to his people: 'My people, why are you doing me harm when you know that I am God's messenger to you?' But when they veered into error, it was God Who caused their hearts to veer, and God guides not a people depraved.

Remember when Jesus son of Mary said: 'Children of Israel, I am the messenger of God to you, confirming what preceded me of the Torah, and I bring you glad tidings of a messenger to come after me called Ahmad.'* When he brought them wonders 61:6 they said: 'This is sorcery manifest.'

Who is more wicked than one who fabricates lies from God while being called to Islam? God guides not a people who are wicked.

They mean to put out the light of God with their mouths, but God shall perfect His light, even though the unbelievers detest it. It is He Who sent His Messenger with Guidance and the religion of truth, to send it victorious over all other religions, even if the polytheists detest it.   61:9

O believers, shall I point you to a commerce that will save you from a painful torment? That you believe in God and His Messenger; that you exert yourselves with your wealth and persons. This would be best for you, if only you knew.   61:11

He shall forgive you your sins and admit you into Gardens beneath which rivers flow, and pure habitations in the Gardens of Eternal Abode – and that is the greatest of triumphs! And yet another bounty, beloved by you, will He grant you: victory from God and an imminent conquest. Give these glad tidings to the believers!   61:13

O believers, be the champions of God, as when Jesus son of Mary said to his Apostles: 'Who shall be my champions before God?' and the Apostles replied: 'We are the champions of God.' So a party of the Children of Israel believed while another party disbelieved.

And We aided those who believed against their enemies, and they ended up victorious.   61:14

Congregational Prayer

In the name of God,
Merciful to all,
Compassionate to each!

Glorifying God is all that exists in the heavens and earth –
Sovereign, All-Holy, Almighty, All-Wise!

He it was Who raised up a messenger from among an unlettered
people, to recite His verses to them, to purify them and to teach
them the Book and the Wisdom, though before they had been
in manifest error – them and others yet to follow them. He is
62:3 Almighty, All-Wise.

This is a favour from God which He bestows on whomsoever
He pleases. God is of favour abounding.

The likeness of those who carry the Torah but do not really
carry it is like a donkey carrying heavy tomes – wretched is the
example of a people who cried lies to God's revelations! God
62:5 guides not a people who are wicked.

Say: 'O you who are Jews, if you claim to be the friends of God,
to the exclusion of the rest of mankind, then pray for death if
you are sincere.' But they will never pray for death because of
what their hands have committed – and God knows best who
the wicked are.
     Say: 'The death you are trying to escape shall come upon you.
Then you shall be returned to the realm of the Invisible and the
62:8 Visible, and He shall inform you of what you used to do.'

O believers, when the call is made for prayer on Congregation
Day, hasten to the remembrance of God, and leave your

commerce aside: this is best for you, if only you knew. When prayer is ended, disperse in the land and seek the bounty of God, and mention God often – perhaps you will prosper. When they spot some commerce or frivolity, they rush towards it and leave you standing.

Say: 'What is with God is better than frivolity or commerce, and God is the best of providers.' 62:11

The Hypocrites

In the name of God,
Merciful to all,
Compassionate to each!

When the Hypocrites come to you, they say: 'We bear witness that you are in truth God's Messenger, and God knows that you are His Messenger.' But God bears witness that the Hypocrites are liars!

They treat their oath as a cover, and thus have barred the path to God – wretched is what they do! That is because they believed, then disbelieved, and so their hearts are sealed and they cannot understand. When you see them, you are impressed by their outward appearance, and when they speak, you listen to their words. But they are like wooden stilts: every shout they hear they imagine to be the enemy. So be on your guard against them. May God strike them down! How they pervert the truth! 63:4

And if told to come so that the Messenger of God might ask forgiveness for you, they twist their heads, and you see them saunter off in arrogance. It is all the same if you seek or do not seek forgiveness for them, for God shall not forgive them. God guides not a people who are depraved. 63:6

It is they who say: 'Do not spend any money on those who are in the company of the Messenger of God unless they leave him.' To God belong the treasures of the heavens and earth, but the Hypocrites have no understanding.

They say: 'When we return to Medinah, the more powerful will expel the weaker.' But power belongs to God, His Messenger and the believers, though the Hypocrites know 63:8   it not.

O believers, let not your wealth or your children divert you from the remembrance of God. Whoso does this – they shall be the losers.

Expend from what We provided you before death befalls any of you and then he says: 'My Lord, if only You held me back a little while, I would have given in charity and been among the virtuous.'

But God holds back no soul once its term has come; and God 63:11   is All-Experienced as to what you do.

Mutual Recrimination

In the name of God,
Merciful to all,
Compassionate to each!

Glorifying God is all that exists in the heavens and earth. To Him belongs sovereignty, to Him be praise! He holds power over all things.

It is He Who created you: one of you an unbeliever, another a believer; and God sees full well what you do.

He created the heavens and earth in truth, and gave you form, and shaped your forms well. To Him is the final return.

He knows whatever is in the heavens and earth.
He knows what you keep secret and what you proclaim.
God knows full well what lies within breasts.   64:4

Have you not heard the stories of those who disbelieved in the
   past?
How they tasted the evil consequence of their acts?
A painful punishment awaits them.

That is because their messengers would come to them with
evident signs, but they would say: 'Are mere humans to guide
us?'
They blasphemed and turned away.
And God had no need of them,
And God is All-Sufficient, All-Praiseworthy!   64:6

Those who disbelieve claim they shall not be resurrected.
   Say: 'Yes indeed! By my Lord! You shall surely be resurrected
and then you shall surely be informed of what you used to do –
a matter easy for God.'

Therefore, believe in God, His Messenger and in the Light We
sent down; and God is All-Experienced as to what you do.
   A Day shall come when He gathers you together for the Day
of Gathering: that shall be the Day of Mutual Recrimination.
Whoso believes in God and does righteous deeds, He shall remit
his sins and admit him into Gardens beneath which rivers flow,
abiding therein for ever. This is the greatest of triumphs.   64:9

But as for those who blasphemed and cried lies to Our revelations, they are the denizens of the Fire, abiding therein for ever
– and what a wretched destiny!

No calamity strikes but by God's leave.
Whoso believes in God, God shall guide his heart.
God is Omniscient.

Obey God and obey the Messenger, but if you turn away, Our Messenger is enjoined only to convey a manifest message.

God! There is no god but He! In God let the believers place
64:13 their trust.

O believers, among your spouses and your children are some who are enemies to you, so be on your guard against them. But if you pardon, disregard and forgive, God is All-Forgiving, Compassionate to each. Your wealth and your children are but a temptation, but with God is a splendid reward.

So be pious before God as best you can, and listen and obey, and expend in charity for your own sake. Whoso is spared his own soul's avarice – these shall win through.

If you loan God a goodly loan He shall multiply it for you and forgive you. God is All-Thankful, All-Forbearing.
64:18 Knower of the Invisible and the Visible, Almighty, All-Wise!

Divorce

In the name of God,
Merciful to all,
Compassionate to each!

O Prophet, if you divorce women, divorce them in accordance with their periods of waiting, and compute that period. And be pious before God your Lord.

Do not expel them from their homes, nor should they leave their homes, unless they commit a flagrant indecency. These are the bounds of God, and whoso violates God's bounds does himself an injustice.

You never know; God may afterwards bring about a change
65:1 of circumstance.

Once they reach their appointed term, hold them back in amity or let them go in amity. And call as witnesses two people of just character among you, and make formal the act of witness before God. This is what is being admonished to whoever believes in God and the Last Day. And to him who fears God, God shall find a suitable outcome, and shall provide for him from where he never imagined. Whoso places his trust in God, God shall suffice him. God enforces what He commands. For all things God has set a measure.   65:3

As for those among your women who have abandoned hope of menstruation, and if you are in doubt, their waiting period shall be three months – so too for women who have not yet menstruated. For pregnant women, their appointed term is their date of delivery. Whoso fears God, God shall grant him ease of circumstance. This is the command of God which He sends down to you. Whoso is pious before God, God shall remit his sins, and greatly enhance his reward.   65:5

Allow them to reside where you reside, according to your means, and do not pester them in order to constrict their lives. If pregnant, you are to pay their expenses until they deliver. If they nurse your infants, you must pay them their wages, and conduct your relations in amity. But if you make life difficult for each other, another woman may act as nurse.

Let every man of means expend from his means, and he whose livelihood is straitened is to expend from whatever God has provided him. God charges no soul except with what He has endowed it. To follow hardship, God shall bring about ease.   65:7

How many a town defied the command of its Lord and His
    messengers!
In consequence, We brought it to a reckoning most grievous,
    and punished it abominably.
And so it tasted the evil result of its conduct,

And it ended in perdition.
To them God has readied a grievous torment.

So fear God, you who are possessed of minds among the believers, for God has sent down to you a Remembrance – a Messenger who recites to you the revelations of God, plain and distinct, to lead the faithful and righteous from the darkness and into the light. Whoso believes and does righteous deeds He shall admit into Gardens beneath which rivers flow, abiding 65:11 therein for ever. God has granted him a goodly provision indeed!

God it is Who created seven heavens, and their like on earth:
Between them the Command descends,
That you may know that God holds power over all things,
65:12 That God encompasses all things in His knowledge.

Making Illicit

In the name of God,
Merciful to all,
Compassionate to each!

O Prophet, why do you make illicit what God has made licit to you, intending to appease your wives? But God is All-Forgiving, Compassionate to each.

God has ordained for you the means to be released from your 66:2 oaths, and God is your Patron, All-Knowing, All-Wise.

Remember when the Prophet let one of his wives into a secret, but when she revealed it, and God acquainted him with the matter, he communicated a part of it and set aside another part. When he informed her of it, she asked: 'Who informed you of this?' He answered: 'The All-Knowing and All-Experienced informed me.'

Should you two seek God's pardon, this is because your hearts have indeed swerved from the truth. But if you two were to come together against him, remember that God is his Patron, as is Gabriel and the righteous believers – with the angels, in addition, acting as reinforcements. 66:4

It may be that, if he divorces you, his Lord may give him in exchange wives better than you: true Muslims, faithful, obedient, repentant, devout, and dedicated to fasting – whether married before or virgins.

O believers, guard yourselves and your families against a Fire whose fuel is humans and stones. Upon it are angels harsh and invincible, who do not disobey God in what He orders them, and carry out what they are commanded. 66:6

O unbelievers, do not plead for forgiveness Today. You shall merely be recompensed for what you did.

O believers, turn in repentance, in sincere repentance, to God. Perhaps your Lord will remit your sins and admit you into Gardens beneath which rivers flow, upon a Day when God shall not discredit the Prophet and those who are with him. Their light shall radiate before them and on their right hands, and they shall say: 'Our Lord, make our light resplendent and forgive us, for You hold power over all things.' 66:8

O Prophet, exert yourself against the unbelievers and Hypocrites, and be harsh with them, for hell is to be their refuge – and what a wretched destiny!

God strikes a parable for unbelievers: the wife of Noah and the wife of Lot. They were both tied in marriage to two of Our righteous servants, and they both betrayed them, but this availed them nothing against God. It was said to them: 'Enter, both of you, into the Fire among those who enter it.' 66:10

God strikes a parable for believers – the wife of Pharaoh, when she said: 'My Lord, build me a house by Your side in the Garden, and deliver me from Pharaoh and his works, and deliver me from a wicked people.'

Then, too, there is Mary, daughter of 'Imran, she who guarded her chastity; and We breathed into her of Our spirit, and she reposed her trust in the words of her Lord and in His 66:12   Books, and was devout in worship.

Sovereignty

In the name of God,
Merciful to all,
Compassionate to each!

Blessed is He in Whose hand is sovereignty, Who holds power
    over all things!
He Who created death and life to test you as to which of you
    is most righteous in deed;
67:2   He is Almighty, All-Forgiving.

He created seven heavens, piled one upon another.
In the creation of the All-Merciful you cannot detect any
    disparity.
Turn your gaze back: do you see any rift?
Then turn your gaze back twice more, and your sight will
67:4   return to you, humbled and flagging.

We adorned the lower sky with lanterns, and made them to be volleys against the demons, for whom We have readied the torment of the Blaze.

And to those who blasphemed their Lord there awaits the torment of hell – and a wretched destiny it is!

When hurled therein, they hear it sighing as it boils over. It almost seethes with rage whenever a batch is thrown in. Its watchmen will ask them: 'Did no warner come to you?' And they shall answer: 'Yes, a warner did come, but we cried lies and said that God had sent down nothing.'

You are assuredly plunged deep in error!

And they shall say: 'Could we but hear or understand, we would not be among the dwellers of the Blaze.'

There! They have confessed their sin! Away with the dwellers of the Blaze!

67:11

But they who fear their Lord in the Unseen shall obtain forgiveness and a great reward.

Whisper what you say or proclaim it aloud:
He knows full well what lies within breasts.
How can He not know, He Who created?
All-Refined, All-Experienced is He.

67:14

He it was Who made the earth subservient to you,
So roam its byways and eat of His provisions; to Him is the
Resurgence.

Or are you confident that He Who is in heaven would not cause the earth to collapse beneath you, as it heaves in turmoil?

Or are you confident that He Who is in heaven would not send you a fire storm? You will surely know what My warning is like!

Those who came before them also cried lies – behold how I reversed their fortune!

67:18

Have they not observed the birds above them, with wings outstretched or clasped? None can restrain them but the All-Merciful. He sees full well all that exists.

Who is it who can act as your troops, to bring you aid, apart from the All-Merciful?

The unbelievers are merely living in illusion.

Or who is it who can provide for you if He withholds His
provision?

They have assuredly sunk deep in obstinacy and aversion from

67:21   truth.

Is he who walks grovelling on his face better guided than one
who walks upright, upon a path that is straight?

Say: 'It is He Who brought you into being, Who provided you
with hearing, sight and hearts, but little thanks do you give.'

Say: 'It is He Who bred you on earth, and to Him you shall

67:24 be mustered.'

They say: 'When will this promise come about if you speak the
truth?'

Say: 'Knowledge of it is with God, but I am just a clear
warner.'

But when they see it coming near, the faces of unbelievers will
grow sorrowful, and it shall be said: 'This is what you asked

67:27 for.'

Say: 'Consider this. Should God make me perish, along with
those who are with me, or else should He show us His mercy,
Who shall offer refuge to the blasphemers from a painful punishment?'

Say: 'He is the All-Merciful. In Him we believe and in Him we
trust. You will surely know who is in manifest error.'

Say: 'Consider this. If your water is swallowed up by the

67:30 earth, who will bring you water from a spring that is pure?'

The Pen

In the name of God,
Merciful to all,
Compassionate to each!

Nun

By the Pen, and by what they trace in lines!
You are not, by the grace of your Lord, a man possessed.
You shall receive a wage, unstinted,
And you are of a character most noble.
You shall discover, and they shall discover,
In which of you lies madness.
Your Lord knows best who has strayed from His path,
And He knows best those who have found guidance. 68:7

So do not obey the deniers,
Who would like you to relent,
That they too may relent.
And do not obey every contemptible oath-swearer,
Every backbiter, spreader of slander,
Forbidder of virtue, aggressor and grave sinner,
Crude and, moreover, a fake –
Even though he owns wealth and progeny.
When Our revelations are recited to him,
He says: 'Fables of the ancients!'
We shall brand his beak! 68:16

We are testing them, as We once tested the owners of the
    garden,
The time they swore they would cull it all when they rose at
    dawn,
But failed to say: 'God willing.'

A calamity from your Lord passed over them as they slept,
And by morning the garden was as if stripped clean.
As they rose up, they called out to each other:
'Go early to your fields if you intend to cull them.'
So they set off, speaking in low voices: 'No poor man is to
enter upon you today.'

68:24

And they hastened at once, resolved in purpose.

When they saw the scene, they said: 'We must have lost our way! Or rather we have been dispossessed!'

The most reasonable among them said: 'Did I not tell you to glorify God?'

They said: 'Glory be to our Lord! We were indeed wicked.'
So they turned upon each other, in mutual reproach.

They said: 'Woe to us! We were truly shameless. Perhaps our Lord will give us one better in exchange. We turn to our Lord, sincere in will.'

68:32

Such is Our torment, but the torment of the hereafter is far more grievous, if only they knew.

To the pious shall be granted Gardens of Bliss, near their
   Lord.
Are We to treat Muslims as We treat villains?
What makes you judge in this manner?

Or do you possess a Book which you study, and wherein you are promised whatever you choose?

Or do you possess a solemn oath from Us, lasting till the Day of Resurrection, that yours it is to judge?

Ask them: which of them will vouch for this?

Or do they have partners? Let them produce their partners if they speak the truth.

A Day shall come when terror is revealed, and they are summoned to bow down, but cannot: their eyes crestfallen, overcome with degradation.

They had once been summoned to bow down, when still
carefree.

68:43

So leave Me with those who reject this Discourse!
We shall lure them on, through ways they cannot know.
I shall grant them respite, but My guile is invincible.
    Or do you demand a wage from them, and hence they are
heavily indebted?
    Or do they have access to the Unseen, and from it they
transcribe?

68:47

Therefore, be patient with your Lord's judgement,
And be not like the man in the whale,
As he called out in great bitterness.
Had not the grace of his Lord intervened to save him,
He would have been cast out into the wilderness, worthy of
    blame.
But his Lord elected him and made him righteous.

68:50

The blasphemers could almost stab you with their glances when
they hear the Remembrance. They say: 'He is possessed.'
    It is but a Remembrance to mankind.

68:52

The Hour of Truth

In the name of God,
Merciful to all,
Compassionate to each!

The Hour of Truth!
What is the Hour of Truth?
But how can you know what is the Hour of Truth?

Thamud and 'Ad cried lies to the Blast.
As for Thamud, they were destroyed by the Scream;
As for 'Ad, they were destroyed by a raging, howling gale,
Which He unleashed upon them for seven nights and eight days,
Uninterrupted.
You could have seen its people strewn dead, like hollowed
    stumps of palms.
69:8 Do you see of them any remnant?

And Pharaoh, and before him, the Towns in ruin, took to
    sinning.
They disobeyed the messenger of their Lord, and he seized
    them with a seizure,
Overpowering.

When the waters overflowed, We carried you away, in a
    surging ship,
That We might make it a reminder to you,
69:12 Grasped by a discerning ear.

When the Trumpet shall be blown, a single blast,
And the earth and mountains are raised up and crushed, a
    single crush,
On that Day, the Calamity shall strike!
The sky shall be rent and, on that Day, be brittle.
The angels shall be on its confines,
And carrying the throne of your Lord above them, on that
    Day, are eight.
On that Day you shall be passed in review,
69:18 And nothing you hide will remain hidden.

And he who is handed his book with his right hand will say:
'Here it is! Take my book, and read it.
I thought I was to meet my reckoning.'
He shall have a life of contentment,
In a lofty Garden,

Whose pickings are within reach.
'Eat and drink in good health, because of your former deeds,
    in days gone by.'   69:24

And he who is handed his book with his left hand will say:
'Would that I had not been handed my book,
Nor known my reckoning!
If only my death had been final!
My wealth avails me not;
My power has collapsed around me.'   69:29

'Seize him and shackle him,
Then scorch him in hell,
Then lash him to a chain, seventy arms in length.
He did not believe in God Almighty,
Nor ever encouraged the feeding of the poor.
Here, this Day, no intimate has he,
Nor any food save the scum of hell,
Which none but sinners imbibe.'   69:37

Yes indeed!
I swear by what you see and what you do not see:
This is the speech of a noble Messenger.
It is not the speech of a poet – little do you believe!
Nor the speech of a soothsayer – little do you remember!
It is a Revelation from the Lord of the Worlds.
Had he put words into Our mouth,
We would have seized him by the right hand,
Then slashed the artery of his heart!
And none of you here could protect him.   69:47

It is a Reminder to the pious.
We know full well that some of you are deniers.
But it is anguish to blasphemers:
It is the truth in all its certainty.
So glorify the name of your Lord Almighty!   69:52

Ascensions

In the name of God,
Merciful to all,
Compassionate to each!

A questioner questioned the imminent torment.

From blasphemers none can parry it,
As it comes from the God of Ascensions.
Angels and the Spirit ascend to Him in a day,
70:4 That spans fifty thousand years.

So bear in seemly patience.
They see it far,
But We see it near:
A Day when the sky shall be like molten brass,
And mountains like tufts of wool.
No intimate friend shall ask about his intimate,
When glances meet.
The wicked that Day will long to ransom himself from
    torment,
In exchange for his sons, his wife, his brother, the clan that
    cares for him,
Indeed, for everyone on earth,
70:14 Who yet might save him.

But No! It shall be the blazing Flame,
The Stripper of scalps!
It calls out to him who had once turned his back and
    departed,
70:18 Who heaped and hoarded.

Man was created restless:
Touched by evil, he is hopeless,
Touched by good, ungenerous.
Except for those who pray,
Who are constantly at prayer,
In whose wealth is a rightful allotment,
To the beggar and the indigent;
Who truly believe in the Day of Judgement,
And fear their Lord's torment –
From the torment of their Lord none can feel secure –
Who guard their chastity,
Save with their spouses and slaves,
When no blame attaches to them;
Though if any covet more than this,
They shall be transgressing;
Who respect their trusts and their contracts,
Who render true witness,
And are diligent in prayer.   70:34

These shall be in Gardens, heaped with honour.
What is the matter with the unbelievers?
Why do they crane their necks in haste towards you,
From right and left, in throngs?
Is every single one of them craving to enter the Gardens of
    Bliss?
No indeed! We created them from what they surely know.   70:39

Yes indeed!
I swear by the Lord of the East and West!
We are capable of replacing them with better than they,
And We shall not be forestalled.   70:41

So leave them to their chatter and amusements,
Until they encounter the Day they are promised,
The Day when they are turned out of their tombs, in haste,

As if racing to some markers,
Their eyes crestfallen, overcome with degradation!
70:44   That shall be the Day they are promised.

Noah

In the name of God,
Merciful to all,
Compassionate to each!

We sent Noah to his people:

'Warn your people before there comes to them a painful torment.'

He said: 'My people, I am to you a manifest warner, that you worship God, fear Him and obey me, and He will forgive you your sins and defer you to a stated term. When God's term
71:4   arrives it cannot be deferred, if only you knew.'

He said: 'My Lord, I call on my people, night and day, but my call only makes them flee further away.

'Whenever I call them together that You may forgive them, they place their fingers in their ears, wrap themselves up in their garments, grow headstrong and swell in arrogance.

'So I invited them openly.

'Then I addressed them in public.

'Then I spoke to them in faint tones.

'I said: "Ask your Lord to forgive you, for He is All-Forgiving, and He will let flow the sky in torrents upon you, furnish you with wealth and progeny, provide you with gardens, and cause rivers to flow for you.

'"Why are you not in awe of God's majesty, though He created you at every stage?

'"Do you not see how God created seven heavens, piled one

upon another, setting the moon among them as an illumination and the sun a glowing lamp?

'"God it was Who caused you to sprout from the earth – and what sprouting! Then He shall resurrect you therein – and what a raising He shall raise you! God it was Who levelled out the earth for you, that you may travel its diverse roads."' 71:20

Noah said: 'My Lord, they have disobeyed me and followed one whose wealth and progeny only increases him in loss.'

And they practised utmost guile.

They said: 'Do not abandon your gods. Do not abandon Wadd,* nor Suwaʿ,* Yaghuth,* Yaʿuq,* nor Nasr.'*

Many have they led astray. Lord, increase the wicked in error!

Because of their sins, they were made to drown and herded into a Fire, finding none to come to their aid save God. 71:25

Noah said: 'My Lord, leave no habitations on earth for the unbelievers. If You let them be, they will lead Your servants astray, and will beget nothing but the dissolute and the blaspheming. My Lord, forgive me, and forgive my parents, as also any who enters my house as a believer. And forgive believing men and believing women, and increase not the wicked save in perdition.' 71:28

The *Jinn*

In the name of God,
Merciful to all,
Compassionate to each!

Say: 'It was revealed to me that a handful of *Jinn* gathered to
    listen, then said:
"We have heard a wondrous Qur'an,
Guiding to righteousness, so we believed in it,
And shall associate none with our Lord.
And we affirm – may our Lord's majesty be exalted! – that He
    took neither wife nor son;
That the impudent among us ascribed to God things far from
    true;
That we never imagined that humans and *Jinn* would forge
    lies about God;
That some men among humans used to pray for safety to
    some men from the *Jinn*,
But they only increased them in insolence;
That they imagined, as you imagine, that God shall resurrect
    no one;
That we probed the sky and found it filled with mighty guards
    and shooting stars;
That we would seat ourselves in seats nearby, to listen,
But whoever listens now is pursued by a shooting star, lying in
    wait;
That we know not whether evil is intended for mankind,
Or whether their Lord intends them good;
That among us there are the righteous, and there are the less
    so – of diverse persuasions are we;
That we know we cannot escape God's might on earth, nor
    escape Him by fleeing;
That when we heard the Guidance, we believed it,

For whoso believes in his Lord fears neither unfairness nor
    injustice;
That some of us are Muslims and some are transgressors;
That as for the Muslims, these have chosen the path of
    guidance,
But the transgressors shall be fire-wood for hell."'   72:15

If only they had kept true to the path, We would have given
    them much water to drink,
To test them therewith;
But whoso turns away from the mention of his Lord, He will
    lead him on the road to a torment ever mounting.   72:17

Houses of worship belong to God, so call upon none besides
    Him;
But when a servant of God began to pray to Him,
They almost fell on him in a mass.   72:19

Say: 'I pray solely to my Lord, and associate none with Him.'
    Say: 'I have no power to do you evil or bring you right
guidance.'
    Say: 'None can grant me shelter from God, nor will I ever
find, apart from Him, any hideout. I merely convey a proclamation from God, and His messages.'

Whoso disobeys God and His Messenger, for him awaits the
fire of hell, abiding in it for ever.
    And when they come face to face with what they have been
promised, they will know who has the weaker and less numerous
supporters.   72:24

Say: 'I know not whether what you are promised is imminent,
or whether my Lord shall set a longer term for it. Knower of
the Unseen is He! He discloses His Unseen to no one, save
to whomever He pleases among His messengers, and then He
stations, before and behind him, sentinels, that He may know

that they have delivered the messages of their Lord. He knows
72:28　all that concerns them, and has tallied everything by number.'

Muffled

In the name of God,
Merciful to all,
Compassionate to each!

You who are muffled in your garments!
Up and awake in the night, all but a little!
The half of it, or diminish it a little!
Or add to it!
And chant the Qur'an in a plain chant.
We shall charge you with a weighty Speech,
And the vigil of night is heavier in burden,
Yet better suited for recitation,
For in daytime you are long preoccupied.
And mention the name of your Lord,
And devote yourself to Him, in consummate devotion.
Lord of the East and West – there is no God but He!
Accept Him as Patron,
And bear patiently what they say,
73:10　And withdraw from them, a seemly withdrawal.

But leave Me to those liars, those men of substance,
And grant them a short respite.
We have heavy chains, and a hell,
And food that chokes, and a grievous torment.
That Day the earth and mountains shall quake,
73:14　And the mountains shall turn into heaps of sand-dunes.

We have sent you a Messenger, a witness to you,
As We once sent a messenger to Pharaoh.

Pharaoh disobeyed the messenger,
And We seized him – and what a calamitous seizure!
So how can you, if you blaspheme, guard against a Day
Which shall turn youths into grey-hairs,
A Day in which the sky shall be rent asunder?
His promise will surely come to pass.
This is a Reminder:
Whoso wills can follow a path to his Lord.   73:19

Your Lord knows that you keep vigil, for almost two-thirds of
the night, or half thereof, or a third, along with a group of those
who are with you.

God, Who disposes the night and the day, knows you cannot
consummate it, so He has granted you pardon.
So recite of the Qur'an what is possible for you.

He knows that among you are the sick, and others who travel
the land, seeking God's bounty, and that still others are fighting
in the cause of God.
So recite of it what is possible for you.

And perform the prayer, and pay the alms, and loan God a
goodly loan.

Whatever good works you lay in store for yourselves you
shall find something better with God, and greater in reward.
And pray for God's forgiveness; He is All-Forgiving,
    Compassionate to each.   73:20

Enfolded

In the name of God,
Merciful to all,
Compassionate to each!

You who are enfolded in your garments:
Stand up and warn!
Magnify your Lord!
Purify your garments!
And abandon impurity!
And give not, hoping to gain more!
74:7   Be steadfast to your Lord!

When the Trumpet is blown,
That shall be a Day grievous to the unbelievers,
74:10   A Day of no ease.

Leave Me to him whom I created frail,
Then granted wealth extensive,
And sons always by his side,
And rendered all things easy for him – all too easy!
And then he covets more from Me!
Ah no!
Inflexible was he against Our revelations!
74:17   I shall inflict a steep ascent upon him.

He reflected and assessed – curse him how he assessed!
And curse him again how he assessed!
Then he paused to consider,
Then he frowned and grew sullen,
Then turned his back and swelled with pride,
Saying: 'This is nothing but sorcery, time-worn;
74:25   Nothing but human speech.'

I shall scorch him in Saqar!*
But how can you know what is Saqar?
It leaves out nothing: it leaves nothing behind.
A scorcher for humans,
Upon it stand nineteen.   74:30

We assigned only angels to rule over the Fire,
And made their tally to be only an ordeal to the unbelievers,
That those granted Scripture may grow certain,
And the believers may increase in belief,
And that neither those granted Scripture nor the believers
    should be in doubt,
And that they in whose hearts is sickness, and the unbelievers
    too,
Might say: 'What did God intend by this as a parable?'
Thus does God lead astray whom He wills,
And guides whom He wills.
None knows the troops of your Lord save He,
And it is nothing but a Reminder to mankind.   74:31

Ah no!
By the moon!
And by the night when it vanishes!
And by the morning when it dawns!
It is assuredly a great calamity,
A warning to mankind,
To any of you who wish to come forward,
Or lag behind.   74:37

Each soul is held to account for what it earns,
Except for the Companions of the Right,
In Gardens, inquiring from the wicked:
'What led you on the path to Saqar?'
And they shall answer:
'We were not among those who prayed;
We did not feed the poor;

And we waded into blasphemy with those who waded.
We denied the Day of Judgement,
Until the Truth came upon us.'
74:48   Of no avail to them the intercession of intercessors!

So why do they turn their backs on the Reminder,
74:51   Like wild asses, stampeding in panic before lions?

Instead, each one of them wants to be handed scrolls
          outspread!
Rather, they fear not the hereafter.
Rather, it is a Reminder:
Whoso wills can remember it;
But they shall not remember unless God wills.
Worthy is He of piety!
74:56   Worthy is He to forgive!

Resurrection

In the name of God,
Merciful to all,
Compassionate to each!

Yes indeed!
I swear by the Day of Resurrection!
Yes indeed!
I swear by the soul that remonstrates!
Does man imagine We shall not reassemble his bones?
Indeed, We can reshape his very fingers!
In truth, man wishes to persist in his debauchery;
75:6   He asks when the Day of Resurrection shall come.

When eyes are dazzled,
And the moon is eclipsed,

And sun and moon are joined together,
Man that Day shall ask: 'Where to escape?'
No, there is no refuge!
To your Lord that Day is the journey's end.
Man that Day shall be informed
Of all his works, from first to last.
In truth, man shall witness against himself,
Even as he advances his excuses.   75:15

Move not your tongue with it, seeking to hasten it along;
Up to Us is its collection and recitation.
When We recite it, follow its recitation,
Then it is up to Us to expound it.
No, but in truth you people love this fleeting life,
And pay no heed to the life hereafter.   75:21

On that Day, some faces shall be resplendent,
To their Lord their eyes are lifted;
On that Day, some faces shall be snarling,
Knowing a back-breaker shall befall them.   75:25

But when a soul has reached the neck-bones,
And a voice is heard: 'Can anyone cure?'
And he knows it is the final parting,
And leg is entwined with leg,
To your Lord that Day is the rounding up.   75:30

But he neither believed nor prayed.
Instead, he cried lies and departed;
Then sauntered homewards.   75:33

Alas for you! Alas!
Then again: Alas for you! Alas!
Does man think he shall be abandoned to futility?
Was he not a sperm drop, to be discharged,
Then became a blood clot, which He created and fashioned?

And made from it a pair, male and female?
75:40 Is such a Being not capable of reviving the dead?

Man

In the name of God,
Merciful to all,
Compassionate to each!

Surely there came upon man a span of time,
When he was a thing not worth remembering!
We created man from a sperm drop of fluids commingled,
That We may test him; and formed him to hear and see.
76:3   We guided him upon the way, be he grateful or ungrateful.

For unbelievers We have readied chains, collars and a raging
    Fire.
But the righteous shall drink from a cup mixed with choicest
    fragrance,
A fountain, at which God's worshippers drink,
Gushing in torrents at their command.
They had fulfilled their vows, and feared a Day whose evil is
    far-flung.
    They had dispensed food, though held dear, to the poor, the
orphan and the prisoner, saying: 'We are feeding you only for
the sake of God. From you we seek neither reward nor thanks.
76:10 We fear a Day from our Lord – lowering, excruciating.'

So God shall spare them the evil of that Day,
And grant them splendour and joy.
He shall reward them, for their patience,
With a Garden, and silk.
They shall recline therein on couches,

And therein shall experience neither burning sun nor piercing
    cold.
Its shades shall hover over them, its plucking made ever so
    easy.
Passing among them are ewers of silver and chalices of crystal,
Crystal-like silver, perfectly proportioned.
They shall be given to drink a cup mixed with ginger,
From a fountain therein, called Salsabil.
Passing among them are eternal youths:
If you see them you would think them scattered pearls.
If only you could see that place, you would see bliss and a vast
    realm.
They shall be clothed in green silk and brocade,
And decked out in silver bracelets,
And their Lord shall give them to drink an untainted draught.
This shall be as a reward to you:
Your venture was worthy of all praise.   76:22

It is We Who revealed the Qur'an to you – a revelation in very
    truth!
So bear your Lord's verdict with patience,
And obey not the blaspheming or sinful among them;
And pronounce your Lord's name, morning and evening.
At night, bow down to Him, and magnify Him all night long.   76:26

These people love the fleeting world,
And turn their backs upon a weighty Day.
It was We Who created them and fastened their sinews,
And, if We wish, We can replace them with their like – in
    every respect!

This is a Reminder.
Whoso wishes may follow a path to his Lord;
And you cannot so wish unless God wishes. God is
    All-Knowing, All-Wise.

He admits into His mercy whomever He wills,

76:31   And for the wicked has readied a painful torment.

Unleashed

In the name of God,
Merciful to all,
Compassionate to each!

By forces unleashed, successively!
By tempests tempestuous!
By dispersers dispersing!
By sunderers sundering!
By carriers of Remembrance,
In pardon or in warning!

77:7   What you are promised shall come true.

When the stars are erased,
When the sky is fractured,
When the mountains are obliterated,
When the messengers are alerted;
To which day shall they be deferred?
To the Day of Separation!
But how can you know what is the Day of Separation?
Alas, that Day, for the deniers!
Did We not destroy the ancients?
Then followed them up with others?
Thus do We deal with the wicked.

77:19   Alas, that Day, for the deniers!

Did We not create you from a trivial fluid,
Which We deposited in a haven, secure,
Until a designated term?
We disposed – how well did We dispose!

77:24   Alas, that Day, for the deniers!

Did We not make the earth a homestead,
For the living and the dead?
And We planted in it lofty mountains,
And gave you sweet water to drink?
Alas, that Day, for the deniers!   77:28

Go forth now to meet that which you once denied!
Go forth to a smoke, thrice-forked,
Offering no shade, and unavailing against the flames,
Which scatter sparks, as from massive logs, coloured like
     tawny camels.
Alas, that Day, for the deniers!   77:34

That will be a Day when they shall fall silent,
When they shall not be permitted to offer excuses.
Alas, that Day, for the deniers!
This is the Day of Separation,
When We shall gather you together with the ancients.
If you can still practise guile, go ahead and beguile!
Alas, that Day, for the deniers!   77:40

The pious shall be among shades and fountains,
And fruits of their hearts' desire.
Eat and drink in good health, in return for your works,
For thus do We reward the righteous.   77:44

Alas, that Day, for the deniers!
Eat and enjoy yourselves for a little while,
But you are in truth most wicked.
Alas, that Day, for the deniers!   77:47

When told to bow down, they do not bow down.
Alas, that Day, for the deniers!
What speech, instead, do they believe in?   77:50

The Proclamation

In the name of God,
Merciful to all,
Compassionate to each!

What is it that they question each other about?
Is it the Great Proclamation, concerning which they differ?
No indeed! They will surely know!
78:5   And again no! They will surely know!

Did We not make the earth a cradle,
And the mountains as pegs?
Did We not create you as pairs?
Did We not make your sleep a time of rest,
And made the night a cover, and the day a time for livelihood?
Did We not build above you seven tight-knit heavens,
And fixed a glowing lantern?
Did We not send down upon you, from rain-clogged clouds,
        torrential water,
To sprout therewith seeds and vegetation, and gardens
78:16   intertwined?

The Day of Separation shall be the date appointed,
A Day when the Trumpet shall be blown, and you shall come
        forth in droves,
When heaven shall be opened, and turn into apertures,
When mountains shall be wiped out, and turn into a mirage.
Hell shall be lying in wait,
For transgressors a final destination, abiding therein for aeons.
Therein they taste neither coolness nor anything to drink,
Save boiling water and filthy scum –
A fitting recompense!
They had had no faith in a reckoning,

And had cried lies to Our revelations – and what lies!
All things We have recorded in a Book.
So taste it! For We shall only increase you in torment.   78:30

But for the pious there lies a path to salvation:
Gardens and vineyards,
Companions, shapely and alike of age,
And cups overflowing.
In it they hear neither gossip nor falsehood:
A reward from your Lord, a free offering, a fair accounting –
Lord of the heavens and earth, and what lies between!
    All-Merciful!
None can address Him.   78:37

That Day, the Spirit and the angels shall stand in rows.
They shall not speak, unless it be one permitted by the
    All-Merciful,
Who shall speak with probity.

That shall be the Day of Truth.
Whoso wishes can follow a path to his Lord's refuge.   78:39

We have warned you of an imminent torment,
A Day when man shall behold what his hands had once
    wrought,
And when the blasphemer shall cry out:
'If only I had been turned to dust!'   78:40

The Dispatchers

In the name of God,
Merciful to all,
Compassionate to each!

By those that dispatch, to the very limit!
By those that speed forth, at full speed!
By those that run smoothly, so smoothly!
By those that race ahead, racing far ahead!
79:5 By those that settle the matter!

The Day when the Quake shall quake,
To be followed by the after-shock!
Hearts that Day shall fill with dread,
And eyes shall be downcast.
They say: 'Are we to retrace our steps, once we are hollow
      bones?'
And they add: 'That would surely be a ruinous rebirth!'
It is but a single Roar,
79:14 And they shall emerge at the surface.

Has the story of Moses reached you?
When his Lord called out to him in the holy valley of Tuwa:
'Go forth to Pharaoh, for he has grown tyrannical, and say to
      him:
"Do you wish to become upright, so I can guide you to your
      Lord,
And you come to fear Him?"'
And he showed him the greatest of wonders.
But he cried lies and became defiant,
Then turned his back and plotted.
He mustered and he proclaimed:
'I am your Lord, most exalted.'

And God seized him with the punishment of the last world,
And of the first.
In this is a lesson to one who fears God.   79:26

Are you more mighty in creation than the sky He built?
He elevated its canopy, and fashioned it to perfection;
He dimmed its night, and drew out its daylight,
And the earth thereafter He flattened,
Bringing forth its water and its pastures.
The mountains He anchored:
All for your enjoyment, and for your cattle.   79:33

But when the great Cataclysm overwhelms,
A Day when man shall remember what he had striven for,
And hell is displayed to whoever can see,
Whoso then has exceeded all bounds,
And preferred the present life,
Hell shall be his shelter.
Whoso feared to stand before his Lord,
And curbed his soul from following its caprice,
The Garden shall be his shelter.   79:41

They ask you about the Hour, and when it shall cast anchor.
But what have you to do with marking it?
Its closure is up to your Lord.
You are merely one who warns those who fear it.
It is as though, the Day they witness it, they had lasted on
     earth
A mere night or its morning.   79:46

He Frowned

In the name of God,
Merciful to all,
Compassionate to each!

He frowned and turned aside
When the blind man approached him.
But how do you know? Perhaps he was seeking to cleanse his
    sins,
Or else be admonished, and the Remembrance might profit
80:4   him.

As for him whose wealth has made him vain,
To him you turn your full attention.
And yet it is not up to you if he does not cleanse his sins.
But he who came to you in earnest endeavour, in piety,
80:10 From him you are distracted.

No indeed! This is a Reminder –
Whoso desires may remember it –
Inscribed in hallowed scrolls,
Sublime, immaculate,
By the hands of scribes,
80:16 Honourable, virtuous.

Perish man, how blasphemous he is!
From what substance did He create him?
From a sperm drop He created him, and gave him shape,
Then made his way easy,
Then caused him to die, and to lie in his grave.
Then, if He wills, He shall resurrect him.
80:23 No, he did not perform what He commanded him.

Let man consider his food.
We poured the water down in torrents,
And furrowed the earth a furrowing,
Sprouting therein grains,
Vines and soft dates,
Olives and palm-trees,
And walled gardens, dense with vegetation,
And fruits and pasturage:
All for your enjoyment, and for your cattle.   80:32

But when the Scream comes to pass,
That will be a Day when a man flees from his brother,
From his mother and his father,
From his wife and his children:
Each one of them that Day will have something to preoccupy
     him.   80:37

Some faces that Day shall be radiant,
Laughing, full of good cheer;
And some faces that Day shall be covered with dust,
Overlaid with gloom.
These are the blasphemers, the dissolute.   80:42

Rolling Up

In the name of God,
Merciful to all,
Compassionate to each!

When the sun is rolled up;
When the stars are cast adrift;
When the mountains are wiped out;
When pregnant camels are left unattended;
When wild animals are herded together;

When seas are filled to overflowing;
When souls are paired together;
When the newborn girl, buried alive, is asked
For what crime she was murdered;
When scrolls are unfolded;
When the sky is scraped away;
When hell-fire is kindled;
When the Garden is drawn near;
81:14   Then each soul will know what it has readied.

No indeed!
I swear by the planets,
Ascending or receding!
By the night when it slinks away!
By the morning when it respires!
This is the speech of a noble envoy:
He is a figure of great power,
In high esteem with the Lord of the throne,
81:21   Obeyed in heaven, worthy of trust.

Your companion is not possessed;
He saw him on the open horizon.
Nor does he hold back what comes from the Unseen.
Nor is this the speech of an accursed demon.
So where are you heading?
This is but a Remembrance to mankind,
To any of you who wish to follow the straight path.
And you cannot so wish unless God wishes,
81:29   Lord of the Worlds.

Disintegration

In the name of God,
Merciful to all,
Compassionate to each!

When the sky disintegrates;
When the stars are strewn;
When the seas are made to erupt;
When graves are dispersed,
Each soul will know what it did,
And what it failed to do.   82:5

O man, what tempted you away from your bountiful Lord?
He Who created you, gave you shape and symmetry,
And framed you in any image He chose?   82:8

It is rather that you deny the Judgement!
But there are watchers over you,
Noble scribes,
Who know what you do.   82:12

The righteous are in bliss,
And the impious are in hell,
To be scorched by it on the Day of Judgement.
Nor will they ever depart therefrom.
But how can you know what is the Day of Judgement?
Indeed, how can you know what is the Day of Judgement?
A Day when no soul can do anything to help another.
That Day, judgement belongs solely to God.   82:19

Those who Shortchange

In the name of God,
Merciful to all,
Compassionate to each!

Woe to those who shortchange!
They who, when they measure from others, obtain their full
    measure,
But when they measure out or balance to others, they defraud.
Do they not imagine they shall be resurrected, on a mighty
    Day?
A Day when mankind shall stand before the Lord of the
83:6   Worlds?

No indeed! The record-book of the dissolute is in Sijjin.*
But how can you know what is Sijjin?
83:9   A record precise.

Woe that Day to deniers,
Those who deny the Day of Judgement!
But only the offending sinner denies it.
When Our revelations are recited to him, he says: 'Fables of
    the ancients!'
No indeed! But stifling their hearts is that which they earned.
No indeed! That Day they shall be veiled from their Lord,
Then shall be scorched in hell.
83:17   It will then be said to them: 'Behold what you once denied!'

No! The record-book of the righteous shall be in 'Illiyyun.*
But how can you know what is 'Illiyyun?
A record precise,
83:21   Witnessed by those drawn near.

The righteous are in bliss,
Upon couches, watching.
On their faces you would discern the radiance of bliss.
They are given to drink from a nectar, sealed,
Whose seal is musk –
For this let contenders contend –
And whose mixture is from Tasnim,*
A fountain, from which those drawn near shall drink.   83:28

Sinners would once laugh at the faithful,
And, when passing them by, would wink and snigger;
Returning home, they would return in high spirits;
Catching sight of them they would say: 'They have surely
     strayed.'   83:32

But they were not dispatched to guard over them.
So on this Day the faithful are laughing at the unbelievers,
Upon couches, watching.
Have the unbelievers received the reward of their works?   83:36

The Splitting

In the name of God,
Merciful to all,
Compassionate to each!

When the sky is split,
In obedience to its Lord,
As is fit!
When the earth is distended,
Throwing up what is upon it, and is voided,
In obedience to its Lord,
As is fit!   84:5

O man, you press on towards your Lord,
With all your might, and you shall surely encounter Him!
And he who is handed his book with his right hand,
Shall be lightly held to account,
And return to his family in joy.
But he who is handed his book from behind his back,
Shall pray for perdition,
But shall be scorched by the Blaze.
He had once been happy among his family,
Imagining he shall never return to life.
84:15 O yes indeed! His Lord always had him in sight!

No indeed!
I swear by the twilight!
By the ingathering of the night!
By the moon full and bright!
You will surely run your course,
84:19 Stage after stage.

So why is it they do not believe?
And when the Qur'an is recited to them they do not bow?
Rather, the unbelievers cry lies,
And God knows best what in themselves they hide.
So give them tidings of a painful torment,
Except for those who believe and do righteous deeds;
84:25 These shall receive a wage, unstinted.

The Constellations

In the name of God,
Merciful to all,
Compassionate to each!

By the sky, with its constellations!
By the Day portended!
By a witness and what is witnessed!   85:3

Perish the People of the Trench,*
With its fire and its faggots,
As they sat above it,
Witnessing what they did to the faithful!
All they held against them was their belief in God,
Almighty, All-Praiseworthy,
He to Whom belongs sovereignty over the heavens and the
     earth;
And God is witness over all things.   85:9

Those who oppress faithful men and faithful women,
And do not repent,
There awaits them the punishment of hell,
And the punishment of the Blaze.
But those who believe and do righteous deeds,
There await them Gardens beneath which rivers flow,
And that is the greatest of triumphs.   85:11

Harsh is your Lord in might!
It is He Who originates and restores,
He Who is All-Forgiving, All-Kind,
August Lord of the throne,
Ever accomplishing what He wishes.   85:16

Has the story of the troops reached you?
Of Pharaoh and Thamud?
And yet the unbelievers continue to deny,
85:20 As God encompasses them from behind.

In truth, this is an august Qur'an,
85:22 In a well-guarded Tablet.

The Night Intruder

In the name of God,
Merciful to all,
Compassionate to each!

By the sky and the night intruder!
But how can you know what is the night intruder?
86:3 A star of piercing dazzle!

Not a soul there is but has its guardian.
Therefore, let man consider of what he was created.
He was created from water, discharged,
Issuing from between the man's backbone
86:7 And the woman's breast-bones.

Surely He is able to raise him from the dead,
On a Day when the secrets of hearts are put on trial,
86:10 When he has no strength, and no supporter.

By the sky, and its seasons recurring!
By the earth and its furrows!
This is speech, decisive;
86:14 It is no jest.

They devise and plot,
And I devise and plot!
So give the blasphemers respite,
A brief respite!   86:17

The Highest

In the name of God,
Merciful to all,
Compassionate to each!

Glorify the name of your Lord, the Highest!
Who created and proportioned;
Who measured and guided;
Who brought forth pastures,
Then turned them into dark stubble.   87:5

We shall dictate it to you, and you shall not forget,
Save what God wishes.
He knows what is proclaimed aloud,
And what is concealed.
We shall ease your way to ease of mind.   87:8

So remind, if reminding profits!
The pious shall remember,
But the wretch shall turn away,
He who shall be scorched by the great Fire,
Wherein he is neither dead nor alive.   87:13

The pure in heart shall prosper,
He who mentions his Lord's name, and prays.   87:15

And yet you prefer the present life,
Though the hereafter is better and more lasting.   87:17

This is all in ancient scrolls,

87:19 The scrolls of Abraham and Moses.

The Overspreading Pall

In the name of God,
Merciful to all,
Compassionate to each!

Has news come to you of the Pall, overspreading?
Faces that Day shall be crestfallen,
Overburdened, haggard,
Scorched by a blazing Fire,
Quaffed by a boiling spring.
No food shall they have but bitter cactus

88:7 That fattens not, nor assuages hunger.

Faces that Day shall be joyful,
Content with their striving,
In a Garden, elevated,
Where no word of immodesty is heard.
In it is a flowing spring;
In it are berths upraised,
And goblets arrayed,
And cushions aligned,

88:16 And fine carpets outspread.

Will they not consider how camels were created?
How the sky was uplifted?
How the mountains were moored?

88:20 How the earth was smoothed?

So remind! For you are but a reminder,
You are not their minder.

But he who turns away and blasphemes,
Him God shall torment with the greatest of torments.
To Us is the end of their road,
And it is We Who will settle their score. 88:26

The Dawn

In the name of God,
Merciful to all,
Compassionate to each!

By the dawn, and ten nights!
By the even and the odd!
By the night as it advances!
Does this oath suffice for a man of reason? 89:5

Have you not seen what your Lord did to 'Ad?
Iram,* of the columns?
Its like was never created in any land.
And what of Thamud, who carved out the rocks in the valley?
And Pharaoh, he of the pegs?
All had grown insolent,
And multiplied corruption on earth.
So your Lord cast down upon them
A lashing torment.
Your Lord lies ever in wait. 89:14

And as for man,
If his Lord tries him,
Honours him, and prospers him,
He will say: 'My Lord has honoured me.'
But if He tries him,
And constricts his livelihood,
He will say: 'My Lord has demeaned me.' 89:16

No indeed!
You do not honour the orphan,
Nor urge one another to feed the poor.
You consume an inheritance to the last mouthful,
89:20 And you love wealth with a love inordinate.

No indeed!
When the earth is crushed, pounded, pulverized,
And your Lord and the angels arrive,
Row after row,
And hell that Day is brought in tow,
That Day man will surely remember,
But how will it profit him to remember?
He shall say: 'If only I had laid up good deeds,
For my afterlife.'
That Day none shall torment as He torments!
89:26 None shall bind as He binds!

O soul at peace!
Return to your Lord,
Well pleased, well pleasing,
And enter among My worshippers,
89:30 And enter My Garden!

The City

In the name of God,
Merciful to all,
Compassionate to each!

No indeed!
I swear by this City,
While you live in this City!
90:3 By a begetter and what he begot!

We created man in hardship.
Does he imagine that none can overpower him?
He says: 'I wasted abundant wealth.'
Does he imagine that none has seen him?
Did We not give him two eyes?
A tongue and two lips?
And guided him to the two highways? 90:10

He did not storm the Steep.
But how can you know what is the Steep?
The freeing of a slave,
Or feeding, in time of famine,
An orphan near in kin,
Or a poor man, dirt-poor,
Then joined those who believe,
Who enjoin patience on one another,
Who enjoin mercy on one another. 90:17

They are the People of the hand dextral.
But they who blaspheme Our revelations,
These are the People of the hand sinistral,
Upon them a Fire, firmly padlocked. 90:20

The Sun

In the name of God,
Merciful to all,
Compassionate to each!

By the sun and its morning glow!
By the moon, in its tow!
By the day, when it burnishes it!
By the night, when it cloaks it! 91:4

By the sky and He Who built it!
By the earth and He Who levelled it!
By the soul and He Who gave it symmetry,
Inspiring it with its perversion and its piety!
Prosperous is he who purifies it;
91:10 Lost is he who stifles it.

Thamud cried lies, in its insolence,
When it followed its most wicked,
As the messenger of God said to them:
'Leave the she-camel of God to drink at will.'
But they called him a liar, and hamstrung her.
So their Lord extirpated them for their sin,
Effacing them;
91:15 Nor did He care for the consequences.

The Night

In the name of God,
Merciful to all,
Compassionate to each!

By the night, when it enfolds!
By the day, when it unfolds!
By Him Who created male and female!
Your striving is disparate.
As for him who is generous and pious,
And believes in God's reward,
We shall ease his way to virtue.
But as for him who is miserly and selfish,
And disbelieves in God's reward,
We shall ease his way to evil.
92:11 Nor will his wealth avail him when he plummets.

It is for Us to point to guidance,
And to Us belongs the Last and the First.
I warn you of a Fire that rages,
At which only the most wicked shall be scorched –
He who denied and departed.
But the most pious shall be delivered from it:
He who hands over his wealth, hoping for purity,
And none has done him any favour that merits recompense,
Save only his desire to find favour with his Lord, the Exalted.
And he will surely be content. 92:21

Prime of Morning

In the name of God,
Merciful to all,
Compassionate to each!

By prime of morning, and night when it settles!
Your Lord has not abandoned you, nor disdains!
The Last is better for you than the First.
Your Lord shall give you, and you shall be content.
Did He not find you an orphan,
And sheltered you?
And found you erring,
And guided you?
And found you dependent,
And enriched you? 93:8

The orphan you must not aggrieve,
And the beggar you must not revile,
And your Lord's blessings proclaim. 93:11

Soothing

In the name of God,
Merciful to all,
Compassionate to each!

Have We not soothed your heart?
Have We not relieved you of the burden that weighed upon
    your back?
94:4 Have We not exalted your renown?

With hardship comes ease.
94:6 With hardship comes ease.

When your work is done, turn to devotion,
94:8 And make your Lord your sole quest.

The Fig

In the name of God,
Merciful to all,
Compassionate to each!

By the fig and the olive,
And by Mount Sinai,
95:3 And this city, secure!

We created man in fairest proportion,
Then reduced him to the lowest of the low,
Save them who believe and do righteous deeds –
95:6 To them belongs a wage, unstinted.

What then can lead you to deny the Judgement?
Is God not the fairest of judges?   95:8

The Blood Clot

In the name of God,
Merciful to all,
Compassionate to each!

Recite, in the name of your Lord!
He Who created!
He created man from a blood clot.   96:2

Recite! Your Lord is most bountiful.
He taught with the pen.
He taught man what he knew not.   96:5

And yet, man grows intemperate,
For he thinks himself exempt!
But to your Lord is the journey's end.   96:8

What do you think of one who forbids
A worshipper as he prays?
What do you think?
What if he were guided aright?
Or commands to piety?
What do you think?
What if he cries lies and departs?
Does he not know that God is watching?   96:14

No indeed!
If he does not desist, We shall drag him by the forelock,
That deceitful, sinful forelock!
Let him summon his gang,
And We shall summon the watchmen of hell.   96:18

No! Do not obey him,
96:19 But kneel down, and draw near!

Power

In the name of God,
Merciful to all,
Compassionate to each!

We sent it down in the Night of Power!
But how can you know what is the Night of Power?
The Night of Power is better than a thousand months.
In it, the angels and the Spirit are sent swarming down,
By their Lord's leave, attending to every command.

97:5 Peace is it that Night, till the break of dawn.

Manifest Proof

In the name of God,
Merciful to all,
Compassionate to each!

The unbelievers among the People of the Book and the idolaters
were of diverse views until there came to them a manifest proof:
a Messenger from God, reciting untainted scrolls. In them are
98:3 canonical writings.

Those given the Book did not splinter except after the manifest
proof had come to them. They had been commanded only to
worship God in sincerity of religion and pristine of faith, to

perform the prayer, and to pay the alms. This is the canonical religion.

98:5

But those who blasphemed from among the People of the Book, and the idolaters, shall dwell in hell eternally.

These are the worst of mankind.

98:6

And those who believed and did good deeds – they are the best of mankind. Their wage with their Lord shall be the Gardens of Eden, beneath which rivers flow, abiding therein for ever. God shall be well pleased with them, and they with Him. This shall be the reward of one who fears his Lord.

98:8

The Quake

In the name of God,
Merciful to all,
Compassionate to each!

When the earth quakes – a shattering quake!
And the earth casts up its loads!
And man says: 'What ails it?'
That Day it shall tell its tales,
For your Lord will have inspired it!

99:5

That Day, mankind will come out in scattered throngs,
To be shown their rights and wrongs.
Whoso has done an atom's worth of good shall see it;
Whoso has done an atom's worth of evil shall see it.

99:8

The Charging Stallions

In the name of God,
Merciful to all,
Compassionate to each!

By the charging stallions, snorting!
With their hooves sparking!
By raiders in the morning,
Dust-raising,
100:5   Amidst an enemy troop appearing!

Man is an ingrate towards his Lord:
Of this he himself is witness.
100:8   For love of wealth he is miserly to excess.

Knows he not that when graves and their contents are strewn,
And the secrets of hearts become known,
100:11   That their Lord that Day is All-Aware of them?

The Battering

In the name of God,
Merciful to all,
Compassionate to each!

The Battering!
What is the Battering?
How can you know what is the Battering?
A Day when mankind shall be like moths, besprinkled;
101:5   When mountains shall be like tufts of wool, adrift.

And he whose scales are weighed down,
He shall have a life of joy.
But he whose scales are light,
His matron shall be the Pit.
But how can you know what that is?
A red-hot Fire!   101:11

Rivalry in Wealth

In the name of God,
Merciful to all,
Compassionate to each!

Engrossed are you in rivalry for wealth,
Until you reach your graves.   102:2

No indeed! For you will surely know!
And no indeed! For you will surely know!
No indeed! Had you known for certain,
You would behold hell!
Afterwards, you shall see it with the eye of certitude,
Then, on that Day, you will be questioned about Bliss!   102:8

Afternoon

In the name of God,
Merciful to all,
Compassionate to each!

By the afternoon!
Man is surely amiss!
All save those who believe,
Who do righteous deeds,
Who enjoin truth upon one another,
103:3　Who enjoin patience upon one another.

The Backbiter

In the name of God,
Merciful to all,
Compassionate to each!

Woe to every backbiter, defamer!
He who amasses wealth, forever counting it,
Imagining his wealth will immortalize him!
No indeed!
He shall be tossed into the Consumer.
But how can you know what is the Consumer?
The flaming Fire of God!
The Fire that laps the hearts!
Upon them it is bolted,
104:9　In columns distended.

The Elephant

In the name of God,
Merciful to all,
Compassionate to each!

Have you not considered what your Lord did
To the People of the Elephant?
Did He not turn their guile into futility?
He sent against them feathered flocks,
Hurling at them stones from hell-fire,
And left them like worm-eaten leaves.   105:5

Quraysh

In the name of God,
Merciful to all,
Compassionate to each!

To bring harmony to Quraysh,
Their harmony being the journey of winter and summer.
So let them worship the Lord of this House,
Who fed them against hunger,
And secured them against fear.   106:4

Liberality

In the name of God,
Merciful to all,
Compassionate to each!

Have you considered him who denies the Judgement?
It is he who drives away the orphan,
107:3 Who enjoins not the feeding of the poor.

Woe to those who pray,
But who are negligent in their prayer;
107:7 Who dissemble, and withhold liberality.

Abundance

In the name of God,
Merciful to all,
Compassionate to each!

We gave to you in abundance,
So pray to your Lord, and sacrifice.
108:3 He who baits you: it is he who shall be childless!

The Unbelievers

In the name of God,
Merciful to all,
Compassionate to each!

Say: 'O unbelievers! I do not worship what you worship,
Nor do you worship what I worship;
Nor will I ever worship what you worship,
Nor will you ever worship what I worship.
You have your religion,
And I have mine.'   109:6

Victory

In the name of God,
Merciful to all,
Compassionate to each!

When there comes the victory of God, and the Conquest,
And you see people entering the religion of God in swarms,
Glorify the praises of your Lord, and ask His forgiveness,
For He is Ever-Pardoning.   110:3

Fibre

In the name of God,
Merciful to all,
Compassionate to each!

Perish the hands of Abu Lahab* – and perish he!
His wealth shall not avail him,
Nor what he earned.
He shall be scorched by a fire, ablaze,
As too his wife, carrying the faggots;
111:5　Around her neck is a rope of fibre.

True Devotion

In the name of God,
Merciful to all,
Compassionate to each!

Say: 'He is God, Unique,
God, Lord Supreme!
Neither begetting nor begotten,
112:4　And none can be His peer.'

Break of Dawn

In the name of God,
Merciful to all,
Compassionate to each!

Say: 'I seek refuge with the Lord of the break of dawn!
From the evil He created,
From the evil of the approaching night,
From the evil of women who blow on knots,
From the evil of the envier when he envies.'   113:5

Mankind

In the name of God,
Merciful to all,
Compassionate to each!   ·

Say: 'I seek refuge with the Lord of mankind,
· King of mankind,
God of mankind,
From the evil of the One who whispers and recoils,
Who whispers in the hearts of mankind,
Of *Jinn* and mankind.'   114:6

Glossary

This glossary is deliberately brief and is aimed primarily at a non-Muslim readership. My intention is to allow readers to come face to face with the Qur'anic text unencumbered by any commentary, as were its earliest listeners, for whom most of the names or terms below would have been recognizable. The first instance of each glossed term is marked with an asterisk in the text.

Abu Lahab Uncle of the Prophet and his fierce enemy.

'Ad A great pre-Islamic Arabian tribe, to whom the prophet **Hud** was sent.

Ahmad A form of the name 'Muhammad' according to the exegetes, the verbal root *h-m-d* being the same in both.

Alif Lam Mim Twenty-nine chapters of the Qur'an begin with the names of Arabic letters in various combinations. These are the so-called 'mysterious letters' of the Qur'an whose meaning, according to most exegetes, is best left with God.

'Arafat The name of a plain and hill to the east of Mecca, central to the rite of pilgrimage.

Assembly, the Highest Arabic *al-Mala' al-A'la*; the angelic host, according to most exegetes.

Badr A well south-west of Medinah, site of the first major Muslim victory over the Meccans in 624.

Bakka Another name for Mecca.

Barbarism, Age of Arabic *Jahiliyya*; the name given in the Qur'an to the pre-Islamic period.

Confederates Arabic *al-Ahzab*; the name given to both contemporary and ancient bands of infidels who fought against Muhammad in 630 and against Noah and other prophets before him.

Dhu'l Kifl An otherwise unidentified figure, regarded as a prophet by some Muslim exegetes.

Dhu'l Qarnayn The 'two-horned'; a mysterious figure, possibly related to the stories surrounding Alexander the Great.

Elias A prophet, possibly related to the biblical Elijah.

Elisha Arabic *al-Yasa'*; a prophet who, according to some exegetes, was a follower of Elias.

Emigrants Arabic *al-Muhajirun*; the name given to Meccan Muslims who emigrated with Muhammad to Medinah in 622 and were among his closest companions.

Haman The minister of Pharaoh who rejected the mission of Moses.

Harut and Marut Mysterious fallen angels of Babylon and teachers of sorcery.

Helpers Arabic *al-Ansar*; the name given to the Muslims of Medinah.

al-Hijr A ruin in north-western Arabia, associated with the tribe of Thamud. Their prophet was Salih.

Hud An Arabian prophet, sent to the tribe of 'Ad.

Hunayn A valley near Mecca, site of a fierce battle in 630, resulting in a Muslim victory.

Hypocrites Arabic *al-Munafiqun*; the name given to a Medinese group who seemingly embraced Islam but disputed the Prophet's political leadership of the community.

Iblis A name for the devil.

Idolatry, Age of *See* Barbarism, Age of.

Idris A prophet, often identified with Enoch or with Hermes Trismegistus.

'Illiyyun A term which refers, according to many exegetes, to a record-book where righteous deeds are kept.

'Imran, House of Arabic *Al 'Imran*; according to most exegetes, the family of Mary, mother of Jesus.

Iram A mysterious tribe or place-name, connected with 'Ad.

Jinn Invisible spirits but, like humans, responsible moral beings.

Korah Arabic *Qarun*; a minister of Pharaoh and enemy of Moses; *see also* Haman.

al-Lat One of a triad of pre-Islamic goddesses of Mecca; *see also* Manat and al-'Uzza.

Luqman A pre-Islamic Arabian sage.

Malik An angel; guardian of hell.

Manat One of a triad of pre-Islamic goddesses of Mecca; *see also* al-Lat and al-ʻUzza.

Midian Arabic *Madyan*; the Midianites, to whom the prophet Shuʻayb was sent, and into whom Moses was married.

Mosque, the Furthest Arabic *al-Masjid al-Aqsa*; generally taken by exegetes to refer to the holy site in Jerusalem where Muhammad led other prophets in prayer and from where he ascended to heaven.

mother's back A pre-Islamic Arabian formula of divorce.

Nasr A pre-Islamic Arabian god.

People of the Book Arabic *Ahl al-Kitab*; a Qurʼanic term denoting religious communities to whom a divine scripture had been revealed. These include Jews, Christians, Sabeans and Magians.

Pharaoh, he of the pegs Arabic *Firʻawn dhuʼl Awtad*; the epithet ʻhe of the pegs' is uncertain in meaning, some exegetes arguing that it refers to his buildings.

al-Raqim A mysterious term possibly referring to a place-name associated with the People of the Cave (*Ahl al-Kahf*), itself a Qurʼanic parable which echoes the story of the Seven Sleepers of Ephesus.

al-Rass According to some exegetes, a well in the territory of Thamud.

Sabaʼ A pre-Islamic South Arabian city and its culture, celebrated throughout the ancient world. Biblical Sheba.

Sabeans An ancient Near Eastern religious community considered by the Qurʼan to belong to the People of the Book.

Sad A mysterious letter which gives *Sura* 38 its name. Many exegetes leave its true meaning with God. *See also* Alif Lam Mim.

al-Safa and al-Marwa Two hills adjoining the Kaʻba of Mecca, a square structure in the middle of the Meccan sanctuary and the centre of Muslim pilgrimage and devotions.

Salih A prophet sent to Thamud.

Saqar A name for hell or for a gate in hell.

Shuʻayb The prophet sent to the Midianites.

Sijjin A term which refers, according to many exegetes, to a record-book where evil deeds are kept.

Suwaʻ A pre-Islamic god.

Tasnim According to many exegetes, the name of a fountain in paradise.

Thamud An ancient North Arabian tribe.

Thicket, People of the Some exegetes locate this thicket near Midian.

Trench, People of the Some exegetes take this to be a reference to a massacre of Christians in a burning trench by a Jewish South Arabian king.

Tubba' Title of rulers of South Arabia in the pre-Islamic period.

Tuwa Commonly taken to be the name of the holy valley alluded to in the same verse.

al-'Uzza One of a triad of pre-Islamic goddesses of Mecca; *see also* **al-Lat** and **Manat**.

Wadd A pre-Islamic Arabian god.

Yaghuth A pre-Islamic Arabian god.

Ya Sin Mysterious letters which give *Sura* 36 its name.

Yathrib The older name of Medinah.

Ya'uq A pre-Islamic Arabian god.

Zayd Adopted and dearly loved son of Muhammad.

read more ◉

PENGUIN CLASSICS

THE BHAGAVAD GITA

'In death thy glory in heaven, in victory thy glory on earth.
Arise therefore, Arjuna, with thy soul ready to fight'

The Bhagavad Gita is an intensely spiritual work that forms the cornerstone of
the Hindu faith, and is also one of the masterpieces of Sanskrit poetry. It describes
how, at the beginning of a mighty battle between the Pandava and Kaurava armies,
the god Krishna gives spiritual enlightenment to the warrior Arjuna, who realizes
that the true battle is for his own soul.

Juan Mascaró's translation of *The Bhagavad Gita* captures the extraordinary aural
qualities of the original Sanskrit. This edition features a new introduction by Simon
Brodbeck, which discusses concepts such as dehin, prakriti and Karma.

'The task of truly translating such a work is indeed formidable. The translator must
at least possess three qualities. He must be an artist in words as well as a Sanskrit
scholar, and above all, perhaps, he must be deeply sympathetic with the spirit of
the original. Mascaró has succeeded so well because he possesses all these'
The Times Literary Supplement

Translated by Juan Mascaró with an introduction by Simon Brodbeck

PENGUIN CLASSICS

THE COMPLETE DEAD SEA SCROLLS IN ENGLISH
GEZA VERMES

'He will heal the wounded and revive the dead and bring good news to the poor'

The discovery of the Dead Sea Scrolls in the Judean desert between 1947 and 1956 was one of the greatest archaeological finds of all time. These extraordinary manuscripts appear to have been hidden in the caves at Qumran by the Essenes, a Jewish sect in existence before and during the time of Jesus. Written in Hebrew, Aramaic and Greek, the scrolls have transformed our understanding of the Hebrew Bible, early Judaism and the origins of Christianity.

This is a fully revised edition of the classic translation by Geza Vermes, the world's leading Dead Sea Scrolls scholar. It is now enhanced by much previously unpublished material and a new preface, and also contains a scroll catalogue and an index of Qumran texts.

'No translation of the Scrolls is either more readable or more authoritative than that of Vermes' *The Times Higher Education Supplement*

'Excellent, up-to-date ... will enable the general public to read the non-biblical scrolls and to judge for themselves their importance'
The New York Times Book Review

Translated and edited with an introduction by Geza Vermes

THE STORY OF PENGUIN CLASSICS

Before 1946 ...'Classics' are mainly the domain of academics and students, without readable editions for everyone else. This all changes when a little-known classicist, E. V. Rieu, presents Penguin founder Allen Lane with the translation of Homer's *Odyssey* that he has been working on and reading to his wife Nelly in his spare time.

1946 *The Odyssey* becomes the first Penguin Classic published, and promptly sells three million copies. Suddenly, classic books are no longer for the privileged few.

1950s Rieu, now series editor, turns to professional writers for the best modern, readable translations, including Dorothy L. Sayers's *Inferno* and Robert Graves's *The Twelve Caesars*, which revives the salacious original.

1960s The Classics are given the distinctive black jackets that have remained a constant throughout the series's various looks. Rieu retires in 1964, hailing the Penguin Classics list as 'the greatest educative force of the 20th century'.

1970s A new generation of translators arrives to swell the Penguin Classics ranks, and the list grows to encompass more philosophy, religion, science, history and politics.

1980s The Penguin American Library joins the Classics stable, with titles such as *The Last of the Mohicans* safeguarded. Penguin Classics now offers the most comprehensive library of world literature available.

1990s The launch of Penguin Audiobooks brings the classics to a listening audience for the first time, and in 1999 the launch of the Penguin Classics website takes them online to a larger global readership than ever before.

The 21st Century Penguin Classics are rejacketed for the first time in nearly twenty years. This world famous series now consists of more than 1300 titles, making the widest range of the best books ever written available to millions – and constantly redefining the meaning of what makes a 'classic'.

The Odyssey continues ...

The best books ever written

PENGUIN CLASSICS

SINCE 1946